CB Hen...

6/19/30

Please return

RIVERSIDE TEXTBOOKS
IN EDUCATION

EDITED BY ELLWOOD P. CUBBERLEY

PROFESSOR OF EDUCATION
LELAND STANFORD JUNIOR UNIVERSITY

RIVERSIDE TEXTBOOKS IN EDUCATION

BY THE SAME AUTHOR

PUBLIC SCHOOL ADMINISTRATION
A STATEMENT OF THE FUNDAMENTAL PRINCIPLES UNDERLYING
THE ORGANIZATION AND ADMINISTRATION OF
PUBLIC EDUCATION

Revised Edition, 483 pp., 37 charts and plans.

RURAL LIFE AND EDUCATION
A STUDY OF THE RURAL-SCHOOL PROBLEM AS A PHASE
OF THE RURAL-LIFE PROBLEM

Revised and enlarged edition, 377 pp., 77 figures, charts and maps
and 32 insert plates.

PUBLIC EDUCATION IN THE UNITED STATES
A STUDY AND INTERPRETATION OF AMERICAN
EDUCATIONAL HISTORY

An Introductory Textbook dealing with the Larger Problems
of Present-Day Education in the Light of their Historical Development
517 pp., illustrations in text, 20 insert plates.

A HISTORY OF EDUCATION
EDUCATIONAL PRACTICE AND PROGRESS CONSIDERED AS A
PHASE OF THE DEVELOPMENT AND SPREAD
OF WESTERN CIVILIZATION

849 pp., 241 illustrations in the text, 17 insert plates.

READINGS IN THE HISTORY OF EDUCATION
A COLLECTION OF SOURCES AND READINGS TO
ILLUSTRATE THE DEVELOPMENT OF EDUCATIONAL
PRACTICE, THEORY, AND ORGANIZATION

A Companion Volume to the above.
684 pp., 375 Readings, 87 Illustrations.

A BRIEF HISTORY OF EDUCATION
AN ABRIDGEMENT OF THE LARGER VOLUME, AND BASED
ON THE SAME VOLUME OF READINGS

462 pp., 101 illustrations, 6 insert plates.

THE PRINCIPAL AND HIS SCHOOL

THE ORGANIZATION, ADMINISTRATION, AND
SUPERVISION OF INSTRUCTION IN
AN ELEMENTARY SCHOOL

BY

ELLWOOD P. CUBBERLEY

PROFESSOR OF EDUCATION
LELAND STANFORD JUNIOR UNIVERSITY

HOUGHTON MIFFLIN COMPANY

BOSTON · NEW YORK · CHICAGO · DALLAS
SAN FRANCISCO

The Riverside Press Cambridge

COPYRIGHT, 1923
BY ELLWOOD P. CUBBERLEY

ALL RIGHTS RESERVED

The Riverside Press
CAMBRIDGE · MASSACHUSETTS
PRINTED IN THE U.S.A.

AUTHOR'S PREFACE

An attempt has been made in this volume to do what in the industrial world is commonly spoken of as "job analysis." The problem set has been an analysis of the work of a principal or supervising principal in the organization, administration, and supervision of instruction in an elementary school in a city, town, or county-unit school system, or of a supervising principal for a small group of closely related elementary schools. In addition, at the beginning of the volume, there is a statement as to the importance and opportunities and possibilities of the principalship as it is possible to make it in our American school systems, and at the close attention is called to the constantly growing outside relationships of the school of which a principal must to-day take cognizance.

This book, like the preceding volumes in this series by the present writer, is an outgrowth of a course offered at Stanford University. In the present case an effort has been made to place before university students of education the special technique of a limited field for which it seemed that definite and specific training should be given. The course has been listed and described in the university announcements as follows:

44. The Principal and his School. A practical course, dealing with the problems of organization and administration of a single school, the supervision of instruction, school extension, community relationships, etc. A thesis on some administrative or supervisory problem required of each student.

4 units, Spring Quarter (*Cubberley*)

After giving this course for a few years, and working over the needed materials, I have now written up the course in book form, not only to give my own students the benefit of clearer and better-thought-out statements and easier access to drawings and tables and references which cannot be so well presented in a lecture course, but also that I may place in the hands of teachers of education elsewhere the results of what I have worked out. I have also materially enlarged my original list of questions and problems for students, and in its present form the book offers plenty of material for a four- to five-unit quarter course or a three- to four-unit semester course.

The technique of school organization, administration, and supervision, from the point of view of the principal or supervising principal, has by now been sufficiently worked out that there is a definite body of concrete experience and scientific information which should be taught to those who are looking forward to becoming principals of elementary schools in cities, towns, or county-unit school systems. Such a course is needed to-day in our schools of education for those men and women in training who are looking forward to administrative service in our public schools. The elementary-school principalship, too, is frequently a beginning position for many capable men who later rise to superintendencies, and it is important that these men be trained for a high grade of professional service during their apprenticeship period.

A course of special training in the technique of the principalship ought also to be offered in our normal schools and teachers' colleges, and be open to those young men and women of executive ability who are likely to find early service as principals of town or county-unit schools, or in city school systems. While the majority of the nearly six thousand elementary-school principals in our cities and towns are men, many very capable women are also entering the work. With the reorganization of our city school systems on the 6–3–3 plan it is probable that most of the six-year elementary schools will in time come to be in charge of women principals, drawn from among those who have been graduated from a normal school or teachers' college rather than from among those who have been university trained. To offer special training that will better prepare their more capable students for such executive work ought to be one of the functions of the normal school and teachers' college. For this purpose a course specifically intended to prepare for the principalship is more directly practical than a course in city school administration.

While designed primarily to organize the subject matter for a new course in school administration of a very practical type, this book also contains much that principals in service will find useful. That the work and duties outlined are greater than a new principal can cover in a single year is readily admitted; that they are greater than a principal should learn to handle is not. On the contrary, the type of elementary-school principal described herein is one that our schools need, and one that schools of education and teachers' colleges must try to produce. As an aid in this work it is hoped that the book herewith presented may be of real service.

It is also hoped that the book may contribute something toward magnifying the importance of the position of elementary principal in our city and town-school organization, by revealing the possibilities for larger professional service, and in consequence may attract better and better trained men and women into the work. The organization of education during the past ten to fifteen years has gone forward by leaps and bounds, and there is every reason to think that the next ten to fifteen years will witness an even greater development in the scientific organization of the instructional process. This will call for sound professional training and genuine administrative and supervisory skill on the part of those

PREFACE

who are to direct our schools, and this in turn must inevitably result in changing the principalship of an elementary school in our cities into a career of quite satisfactory emoluments and large professional importance.

My thanks are due to many students who have provided me with concrete illustrative material covering actual school practices, and to six in particular for plans of the school buildings and grounds reproduced in Figures 5 to 10. I am also especially indebted to Mr. William R. Rutherford, formerly superintendent of schools at Eugene, Oregon, and now in the educational service of the Navy, for help with the bibliographies and for permission to use some half dozen pages from his master's thesis on the supervision of instruction; to my colleague, Professor John C. Almack, for a number of practical suggestions; and to Mr. Howard O. Welty, principal of the Lockwood Junior High School in Oakland, California, for having read the manuscript and suggested a number of changes and additions which his experience as an elementary-school principal indicated as desirable.

ELLWOOD P. CUBBERLEY

STANFORD UNIVERSITY

CONTENTS

PART I

THE PRINCIPALSHIP AND THE PRINCIPAL

CHAPTER I. TYPE FORMS OF ADMINISTRATIVE ORGANIZATION   3

The unit for educational administration — Supervision of the schools — Specialization of the supervisory function — Type forms of school organization — Other types of elementary-school organization — The group, or supervising principal — Desirable use of the group-principal idea — Effectiveness of building supervision — Questions and problems.

CHAPTER II. THE PRINCIPALSHIP AND THE PRINCIPAL . . 18

Position of the principalship — Complementary nature of principal and superintendent — The principal in the administrative organization — Team work within the system — Personal qualities demanded — Special qualifications for the office — The personal equation — Importance of the office — Difficult situations — Personal relationships — What the principalship offers — A student's opportunity — Learning and working — Questions and problems.

CHAPTER III. GENERAL NATURE OF THE PRINCIPAL'S WORK 37

Range of duties — Organization duties — Administrative duties — Supervisory duties — Importance of the supervisory function — Social duties — Saving time for work — Evolving a better working schedule — Laying out one's work — Handle callers expeditiously — Have a working schedule — Outlining the major problems of the school — Questions and problems — Selected references for Part I.

PART II

THE ORGANIZATION OF A SCHOOL

CHAPTER IV. PRELIMINARY CONFERENCES AND ORGANIZATION 59

The problem in the large — Learning the larger outlines of his problem — Seeing the superintendent of schools — Essential purposes of the visit — Building reconnaissance — Preliminary teachers' meetings — The new-teachers' building conference — The building conference for all teachers — General nature of this conference — Planning for the opening day — Suggestions for first-day procedure — Larger aims and purposes — Value of these conferences — Questions and problems.

CONTENTS

CHAPTER V. THE FIRST DAY OF SCHOOL 78

The call for executive ability — The building in readiness — Beginning the work — Starting the school — Beginning school with an assembly — Special conditions — Recess, lines, and assembly — The afternoon teachers' meeting — Questions and problems.

CHAPTER VI. INTERMISSIONS, LINES, AND DRILLS . . . 93

1. Intermissions and lines — Size of grounds a limiting factor — Handling recess periods — Lines and marching — The argument for lines and marching — Organizing the lines — The argument against lines — Minimizing the marching procedure — Building up self-control.

2. Fire-drills — Purpose of the drill — Organizing the fire-drill — Directions for fire-drill — Cautions to be observed — Special points to be looked after — Questions and problems.

CHAPTER VII. YARD AND BUILDING ORGANIZATION . . 117

1. Yard organization — Varying problem — The teachers and yard duty — Dividing off the play space — Apportioning the grounds and apparatus — The small school grounds — A satisfactory playground outfit — Supplies, and use of grounds — Supervising the play — Advantages of good play organization — Supervision at the lunch hour.

2. Supervision of toilets and basements — Toilets a strong influence — Shaping conditions — Use and supervision of the toilets — Stopping trouble — Handling through school organization and teaching — The basement — Questions and problems — Selected references.

CHAPTER VIII. THE CROWDED-BUILDING PROBLEM . . . 140

The principal and the problem — Solutions for the crowded-building problem — Shifting the district lines — Using portables and renting rooms — Part-time instruction — Other expedients to increase the carrying load — Building reorganization to increase the carrying load — The companion-class plan — The platoon plan — Applying the platoon plan to an old-type building — How program such a school — Applying the platoon plan to a modern building — Administrative details to be considered — Educational advantages of the plan — Questions and problems — Selected references.

CHAPTER IX. PROGRAM-MAKING 162

Different types of programs — Principles in program-making — Special supervisors and the programs — Program standards — Departmental type programs — Other special-type programs — The companion-class and the platoon-type programs — The chief difficulties encountered — Questions and problems.

CONTENTS

PART III

THE ADMINISTRATION OF A SCHOOL

CHAPTER X. BUSINESS ORGANIZATION AND ADMINISTRATION 185

1. The office and its work — The principal and office routine — System and the man — The school without an office clerk — Classifying duties and organizing a working schedule — Minor schemes for saving time — The school with an office clerk — Office hours.

2. Supplies and the storeroom — Types of supplies required — Ordering these supplies — Giving out the supplies — Keeping records and charging.

3. A small school budget — Need for and use of — Apportionment and accounting.

4. Blank forms and reports — Blanks for pupils and parents — Other blanks and forms used in the school.

5. Relations with the central office — Punctuality and proper form.

Questions and problems — Selected references

CHAPTER XI. THE SCHOOL JANITOR AND HIS WORK . . . 209

The position, and janitorial types — Varied nature of the janitor's work — The task of the school principal — Administrative principles in dealing with the janitor — Placing responsibility for service — Reasonable standards for work — Estimating the janitor's work — The daily building inspection — The janitor as a helper — Questions and problems — Selected references.

CHAPTER XII. HEALTH AND SANITARY CONTROL . . . 223

A principal's work in health matters — Child hygiene — Health teaching — What any school may do — A campaign of health education — Malnutrition, school feeding, fresh-air rooms — First-aid work — The first-aid case — First-aid teaching in the school — Utilizing the Scouts — Organization of a school health department — Junior Health Leagues — The Junior Red Cross — The school nurse and health supervision — A professional school health service — Questions and problems — Selected references.

CHAPTER XIII. THE ATTENDANCE OF PUPILS 247

A universal problem — Causes of irregular attendance — Handling the problem — Checking the school census — Locating the missing ones — The daily classroom check — Some principles to be followed — Devices for stimulating attendance — Principal and teachers and the home — The visiting teacher — The spirit of the school and attendance — Use of stronger methods — Questions and problems — Selected references.

CONTENTS

CHAPTER XIV. DISCIPLINE AND CONTROL 265

Inheriting an unruly school — Transforming an unruly school — Minor disorders in the school — Fighting among pupils — After treatment for fighting — The school bully: promoted fights: gang fights — Lying and stealing — Vulgarity and obscenity — The principal as judge — Making discipline productive — Decreasing discipline by prevention — Questions and problems — Selected references.

CHAPTER XV. THE TEACHER AND GOVERNMENT . . . 284

Relation of principal and teachers — Different classes of teachers — Shaping conditions to be of service — Strengthening the teacher in government — Causes of poor control — What a new principal may find — Supporting the teacher in government — Supporting the teacher when wrong — Protecting the teacher — The complaining parent — The irate parent who comes to the school — Improving relations with parents — Questions and problems.

CHAPTER XVI. BUILDING UP A SCHOOL SPIRIT 302

The school without spirit — What is school spirit? — The principal creates this spirit — What means to use — Make the instruction good — Monitorial service — The playground games — Organization of group activities — Scouts and Leagues — School entertainments — The school assembly — The school savings bank — Outside influences that help — The pupil-government idea — Partial plans and adaptations — The school council — The school-captains plan — The School Congress idea — Results of such pupil-control plans — Need for this work in our modern society — Difficulties the principal will meet — Questions and problems.

CHAPTER XVII. USE OF THE ASSEMBLY PERIOD . . . 320

Arranging for school assemblies — Importance of the assembly period — The principal and the assembly period — "Heart-to-heart" talks — Types of assemblies — Types of assembly programs — Class responsibility for programs — A month's program — The platoon school or Gary-type assembly — Other values of the school assembly — Questions and problems — Selected references.

PART IV

THE SUPERVISION OF INSTRUCTION

CHAPTER XVIII. KNOWING THE SCHOOL 337

Preparing the way for supervision — Knowing his community — The census reports and his school — The age-and-grade distribution sheet — The type of school revealed — Causes for this condition — Promotional-failure studies — A new aid in pupil classification — Use of intelligence testing — What intelligence tests

CONTENTS

may reveal as to class groups — Importance of graphic methods and of the new psychological tools for the school principal — Questions and problems — Selected references.

CHAPTER XIX. CLASSIFYING AND PROMOTING THE PUPILS . 358

The principal and promotional procedure — Type plans for school classification — Special plans sometimes used — Homogeneous working groups — Means for obtaining homogeneous working groups — Promotional rules — Special promotions — Securing results by individual study — Value of, in school administration — The special, or ungraded room — Best use of such a room — Use of as a clearing house — Acceleration and retardation in a parallel-course school — The promotional problem in the differentiated-course school — Special promotions and progress under this plan — Combination promotional plans — Adaptations for the slow and the capable — Questions and problems — Selected references.

CHAPTER XX. OBTAINING RESULTS FROM THE COURSES OF STUDY 388

Types of courses of study — Using the course of study as a stimulus to thinking — Mapping out the instruction — Use and abuse of lesson plans — Assistance to teachers — Plans a means to an end — The course of study not an end in itself — Getting results by drives — The question of home study by pupils — The home and home study — What is good teaching? — New work for the school principal — Organizing a school for directed study — Redirecting the instruction — The teacher's part in the work — Where directed study is needed — What directed study may add — Questions and problems — Selected references.

CHAPTER XXI. THE SPECIAL TEACHERS AND THEIR WORK . 414

Types of special teachers — The primary- or grammar-grades' supervisor — The problem of the special supervisor — The principal and the special supervisor — Types of difficulties encountered — The place of the principal in special instruction — Coöperation with the supervisors — Best use of the supervisor's time — The special supervisor in the classrooms — Departmental-type organization — Platoon-type organization — The supervisory work of the principal — Questions and problems — Selected references.

CHAPTER XXII. PLANNING THE SUPERVISION 431

Supervision a supreme duty — Supervisory mistakes — Beginning supervision in a new school — Good introductory plans — Planning what is to be done — Types of supervisory plans — Definite long-time supervisory planning — Professional leadership — Paving the way for helpfulness — The technique of visitation — Visitation records — Offering constructive criticisms — Keeping the conference informal — Keeping the criticism constructive — Supervision should liberate the teacher — Questions and problems — Selected references.

CONTENTS

Chapter XXIII. Helping the Teacher 459

Types of teachers — Types of service — The beginning teacher — Building up the beginner in teaching skill — The group conference — Demonstration teaching — A visiting day — Special teaching problems — A teaching problem illustrated — Course of study problems — Professional reading — Discovering special ability — Training in working habits — Rating the teachers — Questions and problems — Selected references.

Chapter XXIV. Measuring the Instruction . . . 485

New scientific tools — Uses of these new tools — The so-called informal tests — Use of standardized tests — Diagnostic value of the tests illustrated by handwriting — By spelling — By reading — Use of the tests to measure school progress — What achievement tests do not reveal — Importance of the mental age (I.Q.) — New achievement norms — Importance of the achievement quotient (A.Q.) — The principal and educational measurement — Teachers' marks and report cards — Vocational guidance uses — Intelligence requirements of the vocations — Questions and problems — Selected references.

Chapter XXV. Making Teachers' Meetings Profitable 513

The teachers' view — Reasons for this attitude — Objectionable types of meetings — Responsibility of a principal — Types, time, frequency, and method — Have definite objectives — Types of objectives — The principal as the professional leader of the group — Rules and cautions — Questions and problems — Selected references.

PART V

SCHOOL EXTENSION

Chapter XXVI. Extra School Activities 533

1. Special school occasions — Changed conception of the school — Building up school support — Special school visitation days — Special program days — Annual exhibit days.
2. Entertainments to raise money — The arguments against — The opposite point of view — Handling such an entertainment — Minimizing the work of preparation.
3. Inter-school contests — Value of if properly controlled — An opportunity to teach important lessons — Rules for handling inter-school contests — Selected references.

Chapter XXVII. The Parent-Teacher Association . 548

The new school-and-home organization movement — When to organize an association — Troublesome organizations — Need for a constructive program of work — Meetings, and types of work — Working through these organizations — Selected references.

CONTENTS

Chapter XXVIII. The Principal as a Leader in the Profession 560

His duty in leadership — The professional spirit — The professional spirit has its basis in knowledge — Marks of the professional leader — Maintenance of professional standards — Selected references.

Index 567

FIGURES IN THE TEXT

1. A Typical Small-City School System 7
2. Same City as in Figure 1, but with more Children . . 9
3. Two Types of the Group System 12
4. Illustrating Another Method of using the Supervising Principal Idea 13
5. An Old-Type Fourteen-Room One-Exit School Building 95
6. An Old-Type Frame Three-Story-and-Basement Twenty-Room Building. 96
7. A Frame Sixteen-Room Elementary-School Building . . 98
8. A Twenty-four-Room California Elementary School . . 99
9. A One-Story-and-Basement Town Consolidated School . 101
10. A Modern-Type Fireproof City School Building . . 103
11. Yard Duty Assignments for a Fifteen-Teacher School . 121
12. Age-Periods for Plays and Games 123
13. Showing how Congestion may be relieved by moving District Lines 143
14. A Fifth-Grade Program in a Companion-Class School . 149
15. A Classroom Weight Record 229
16. Results from Accident-Prevention Instruction in Detroit 236
17. Acceleration and Retardation shown graphically . . . 343
18. Results of a Five-Year Study of Pupil Progress in one School 345
19. Age-Distribution of the Pupils of Grade 5B, Table VIII, School 346
20. Percentage of Pupils in each Grade not promoted at Last Four Semi-annual Promotions 347
21. Results of the Binet Intelligence Test as Applied to 397 Entering (1B) Pupils, Oakland, California. . . . 351
22. Chronological and Mental Age compared for the Pupils of Grade 5B, Table VIII, School 353
23. The Parallel-Course Plan 359
24. The Differentiated-Course Plan 361
25. A Handwriting Specimen Analyzed 490
26. Results of a Spelling Test with Three Fifth-Grade Classes. 491
27. The C-Course Spelling Class analyzed 492

28. Showing the Scores of a Sixth-Grade Class on the Courtis Silent Reading Test, No. 2 494
29. Median Scores of a Sixth-Grade Class in September, and the following April, as measured by the Courtis Standard Research Tests in Arithmetic, Series B . . . 495

LIST OF TABLES

1. Suggested Time Distribution for Primary Grades . . 168
2. Suggested Time Distribution for Grammar Grades . . 169
3. Program for a Fifth Grade in a Grade-Type School . . 171
4. Departmental Program, Grades 6–8 173
5. Teacher Distribution for a Twelve-Class Platoon-Type School 176
6. Weekly Class Program of a Twelve-Class Platoon-Type School, by Classes 178–179
7. Weekly Room Program of a Twelve-Class Platoon-Type School, by Rooms 180–181
8. An Age-Grade School Distribution Table 341
9. Causes of Non-Promotion, by Subjects and Grades . . 349
10. Showing the Working Capacity of Nine Fifth-Grade Pupils 502

LIST OF FORMS

1. A Principal's February Working Schedule 51
2. A Monthly Attendance Record Sheet 253
3. A Card Lesson-Plan Form, filled out 393
4. A Classroom Supervision Outline 441
5. A Classroom Supervisory-Visit Record 448
6. A Visiting-Day Direction Form 472
7. A Teacher-Efficiency Score Card 481
8. Pupil Diagnosis for Teacher of Ungraded Room . . . 493

THE PRINCIPAL AND HIS SCHOOL
..
PART I
THE PRINCIPALSHIP AND THE PRINCIPAL

THE PRINCIPAL AND HIS SCHOOL

CHAPTER I

TYPE FORMS OF ADMINISTRATIVE ORGANIZATION

The unit for educational administration. The unit for educational administration with us is the school district, though we have many different types of districts, and these vary much in size and in the scope of the school system which they maintain. We have rural-school districts, village-school districts, incorporated-town school districts, consolidated-school districts, county-unit school districts, small-city school districts, and large-city school districts. At one extreme is the little Southern or Western mountain school district, under the immediate control of three local trustees, and employing but one teacher. At the other extreme is the metropolitan-city school district, under a board of education and employing a staff of supervisory officers and thousands of teachers for the hundred or more schools it directs and maintains. Between these two extremes in size we find the village, town, consolidated, and small and medium-sized city school districts, each having problems of organization and administration more or less peculiar to itself.

A common feature of practically all types and sizes and forms of school districts is the presence of a governing board, known as a board of school trustees, school committee, board of school directors, board of education, board for school control, or some similar title, which represents the people on the one hand and the State on the other in the organization and administration of the schools. Only in some of the recently-organized commission-governed or business-manager type of cities do we find the board for school control lacking. This board, acting under the school laws of the State, but also more or less independently, organizes and directs the administration of the schools under its charge.

Supervision of the schools. The board, though, acts only when meeting as a body, and by recorded vote. Individually, and outside of the board meeting, the members have no actual authority, though this is often assumed. To the teacher, if there be but one; to the principal, if there be two or more; and to a supervising principal or superintendent, if there be a number of schools, the board must entrust many of the details of organizing, supervising, and administering the work of the schools. As the school increases in size the number of functions and duties which must be entrusted to the principal and the superintendent naturally increase.

In a large school building in a town, or in a city school system maintaining many schools, the principal of a school has many important duties and responsibilities. Upon him must rest, to a very large extent, the responsibility not only for the immediate supervision of the instruction in the school but for the smooth running of its administrative machinery as well. He must look after the details of organization and administration, settle difficulties and problems as they arise, supervise the instruction, and direct and administer his school as a unit in a larger organization or system.

Specialization of the supervisory function. The tendency of our cities has been to specialize the supervisory function. Not only has the superintendent been given additional powers, special supervisors been appointed, and bureaus for the study of supervisory problems created, but the principal has been freed more and more from teaching and from clerical duties that he may devote a larger percentage of his time to the close supervision of the instruction in his school. More and more has the tendency grown to impose on him the responsibility for the successful organization and administration of his school and for the proper progress of the children in it. While this tendency has perhaps been more marked in the cities, where a principal directs but one of a number of units in a large school system, it has also been quite in evidence in town-school organization, where the school system is represented wholly or in large part by one large school building.

To carry out the supervisory function successfully in a city calls for the organization of an adequate supervisory corps, under the general direction of and responsible to the superintendent of schools, and the unifying of the work of this corps that it may render effective service. To the principal of the high school, one division and kind of work will fall; to the principal of the junior high school, another; to the elementary-school principals, another; and to the special supervisors, still another. Of all of these the principals of the elementary schools occupy a position the importance of which has seldom been fully realized or attained.

It is of the work of the principal of an elementary school in a city, or the supervising principal in a city, town, or county-unit school organization, with which this volume of the series will be concerned. Before taking up the work of such a principal in detail, we shall first examine briefly the type forms for school organization which have so far been evolved, that we may have before us the different types of organization and work which we have to consider. We shall also examine briefly the personal character of the service which the principal himself is expected to render.

Type forms of school organization. Passing at once to an examination of school organization as it relates to the principalship, we find a number of type forms in use in our American cities and towns. The simplest form is the village or city elementary-school principalship, the principal being in charge of a small building containing from eight to twenty teachers in charge of the different school grades. The following organization for a twelve-room elementary-school building may be regarded as fairly typical of that found in many towns and cities in different parts of the United States.

> 1 principal, not teaching.
> 12 teachers, in charge of grades, as follows:
>
> | | |
> |---|---|
> | 1. Kindergarten | 7. 4 B and 4 A |
> | 2. Receiving class, and 1 B | 8. 4 A and 5 B |
> | 3. 1 B and 1 A | 9. 5 B and 5 A |
> | 4. 2 B and 2 A | 10. 6 B and 6 A |
> | 5. 2 A and 3 B | 11. 7 B and 7 A |
> | 6. 3 A | 12. 8 B and 8 A |
>
> 1 school janitor.
> Total, 14 persons.
> Average daily attendance, about 400 pupils.
> School grounds cover a quarter of a city block.

A school system consisting of three or four such elementary-school buildings, two or three smaller buildings in which the principals may also teach a class, and one high-school building, and employing a total of 75 teachers and principals and having an average daily attendance of approximately 1800 pupils, would be fairly representative of many cities in this country which have a total population of from 15,000 to 18,000 inhabitants. Such a city might be represented by the distribution shown in Figure 1. Quite frequently a city of such population-size would have a larger number of small school buildings and fewer large ones.

In a compactly built Massachusetts manufacturing city, on the contrary, we find one third of the teaching force and

TYPE FORMS OF ORGANIZATION

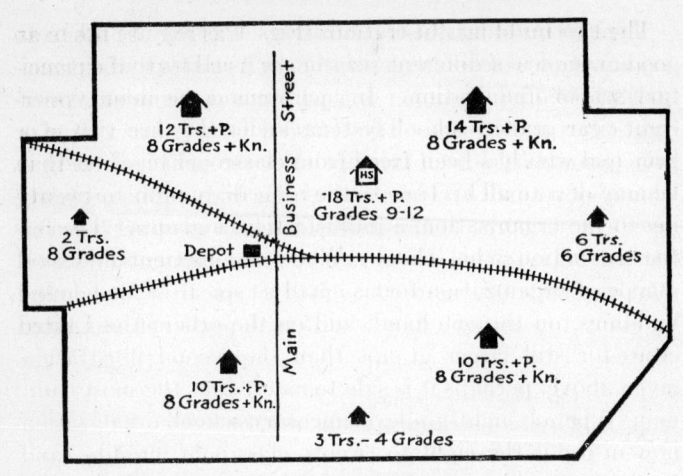

FIGURE 1. A TYPICAL SMALL-CITY SCHOOL SYSTEM

Total teachers employed, 75; principals who do not teach, 5; one central high school; four large elementary schools having eight grades and kindergarten; and three small elementary schools.

one third of the pupils of the city in one elementary-school building, with the following teaching and supervisory force:

I. Non-teaching force (8)
    1 Principal
    1 Assistant Principal
    1 Sub-master
    1 Assistant to the Principal
    1 Office clerk
    3 Janitors

II. Regular Teachers (43)
    3 Kindergarten teachers
    5 First-grade teachers
    6 Second-grade teachers
    5 Third-grade teachers
    7 Fourth-grade teachers
    5 Fifth-grade teachers
    5 Sixth-grade teachers
    4 Seventh-grade teachers
    3 Eighth-grade teachers

III. Extra and Special Teachers (11)
    1 Substitute teacher
    1 Special teacher — Boys
    1 Special teacher — Girls
    1 Ungraded-room teacher
    1 Open-air-room teacher
    6 Non-English teachers

Total force, 62 persons.
Average daily attendance, about 1800 pupils.
Building, 50 classrooms, offices, and assembly hall.

The two building illustrations (Figs. 1, 2) may be taken as good examples of different sizes of the usual type of elementary-school organization. In each we find the older type of eight-year graded school system, under the direction of a principal who has been freed from classroom teaching that he may devote all his time to the immediate problems relating to the organization, administration, and supervision of the instruction in his school. While we sometimes find such a type of organization for as small as six- to eight-teacher buildings, on the one hand, and on the other in our large cities for still larger groups than the second illustration given above, perhaps it is safe to assert that the most common type of eight-grade elementary-school organization now in use is the eight to twenty classroom building, and for each of which a principal who does not teach is employed.

Other types of elementary-school organization. The simplest form of variation from the type just described is that in which the two upper grades, and not infrequently the three upper grades, have been reorganized under what is known as the departmental type of upper-grade organization. Under this plan the lower grades are still taught by grade teachers, but the upper grades are taught by subjects and the pupils move about from teacher to teacher. Such a plan of combined grade and departmental organization may be worked out easily in any large elementary-school building.

Another simple variation from the grade type of organization is that in which some of the upper grades have been omitted. Where the junior high school type of school has been established in a city, the seventh and eighth grades are usually missing from the grade schools, these, together with the ninth grade from the high school, having been concentrated in one or more central schools and organized under a departmental plan of instruction. Sometimes one finds only the first five or four, or even three grades present in a school building, but in such cases the school is usually a primary school, feeding into some other elementary school not far away.

The junior high school type of organization, or rather reorganization, has frequently been introduced as much as a means of economically handling a congested-building problem, presented by a city growing in population and not expanding in area, as because of its educational merits. Such a situation is well shown in Figure 2, which shows how the

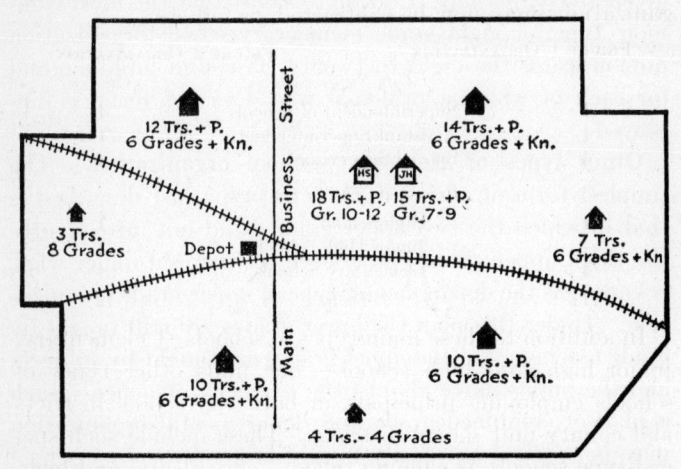

FIGURE 2. SAME CITY AS IN FIGURE 1, BUT WITH MORE CHILDREN

Due to increase in population without increase in area, all schools became congested, and the solution was found in the building of a junior high school, near the high school building. The city now employs 93 teachers, and 6 principals who do not teach.

same city used in Figure 1 handled a somewhat evenly distributed population growth sufficient to necessitate the employment of eighteen additional teachers, and by the erection of but one new school building. One new junior high school building, erected at a central location, relieved the high school building of caring for the ninth grade, and also took from all the elementary schools the seventh and eighth grades. These latter now become six-year elementary schools, and the school system has been changed from the 8–4 plan of organization to the 6–3–3 plan. The new children in the first six grades in the city represented by the eleven additional teachers for grades one to six have been accommodated in the most economical manner possible, and at the same time a better form of educational organization has been obtained.

The old (Figure 1) and the new (Figure 2) supervisory organizations may now be contrasted, as follows:

FIGURE 1 ORGANIZATION		FIGURE 2 ORGANIZATION
	City Supervisors	
1	Superintendent of Schools	1
1	Assistant Superintendent	1
4	Special Supervisors	4
	Principals who do not teach	
1	High School	1
–	Junior High School	1
4	Elementary Schools	4
11	Totals	12

In addition to these main types of schools — elementary, junior high, and high school — one finds other types of schools employing principals, in both city school districts and county-unit school districts. These include such special-type schools as evening schools, agricultural and technical high schools, and special schools for some form of special instruction, such as industrial schools, parental schools, schools for defectives, etc.

The following is typical of the administrative organization in a city school district employing a teaching and supervisory staff of approximately 200, or in a county-unit school system employing approximately 150 teachers and supervisors.

TYPE FORMS OF ORGANIZATION

City District	County-Unit District
1 City Superintendent	1 County Superintendent
1 Assistant Superintendent	1 Assistant Superintendent
1 Supervisor of primary work	1 Supervisor of primary work
3 Supervisors of special subjects	3 Supervisors of special subjects
1 Supervisor of health and play	1 Supervisor of health and play
1 City attendance officer	1 County attendance officer
1 High school principal	1 Principal of county agricultural high school
6 Elementary-school principals, who do not teach	4 Principals of consolidated schools, who do not teach
2 Elementary-school principals, who teach	7 Principals of consolidated schools, who teach
1 Principal of a vocational school, who teaches part time	

The group, or supervising principal. In all the types so far studied we have considered only the building principal. In a few of our cities another type of organization for the administration and supervision of schools has been worked out, which is known as the group or supervising principal. The essential features of the group plan are shown in Figure 3, two forms or types of the group supervisory system being given. In each case a small group of schools is placed under the immediate control of a supervising principal, who looks after the larger details of administration and supervises all the schools of the group, assisted usually by vice-principals in each of the buildings. These vice-principals usually teach a class, and hence have no time for supervisory and not much time for administrative duties.

In cities having a number of small school buildings, located but short distances apart, some form of group supervisory organization is almost a necessity if economical and effective supervision is to be secured. In many cities now employing the group-principal plan for supervision, the real reason for so doing is the large number of small buildings located in close proximity to one another. Where large buildings not too close together can be had, better school administration and supervision can usually be secured by having a principal who does not teach for each elementary-school building.

Desirable use of the group-principal idea. There is, however, a certain use which may be made of the group- or supervising-principal idea which probably would lead to greater effectiveness in school administration and super-

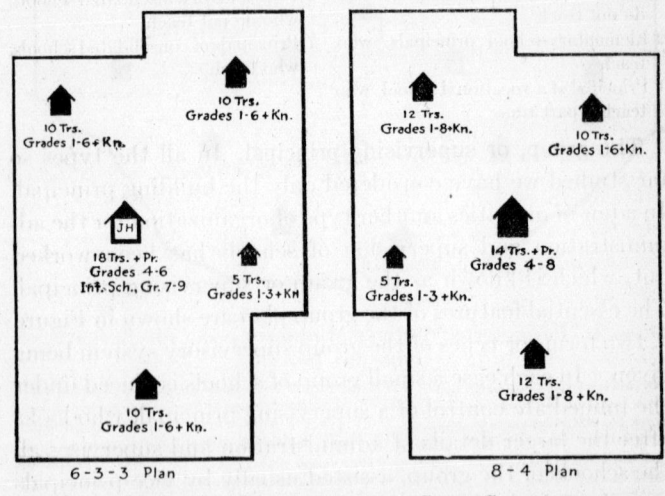

FIGURE 3. TWO TYPES OF THE GROUP SYSTEM

Each group requires 53 teachers and a supervising principal. Each may be assumed to represent a section of a city, and to be bounded by street lines. The organization to the right is based on an eight-years' elementary school, and a four-years' high school; the one to the left on a six-years' graded elementary school, a three-years' junior high school, and a three years' high school. Grades four to six have been retained in the junior high school building because of building and neighborhood necessities.

vision. It would not, however, be materially cheaper, and might even cost more. It is based on a combination of the two ideas of (*a*) so reorganizing education as to provide better opportunities and instruction for children, and of (*b*) providing sufficient supervision and specializing it somewhat in kind. Figure 4 illustrates the idea very well for a city of approximately 35,000 inhabitants, and employing a teaching staff of approximately 220 teachers and supervisory officers.

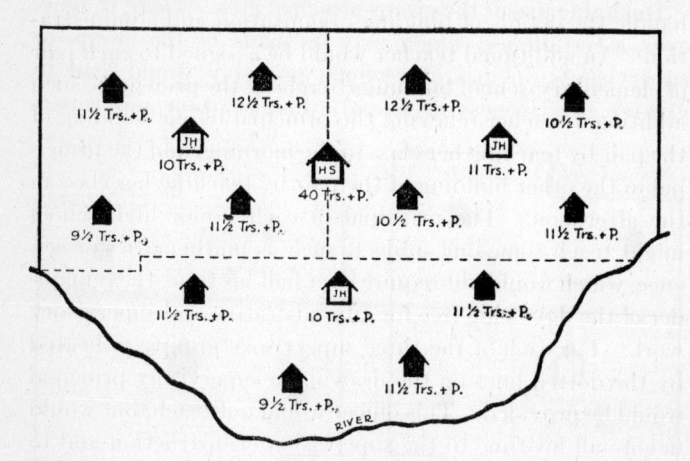

FIGURE 4. ILLUSTRATING ANOTHER METHOD OF USING THE SUPERVISING PRINCIPAL IDEA

In this river city of approximately 35,000 inhabitants the schools are so located and of such size as to permit of the organization of the city into three groups of five schools each, employing 55, 56, and 54 teachers respectively, and for each of which groups a supervising principal is employed. In addition the principal for each elementary-school building is freed from class work half of each day for the administration and supervision of the school. The central school in each group is an intermediate, or junior high school, and the three junior high schools send their pupils to the central city high school. Each supervising principal here is in effect an assistant superintendent of schools. As is explained in the text, this might also be a county-unit school system.

The city, as will be seen from the drawing, is divided into three school groups, each group having four elementary schools and a junior high school. The kindergarten and only the first six grades are to be found in each of the elementary schools. The junior high schools contain the seventh, eighth, and ninth grades, these being organized on the departmental plan. The central high school contains the tenth, eleventh, and twelfth grades of instruction.

Under the plan shown in Figure 4, a woman probably

would be placed in charge of each elementary school as principal. This principal would teach half of each day, the schools here being small in size, and in addition she would handle the details of building organization and administration. An additional teacher would be assigned to each pair of elementary-school buildings to relieve the principals, such additional teacher relieving the principal in one building of the pair by teaching her class in the morning, and the principal in the other building of the pair by teaching her class in the afternoon. The principal in each junior high school might teach some one subject, such as mathematics or science, which would not require over half his time, the remainder of the day being free for administrative and supervisory work. For each of the three supervisory groups, indicated by the dotted lines on the drawing, a supervisory principal would be provided. This officer would not teach, but would devote all his time to the supervision of instruction and to the larger features and problems of the organization and administration of the five buildings of his group. Details of administration would be handled by the building principal. The three supervising principals under such a plan as is shown in Figure 4 would be in effect assistant superintendents for the schools of the city, but with definite supervisory areas and duties assigned to them.

This same plan of group-principal organization would apply equally well to a county-unit type of school organization. If we imagine Figure 4 to represent a county school district, instead of a city, the fifteen schools of the drawing each to be a consolidated rural school under a principal who probably teaches part of each day, the high school to be a central county agricultural high school, and the three groups as shown to represent three subdivisions of the county for supervisory purposes, we would have a county-unit supervisory organization well worked out, such as might be found in Utah or Maryland. The administrative principles involved would be practically the same, in either case.

Effectiveness of building supervision. Whatever plan or combination of plans may be worked out for providing the needed supervision of instruction and the details of school building administration, either in city or in county-unit school systems, there can be no question but that plenty of close professional supervision pays and pays well. The hundred and one little details of building organization and administration need constant attention if smooth running conditions are to be expected. Where little things are constantly looked after big things seldom arise. The oversight of the material and educational surroundings of three to four hundred children assembled in one school building, if properly done, will give a building principal plenty of occupation without any regular fixed classroom service. The physical conditions surrounding the work of instruction need to be looked after, the playground properly handled, children's needs and difficulties attended to without undue delay, the school morale built up and maintained, parents seen and treated courteously, the progress of the children through the school watched and studied, and teachers helped and stimulated to do their best work. Upon the building principal falls very largely the task of creating the right conditions and atmosphere for the school. "As is the principal, so is the school," is a much truer statement than the similar one relating to the teacher.

Viewed from the standpoint of educational efficiency alone, a good school principal should pay for his services by reason of the more economical progress of the children through the grades. The acceleration ought to be greater and the retardation less by reason of the more scientific placement of pupils. The few comparative studies which have been made show that this is the case. The small outlying schools of a city which do not have a principal freed from classroom instruction usually do not make the educational progress of the large well-supervised city school, while the larger amount of retardation in our rural and small town schools, as compared with good city schools, is a matter of common knowledge. The business of the school should be to get the children through the grades as rapidly as their abilities will permit. Not only do all our studies reveal the heavy loss from school of retarded pupils, but also that children who reach the high school late usually make the poorest success with high school studies. On the other hand the bright pupils, who need to be singled out and helped along, because they are usually held back too much by the teachers, are the ones who should be pushed forward to the high school and given extra advantages. Such useful and economically important service pays largely, and amply justifies the presence and expense of a good building principal.

How to organize and administer a school and produce conditions leading to most effective building or group supervision is a problem that should interest every building or supervisory principal, in all types of school organization, and will be the subject of this volume in this series of textbooks. Before proceeding to the details of building organization, administration, and supervision however, we wish to devote two chapters to a consideration of the nature and work and opportunities of the principalship itself.

QUESTIONS AND PROBLEMS

1. State the disadvantages in school administration when the principal teaches the entire school day.
2. If a principal were obliged by regulation to teach one hour a day, would it be better that he teach one fixed class at the same period daily, or that he have no fixed assignment and move about? Why?

TYPE FORMS OF ORGANIZATION

3. On the basis of salaries in your neighborhood, 35 pupils on an average to a teacher, and a 180-day year, calculate the cost per pupil per day and per year for supervision by having a principal who does not teach in
   a. a ten-room building:
   b. a sixteen-room building:
   c. a twenty-four-room building.
4. Calculate, similarly, the cost per teacher which such supervision adds.
5. Calculate costs for supervision on the same basis as in 3, for the group of schools shown in Figure 3 for each of the following plans:
   a. Assume that the four large schools have individual principals who do not teach and the small school a principal who teaches, but no supervising principal.
   b. Assume a supervising principal for the group, principals who teach for the small school and the large central school, and principals who do not teach elsewhere.
   c. Assume a supervising principal for the group, a principal who teaches in the small school, and two additional teachers employed to relieve the principals of the other schools each a half of every day.
6. Make comparative calculations for the schools of Figure 4, for each of the following plans:
   a. Organized as described in the text.
   b. Drop the half-day teacher in each elementary school and the supervising principal for each group, and substitute principals who teach and one assistant superintendent for the city, for supervision.
   c. Drop the assistant superintendents entirely and provide principals who do not teach at all schools.
7. Calculate the total cost per day, on basis of local salary schedules and prices, for a twenty-room school, for teachers, principal supervision, janitor service, heat, light, and supplies.
8. In both problems 5 and 7, what are the percentages for "overhead"?

CHAPTER II

THE PRINCIPALSHIP AND THE PRINCIPAL

Position of the principalship. The principal of a school in a city school system occupies a peculiar and somewhat confidential relationship to the superintendent of the school system, and his connections with the superintendent's office must be on a higher plane than if he were merely a teacher. The relationship is analogous in the business world to that of the manager of a town branch of a public utility to the general superintendent of the business; to that of the manager of a single department to the general manager of a department store; to that of the superintendent of a division of a railroad to the president of the company; or to that of the colonel of a regiment to the commanding general of an army. In each case the manager or superintendent or president or general is responsible directly to the directors of the business or to the public authorities in charge for the larger outlines of policy and for the general success of the undertaking, while the subordinate in charge of a branch or a division or a regiment or a school is responsible only indirectly to the highest authorities, but is immediately responsible to the officer above him for the success of the division or unit entrusted to him for management and control. Still more, he is responsible for the management and control of his division or unit in accordance with the larger lines of policy decided upon by the commanding officer and the directors of the business, regardless of whether or not he approves or knew of or had any part in formulating the policy to be followed. On any other basis a business courts bankruptcy, an army disaster, and a school system disorganization and inefficiency.

Complementary nature of principal and superintendent.
The principal of a school and the superintendent of a school system hold somewhat complementary positions in the administration of a system of public instruction. The superintendent of the schools is primarily responsible to the school board and to the people of the whole city for the successful conduct of the whole school system; the principal is primarily responsible to the superintendent for the successful conduct of a single school, or, in the case of a supervising principal, a group of related schools. It is primarily the function of the superintendent to think and to plan and to lead; it is primarily the function of the principal to execute plans and to follow and to support. It is also the function of the superintendent of schools to pass upon and decide the more important matters referred to him from the schools and by the school board; it is the function of the principal to decide as many matters of a local nature as is possible, and to refer for decision only the more important questions to the central office above. A principal should be able to sense the superintendent's policy, and to carry it out without bothering him continually for details. He should also note the results of the policy in action, and should be willing to call the attention of the superintendent to what seem to him to be needed changes or to danger ahead. Both superintendent and principal must be alike able and willing to shoulder responsibility, to be frank and helpful to one another, and at times each must stand firmly in defense of the other. In a school system in which rapid progress is being made this is particularly important, as in such cases the progress in the schools often outruns the thinking of the people, and sooner or later a reaction is almost inevitable.

Such a relationship calls for many important executive qualities, some of which unfortunately are not possessed by the majority of school people. Especially does it call for tact, intelligence, convictions, good common sense, deep personal loyalty, technical knowledge, and a type of professional skill not always found in those who think they would make good school principals.

The principal in the administrative organization. The larger the school system becomes the more marked will the relationship described above become. Often new plans will be considered in conference, and sometimes so decided, but often instead matured plans will merely be given to the group to execute. Whether or not the principal has had a part in the maturing of the plans so promulgated, he must now feel a personal responsibility for their application and detailed working out in his particular school, and must coöperate fully in an effort to insure the success of his part of the common undertaking. Success or failure, too, usually depends upon him alone. Closely as he is in touch with his teachers, he can determine almost absolutely the fate, in his school, of any policy the superintendent may inaugurate.

Detailed conferences with subordinates are not possible in a large city school system. The superintendent of schools and the heads of departments under him, acting in conjunction with the board of education, must settle many of the larger features of policy and plan in the administration of a large city school system, and this without taking the time to confer over each detail with the principals and teachers. There are too many things to be done in a large school system to proceed by a plan so wasteful of time and effort. Much of what is so decided upon the principal must take for granted, and as the basis upon which his own work is to begin and to be carried on. His functions will be much more those of execution, in his own school or group of schools, of plans which have been decided upon by authorities of larger scope, than of helping to formulate new plans and policies for the school system as a whole. The superintendent, too, must often of necessity deal with problems only in the large, but the principal must work with these same problems in a much more limited and much more concrete way. The superintendent, too, often can present only the larger outlines of a plan which has been decided upon, and must leave to the principal the working out in his school of its smaller details.

It is such whole-hearted coöperative team work that insures a successful supervisory organization. To refuse to coöperate whole-heartedly because he was not consulted, or because he does not approve of the new plan, represents a form of bumptiousness running very close to actual disloyalty. Its exhibition ought to be clear notice to a superintendent and to a school board that a principal showing such characteristics is not one whom they can afford to advance further in the school system. If the new plan is fundamentally wrong it will in time so demonstrate its defects that it will have to be withdrawn, and a succession of such failures means the ultimate withdrawal of the superintendent promulgating them. This, however, is for the board of education rather than the principal to decide.

Team work within the system. The conduct of all coöperative undertakings, whether in business, sports, warfare, or education, calls for good team work on the part of all holding responsible positions on or in the team. Without team work, full and complete victories, in which all in a way share, cannot be won. Not only does each member of the team have a particular place to play and to fill, but for success each must also know the essential details and working rules of the game as a whole. The full philosophy of the game all do not need to know — that may be left largely to the leaders or directors. In school work this calls for intelligent direction and oversight from the top. On the part of those responsible for the success of the different administrative units of the school system — the principals — it calls for a high degree of individual efficiency, ability to shoulder responsibility, willingness to coöperate wholeheartedly, unity in carrying out a purpose, loyalty in support and defense of a plan, and at times self-effacement for the good of all.

One of the places where self-effacement is most frequently called for in the practical work of administering a school system is in the matter of credit for new ideas and achievements. Some otherwise satisfactory people seem incapacitated for team work in this respect. They not only want more than full credit for any new ideas they may develop, but not infrequently they want to keep a monopoly of the good ideas to themselves, so that their schools may seem better than the average of the system. They seem never to have learned that there is always glory enough to go around for all who deserve it. Not infrequently the same bad spirit manifests itself in jealousy of more progressive and more capable principals. They utterly fail to see that all energy spent in jealousy and internal dissension not only destroys their own highest efficiency, but also seriously interferes with effective team work within the system. The man filled with envy or carrying a constant "grouch" never inspires confidence, and is always relatively ineffective in any position that calls for leadership.

Personal qualities demanded. The position of principal in a school system, then, is a position of strategic importance. The larger the school system becomes the more strategic becomes the position of principal. A superintendent is almost entirely dependent upon the frankness and loyalty of a principal for information regarding the school and the community, and for recommendations as to needed changes in the work of the school. Upon the educational insight, largeness of vision, good nature, ability in administration, discretion, tact, personal loyalty, and frankness in discussion of the principals of a school system the success or failure of the policies evolved for the conduct of a school system in large part depends. The principal should feel that he represents the administration before the teachers, before the children, and before the parents, and that he acts largely in the place of and in the name of the superintendent of schools.

Misunderstandings of policy, manifestations of narrow-minded personal enmity, bitter political attacks, and severe newspaper criticism of the schools must at times be expected, so long as human nature remains what it is. To be frank enough to discuss plans freely with the superintendent, when asked; to be discreet enough not to talk outside about matters still under discussion; to be able to retain confidences granted; to be willing whole-heartedly to try to put plans into operation, even though they differ from what one might have wished; to labor to prevent or to remove misunderstandings by explaining plans and purposes; to bear responsibility without shirking; and at times to put one's back to the wall and stand solidly in defense of the system — calls for personal qualities that always command a good market price because they are not overabundant in this world. To be able and willing to give an opinion when requested, to state one's evidence and to draw conclusions, to shoulder responsibility when occasion demands, and to carry through necessary but disagreeable duties, calls for a quality of intelligence and a degree of courage and loyalty that will always command a premium in this world.

Special qualifications for the office. In addition to the right personal qualities, the position of school principal also calls for certain special qualifications. To be a good principal one should be a good teacher, should know the details of school organization and administration, and should have a reasonably satisfactory philosophy of the educational process which he is to supervise. These may be regarded as rather fundamental prerequisites. The principal ought to be able to take a class from any teacher and teach it well, and he ought to know the details of school organization and the reasons for doing things in certain ways better than all except a few of his older and more capable teachers. In educational grasp, as shown by his ability to supervise and to give reasons for doing things, he ought to be distinctively the educational leader of his school.

In addition to these purely educational qualifications, the person who would be principal must also possess that something so hard to test for or to define but which is known and recognized as executive capacity. This is a compound of many personal qualities and working habits. On the personal side, cleanliness, courtesy, good manners, and kindliness are important. A good executive is seldom a sour, discourteous, ill-mannered boor. Good working habits — promptness, speed and accuracy in work, a sense of order and system, and a good time sense — all are important. Without a feeling for punctuality and order and accuracy, and that sense of proper values which makes one continually conscious of passing time and the value of minutes, work is almost certain to pile up and the would-be executive will find himself continually behind in his work and late to his engagements. Still more, he is not likely to attract the attention of men who possess these fundamental traits.

A good sense of proportion, too, will be of use in revealing relative values, and in indicating relative time-worths of different executive details. Some things need to be done now, other things can wait until to-morrow. The ability to grasp details, to see the problem almost before it has been fully stated, to see what ought to be done and why, and to decide quickly and accurately on most questions that come up, are also very important ear-marks of an executive. The man who cannot decide anything without thinking it over at length, or whose quick decisions are twenty-five per cent wrong has little business in an executive position. Ninety per cent of the administrative questions and problems that come to an executive are questions and problems that he ought to be capable of deciding quickly and accurately, and then promptly dismiss them from his mind. Only a few questions and problems need sleeping over.

Ability to grasp and hold in mind numerous details, and to see details in their proper places and relationships, is another important characteristic of an executive. The man who cannot remember what he did yesterday, who has to keep and refer to notes as to his actions, and who cannot distinguish details from important central ideas, is not likely to make a very successful executive. Still another executive characteristic is the ability to shed details, to get them handled by others, to avoid deadening office routine, and to save time for the more important things that are to be done about a school. Not to do for long what others can do, in order to find time to do what others cannot do, is an important mark of executive capacity.

Every one has been told that the way to get ahead in this world is to do more than is expected of him, but not every one knows how to carry this precept into action. The qualities which most frequently impede the progress of men are lack of knowledge, lack of self-confidence, and idle habits of thought without the thought leading to action. Perhaps the best possible prescription for overcoming the first two and correcting the third is to daily do something that is in addition to one's daily duties. The effort to be useful in some new way, or to master some new idea or process, leads to the acquirement of knowledge, gives self-confidence, and carries thinking into action in one of the best of ways. Men who continually do this soon set themselves off from their fellows by reason of their larger knowledge, ability to do new things, and their habit of being serviceable in some new and unexpected way. They soon come to know so much and to be so useful that they make themselves indispensable. Ordinary natural ability and hard work are worth more than genius here.

The personal equation. Frequently otherwise good principals fail to achieve a high degree of success because of what for lack of a better term may be called "the personal equation." Every principal ought, once in a while, seriously to inquire of himself if he is, in his personal and official relations with teachers, pupils, and the public, all that he is asking his teachers and pupils to be. To many a boy and girl in school the principal is the only example of a man in the teaching profession they will ever come in close contact with, and the estimate of the profession, good or bad, of many a citizen of to-day goes back to the impressions of his school days. The principal must remember that he holds a particularly responsible position as a model in his community, somewhat corresponding to that of the priest in the parish under the old régime of the church. He must, in his dress, his manner, his speech, and his bearing so conduct himself that he will easily win and hold the respect of those teachers and pupils who have grown up under the best home influences, and who know the best social usages and practices of the world.

To this end he must remember to carry himself at all times as a gentleman of the world should and would. He must be clean, both in his person and in his speech and acts. His clothing, his cuffs and collar, and his shoes should be kept in good condition. His hair should be trimmed frequently, and kept clean and neatly combed. He must be careful to shave every morning. There must be nothing offensive about his breath or his person. On the streets and about his school, at least, he must not smoke. He must not frequent places where gentlemen do not go. In his dealings with his teachers he must be impartial, considerate, and just, and must show no special attentions and play no favorites in the group. His statements must be absolutely reliable; he must not shilly-shally to and fro; and his loyalty and support of both teacher and superintendent should be unquestioned.

Every executive, too, needs a good saving sense of humor. Many a situation is partly solved by laughing over it, or at least seeing its humorous side. In all his contacts with teachers, pupils, and parents he must seem both genuine and human. Pompous dignity will count for nothing, nor will a too familiar manner inspire respect. Freakish clothes, a singular manner, obsequiousness, or roughness and lack of consideration for others must all be equally avoided.

Given good personal qualities, good training, good executive sense, energy, industry, the ability to concentrate his efforts, studious habits, and the willingness to postpone present pleasures for the sake of a larger future, a young man or woman, entering the principalship in a city school system to-day, should be able to succeed in a large way. The service is important, and the scope of one's influence larger than most principals realize.

Importance of the office. We are not likely to overestimate the importance of the office of school principal. As the superintendent of schools gives tone and character to the whole school system, so the school principal gives tone and character to the school under his control. In the administration of a school system the superintendent should tend to magnify the office of school principal. Whatever can be done to add strength and dignity and responsibility to the office should be done, with a view to making each principal feel that his work is large and important, and that he must keep growing constantly if he is to continue to measure up to the demands of the position. Everything pertaining to his school should pass through his hands, and the position should be made one of definite and fixed responsibility.

The knowledge, insight, tact, skill, and qualities of helpful professional leadership of the principal of the school practically determine the ideals and standards of achievement of both teachers and pupils within the school. The best supervisory organization cannot make strong schools where principals are weak and inefficient, while a strong and capable principal can develop a strong school even in cities where the general supervisory organization is weak and the professional interest of teachers is low. The mere fact that helpful supervision is so predominantly personal in its nature and methods gives to the office of school principal large potential importance.

That our school principals, speaking generally and of the United States as a whole, realize the full possibilities of their position, few who have carefully observed principals at work would contend. Many principals give their time almost entirely to administrative duties and do little supervisory work, though the latter ought to be their most important function. Of those who do supervisory work, many fail to make their supervision helpfully constructive to the teachers supervised.

Often the principals are not wholly or even largely to blame for such a condition. Where the principal is given little authority to vary anything, or to depart from a prescribed uniformity, supervision easily degenerates into inspection and the office work exerts the strongest pull. Even good principals gradually lose their energy and their capacity for usefulness under such administrative conditions. The breaking up of uniformity and rigidity in administration, the placing of authority with and responsibility on the principals, and the awakening on their part of a desire to excel, are among the best means a superintendent can employ to improve the work of the school principal. If principals do not know it, the difference between office-chair administration and clerical perfection on the one hand, and helpful and constructive supervision on the other, should be clearly set forth and emphasized in the administration of the system.

Difficult situations. Sometimes a principal finds himself in the peculiar situation of sensing much more clearly what ought to be done than do the supervisory officers over him, and he finds himself chafing under the directions given as to work, or the limitations and restraints and office detail which the administration imposes upon him. The question now arises as to what should be the principal's attitude and action under such circumstances.

In the first place, the principal should be very sure that he is in the right. Possibly he is setting himself up as an authority in opposition to the superintendent on very inadequate grounds. The superintendent may know what ought to be done better than he. The public presumption is likely to be in the superintendent's favor in case of any conflict, and opposition may be regarded, as it not infrequently is, as mere bumptiousness on the part of a young fellow who is beginning to feel his oats.

On the other hand, the principal may be right, and in such a case he needs to consider his actions and attitude very carefully. He is always at liberty to talk over the situation with his superiors, and, if he is pleasant about it, and uses ordinary tact in selecting his time and method of approach, he will seldom encounter any difficulty in having his point of view heard and considered. Should he find himself unable to convince his superior officers that they are wrong and that he is right, he ought either to follow instructions and execute policies or resign. Refusal to obey instructions is not likely to accomplish anything. Only in the rarest of circumstances is one warranted in open rebellion, and he who chooses this method should remember that there are very few successful rebels in history, and that failure means professional disaster.

It is a truism that if one is to command he ought first to have learned to obey. This does not mean that a principal surrenders his professional opinions to a school board or to a superintendent when he becomes a paid employee in the school system. His right to these he retains, and as a citizen or in an educational meeting he is privileged to vote and speak as he thinks. His right to exploit these ideas in the administration of his school, however, in opposition to the expressed wishes or directions of those in positions of larger responsibility over him, is not a right which he retains when he enters employment as principal of a particular school in a particular school system. By entering the employment he from that time forth owes allegiance to the policies and plans as regularly determined for the school system, and if he cannot render such allegiance he should resign and find employment in a school system where he is in sympathy with the policies, and can coöperate fully and loyally with the authorities.

Personal relationships. Sometimes the problem which a principal faces is one of personal relationships between the superintendent and himself. He may not feel that the superintendent treats him properly, that he does not allow him to exercise proper authority in his school, that he does not uphold him in his actions and decisions, or that the superintendent decides against him without giving him an adequate hearing. Such situations at times arise, but before taking any action the principal ought to be very sure that he is not himself mistaken. A slow, retiring, somewhat moody, and quite sensitive principal may easily imagine difficulties of this type which have no real existence, and may take as personal slights the inattention or quickness of decision of a very busy man. The stronger the superintendent and the larger the problems he faces, the more likely he is to think and act quickly. Often he will sense the situation and make a quick decision before the principal thinks he has had time to grasp the problem. Often, too, he has too many things to do in a day to waste time in listening to long stories, reading and answering long letters, or spending an undue proportion of his time on any one case. Every executive is familiar with the type of man — with school people more common among men than among women — who cannot state a case quickly, who cannot set forth the crux of a situation without burying it under a mass of irrelevant details, who writes letters pages long, who feels that if he gets a quick decision his case has not been properly considered, and who often experiences difficulty in getting away from the office after his business is done. Such people often feel slighted and hurt when the trouble lies with themselves.

On the other hand, the superintendent ought to be very careful to treat the principal as the executive head of a school should be treated, to uphold and strengthen his authority as the head of the school, and to be very considerate of his feelings if at times he feels compelled to reverse his decisions. The superintendent is more likely to see a situation from a larger point of view than the principal, and an intelligent man will accept occasional reversals in a good spirit and in no way as a personal slight.

If, on the other hand, the principal, after long and careful thinking over the matter, feels that the superintendent does not treat him in a professional manner, and that the superintendent's attitude toward him and his work is undermining his usefulness as principal of the school, the thing to do is to await a good opportunity and then lay the matter frankly before the superintendent. If done at a time that is opportune, and done without bitterness and in apparent good spirit, there are few superintendents who will not listen carefully to a principal's statement of his case and try to make him feel satisfied in the future. In presenting his case the principal must do it tactfully, frankly, and without any evidence of bad temper, and he should accept the superintendent's assurances as genuine and drop the matter. If no improvement in relations then results the principal has three courses open to him. One, and probably the best one, is to go ahead and do his work and try to forget the whole matter. A second is to appeal over the superintendent's head to the board of education for just treatment. The third is to move to some position elsewhere where he may expect to be treated differently. Which one of these lines the principal should follow must depend on the particular situation involved, and will call for the exercise of the principal's best judgment.

What the principalship offers. The principalship of a school in an American city to-day offers unusual opportunities for personal growth and for community service to the person who is studiously inclined and interested in children. Of all places in the school system, if the principal uses his time well, the principalship offers the largest opportunities for study and personal growth. This is equally true whether one regards the position as a permanent career or as an apprenticeship for a superintendency elsewhere. As a permanent occupation the position offers large opportunities and leisure to the student. The monetary prizes are not so large as in business or the professions, but on the other hand there are few blanks. Success and steady employment are more certain, and failure and bankruptcy much less common. To the student the position makes a strong appeal. The school work, day by day, can be made experimental and fruitful, professional books and magazines can usually be had free of cost for reading and study, and the regularity of work and the long vacations permit a planning of one's life work not possible in most lines of human endeavor.

To one to whom some form of social service makes an appeal, the position of school principal offers advantages almost unequaled elsewhere in a city for a very important and useful type of community service. Few who serve a city have such opportunities for constructive work. Many of our cities have men and women who have served twenty-five to thirty years or more as the principal of one school building, and whose work has in consequence deeply moulded the lives of a generation of the people. Not infrequently we find new school buildings named after such principals, in grateful recognition of long and devoted service.

A student's opportunity. Viewed from the standpoint of an apprenticeship for larger work later on, the principalship is also a student's opportunity. Four or five years may well be spent in an elementary-school principalship by one who desires to train himself for a school superintendency. Such an apprenticeship, if rightly used, more than doubles the effectiveness of his previous collegiate and professional preparation. During these years the principal must be a student of educational processes in his school, and must save as much time as possible for careful reading and study along the lines of his future profession.

He should also, during these years, gradually crystallize for himself a good working educational philosophy, to guide him in his later work and to vitalize all his later educational procedure. He must seize intelligent hold on the conception that education stands for the higher evolution of both the individual and the race, and must relegate to their proper place in the educational scheme all the details of organization, administration, and instruction. Without such a guiding conception administrative work soon becomes dull and fruitless routine, and the principal sooner or later sinks, as so many do, to the level of a professionally dead and ineffective office worker.

Learning and working. During these years of apprenticeship one who would rise to a superintendency should accumulate a good working library along the line of his major interests. He should keep closely in touch, too, with all advancements and important experiments in his field, and with what other workers elsewhere are doing. He should welcome new school tasks, making himself as professionally useful as possible, and should take a deep personal satisfaction in doing difficult things. He should give himself practice in developing an ability to speak easily and briefly, and to write clearly and convincingly. He should mix somewhat with practical men of affairs, partly to counteract his daily life with women and children, and partly because from such men he can learn much that will be very useful to him later on. The acquaintance of some successful and older doctor, or lawyer, or banker in the community may prove well worth his time and attention. If the opportunity offers to join a discussion club, especially if composed of men older and more mature than himself, he should avail himself of it. Lodges, purely social organizations, bridge-whist clubs, and similar affairs he will probably do well to keep out of. Unless he is in need of social polishing, dances and parties should be indulged in rather sparingly, they being wasteful of time and energy and having in them little that is of permanent value. If his salary does not seem large enough to cover both married life and study, he should for a time resolutely put marriage aside. If he does marry, he should be very sure that the woman he marries is in sympathy with his work, is his equal in education and ambition, and is in other respects his superior. With so many good women in the world a man should never marry beneath him.

It requires concentration of effort and will power to carry through such a program, as well as a willingness to make social and other sacrifices for the sake of the larger future. These many young people are not willing to make, but, given brain power, and manners, and tact, and quickness of action, those young people who are willing to sacrifice the present for the sake of the future will inevitably hold the important places a decade or two ahead.

The young man must, during these years of apprenticeship, willingly accept work and burdens that lead toward his desired goal, and resolutely reject those which do not. He should know and remember that the habit of hard and faithful work is one that is established but slowly; that it requires close watching of one's pole star to establish it; and that it is not fully established in most men before thirty-five to forty years of age. He should also remember that it requires thirty to forty years of careful preparation to get ready to do something really large in life. Too many men never accomplish much because they dissipate their energies in pleasure, in family life, or in taking part in dozens of things they ought to let alone. One must concentrate his energies to a purpose and work hard if he expects to accomplish much in this world.

The principalship of a school then must be considered as one of the most desirable of all educational positions. In opportunities for a studious life, as well as in salary, it ranks fairly well with that of a teaching position in a college. To the man with the habits and instincts and aspirations of a student there are few vocations in which one can realize better the ideals of his life. No other person in the school system can do so much good at first hand, no other person in the community can so immediately mould its life and shape its ideals, and the opportunities for personal culture and pleasure are very large to the man or woman who will use them.

QUESTIONS AND PROBLEMS

1. What about the common excuse, given so often by schoolmen for failure to follow instructions or a plan, that they are too deeply interested in the child — that the child is more important to them than the system?
2. Show how a principal may help to ward off criticism of a city school system, or may help to bring it on, by the way in which he handles his administrative duties.
3. Show that people lacking a time sense, regardless of ability, must always work on a lower plane of efficiency than those of equal ability who have it.
4. It is often stated that successful people are set off from unsuccessful people largely by their practice of utilizing little opportunities to improve themselves or to be useful, which opportunities unsuccessful people neglect. Illustrate.
5. If the principalship is such a strategic position, how do you account for our long failure to realize the possibilities of the office?
6. Distinguish between the rights and the obligations of a principal when in his official relations and when out of school as a citizen. Even as a citizen does he have complete liberty?
7. Explain more fully what is meant by the statement that the principal should build up for himself a guiding educational philosophy, and the importance of doing this.

CHAPTER III

GENERAL NATURE OF THE PRINCIPAL'S WORK

Range of duties. The range of duties devolving upon a building principal is determined somewhat by the size of the school system in which he works. If the system is a small one and the superintendent is teaching part time in the high school, or if the system is a large one and the superintendent is engrossed with problems of policy and procedure and can give but little time to supervision — then in either case the work of the principal must include many duties and responsibilities, in both school organization and administration, which do not come to a principal working in a school system of medium size. The three classes of situations commonly met with may be briefly described, as follows:

A. Small city system. City of 6000 to 10,000 inhabitants.

Superintendent also principal of high school, and teaches part time. Two to three grade schools, with principals. Many administrative duties on superintendent, and little office assistance. Principal here must assume many administrative and supervisory duties.

B. Medium-sized city system. City of 20,000 to 60,000 inhabitants.

Superintendent does not teach, and has time for supervision. One high school, and four to eight grade buildings under principals. Principals now partially relieved of many administrative and supervisory functions, or carry these out in conjunction with the superintendent.

C. Large city system. City of 75,000 inhabitants and upward.

Practically no supervision by superintendent. Principals responsible for organization, administration, and supervision of buildings. Can make or break the superintendent, as far as work in his building is concerned. Loyalty to policies now extremely important, and more often lacking than in **B** or **A** types.

From the above classification it will be seen that not all principals perform the same duties or shoulder the same responsibilities. All principals, though, perform the same general types of duties, and these general types may be classified under four main heads:

1. Organization duties.
2. Administrative duties.
3. Supervisory duties.
4. Social duties.

We shall consider each of these briefly here, and more in detail in the four main divisions of the book which follow. In each of these four aspects of the work the principal must possess a reasonable degree of knowledge and skill if he is to become a successful worker.

Organization duties. As an organizer a principal will naturally be given greater liberty in some school systems than in others, even of the same size and type, but in all school systems a certain amount of organizing will have to be done. In a school in a type A school system, the amount will be small. In a school in a type B school system, though the amount may be large, it will be carried on so closely in conjunction with the superintendent that the actual thinking required of the principal may be less. In a school in a type C school system, the amount may be quite limited, due to all being required to work under uniform regulations, or, on the other hand, it may be quite large, due to the initiative given to principals to effect independent organization. Much will depend here on the character of the superintendent and the traditions of the school system.

In any case, though, and wherever he works, the principal will be called upon to think out his peculiar local problems and to organize his school in the best manner possible for effective coöperative service. With the tendency, now fortunately becoming more and more common, to magnify the importance of the office of school principal and to give to the principal more and more authority to organize his school and his work along more individual lines, and then to hold him responsible for educational results rather than for details of organization, a knowledge of the forms and practices and problems of school organization tend more and more to become important elements in the equipment for success of a school principal. In the chapters which follow we shall accordingly deal with organization first.

Administrative duties. After a consideration of the problems of organization, we shall next take up the administrative work of a school principal. As an administrator the principal stands responsible to the different authorities above him for the successful administration of his unit in the school system. He is the intermediary between the board of education and the central office on the one hand, and the teachers, children, and parents of his school on the other. Standing, as he does, in close touch and harmony with the teachers of his building, he can usually determine the success or failure in his school of any new administrative policy which is proposed.

As an administrator the principal looks after all administrative details relating to janitors and their work, and the needs of the teachers; oversees the attendance and conduct and health of the pupils; orders and receives and often gives out the supplies; has charge of, and inventories, and keeps up the stock room; is responsible for the contents and care and often of the minor repairs of his building; directs the work of his office clerk, if he is fortunate enough to have one; and makes reports as required by the central office. He naturally works here largely under the laws of the State and the rules and regulations laid down by the board of education. Regarding this aspect of a principal's work, the laws and rules are usually very explicit — so much so, in fact, that one reading the usual board rules might easily infer that the principal is only an odd-job clerical worker rather than a professional supervisor.

To show still better the nature of the administrative duties of a school principal the classification adopted by Nutt is here reproduced.

A. ADMINISTRATIVE DUTIES.
   1. *Annual and semi-annual.*
      a. Supplies and equipment (Orders often placed monthly).
      b. Promotion and transfer of classes.
      c. Individual promotions.
      d. Classifying new pupils.
      e. Checking up permanent records.
      f. Reports to the superintendent.
      g. Commencement exercises.
      h. Schedules.
   2. *Daily routine.*
      a. Inspecting building and grounds.
      b. Inspecting janitor service.
      c. Care for pupils before school opens.
      d. Excluding pupils.
      e. Attendance.
      f. General and special discipline.
      g. Care for luncheon pupils.
   3. *Miscellaneous.*
      a. Fire drills.
      b. School enterprises and activities.
      c. Parent-teacher organizations.
      d. Teachers' meetings.
      e. School exhibits.
      f. General.

This phase of a principal's work calls for good practical business sense, a good time sense and sense of proportion, punctuality in all official relationships, some genuine political skill in handling difficult people, frankness combined

NATURE OF PRINCIPAL'S WORK

with courtesy when frankness is called for, and at times courage and conviction. Occasionally he will find it necessary to assume control and command the situation; at other times he will offer good advice; again he must be a petitioner and take what he can get; and at still other times he must execute orders and not question why. It will call for much good judgment to know which rôle to assume as different situations present themselves. He must know his rights and also his duties; know when to stand firm and when to go slowly; have a genius for quickly getting close to the heart of every situation and deciding what ought to be done; know the meaning of loyalty to the decisions of those in authority; be able to establish fixed places of authority in his school and to have that authority met; and know how to handle difficult situations with both firmness and tact. To have a good grasp of the fundamental principles involved in proper school administration, and to settle problems arising in the light of these principles, is one of the surest means of handling difficult situations correctly.

It should be the aim of every principal to settle wisely and satisfactorily as many difficult situations as possible; to refer as few cases as possible to the central office for decision; and to have the smallest possible number of appeals from his decisions go to the central office. Few surer means than just this ability could be thought out for winning the approval of those above for his administrative skill.

Supervisory duties. It is upon the two aspects of organization and administration that many principals spend most of their time and energy. Often clerical and administrative duties are allowed to so monopolize the principal's time that the central office can usually depend upon finding him at work in his office chair at any time in the day they may call him on the telephone. Gilbert has well described this older type of office principal, in the following words:

The encroachment of petty duties is insidious. The many little demands upon the principal's time, calls for books or supplies, cases of discipline, long visitations with callers, answering the telephone, and reports — always reports — are so insistent that, unless he is very watchful, more and more time will be given to them until he becomes that most ineffectual, that deadest of pedagogues, the office principal. Every superintendent knows him. He is always there, in his chair at his desk. Seldom can he be surprised away from his customary spot and if he is, he apologizes.

It is because this description is so often true, and because the newer demands on the school require that it be changed, that we have recently heard so much criticism of the work of the school principal.

Board-of-education rules place their emphasis here, and neglect of administrative duties is hard to conceal from the central office. The emphasis placed on this aspect of a principal's work may be seen from a recent tabulation of duties by Boggs, covering the rules and regulations as to principals in thirty selected American cities.

DISTRIBUTION FOR THIRTY CITIES

TYPE OF DUTY	NUMBER OF DIFFERENT REQUIREMENTS	TOTAL NUMBER OF RULES AS TO
1. Clerical duties	15	101
2. Routine relating to building and equipment	27	171
3. Routine relating to personnel	28	153
4. Discipline	6	72
5. Teaching duties	1	9
6. Supervisory duties — Vague general statement	2	42
7. Supervisory duties — Specific statement	6	52

In contrast with this is a recent study by McClure, in which the judgment of fifteen university professors of education was sought and combined. This gave the following distribution:

Rank of Importance	Function	Median Percentage of Time for	Ranges
1	Supervision of instruction...	40 per cent	25–65 per cent
2	Administrative duties.......	20	10–40
3	Community leadership.......	15	10–25
4	Professional study..........	11	5–30
5	Clerical work...............	10	0–20

Sometimes the office type of principal is, in addition, quite a community leader and organizer, and renders useful service in lines of civic betterment and school improvement. This often tends to excuse his failure in supervision. The organization and administration of his school is excellent, and he is a leader in community welfare. This is all very good in itself, but the teachers in his school receive but little helpful supervision from him.

Importance of the supervisory function. Yet the supervision of instruction, that the education of children may proceed under better conditions and be more effective in results, is the prime purpose of freeing the principal from teaching, and is the end and goal toward which the organization and administration of the school should tend. All other work is in a sense preliminary to this larger function. The broader professional knowledge and insight of the principal must find expression in the daily work of the teachers and pupils if his largest usefulness as a principal is to be rendered. To this end he must reduce his office work and economize his time, that he may be found as much as possible during school hours in the classrooms of his school. He should at all times know what his school is doing, be able to determine accurately the efficiency of the instruction given in it, know that the pupils are classified as they should be, be able to give demonstration teaching, get real team work out of his teachers by coördinating their work, and be able to approach the instructional problems of his school with a degree of expertness which is based only on the objective and quantitative testing of results.

He must be able to direct and build up the work of apprentices and new teachers, to assist them in making their programs more scientifically, and to hold helpful meetings with his teachers for the planning and discussion of instruction and the interpretation to them of the policy of the school system. The larger lines of policy will probably be planned by the superintendent, or decided upon in conference, but upon the principal rests the responsibility for the successful carrying into practice of the ideals of the superintendent and the upbuilding of his own school. His ability to do this will be determined largely by the thoroughness and professional character of his knowledge of his own school problems and conditions. The highest degree of skill is required for the proper carrying out of this division of his duties, and, in consequence, the supervisory functions are usually much less satisfactorily carried out than are the administrative functions.

Social duties. Under this heading is included a relatively new but increasingly important group of duties or functions that represent quite an extension of the older conception as to the work of a school principal. Under this heading must be included the playground and athletic activities of the pupils, inter-school games and sports, school entertainments, thrift work, Scout work, Junior Red Cross work, and similar student activities which now demand supervisory oversight. In addition, the principal can render a very important service by working with the Parent-Teacher Association, looking after the out-of-school needs of his teachers, organizing special school programs, coöperating with the public library and important civic movements, and assisting his community in an intelligent, wider use of his school plant. In a very real sense, the principal acts as an interpreter to the people of the meaning and importance of their own schools. He also owes a duty to his profession, both in the community and in the state.

All these new functions are becoming increasingly important in building up a school and community spirit favorable to good school work, and an ability and a willingness to back the schools and the school policies against hostile attacks. The proper encouragement and guidance of such extra-school activities and interests require careful planning, and the expenditure of much time and energy on the part of the school principal, but the results achieved by such work are so fruitful that the time spent on them after all gives large returns.

Saving time for work. Most principals who find themselves swamped with routine administrative duties could emancipate themselves if they desired to do so. A first step would be to make a careful analysis of what they actually do. One good means is to make an accurate record by minutes of what one does during each school day, for a week or two at a time, and analyze this record into percentages of a day. Then, with such a table before one, raise the question for each item as to whether the time spent on it was time well spent.

For example, one principal of the writer's acquaintance who found himself "swamped by administrative routine," followed this suggestion and found that, for the first week for which he kept an accurate record, his ordinary run of duties averaged, for each five-hour day his school was in session, as shown in the table on page 46.

Such a time distribution is exceedingly poor and exceedingly wasteful. Taking the total cost for salaries, janitor service, supplies, and heating and lighting, and dividing by the number of school days per year, this principal found that his school was costing approximately $195 a day, or $39 an

Time Distribution Found	Per Day		
Seeing and talking with parents	50 minutes, or 17%	}	
Seeing callers, other than parents	15 " " 5%	}	29%
At the telephone	21 " " 7%	}	
Dealing with pupil cases	35 " " 12%	}	15%
Attendance-officer work	10 " " 3%	}	
Building inspection and supervision	15 " " 5%	}	
Messages to and errands for teachers	13 " " 4%	}	16%
Doing virtually janitor work	21 " " 7%	}	
Writing notes and letters	25 " " 8%	}	
Office work, records, and reports	35 " " 12%	}	25%
Work connected with storeroom	15 " " 5%	}	
Left for schoolroom supervision	45 " " 15%		15%
Totals	300 minutes, or 100%		100%

hour. His own salary, on a five-hour day, was $3.10 an hour. To the supervision of instruction in the school and the improvement of the education of 550 boys and girls he was giving but three and three quarter hours a week, or but fifteen per cent of his school time. Such a small percentage is very likely to be mere "room visitation," aimlessly carried out, and without any very definite results.

Evolving a better working schedule. Certainly an average of fifty to sixty per cent of a principal's time, during each school week, once the school is organized and under way, ought to be given to carefully planned supervision of the instruction in his school. In the above-mentioned case to find that amount of time required the complete reorganization of the principal's activities and methods of work. This he proceeded to do. The janitor was given the janitor work to do. The messages to teachers and errands for them were provided for by a system which utilized a mail-box system, combined with monitors at recesses and other non-school time. By being in the office much less, the telephone naturally required less attention. Storeroom work, record and report work, and building supervision and inspection were all relegated to before-school and after-school hours. The handling of pupil cases and the seeing of parents was systematized and expedited, and the time spent on callers materially lessened.

The principal made the transition by at once taking three hours a day for classroom supervision, the other work being permitted to pile up, and pile up at first it did. This for a time required much after-school time and some home work, but the introduction of system soon reduced very materially the time required. He finally reduced his daily work to approximately the following schedule, saving his best hours for the help and inspiration of pupils and teachers, and performing his office duties at times when they could be done most economically.

TIME DISTRIBUTION SUBSTITUTED

8.00 to 9.00	Building and yard inspection, school business, office work, and seeing parents, teachers, and pupils.
9.00 to 9.30	Pupil and attendance cases, parents, hasty glance over morning mail for anything of importance.
9.30 to 12.00	Classroom supervision. Only emergency calls for other work attended to.
12.00 to 2.00	Luncheon, building and yard oversight, office business, mail, pupil cases.
2.00 to 3.00	Classroom supervision.
3.00 to 4.00	Seeing parents and teachers, teachers' meetings, and cleaning up day's work in office. Leave building by 4.00 to 4.30. Rest and relaxation until evening.
Evening	Reading, and study on the larger problems of the school.
Note.	Program for hours 1.00 to 2.00 and 2.00 to 3.00 to alternate, as needed for supervision.

Laying out one's work. Learning system and perfecting organization seems particularly difficult for many people. One finds in almost every school system principals who are slow in thinking and acting, halting in decision, weak and ineffective in organizing power, and who in consequence accomplish little. Many of these are otherwise good men, but they have followed an uneconomical routine for so long that they cannot now learn new ways of working. A young person entering the principalship, though, ought from the first to develop a more intelligent organization of the work to be done. Many little methods and plans and tricks in work can be employed effectively by a quick and intelligent principal. A few such may be mentioned briefly here.

In the first place, one should organize his desk and his office for expeditious and effective work. Have ink, paper, blotters, envelopes, printed forms, order blanks, etc., in well-organized and convenient places, so that it is easy to do work whenever there is work to be done. Carry a pad or card in the pocket on which to note down things to be done or to be attended to later. Use printed forms and correspondence cards freely, and save the writing of letters. Learn to condense the letters that must be written to as small a space as possible, and only under exceptional circumstances write a letter of more than one page. A half-page letter is nearly always better. Organize a bulletin-board and letter-box service for teachers and janitors, and have a time when notices and bulletins are put there and when they are expected to look for them. Organize the storeroom for expeditious handling, and the charging system for supplies and books in as simple and effective a manner as possible. Avoid elaborate filing devices which require time, and in which things usually get lost. Have but few files, and these well systematized. Have the janitor do and look after many things that save the time of principal and teachers, and train teachers to do their work without calling upon the principal to do their errands for them. Do not begin that way.

Systematize, as much as possible, the work on pupil cases, and have stated times, well advertised, when parents will be sure to find you. If parents know that they can see you best at certain hours, they will in time tend to come then only. Give the central office your working schedule, and gradually train this office to call you only at your office periods. At other times let the telephone ring; if you have no clerk and are not in the office, it will not have to be answered. There are very few messages that will not keep a few hours.

Handle callers expeditiously. In handling callers, be polite, but at the same time handle cases quickly. Get rid of persons who come to try to interest you in something. Do not waste much time on casual callers, either. If they want to see the school, send or take them to the classrooms; if they merely want to talk, tell them that you have important duties elsewhere. In dealing with parents who call, treat them politely, but handle them expeditiously. If they want to linger, send them to the rooms where their children are. Be resourceful in devising polite ways of moving people along. Use pupils as guides or messengers, and save your own steps and time. Let the superintendent, when he comes for inspection or supervision, go about alone, unless he shows a desire to have you accompany him, and then try to show him what he came to see in your school. If he seems to have no definite objective, show him the high spots or the low places in your school, and let him see that you know how and in what direction your school is traveling.

Do not make your callers too comfortable, as too many people do not know how to get up and get away when their business is over. To sit at one's desk and have a fixed chair for each caller is very wasteful of time if many are to be seen. It is usually better to stand, or to use a light chair and move it about the room yourself, and to see parents anywhere — at the door, in the hallway, or on the playground — rather than to take them to the office and seat them properly before taking up their errand. To know how to meet people graciously, to get their case quickly, to render a rapid and satisfactory decision, and then to help them to get away without offending them, while you get on to the next case, is an art which every executive who has much work to do has to learn.

Have a working schedule. A tentative working schedule will also help a principal to use his time economically. Such a general working plan as is given on page 47 will be found helpful. One will need to vary from any working plan, from time to time, but week by week the general plan should be adhered to. Keep a clock in the office or on the desk, and keep an eye on the clock as you work.

In addition to a daily schedule of work, a principal should have a monthly and a yearly schedule, and should look at these frequently. They will help to anticipate work ahead, and prevent oversights and an undue accumulation. Such a schedule could be made up on good-sized cards, one for each month, or could be put on sheets of paper in a loose-leaf folder and then bound. The leaf from a yearly schedule made up by one principal, given on page 5, will illustrate the nature and use of such a schedule for work.

Outlining the major problems of the school. Another type of working schedule or plan for work is one which outlines the major problems which the school will attempt to meet during the year. The outlining of these problems will not be as easy for a new principal as for one who has been in the school before, and hence knows needs and conditions. Still, it will not be difficult after a little study of a situation. These major problems should be definite and concrete, and perfectly capable of solution by the teachers working together. The formulation of such problems furnishes working objectives for the year's activities, and gives an additional interest both to classroom instruction and to teachers' meetings. Sometimes these objectives are formulated for the whole school system by an energetic and studiously inclined superintendent of schools, but more commonly they must be outlined by each individual school. In any case, each school has its individual problems, and can supplement any general city-wide program.

NATURE OF PRINCIPAL'S WORK

FEBRUARY WORKING SCHEDULE

Week	Day	Administrative Duties	School Events	Outside Duties and Events
1st	M. 31	Jan. Teachers' Rpts. due. New pupils — Regroup classes. Rpt. enrollment to office.	2D TERM BEGINS.	
	Tu. 1	2d rpt. on enrollment due.	Teachers' Meeting, 3.15 P.M.	
	W. 2	Jan. monthly rpt. due. Jan. promotion rpt. due. Jan. visitation rpt. due.	School Assembly, 9 A.M.	*Principals' Meeting,* 2 P.M.
	Th. 3	Final term rpt. due. 3d rpt. on enrollment due.	Parent-Teacher Meeting, 3.15 P.M. Invite parents Lincoln day exercises.	
	F. 4		Jr. Red Cross Council, 3.05 P.M.	
	Sa. 5			*Janitors' Conference,* 9 A.M.
2d	M. 7	Fire drill this week		
	Tu. 8		Conference 3.15 P.M. Teachers Grades I–IV — Supervisory results in reading.	
	W. 9	Teachers' Programs. Seating-Charts, and age & grade sheet distribution, 2d half-year, due.	School Assembly, 9 A.M.	Teachers' Study Group, High School, 7.45 P.M.
	Th. 10			
	F. 11		Lincoln's Birthday exercises all rooms, 2 P.M.	Lecture, High School, on Lincoln, 8 P.M. General notice.
	Sa. 12			
3d	M. 14			Meeting, Course of Study Committee, Supt's. Office, 7.30 P.M
	Tu. 15		Teachers' Meeting, 3.15 P.M.	
	W. 16		School Assembly, 9 A.M.	*Principals' Meeting,* 2 P.M.
	Th. 17		Parent-Teacher Meeting, 3.15 P.M.	
	F. 18		Reception, 7th & 8th Grades to "Over-Seas" Men. Moving Pictures of War, 8 P.M.	
	Sa. 19			Special story hour for children, by city librarian, Lowell Sch. Auditorium, 10.30 A.M.
4th	M. 21	Fire drill this week.	Washington's Birthday exercises. HOLIDAY — Flag up. School Assembly, 9 A.M.	
	Tu. 22	Washington's Birthday.		
	W. 23			Teachers' Study Group, High School, 7.45 P.M.
	Th. 24	Preliminary monthly pay roll to office.		
	F. 25	Phone pay roll, final report.		
	Sa. 26	Monthly requisition for supplies due.		*General Teachers' Meeting,* High School, 10 A.M.

FORM 1. A PRINCIPAL'S FEBRUARY WORKING SCHEDULE

Only one or two of these major problems or objectives should be undertaken in any one year. Each should be definitely formulated and stated, each should be based on a study of existing conditions and needs, where possible each should be set before the teachers in the form of graphs and diagnostic charts showing conditions and needs, progress made during the year should be similarly reduced to graphic form, and every effort should be made to make the study and work on the problems contribute to definiteness in classroom work and to economy in procedure throughout the year. In such formulation of objectives older and more mature teachers can render valuable service, and the selection of objectives for each year may well be done by the teachers in meeting. The principal, though, must still be the guiding spirit, suggesting and directing the study, coördinating and integrating the results, stimulating new inquiries, and carrying on far more extensive observation and reading on the problems than he can expect any of his teachers to do. By his larger grasp of the problems he must show his qualities for professional leadership.

A few such major objectives, each suitable for the work of a year or more, may be stated to illustrate what is meant:

1. A study of age and grade distribution, promotions, and the course of instruction, with a view to discovering causes of and means for reducing retardation in the school.
2. A study of retardation among the brighter pupils, the effect of this on their work and progress, and means for speeding up their instruction.
3. Improvement of the manners of pupils, better care of building and grounds, decrease in quarrels and personal injuries, and the development of a big-brother attitude, objectively measured in the rise of a better school and community spirit.
4. A study of reading throughout the grades, with a view to its analysis and improvement. Both silent and oral reading considered.

5. An analysis of handwriting difficulties, progress, and standards, with objective measures of results.
6. A similar study for spelling, or composition.
7. Objectives in geography, history, or arithmetic, and means for motivating the instruction in these subjects.
8. A study of minimum essentials in any elementary-school subject, or group of subjects.
9. A program for Americanization work throughout the school, and among the parents as the school may reach them.
10. Better health and nutrition, and support of a Health Center.
11. The teaching process, and the improvement of teaching technique.
12. Project work in the grades.

It is by some such laying-out of one's work, by the formulation of programs for economical and effective work, and by the concentration of attention on important fundamental objectives in work that a principal can best emancipate himself from the routine of office and administrative duties and find time for his really important function of a supervisor of instruction and a helpful leader of his teachers in the school.

QUESTIONS AND PROBLEMS

1. Show how a principal's daily contact with parents may
    a. Add strength to his position and control of his school;
    b. Prove his ultimate undoing.
2. Give concrete illustrations to show the different attitudes a principal must at times assume, as stated on page 41.
3. Illustrate the importance to a principal of (*a*) a good time sense; (*b*) a good sense of proportion; (*c*) easy and refined manners; (*d*) a good sense of humor; (*e*) quick and accurate decision; (*f*) human sympathy.
4. Show that a definite program for work will help a principal to transform his work from routine into constructive service.
5. Make up a working program for the month of December.
6. Make up a working program, based on the principal teaching half of each day.
7. Some principals have teachers' mail boxes outside their office door, and expect teachers to look in these twice a day for any notices. What do you think of such a plan? Why twice? Why outside?
8. List five other worthy objectives for an elementary school.

9. Outline, more in detail, any one of the major school objectives given above.
10. Explain how and in what ways a principal "acts as an interpreter to the people of the meaning and importance of their own schools."

SELECTED REFERENCES FOR PART I

Bardeen, C. W. *Teaching as a Business.* Syracuse, 1901.
A series of very sensible essays on teaching as a profession.

Bird, G. A. "Teachers' Estimates of Supervisors"; in *School and Society,* vol. 5, pp. 717–20. (June 16, 1917.)
A summary of the opinions of 100 experienced teachers when asked to name the most noteworthy qualities of principals and supervisors they had known.

Bobbitt, Fr. "The Building Principal in the Surveys"; in *Elementary School Journal,* vol. 19, pp. 106–20. (October, 1918.)
Tabulates duties and recommendations as to qualifications as stated in the recent school surveys.

Bobbitt, Fr. "Mistakes often made by Principals"; in *Elementary School Journal,* vol. 20, pp. 337–46, 419–34. (January and February, 1920.)
Lists fifty common mistakes; a list that no principal will be harmed by reading.

Boggs, J. "School Board Regulations concerning the Elementary-School Principalship"; in *Elementary School Journal,* vol. 21, pp. 730–42. (June, 1920.)
A tabulation for thirty American cities, and distribution according to groups as proposed by Nutt, Reavis, and McMurray. Numerous extracts from rules.

Boynton, F. D. "Coöperation in a School System"; in *Educational Review,* vol. 53, pp. 329–40. (April, 1917.)
A general, but thoroughly sound article.

Davidson, P. E. "The Professional Training of School Officers"; in *Educational Review,* vol. 46, pp. 473–91. (December, 1913.)
States needed preparation, and analyzes duties.

Fairchild, R. W. "The Measure of the Administrator"; in *American School Board Journal,* vol. 57, pp. 23–24. (December, 1918.)
Value of tact, clothes, degrees, personal bearing, etc.

Farrington, F. E. "The Equipment of a School Principal"; in *Educational Review,* vol. 35, pp. 41–51. (January, 1908.)
Very good on general qualifications.

Gilbert, C. B. *The School and its Life.* 259 pp., New York, 1906.
Chapter XXI a general discussion of the functions of the school principal.

Gowin, E. B. *Developing Executive Ability.* New York, 1921.
A good presentation of the importance of initiative, efficiency, concentration, and executive capacity for business and civic activities.

Gray, W. S. "Work of the Elementary-School Principal"; in *Elementary School Journal,* vol. 19, pp. 24–35. (September, 1918.)
A good general article on the supervision of instruction.

Horn, P. W. "Team Play in the System"; in *Proceedings, National Education Association,* 1913, pp. 116–22.
A good statement, well worth reading.

Judd, C. H. "The High School Principal"; in *School Review*, vol. 26, pp. 641–53. (November, 1918.)
: Has a number of good suggestions for elementary-school principals.

Maxwell, W. H. "The Duties of Principals"; in his *A Quarter-Century of Public School Development*, pp. 16–24.
: A good study of the work of an elementary-school principal.

McAndrew, Wm. *The Public and Its School.* 76 pp., Yonkers, 1916.
: Contains many valuable suggestions for both principals and superintendents.

McClure, W. "The Functions of the Elementary-School Principal"; in *Elementary School Journal*, vol. 21, pp. 500–14. (March, 1921.)
: Tabulation of replies to a study made by the Principals' Association of Seattle. A valuable study.

McClure, W. "Professionalizing the Principalship"; in *Elementary School Journal*, vol. 21, pp. 735–43. (June, 1921.)
: A study of tendencies in our cities.

Neson, B. E. "How can the Ward Principal be of Most Service"; in *Proceedings, National Education Association*, 1909, pp. 324–26.
: General on administrative and supervisory duties.

Nutt, H. W. "The Duties of an Elementary-School Principal"; in *Elementary School Journal*, vol. 19, pp. 174–97. (November, 1918.)
: Duties of principals in school systems of different sizes. A well-organized article.

Perry, A. C., Jr. *The Management of a City School.* 2d ed., 434 pp., New York, 1919.
: Chapter IV on the principal's relation to the authorities, and Chapter X on the principal and the principalship.

Potter, M. C. "Qualifications and Functions of the Ward-School Principalship"; in *Proceedings, National Education Association*, 1909, pp. 322–24.
: A good but somewhat general discussion on his personal qualities and work.

Reavis, W. C. "Duties of the Supervising Principal"; in *Elementary School Journal*, vol. 19, pp. 279–84. (December, 1918.)
: Divides duties into managerial, professional, and social, and characterizes each group.

Spaulding, Fr. "Coöperation in School Administration"; in *School Review*, vol. 26, pp. 561–75. (October, 1918.)
: An excellent article, quite to the point.

Weet, H. S. "The Duties of a School Principal"; in *Elementary School Journal*, vol. 20, pp. 253–62. (December, 1919.)
: A good general article.

Wilde, A. H. "The Principal's Duty in Improving Instruction"; in *School Review*, vol. 24, pp. 617–25. (October, 1916.)
: A very good article on the principal and his work.

PART II
THE ORGANIZATION OF A SCHOOL

CHAPTER IV

PRELIMINARY CONFERENCES AND ORGANIZATION

The problem in the large. Every principal of a school, whether new to the school or not, faces certain preliminary conferences and duties at the beginning of each school year. These naturally vary with situations and circumstances, and also differ according as the principal is merely assuming charge of a school he has directed for years, is taking charge of a school to which he is new but in a city in which he has worked and with which he is familiar, is starting a small new school, or is a stranger to the city and is taking charge of a school some one else has previously managed. In all these situations, though, certain common duties will appear, and these may be indicated most easily by describing the problems facing the principal coming to a city new to him to assume charge of an established school.

This type of situation calls for the exercise of good sense that a proper first impression may be made, and then later the ability to live up to this first impression. To a certain body of teachers, and to hundreds of parents and children, he comes as a new and untried personage, one who may deeply influence their work and lives in the right direction, or one who may antagonize teachers, parents, and children by his lack of tact, arbitrary manner, and lack of understanding of them and their ways and their problems. If the principal before him has been a strong, capable, and much-beloved executive, it is much in the newcomer's favor if at the start he seems to measure up to his predecessor, and later can continue to hold such feeling. If he, too, is strong he will keep all that is good which has been established, and add to it as he can. He will also find that such a principal has established many traditions in the school — some good, and some bad — and these he will need to recognize and deal with carefully.

If, on the other hand, the principal before him was weak, or incompetent, or lazy, or coarse, his work will in a way be easier. If he shows ability to do, and seems to understand what leadership and good work are, his work will win favor quickly by contrast with that of the man who preceded him. In other respects his work will be harder, because he will find that his predecessor has left him a legacy of lax methods, weak discipline, poor organization, little or no classroom supervision, and often few or no records, and these will require time and patience and hard work to overcome and correct. He will experience a pleasure in accomplishment, though, which will more than compensate for the difficulties he has to meet.

In any situation which may confront him, however, the ease with which he grasps the essentials, and the quickness, force, and correctness of his responses, will largely determine his success as principal and that of the school under his charge.

Learning the larger outlines of his problem. Assuming, then, the case of a principal new to a school system and a city, along what preliminary lines would he best proceed?

In the first place, during the preceding summer vacation period he ought to have familiarized himself, as much as can be done from printed material, with the educational conditions in the city and the State in which he is to work. This may best be done by studying carefully the *Annual Report of the Superintendent of Schools* for the city, and working over its statistical tables; the printed *Course of Study* for the city, including the textbooks used; and the *Rules and Regulations* of the Board of Education for the city. If a school survey of the city has ever been made and printed, he should study this with the greatest care.

If new to the State, the *Report of the Superintendent of Public Instruction* for the State should be looked over for its general view and statistics, and the *School Law* and the *Rules and Regulations* of the State Board of Education, in so far as these apply to principals, teachers, and pupils, should be made familiar. It is good to learn more than probably will be needed, and to know fairly well not only the duties and powers and prerogatives of one's own position, but of the higher authorities as well. In every business the clerk who is studying the work of his superior officers as well as his own will be, given equal ability, the one most likely to be singled out for promotion.

Some study of the city, too, if unfamiliar, will also be helpful — its size; character of its population; comparative wealth; comparative expenditure for its schools; its railroads, commerce, and industries; and its peculiar social and educational problems. All such information is likely to prove useful many times in the early days of one's work. When the time approaches for the opening of the schools, the principal should go to the city several days in advance — a week to ten days is not too long — in part to locate comfortably, and in part to have a day or two to look over the city quietly by himself, so as to get a better preliminary grasp of its peculiar characteristics and problems. A new principal ought also to take the boundaries of his district and walk up and down the streets to see what his district is like, and he should also walk from his boundaries to the nearest school in each direction, to get distances, and note any differences in the character of the population.

Seeing the superintendent of schools. The first official call should be upon the city superintendent of schools. This should be arranged for in advance, by letter or telephone, and the principal should be at the office at exactly the hour set. If it is a large office, where he may have to send in his card and pass a number of clerks, a few minutes should be allowed for this. In a large city he probably will not see the superintendent, at least at first, but may be asked to see instead an assistant or deputy superintendent. In a small city he may find it necessary to see the county superintendent of schools as well, to arrange as to his teaching certificate and other matters. In a small community, where he is to be a supervising principal and there is no city superintendent of schools, his first call should be upon the county superintendent of schools instead, and this should be similarly arranged for by letter or telephone. This preliminary call and conference is partly to report for duty, partly to see and be seen, and partly — largely — to obtain such preliminary information and instructions as the superintendent of schools sees fit to give individually. All general instructions he may be assumed to communicate to the teachers in a body at the preliminary teachers' meeting on the coming Saturday, or by printed forms, and his time need not be taken for these at this first interview.

The purpose of this visit should be thought out in advance, and the information to be sought and the main questions to be asked should be got in mind. On the back of an envelope or the edge of a newspaper, to be held in one's hand and casually glanced at, the main topics to be brought up may be jotted down. This will give a purpose to the meeting and materially expedite the interview. The peculiar problems of the particular school one is to manage, the policies for it the superintendent has in mind, and any information the superintendent cares to impart as to the work of the preceding principal and the teaching and janitor staff of the school, might well constitute important items on one's list. The main educational objectives the superintendent

PRELIMINARY ORGANIZATION

has in mind for the year, and the type of general teachers' meeting he will hold before the opening day may well be other important points. One may also ask for any needed information as to one's certificate, and request, at the close, to be referred to the clerk or other person or persons who can give detailed information as to reports, blank forms, supplies, orders, teachers, and other administrative details that the superintendent may be assumed to delegate to others. One ought also to make the acquaintance of all the office force one is likely to have dealings with later on.

Essential purposes of the visit. The principal should keep clearly in mind that he has called on the superintendent of schools on one of his busy days, and that he should stay only as long as the superintendent seems to desire to have him stay, and not long in any case. He has also called to be seen, and to secure information and advice, and it is the superintendent and not he who should do most of the talking. Should the superintendent turn the interview about and begin to ask questions, he should answer frankly and to the point, but rather briefly. The principal should assume that the superintendent does not want to be forced to listen to any disquisition on the principal's educational views, past service to the cause, or ability to do fine things. When he has finished what he came for, let him show that he knows how to terminate an interview and get away. The officials over him are much more likely to think well of him if he states his business promptly, asks questions to the point, gets quickly what he came for, and leaves before they really want him to go, than if he stays so long that the line piles up behind him and he finally has to be helped out of the office. There will come occasional times, either when some unexpected emergency has arisen, or when business is very slack, when the superintendent may desire to talk and one is warranted in remaining for something of a visit, but these times do not come often, and it is for the superintendent rather than the principal to indicate when one of the occasions has come. On the other hand an excess of timidity is not desirable, as it is nearly always regarded as an evidence of immaturity and does not inspire confidence.

From the subordinates and clerks in the office the principal may assume he has a right to expect all necessary information. The blank forms he and his teachers must use, the times and forms of reports to be made, the ordering of supplies and repairs, the handling of a petty expense account if such be allowed, the keys to his building, what he may expect and require of his janitor — all these and other similar items he may inquire about. Even though he be told that supplies of all blank forms will be found in his building, he may ask for a sample of the important ones and on these make notes as to when expected, and other information given. He may well ask to see the store and supply room, to learn what the school system keeps and provides. He should also obtain a full list of all teachers, janitors, clerks, and other persons who are assigned to his building, together with the following information concerning each of his teachers, and part of it also for the janitors and clerks.

1. Name in full.
2. Grade assigned to. Salary.
3. New teacher.
    a. To city system.
    b. To particular building.
4. Education.
5. Teaching experience, summarized by years and types.
6. General characteristics of.

Such information, excepting 6, is always on file at the central office, and the principal may ask to be permitted to copy it for his own information and guidance, using a separate card for each teacher and other employee he will have under him.

PRELIMINARY ORGANIZATION

With such information he is now ready to take up his work at his building, though he may have been to and taken a hasty look over his building and grounds before visiting the central office.

Building reconnaissance. The next step probably would be to make a careful reconnaissance of the school plant he is to supervise. He should go over his building and grounds thoroughly, and make notes for his information and guidance during the early days of his work. This should start at the office. Here he should go through his desk, find what it and his office contain, and organize his desk and cases and shelves and files and working materials, so that he will know what he has and needs, and where things are and should be. The same should be done for the stores, supplies, and books, with the amounts on hand and to be sent checked and recorded.

Probably best accompanied by the janitor, he should next examine each class- or special room, noting the teacher's supplies and storage, contents of desk, number and kind of seats in room (sizes, fixed, adjustable), size, lighting, and general condition. The hallways, staircases, the number and condition of the toilets for each sex, the heating and ventilating plant, drinking facilities, the lighting system, the facilities for cleaning and repairs, the fire-control provisions, and the signal system are points of importance in the inspection. The nature, size, and use made of yard and streets, and play apparatus on the yard and in store should also be noted. If the school has an assembly hall, its size and possible usefulness should be noted.

The next point might well be a careful examination of the building records, to see what they tell. The number of pupils for each classroom and for the school should be estimated from the registers of promotion and school-growth records. The health records, the attendance and tardiness records, the truancy and disciplinary records, the petty-expense records, and the permanent pupil-records should be examined. For some, and often for many of these items, there will be no records to examine. This, however, is good to know. The age-and-grade-distribution records, the failure and promotion records, the records as to nativity and occupation of parents, the transfer and withdrawal records, the faculty-meeting records, the parent-teacher-meeting records, the medical-inspection records, and any standard-test examination records that may be available should be gone over. The teachers' classroom *Registers* should be looked over to see what they contain, and how they have been kept. All that a principal can learn about his school and its work before he sees his teachers and begins work with them will be of value. He will not need all this information, but the man who succeeds best and most easily is the man who knows more than he is expected to know. All this knowledge will help him to shape his plans for meeting any unexpected conditions and emergencies during the opening day and week.

Preliminary teachers' meetings. The number and types of preliminary teachers' meetings the principal himself will want to hold, before the opening day of his school, will depend much upon the number and type of meetings the city superintendent holds. In some of our cities the opening of school in the autumn is preceded by a two- to three-day general institute, and in some cities even five days are given to this work. In such a case much of what the principal would otherwise present is given to all teachers at the general institute. The more common plan, however, is for the superintendent to hold a single meeting of all teachers on the Saturday morning preceding the opening Monday, at which only quite general instructions are given. In the latter case more preliminary work will fall to the principal of each building.

Something will also be determined by the number of teachers new to the system who are to begin work in the principal's building the coming year. If there are no new teachers the meeting problem is somewhat simplified, and one meeting, on Saturday, probably will suffice. If, as usually happens, from two or three to six or eight or ten new teachers are to begin work in the building the coming year, the principal should first hold a preliminary teachers' meeting with these new teachers alone, on the preceding Friday morning. At the time new teachers are elected they should be notified to be on hand for such a meeting, at the building, at a fixed hour. In some cities this preliminary conference with new teachers takes place on Thursday morning, Friday is devoted to meetings of new teachers from all buildings by grades, and on Saturday comes the general meetings of all teachers, new and old.

The new-teachers' building conference. The preliminary conference of the principals with the teachers new to their buildings, let us assume, is set for Friday morning at 9.30 o'clock. At this time each principal will meet only the teachers new to his building. The purpose of this is largely to initiate them into the ways of doing things in the city, and in his particular building. If the principal, too, is new, the importance of his previous study of all the conditions and regulations surrounding his work will be apparent. After the principal has been in the building, or even in the school system, a short time, he can conduct such a conference with greater ease and effectiveness.

The program of such a preliminary conference with the new teachers should be, in a general way, to get acquainted with them, to show them their rooms, to initiate them into the procedure to be followed, to help them plan their programs and work for the first few days, and to indicate to them something of the spirit of the school and the keynote of the principal's educational creed.

More specifically, the principal should explain to them the regulations for and the plan of management to be followed in the conduct of the particular building in which they are to work, indicate strong and weak points for their guidance, explain the plan followed for filing in and out, recesses, passing to toilets, usage in conducting fire drills, the signal system, the use of monitors, play periods, use of the assembly hall, degree of self-government practiced, yard games, yard and basement supervision, special details for duty, the lunch room, the health work carried on, the sick room and the first-aid cabinet, supplies available and how distributed, the building keys and regulations, the permanent-record cards, blank forms to be used, reports to be made and how and when to make them, how to use the janitor and his duties, handling of tardiness and truancy, obstreperous cases, sending pupils to the office, keeping pupils in, punishments, teachers' hours and general duties, unexpected absence and how to report it, the grading and promotion system, special promotions, use of the ungraded or disciplinary rooms, the textbooks in use, desk and supplemental books and how and where to get these, use of the public and the teachers' libraries, the course of study, its administration, lesson plans, the vacation days and periods, the retirement fund, salary payments, the tenure system, building and grade teachers' meetings, the general teachers' meetings, and any other special requirements of the state laws or the rules and regulations of either the State Board of Education or of the City Board of Education, with which the older teachers may be assumed to be familiar and which new teachers ought to know.

Plenty of opportunity should be given for the teachers to ask questions, so that a clear understanding of all points may be attained. It may be that a second afternoon meeting will be necessary to cover all that is to be imparted.

Should there be a general city meeting, by grades, of all new teachers to go over course of study and promotional procedure, the building conference outlined above can be materially shortened. It may also be shortened, and perhaps improved, by taking up only the matters and items likely to be needed for guidance during the first few days of school, reserving for a second conference, to be held some afternoon toward the close of the first week, or on the following Saturday morning, all those matters dealing with school procedure not likely to be needed the first week of school.

The building conference for all teachers. Assuming that the superintendent holds a general teachers' meeting on Saturday morning, the principal should then hold a general teachers' meeting of all teachers of his building, old and new, following this general meeting. Just when and where this meeting should be held will depend a little on the usage previously followed in the city, and somewhat on the condition of the weather that day. In some cities it is the practice to hold the general teachers' meeting at 9.00 or 9.30 in the high school or other school building auditorium, adjourning this by 10.30 to 10.45, and then have all teachers meet with their principals for a building conference from 11.00 to 12.00, in the different classrooms of this same school. If this is the general city practice the principal would better adhere to it, though there is a psychological advantage in holding the building conference in the building in which the teachers are to teach. To require this, though, contrary to general practice, only means to incur unnecessary opposition at the start which more than nullifies the slight advantage to be gained.

On the other hand, one frequently finds the general teachers' meeting held at some central place at 10.00 or 10.30, this lasting an hour and a half or so, and then building conferences are scheduled for 3.30 or 4.00 o'clock, at each of the school buildings. This is not a heavy program, gives plenty of time to rest after lunch and escape the heat of mid-afternoon, and has decided advantages. Under such a plan a tactful and considerate principal can make such a meeting a very pleasant as well as a profitable occasion.

As the meeting is partly an acquaintance and reunion meeting, as well as for business, it may well be partly social in nature. The principal, either himself or with the aid of the older teachers, might do much to start things off well by receiving each teacher in person and offering a cup of tea or some light refreshment. A bowl of punch, or ice cream and cake, may prove very acceptable on a hot afternoon, as opening days are apt to be, and will give an opportunity for introductions and general conversation which will do much to create a spirit of friendliness. The meeting can be formally called together later, or may gradually develop out of the social circle thus formed. The latter plan retains the informality of the gathering, which is useful at this first meeting. A woman principal can handle such an affair with ease and grace; it is much harder for a man to do so.

If the principal has carefully thought out what he wants to accomplish at this meeting, and knows about what he is to do and say, much can be accomplished in a short time. A principal new to the city will need to feel his way and ask for information, and, unless he is quite sure he can improve on plans previously followed in the school, he would best accept these and carry the school along on the opening days as has previously been done. If the plans are not good they can be changed later, when there is more time to train teachers to a new procedure and when change will savor less of a mere exhibition of authority. If, on the contrary, the principal is old to the school he will know very definitely what to do and say, and if most of his teachers are familiar with the school procedure he can proceed quite rapidly.

Any new plans, though, will need careful explanation to all.

General nature of this conference. This preliminary building teachers' meeting may begin with a brief statement by the principal of his purpose in getting the teachers together, and may well proceed along four lines, and perhaps best in the following order:

1. A brief résumé of such general regulations as need mentioning for a clear understanding of duties, and such regulations as have been changed since last year and now need restating.
2. The work and management of the first day or days of school.
3. Certain classroom organization details that may be useful.
4. Some general statement as to aims for the year's work.

The whole discussion of the above topics can proceed more informally at this first meeting than will be the case later, and there should be ample opportunities for questions by both the teachers and the principal. The latter, however, needs to have in mind, and probably still better on a card, a definite outline of points to be brought up for consideration, that important matters may not be overlooked. He may find it desirable, and certainly economical of time, to give to each teacher, in mimeographed form, certain general information which all need to have. This may include such items as:

1. Skeleton outline for a daily program, with times for beginning, recesses, assemblies, and dismissals indicated.
2. A time-limit sheet for subjects and grades.
3. Rules as to books and supplies.
4. The signal system used in the school, and dismissal plans.
5. Time different reports are due and expected.
6. A statement of the standards for promotion and method of grading, if such have been formulated for the school system as a whole.

All the above in printed form avoids misunderstandings and saves time.

Having gone over the details of school management previously with the new teachers, there will be little need for repeating many of such details now. Any new regulations, or important changes in the old regulations, not explained at the general morning meeting, will of course need attention. Any reports to be required during the first day and week will be stated, with times when the principal will expect them for use. An old principal should briefly explain the method to be followed in handling pupils, and a new principal will wisely find out from the teachers the general scheme which has been followed for assembling and dismissing pupils, regulating yard and basements, handling supplies, dealing with new pupils, etc., as well as any criticisms and suggestions for improvement. These may be considered later. He can learn how much responsibility has been placed on teachers in the past, and can give them new responsibilities under the guise of getting them to assist him. In a general way all teachers may be asked to take up the work they have previously handled. If any new or general type of program is to be instituted this will need careful explanation. The work of the special supervisors may need mention and explanation also.

Time should not be spent in passing out supplies needed; instead the janitor should have placed all these in the rooms, ready for the teachers to put away for use. The teachers should be expected to see that their rooms are properly supplied with books, equipment, and supplies for the first day's work, so that no time need be taken the first day with these details. The first day will be needed for the children only.

Planning for the opening day. An understanding will need to be arrived at and clearly understood as to plans for handling the pupils and parents on the opening day. Each teacher should be provided with a list of the pupils promoted to her room and who presumably will constitute her class for the coming term. Such lists will help teachers in identifying and checking up lost children, and it has a good effect on the children to be called by name as individuals. Explain the card forms to be used and data to be obtained from the children. Yard and other extra duties will be indicated for the first few days, at least.

A good general plan is to have all regular pupils on assembling proceed to the room of the grade to which they were promoted at the close of the preceding year, where their credentials will be examined by the teachers, as they come, and, if not properly placed, they will be directed by the teachers to the proper rooms. Have pupils coming with transfers from other schools in the city looked after by Miss A, transfers from other cities by Miss B, special cases — left-overs, irregulars — temporarily classified by Miss C. The older and wiser teachers should be requested to assume these positions, and how and where they should carry on their work as the children arrive be indicated. Have the kindergarten and the primary teachers look after the little folks and their mothers, and get them sorted out and started contentedly. The principal will reserve for his personal attention the more difficult cases referred to him for classification by the teachers. Should the school be in a foreign quarter better provision for pupil and teacher assistance will need to be made, and more teachers used in handling the crowds of mothers and children, collecting residence and other needed data, supplying books to indigents, etc. Everything comes with a mad rush in a big school in a foreign quarter of a city, and the principal must keep himself free from detail work to look after the emergencies that arise.

Suggestions for first-day procedure. After a general first-day plan has been determined upon, the principal may well offer a few suggestions as to first-day procedure, of which the following may be taken as a type:

1. Be on hand early. See that you have what you need for your room, and that it is in good order. Order and method lead to effective work. A touch of beauty — flowers if available — add much to a favorable first-day atmosphere.
2. Have a definite plan in mind for seating and sorting the pupils, passing materials, distributing books, and getting the school under way in the shortest possible time. Use seating charts to locate pupils and fix names quickly.
3. Have and follow a very definite program the first few days. You may be more flexible later, but at first be definite and decisive, for its effect on the children.
4. Remember that pupils are "sizing up" the teacher, and that you have a problem of class psychology to deal with. Take for granted that the children are with you, keep your eye on them as individuals, but treat the problem as a class problem — at first.
5. Have plenty of work ready, and try to open up some class or group problems the first day that will carry over to succeeding days. Motivate your work from the first.
6. Insist on good working habits from the first. Have things done properly. Keep everyone busy. Do not worry if you do not teach much the first week; the establishment of the right atmosphere in the school and the right type of responses on the part of the children are more important at the start than subject matter.
7. Keep yourself in the background as director and master, but be in control from the first. Avoid talking too much, but get the pupils so busily at work that they will want to do the talking.
8. Keep yourself cheerful and natural and human, and do not fail to see the funny side of things with the children. Do not expect too high a degree of perfection, either in conduct or work.
9. Remember that the children have just come in from a long vacation, and that both they and you are working at a problem of adjustment.
10. Watch your own habits of work, and determine whether they are such as you would wish your children to imitate.

Tell the teachers that you will call a brief teachers' meeting after school the first afternoon, and ask them to note down,

PRELIMINARY ORGANIZATION 75

during the day, the special problems they meet. Also tell them the main purpose of this first after-school meeting.

Larger aims and purposes. When these matters have been disposed of, and a business-like program for the first day's work has been arrived at, the principal may take a few minutes to state what he conceives to be his function as principal, emphasizing his desire to minimize administrative routine, stress his supervisory functions, uphold his teachers in every way he can honestly, and help them in all ways where his experience and advice might be of value. In particular he wishes to be of help to them in planning their work, interpreting the course of instruction, improving instructional procedure, and in professional advancement. While assured of full coöperation and support, he nevertheless expects them, in large measure, to handle their own class and individual problems, not because he is unwilling to help but because they will be worth more to the children if they are able to do so.

The principal may well conclude the conference by a short talk as to the larger aims and purposes for the year. Like a skillful general, he may review the past accomplishments of the school, if new to the work then as he has come to understand them, and will open up to his co-workers some broad outlook on the work still remaining to be done. If an objective or two for the year's work has been decided upon previously by the teachers, this may be touched upon and its larger possibilities pointed out, and if none has been selected he may suggest certain ones and say that he will bring this matter up again a little later for consideration. The meeting can thus fitly close with a brief discussion of aims and ideals and means of attainment, and the principal can fire his teachers with some of his own enthusiasm for the work that lies ahead.

In this first real contact the principal must remember

that his measure is being taken by the teachers, and the importance of a good first impression should not be overlooked. Tact, courtesy, kindliness, appearance, and manner all count, but after all the most important thing is his fullness of grasp of the problems and work, and his ability as an educational and inspirational leader. Nothing can be subordinate to this fundamental requirement.

Value of these conferences. Some such scheme of preliminary conferences, if well conducted and profitably carried out, practically always wins the approval of the teachers. Newcomers find such preliminary conferences as to detailed procedure very helpful. What teachers object to is attending meetings to listen to what they already know, to oral instructions that would better be given in mimeographed form and that do not concern their immediate work, to dictatorial statements and directions, to long explanations of "my policies," and possibly to criticisms and scoldings. From all such conferences they get little that is helpful and inspiring. Teachers are by nature a body of enthusiastic idealists, and they will respond quickly to one who knows how to fire them with new conceptions as to procedure or purpose in what they do.

These meetings can be made as important as any other part of the work of the term, and they do much to start the school under proper "control," but the amount teachers get out of them is directly proportional to the work put on preparation for them by the principal and the skill and professional enthusiasm he evidences while conducting them. He must be careful not to stress too much what *he* wants done, but rather should endeavor tactfully to gain the confidence of his teachers by his sympathetic attitude toward their problems, and especially by being a good listener if the teachers will talk. The principal who can, in such a conference, so manage things that the teachers become the chief conferees has taken a long step toward efficient organization of his staff.

One caution is of importance — have an eye on the clock, keep things moving along, and do not delay the teachers so long that they will be late in getting home for their dinners.

QUESTIONS AND PROBLEMS

1. Show that it is easier for a good principal to follow a good principal than a poor one.
2. Show the importance of a preliminary study of his district which a principal ought to make.
3. Illustrate, in the case of a school principal, the common business-world statement that "only the man who is larger than and overruns the outlines of his calling is safe."
4. Indicate something you would add, not listed in the text, to the preliminary conference with new teachers on Friday.
5. Do the same for the general building conference on Saturday.
6. What is your judgment as to where and when to hold the Saturday building meeting? Why?
7. Should the teachers be given the room registers and lists of pupils at the building meeting on Saturday, or should they find them on their room desks? Why?

CHAPTER V
THE FIRST DAY OF SCHOOL

The call for executive ability. The first day of school is a critical day, and probably no day in the whole year will test so severely the principal's qualities of leadership. Especially will this be true for a principal new to the school. It is now that his work in studying the building and records, organizing his office and supply room, planning his work, holding conferences, and distributing duties, in all of which he has tried to anticipate difficulties and pave the way for smooth and expeditious activity on the first day, will yield abundant fruit. The more thoroughly he has planned, the more little details he has looked after, and the more difficulties he has anticipated, the better will he go through the critical first day. It is at best a trying time for every one — principal, teachers, children, and parents. The weather is likely to be hot, everything has to be done rapidly, there will be little time for conversation, and nerves may easily get on edge. With a new principal in charge and a number of new teachers in the building, it is with them, as with the children in the rooms, "a psychological problem in the adjustment of personalities."

If the last principal was a popular one, then the test on the part of both teachers and pupils is likely to be more severe. To handle the situation the principal must have anticipated the main difficulties likely to occur. The larger the school the more must he keep himself free from detail work so as to have time to move about and be on hand where needed. The teachers will work into the new régime more easily if they are given quite a share in the handling of details. The principal must be courteous, decisive, and yet ready to accept any good suggestion that may be offered. He probably will be told, frequently, that "Principal So-and-So did this way," and he will be foolish to resent or to turn such a suggestion aside without giving the plan serious consideration. It may be best to say, with a smile, "Very well, let us continue that way, at least for the present."

Beside the mutual adjustment problem, the day is very likely to test the principal's qualities for leadership. He may be accepted by teachers and pupils as a nice man or a good fellow, but if this is all he will not get very far. He must in addition establish clearly his ability for leadership, not by driving or by arbitrary commands, but by real worth. To get the work done with the greatest dispatch and the least friction must be his aim. In all the work and decisions of the day, his must be the outstanding personality in the school if he is to hold the admiration and respect of teachers and pupils. Courtesy, an unruffled exterior, quick and correct decision, a quiet manner betokening plenty of reserve force, complete confidence in himself without evidence of egotism, and a sane and tempered enthusiasm for the work will do more to give evidence that the principal is as large or larger than the job than almost any other qualities he can display on this opening day.

The building in readiness. The conferences with new teachers, the preceding week, will have done much to initiate them into the work and ways of the school, and the preparatory work in planning and assigning will have helped materially to care for any rush the first morning. The principal should see to it that the janitor has distributed chalk, erasers, paper, scratch pads, pens, pencils, ink, blank forms needed, maps, and other standard supplies to the rooms the preceding Saturday, so that there will be no waste of time in securing these on the opening day. Lists of pupils to be advanced, classification blanks, the cumulative record cards for each pupil expected, and the reports and amount of work covered the preceding term should also be placed in each room. The teachers should select the needed desk books and supplemental books for first-day use from the storeroom the preceding Saturday, and have them charged and delivered also by Monday morning. The old teachers will know how to do this, but the principal may need to initiate the new teachers into this procedure. If free textbooks are provided, supplies of these will need be ready to be charged and given out. If they are not provided, then printed book lists, to be checked and sent home with each pupil, will be needed, as well as application blanks for free books on the part of those claiming inability to purchase. In schools not providing free books, a good stock of supplemental reading material, and good plans by teachers for written and other work, will need to be looked after. The chances of first-day difficulties will be lessened if all such matters are carefully attended to in advance.

To sort and handle pupils and parents, large printed signs, put up at the outer door and in the main hallways, and giving directions as to where to go and whom to see, will prove very useful. A movable blackboard may be used for the purpose, but it is less satisfactory than the printed cards. These can be read by all children above the second grade at least. A number of boys and girls, selected by the teachers or principal from the highest class, can be used to good advantage as ushers. If a form of pupil government is in use, this can be planned for at the close of the preceding school year, and the pupils be in readiness to assume the service. The boys can direct pupils and parents, assist in errands, answer the telephone, give bell signals as directed, carry and place chairs, and perform similar simple duties. The girls will be especially useful in ushering parents and in taking the little children to the kindergarten and first-grade rooms.

A few leaders of both sexes can take charge of the yard, run up the flag, start games, and probably prevent trouble.

The principal should have had the janitor place from thirty to forty chairs about the lower hallway, and a few in each of the rooms, for parents to occupy. Parents are of course much interested, and often very useful with little children in giving names, quieting fears, caring for personal needs, etc. Signs on the doors of all rooms should indicate what classes of pupils or parents are to go there. The principal probably will do well to have a table or his desk put out in the hallway and work there, unless he has a very large outer room. A small office is easily crowded, and if there is but one door for entrance and exit the congestion is likely to slow up procedure and prove irritating. He would also best work standing. If he uses his office, he would best have all chairs removed from it for the day. On this day particularly he must not be tied to his desk or the telephone, but must be able to move people along rapidly and move himself as needed. The advantage of having his desk out in the hallway is obvious. He also needs to keep three or four files, on which he can string and classify slips of paper bearing notes, permits, things to be attended to later, and other special items. On a card, carried in his pocket, he should make notes for the afternoon teachers' meeting.

The principal should also have taken some preliminary estimate of his school neighborhood, and should have some idea as to the increase in enrollment likely, in what grades it is likely to be, and what he will do with it. If his school is likely to be overcrowded, maps of his district, showing streets, and on which he can locate his extra pupils by grades, will be very useful if he has to shift pupils to other schools. If he has any vacant rooms he will need to plan how best to use them.

Beginning the work. In many city schools it is customary for the principal and teachers to arrive early, to see that all is in readiness, and then for the doors to be opened at an advertised time, such as 8.30 or 8.45. Where there is likely to be much early crowding this may be desirable. Where this is not the case the doors would best be opened as soon as the teachers arrive, and the pupils be allowed to enter and be sorted and placed as they come. The great task for the first hour will be classification. With teachers in their rooms or at stations in readiness, particular teachers designated to handle special cases, any unclassified or substitute teachers available on hand for special service, the teacher of say the two highest grades in the school assuming important duties in classification, the principal keeping himself as free as possible from small details, the signs up giving directions, and pupil ushers busy in guiding and directing, the work can proceed quite rapidly and without much confusion.

When parents or children are familiar with the building they can find their way easily. The student ushers can direct any who are not quite sure. The signs on the doors will further help. Strangers are referred to the proper teacher, who classifies quickly, and the assisting young people show the pupils to the proper rooms. Some pupils will come without credentials and give evidence of an uncertain type of preparation. These will have to be classified experimentally, and find their proper place later on. Plenty of cards or slips of paper, about three by four inches in size, on which to write "Room No. —," "Classification," "Temporary Placement," "Week's Trial," etc., will prove useful. The teachers receiving transfers similarly classify and sort. The left-overs, irregulars, and conditioned pupils, handled by Miss C, may be temporarily sorted, held in their old rooms for a few days, or sent to the ungraded room for work until they can be dealt with by the principal. Slips for all these cases should be sent with the pupil to the teacher, and saved by her for consultation with the principal. It may take some days, or even weeks, to adjust these special cases properly.

The kindergarten and first-grade teachers, probably assisted here by any substitute or special teachers available for service, will sort out the little ones. The kindergarten room is large and specially well suited for caring for a crowd, and is the proper place for all beginners. Those too young for school will be sent home, and the others temporarily classified. If the number of little ones exceeds provisions made, the substitute teacher can be given a class temporarily in one of the vacant rooms, if there be such, and if not she can help the first- or second-grade teacher.

The purpose is to get a quick classification, and only as good a one as can be made in approximately half an hour to an hour. Of necessity there will have to be many cases of re-classification during the week, and some temporarily admitted may be found mentally too young and may have to be sent home if no development class is available. With this in mind, in all cases of doubt classify low rather than high; it is much easier to move pupils up than down. In all temporary-classification cases, hold back book-purchase lists until the case is decided. Have the teachers test these pupils as rapidly as possible and re-classify when the case is obvious, leaving decision to principal only when the proper position of the pupil is in doubt.

Many parents will want to see only the principal, or at least to see him first. Hence the advantage of his being out in the open, and standing, with no chairs about his desk this first morning. He must greet them, find their wants, send them on by an usher to the proper teacher or room, and get to the next in line. Most cases he can refer to some teacher, or settle on the spot, and it is a great waste of valuable time to have these people file into an office, sit down, take their turn in line, and have to get up and get out again before he can attend to the next case. The more difficult cases he can make a note about, make a temporary decision, and put the note on one of his files for later consideration, having the parent or pupil call again in a day or two. Parents who want to talk he can move along, if he is tactful, by accepting their profession of interest, etc., etc., and inviting them to be present at the first meeting of the Parent-Teacher Association, at 3.15, on a week from the following Thursday, when there will be time for them to set forth their views more at length.

Starting the school. At 9.00, let us say, bells will give the signal for all children to go to their rooms. No attempt at lines or formal passing need be made. Teachers and ushers can soon get the children in and placed. The teachers in each room can quickly sort over those present, determine who should be sent elsewhere and who are to remain, enroll, and seat. Pupils not in the right room can be sent where they belong. Pupils from outside the school district are handled as the regulations direct. In many schools it is customary for the pupils to go first to the room they occupied the preceding year, and then, at a signal, to pass to the new room they are to occupy. The plan is more wasteful of time and effort, and adds nothing to the effectiveness of organization. A good administrative principle, especially for first-day organization, is to proceed by the most direct and most economical route, save unnecessary motions, and get instruction under way as early as possible.

A still better plan, in schools where there is not much change in clientèle, is for the principal to make all promotions just before recess the last morning of the preceding school year, send the pupils with their wraps and books to the room they will occupy the following year, and then conduct the classes the remainder of this last day in the new rooms. Everything then is in readiness to begin work promptly the first day in the Autumn, and classes can start to work within five minutes after the pupils reach the rooms. This avoids all delay, and gives the pupils the impression that the school means business from the start.

As soon as can be done, ordinarily by or before 9.45, the teacher should send a pupil to the principal with a slip of paper containing the following information:

>   Room No. 12
>   Teacher *Mabel Brown*
>   Pupils in 6 B Grade 26
>   Pupils in 6 A Grade 23
>   Total No. of pupils 49
>   Number of seats 42

By ten o'clock the principal can have transferred these items to a printed single-page Classification Report Sheet, and have a first temporary view of his grades and seating space to look at and figure from. Re-classifications and additions in the afternoon will change his first tally, but it is useful to have such early preliminary returns. Probably the superintendent's office will telephone for such a report before noon, and figures are better than guesses.

The teachers now proceed at once to organize their classes. On the blackboard a temporary program should have been placed, which the pupils are told will be followed for the present. On the blackboard should also be found, and explained by the teacher, the bell-signal system of the school. These signals should remain on the board for a few days, until the pupils have become thoroughly familiar with them. If there are any absolutely necessary rules that should be stated to all, this is the time to explain them and the reasons for making them. Teachers should be instructed, though, to make at first no rules not needed, and none which they do not expect to enforce. Rules should proceed out of needs. The principal should follow the same idea in his work. There are usually few cases of discipline on the first day, though the measure of principal and teachers, especially the new ones, is being taken by the more aggressive youngsters of the school.

The next step is to arrange the pupil-monitors by rows, pass out the necessary supplies and books, charge any books permanently loaned to pupils, and start the work of the school. For this every teacher should have a tentative program of work laid out, so that she will know about what she is going to do this first day. The new teachers may need some special help here, though this difficulty ought in large part to have been anticipated at the Friday morning new-teachers' meeting. Teachers who are not only new to the school but beginners in teaching as well may need special attention the first few days, though if they can handle their problems it is better to let them do so, even at the cost of some mistakes. The effect on the children is better. By 9.40 to 10.00 instruction ought to be under way, so that one group or grade may be set to work studying and the other have one recitation before the morning recess time comes. A quick and energetic start, with plenty of well-organized work the first day, makes a good impression and tends to ward off disciplinary trouble.

Beginning school with an assembly. All that has been said so far has been on the assumption that the school does not have an assembly hall where all the pupils can meet together, as most of the older elementary-school buildings, such as those shown in Figures 5, 6, 7, and 8, pages 95–99, do not. In such schools as are shown in Figures 9 and 10 the situation is different, and in these the best procedure would be to begin the school with a general assembly of all of the pupils. For this the principal should have prepared with some care. It must be an inspirational and enthusiasm-

THE FIRST DAY OF SCHOOL

awakening occasion, and if carried through with some spirit it can be made of large usefulness in putting the pupils once more into the spirit of the school and in starting things off right. An interesting program should have been thought out and prepared for in advance, and this should be run through with some "snap." Every one should leave the assembly with a good feeling for the school, and the principal and the teachers should feel that a good start has been made.

At the 9.00 signal all pupils would then go to the assembly hall instead of to their rooms. Placards should announce the meeting and point the way. All cases with pupils and parents should be postponed until afterward, and all be invited to go to the assembly hall. If the school has any good music — orchestra, piano and cornet, violin, or a teacher who can sing well — start with a selection, and if not try to get a well-known song started. A good leader is important if a song is to be sung. The principal would best be in charge of the assembly, regardless of what procedure may be followed at other times. Give variety, as well as interest and spirit to the program. Do not do any one thing very long. Make the program constructive; do not lay down the law, or scold, or preach a sermon.

The following program, carried through by a principal, is suggestive of what may be done:

9.00 — Bell signal; pupils file in. Boy Scouts used to direct and usher, and bring in stragglers. No special order insisted on, and only reasonable quiet expected.
9.05 — Music by the school orchestra; two short selections.
9.20 — Welcoming talk by the principal. Kindly, sympathetic, constructive, and inspiring for the work of the new year. No fault-finding, no regulations, no rules.
9.28 — President of the School Council (boy). Short talk, calling for coöperation, school loyalty, team work, and explaining half a dozen of the important rules of the school.
9.33 — An eighth-grade Girl-Scout pupil. A few words to the

girls on what the girls can do for the school, and appealing for coöperation and a fine school spirit.

9.38 — Announcements by the principal. Directions as to what to do and where to go, and a few final words as to starting to work promptly and making this the best year of their lives.

9.45 — Dismissal, pupils pass out and to rooms, orchestra playing a march tune.

9.48 — Bell signal to begin work in the rooms.

The teachers now begin sorting and enrolling the pupils, as previously described, and get the work of instruction under way as rapidly as is possible. The principal at once resumes work at his desk in the hall, handling parents and pupil cases, and the preliminary classification report slips are expected from the teachers by or before the morning recess.

Special conditions. If the school is small, or happens to be one of a number of elementary schools constituting a supervisory group (as in Figure 3, page 12), and in which the principal also teaches a class, it probably will be necessary, if no substitute or special teacher can be provided to relieve him, for him to enroll his class on arrival, give them the necessary directions for the following day, and then dismiss them for the day that he may have time to look after the organization of his building as a whole.

Again, if the upper grades of his school have been reorganized on the department plan, or as a junior high school, a special procedure will need to be followed for these grades. In such a case some such plan as the following may well be carried out:

1. All old pupils to report to their "home room" of the preceding term on coming to the school.
2. Pupils promoted from the grades below to the departmental work to go to a designated room and teacher for classification.
3. Pupils new to the system to go to another room and teacher for classification.

4. Both 2 and 3 might better meet in the auditorium, if there be such a room.
5. Home-room assignments made (9.00–9.15), and pupils sent at signal to new home-room, where teachers seat and enroll as in the grades.
6. The pupils now, with the assistance of the home-room teachers, make up their individual programs from the room program on the blackboard and the schedule key in the hands of the teacher.
7. Pupils promoted in all subjects and regular simply copy the room or class program; pupils irregular are given variations by the teacher from the schedule key she holds.

The above, together with book lists, book charging, and announcements probably will occupy from a half to three quarters of an hour. It probably now will be an advantage to run through the day's program of room changes, using eight- to ten-minute periods, until the home room is again reached. This will familiarize the pupils with the changes, give the different departmental teachers an opportunity to assign places and make announcements, and get everything ready for starting on the regular program immediately after the morning recess. In a small school this experimental run of the room changes is hardly necessary; in a large school, and especially in a regularly organized junior high school, it is quite desirable.

Again, if the school as a whole happens to be organized as a Gary-type, companion-class, or platoon school, a still different type of preliminary organization will be needed for all pupils, though many of the details as to procedure previously given will still apply. Under any one of these plans, as will be described further on, there are more pupils than there are classroom seats, there being virtually two companion schools in the building at the same time. While one of these schools (A) is reciting in the classrooms, the other school (B) is at work in the shops, special rooms, or on the playground. The building is thus made to carry two schools. The details for such a type of organization will be given later.

Recess, lines, and assembly. The different teachers will have been instructed, at the preceding conferences, as to dismissals, stairways to use, signals, etc., and will have been told, assuming that lines have been in use in the school, that at the first recess period the temporary yard organization will be perfected. Yard and basement assignments for teachers will also have been made, if the school has in the past followed this plan.

At the close of the recess period, a short time will be taken to form and place the lines. Each teacher and class will take the position assigned to it by the principal, according to a worked-out plan, the details of which will be given in the following chapter. The position of each class will be determined by the shape of the yard, position of entrances, and scheme of movement. The necessary instructions are given to the pupils, the music is started, and the classes march in in the order called and pass to their rooms. After a few attempts the order and plan will become mechanized. The same oversight will be given to the lining up and marching in at the afternoon assembly, recess, and for a few days thereafter.

After the recess the remainder of the morning will be devoted to regular classroom instruction, and the school will be expected to settle down to its routine procedure as rapidly as possible. The afternoon session will find a few new pupils, mostly pupils coming by transfer from other schools, but ordinarily these will be so few in number that the principal can handle and classify them alone.

The great advantage of all the preliminary planning and conferences on problems of organization will early be apparent. A carefully planned and businesslike way of handling the difficulties which always present themselves on the opening day creates a healthy and lasting impression on pupils, teachers, and parents, insures for the school a higher degree of efficiency, and does much to make all concerned feel that the principal is master of his work.

The afternoon teachers' meeting. The principal will naturally have been moving about over his building during the day, looking in here and there and seeing conditions, answering questions of teachers, settling problems at least tentatively, helping in the revision of other tentative decisions of the morning, making adjustments of pupils and classes, and other similar work; but, notwithstanding all that may be done in this manner during the day, and it should be much, there will of necessity be many questions and problems that will need a hasty talking over by the group. For this an afternoon teachers' meeting in the building will be desirable. This should be called as soon after school closes as the teachers are free. The principal should clear his office rapidly so as to get to this. The teachers are tired, and they ought to be allowed to go home as soon as can conveniently be done.

The meeting ought to be carried through rapidly, without wasting time in considering matters that can wait, or in prolonged discussion of any point. The principal again needs to have in mind, or still better on a card, a program of what he intends to take up, and matters that are not then important should either be quickly and tentatively ruled on or be reserved for consideration at a later meeting.

The teachers should bring to this meeting a final day's Classification Report, and each class and grade can be quickly called for and noted down on a final first-day's Room and Grade Classification Report Sheet. Each teacher should also bring in a written list of all pupils who ought to be in attendance, according to the promotion lists, and have not yet appeared. It is likely that each teacher will have problems — pupils, organization, seating, supplies, etc. — that she will want to raise questions about, and on many of these the principal will want to make a note for action before the following morning. The principal, too, will want to bring up matters noted during the day on his pocket card, or on the slips on his office files, and also probably to ask about particular cases, though much time should not be taken in considering any case or problem of interest to only one teacher. Marching plans, yard organization, the fire drill, basement and toilet supervision, and play direction are also subjects that it may seem desirable to take up for brief consideration. If the principal is new to the school these would better be left, for a time at least, as they have been in the past, any discussion now being merely to make action clearer or more forceful the following day.

Before leaving for the night the principal should report to the office of the Superintendent of Schools the condition of his building as to pupils and seats, and any other important matters. He will take home with him the serious problems of adjustment which he faces, that he may think them over and plan for the following day.

QUESTIONS AND PROBLEMS

1. Show that executive skill consists in part in the ability to get others to coöperate and carry the details of an undertaking.
2. Suppose the janitor to be new and not possessed of much head; how handle the preliminary supply distribution so as to get the results desired?
3. Map out a plan of teacher and pupil coöperation and assignment for each of the buildings shown in Figures 5 to 10, Chapter VI.
4. State how you would handle the pupil entry and classification in each of these buildings.
5. Draw up a supposed first-day pupil and grade Classification Report Sheet for any one of the buildings.
6. Why keep the principal's office free of chairs? Why is it best for him to stand the first morning?
7. To carry through the first day's work properly and expeditiously, list the things a teacher would need to plan, have, and write on the blackboard before the school began the first day.
8. What types of questions would you expect to take up at the teachers' meeting the evening of the first day?
9. What types of problems would the principal probably need to take home with him the first night?

CHAPTER VI
INTERMISSIONS, LINES, AND DRILLS
1. *Intermissions and lines*

Size of grounds a limiting factor. Just how a principal shall arrange his recess periods, and handle his playground at other times, depends much on the size and character of his play space, as well as on the number and grade-distribution of the children in his school. In a school which has plenty of play space all the children can be on the grounds at once, the recess period can take place simultaneously for all, and the before-school period will not give any particular trouble. Many schools are not so fortunately situated, however. Especially in eastern cities are the school grounds, for the older buildings at least, very commonly small and ill-suited to modern play needs, and principals of such schools are frequently called upon to exercise a large amount of ingenuity to care for the recess and play needs of their children. Sometimes, where street play is not permitted by the city authorities, standing room only is all that is available, and the recess periods are merely walking-around and fresh-air periods.

In an average city, not suffering specially from congestion of population, a school site ought properly to contain somewhere near 200 square feet (c.14′×14′) for each child. This would be 218 children to the acre, or would require a site of about four and a half acres for a school of 1000 pupils. The percentage of the site taken up by the building will also materially influence the playground possibilities. A fifteen-room elementary-school building, with a carrying load of 500 children, located on a quarter of a large city block with grounds but 200 × 225 feet in size, would have only about 60 square feet (7½ × 8 feet) per pupil. In such a case, dismissals, games, and sports will need to be organized quite differently from what would be the case were the same school to have a whole block of land. Assuming a full block, and making the same allowance for the building as before, there would then be about 300 square feet (15 × 20) of play space per pupil. This would give plenty of room for games requiring space, simultaneous recesses, plenty of free play, and parts of the grounds could be set apart for special purposes.

Handling recess periods. The first problem that a principal faces in the matter of his recess periods is that of the size and nature of his school grounds and the use he can make of his streets. While usually he cannot change conditions, and must deal with situations as they exist, he must arrange his intermissions and organize his playground activities with these limitations clearly in mind. Figures 5 to 10, given on the pages which follow, and which have been drawn from actual situations, show the many different types and conditions of buildings and grounds which a principal may meet. Each of these presents an entirely different problem in organization, both for recess periods and for play. Games suitable to the larger and less-crowded grounds are not possible on the smaller sites. Streets scarcely need be used where the site is large, but must be used, if permitted, where the site is small. The handling of the street play, and its policing, becomes an additional problem where the site is small.

In the schools represented in Figures 7, 8, 9, and 10 there is room for all children to be on the playground at one time, and in 8, 9, and 10 no use need be made of the adjacent streets. Even in Figure 7 the use of streets could be dispensed with, if necessary, but their use is desirable if possible as the children are thus spread out more, the play is

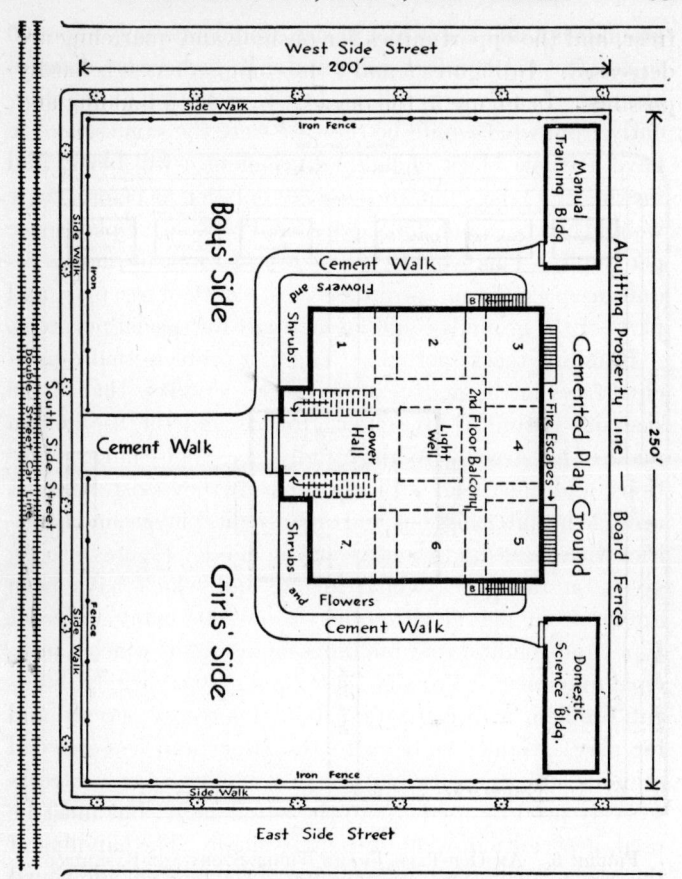

FIGURE 5. AN OLD-TYPE FOURTEEN-ROOM ONE-EXIT SCHOOL
BUILDING

Seven rooms on each floor, and the principal's office on the second floor, over the front entrance. The building is a brick shell, with wooden interior, and has the heating plant in the basement. It is located on half of a city block, a trifle over an acre in size. The carrying load of the school is 475 pupils, which gives, counting building, 105 square feet per pupil. A part of the grounds has been taken by two portables, located at the rear, and by planting, so that the available play space is much lessened in consequence. Two small indoor playrooms, though, are provided in the basement, and the large lower hallway, which is lighted by a skylight, is also used on rainy days. Street play is forbidden by city ordinance. There is no play apparatus on the grounds. The school has no kindergarten, and grades 1 to 8 are on the grade plan.

freer, and the opportunities for pushing and quarreling are decreased. In Figures 5 and 6 the common recess is hardly possible. In Figure 5, the one exit from both building and

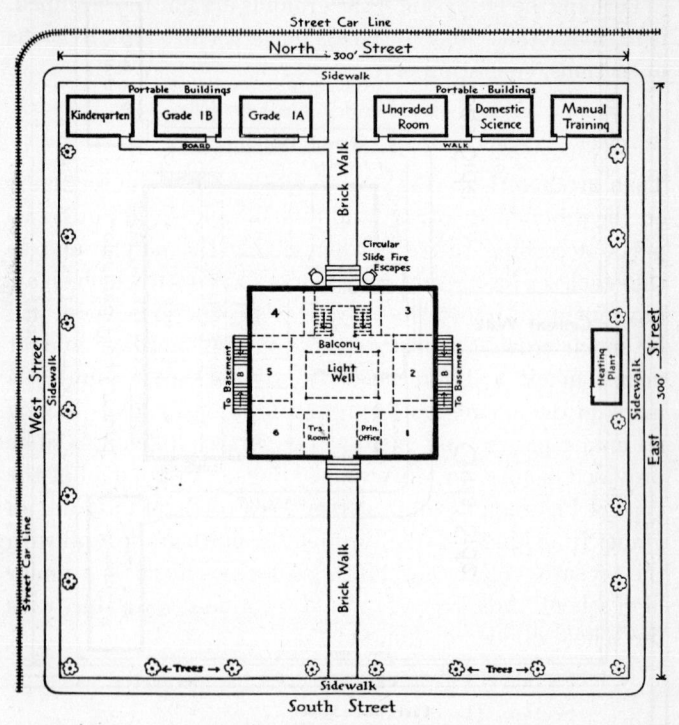

FIGURE 6. AN OLD-TYPE FRAME THREE-STORY-AND-BASEMENT TWENTY-ROOM BUILDING

A wooden building of an old type, located in the center of a city block of a little over two acres. Six portable buildings have been set up in the yard to carry the increase in attendance. The school has 24 classroom teachers, and special teachers for domestic science and manual training, and a carrying load of 840 pupils. This gives 107 square feet per pupil, counting building space. Street play is prohibited by city ordinance. No play apparatus is provided for the grounds. The school has nine grades and kindergarten, grades 7 to 9 being on the third floor and organized as a junior high school. On the second and third floors another classroom is located over the south entrance. Good playrooms are in the basement, as are the toilet rooms. The basement may be entered from both sides of the yard, as well as from the inside. The large central lower floor is also used for play in bad weather. There is but one large double stairway, but this has been rebuilt in iron, and two circular slide fire-escapes have been attached to the landings.

grounds, and in both Figures 5 and 6 the very limited play space, make the use of the simultaneous recess almost impossible and the use of the streets for play very desirable.

Perhaps the best plan, if the grounds are not too cramped, is to divide the school for recess purposes into two divisions or sections, consisting of:

> Section I — Grades 1 to 4 inclusive.
> Section II — Grades 5 to 8 inclusive.

Then arrange the recess periods so that only one section is on the grounds at a time, and divide each section into two parts, according to sex. Then divide the playground so that each sex has its own play space. Even with such an arrangement, which covers only the recess periods, there will be much crowding before school in the morning and at noons, unless a difference of twenty to thirty minutes is made in the opening and closing times. In schools having no indoor playground there will be further difficulties to be provided against on rainy or cold days. In a school of the type of Figure 6, having small and crowded grounds and all grades from kindergarten through the ninth grade, and with the seventh, eighth, and ninth grades organized as a junior high school, three recesses would seem most desirable, with the school divided as follows:

> Section I — Grades 1 to 3, and kindergarten.
> Section II — Grades 4 to 6.
> Section III — Grades 7 to 9.

All these contingencies may require two series of programs, one for good weather and one for bad, and different playground arrangements for morning and noon on the one hand, and recess periods on the other. Not only will the disposition of the play space need to be different for the different contingencies, but the arrangements for dismissals will need to be different also. In such schools as are shown

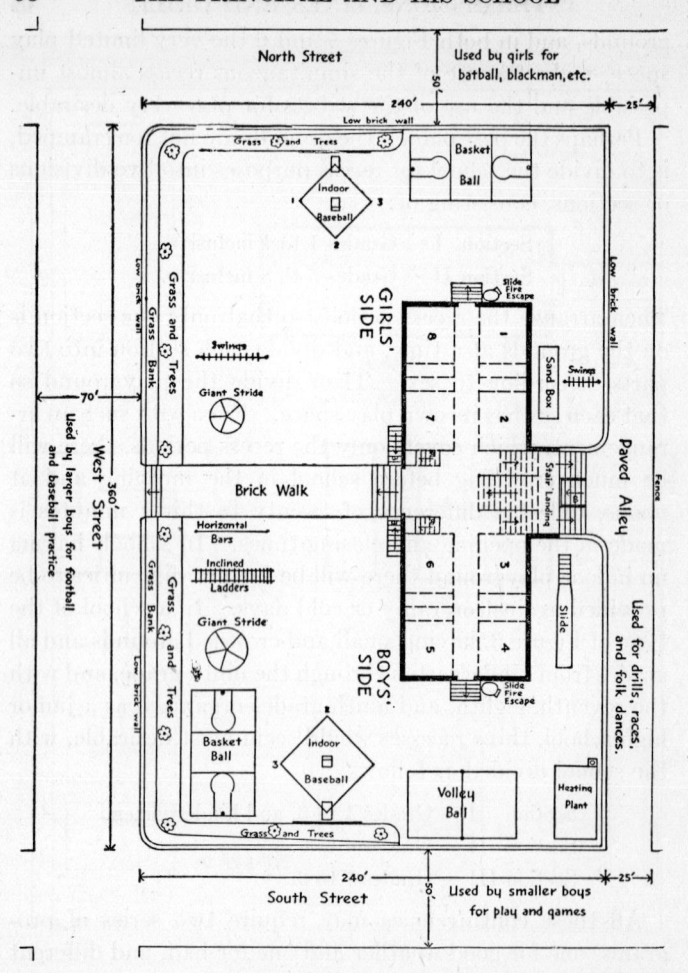

FIGURE 7. A FRAME SIXTEEN-ROOM ELEMENTARY-SCHOOL BUILDING

A relatively modern sixteen-room frame building, carrying a kindergarten and eight grades. The school has a principal and 16 teachers, and a carrying load of 560 children. The combined yard and building area gives 154 square feet per pupil; including streets and alleys 275 square feet are available. The rooms of the first floor are indicated, as well as the exits. On the second floor eight additional rooms are over the ones below, and the principal's office is over the back hallway. In the basement, reached both from within and without, are toilet rooms, two small indoor playrooms for use in bad weather, a room for manual training, and one for domestic science. The school has no assembly hall.

INTERMISSIONS, LINES, AND DRILLS 99

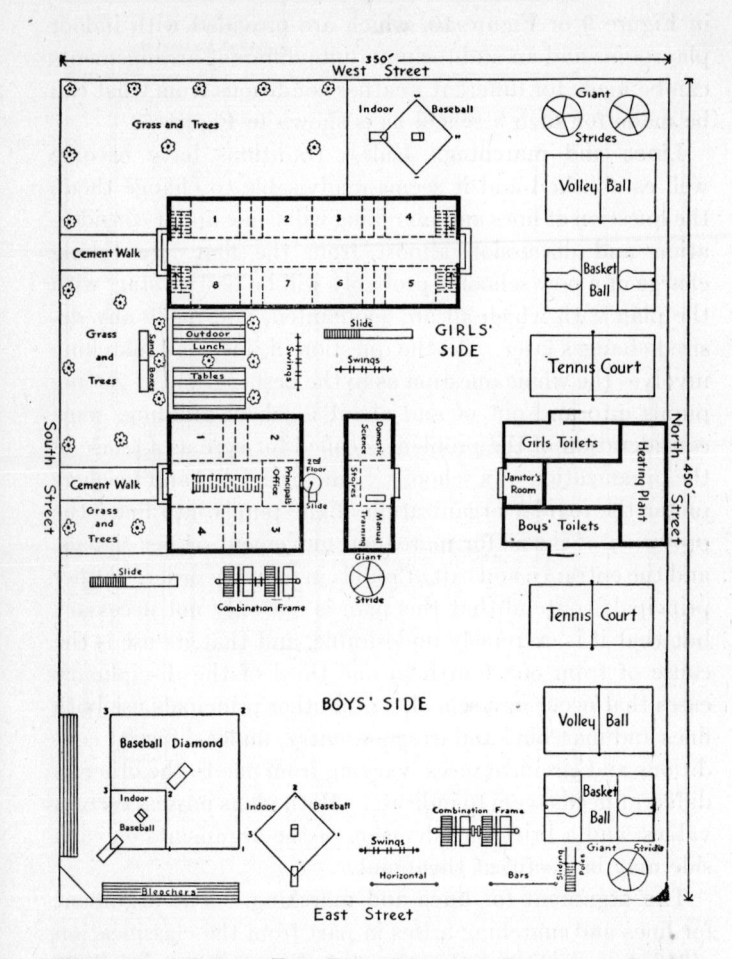

FIGURE 8. A TWENTY-FOUR-ROOM CALIFORNIA ELEMENTARY SCHOOL

Located in a small city, on a block of approximately three and a half acres. The original school was an eight-room building. With increasing population a new building of sixteen rooms was erected, as well as a special building for manual training and domestic science. Twenty-two rooms are now used for nine grades, grades 7, 8, and 9 being organized as a junior high school. The building now carries 625 pupils, which gives, counting buildings, 252 square feet per pupil. The second floor of each building is a duplicate of the first, except that in the old building the space over the principal's office is given to a broad stair landing, leading to the circular fire-escape.

in Figure 9 or Figure 10, which are provided with indoor playrooms and an auditorium, quite different arrangements can be made for different weather conditions from what can be made for such a school as is shown in Figure 5.

Lines and marching. Unless traditions have become well established and it seems inadvisable to change them, the question of lines and marching will come up for consideration and discussion almost from the first. In taking charge of a new school it probably will be best to start with the plan with which all are acquainted, and make any desired changes later. As the question of lines and marching involves the whole question as to the best method of getting pupils into and out of and about a school building, some consideration of the problem is called for here as a phase of the organization of a school. Some principals and teachers prefer the regular organization of the pupils into lines, the provision of music for marching, movement as per signals, and the entrance and exit of pupils in military order. Other principals contend that this plan is not only not necessary but that it is extremely undesirable, and that its use is the cause of from one fourth to one third of the disciplinary cases that occur in a school. Still other principals use both lines and marching and irregular entry, under different conditions and circumstances, varying from one to the other as different needs seem to indicate. Both plans possess certain values, and a brief consideration of the arguments on each side may be useful at this point.

The argument for lines and marching. The argument for lines and marching arises in part from the classification of this as a routine, rather than a judgment factor in school organization and control. Especially is this true for a school located in a foreign section of a city, or a school where discipline and orderly procedure are lacking. As a routine factor it of course ought to be transformed into mechanized

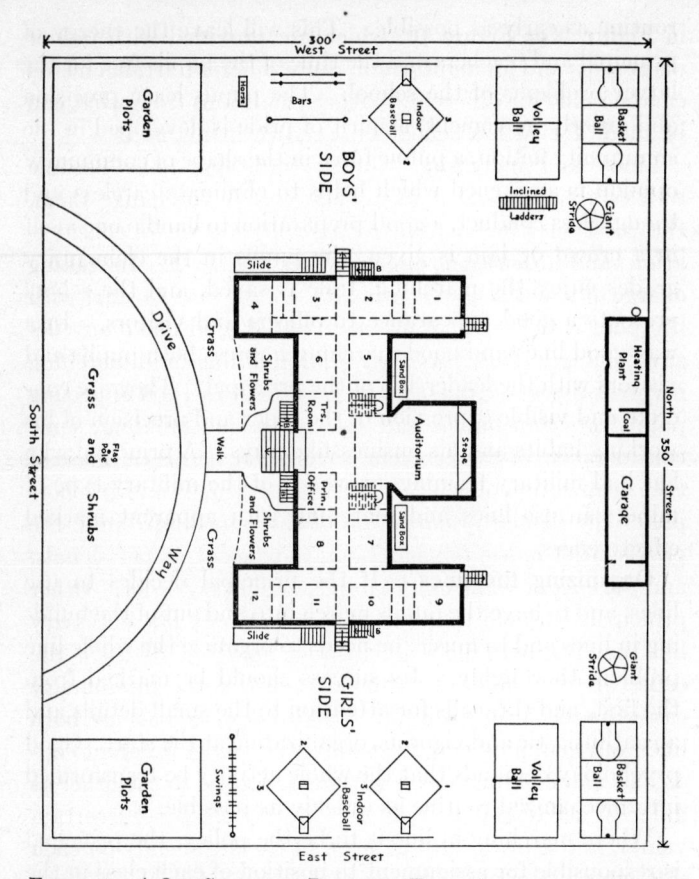

FIGURE 9. A ONE-STORY-AND-BASEMENT TOWN CONSOLIDATED SCHOOL

This building is of wood construction, and is one story high with a high basement. It is located in the center of a block of approximately three acres, in an incorporated town, and to it children are brought in automobile busses. The main floor has twelve regular classrooms, office and teachers' room, and an auditorium. In the high basement are located a gymnasium under the auditorium, toilet rooms, a lunch room, and rooms for manual training and domestic science. The school has a kindergarten and grades 1 to 8, grades 6, 7, and 8 being organized on the departmental plan. Twelve teachers and a principal are employed. As a grade school the carrying load is 420 pupils, which gives, counting space occupied by buildings, 250 square feet per pupil. This building is so arranged that it could be reorganized as a platoon-type school, as will be pointed out in Chapter VIII, carry twice the load, and still have 125 square feet per pupil.

routine as early as possible. This will leave the energy of principal and teachers and the time of the pupils free for the larger problems of the school. The pupils learn precision and orderly movement, a spirit of pride is developed in the community action, a public force in the shape of community opinion is awakened which helps to eliminate careless and thoughtless conduct, a good preparation to handle one's self in a crowd or jam is given, the pupils in the elementary grades enjoy the marching, time is saved, and the school presents a good appearance to officers and visitors. In a way good lines and good marching impress both pupils and visitors with the leadership of the principal. They are concrete and visible expression of the order and precision of his working habits and his businesslike ways. A principal who has had military training, or who is of the military type of mind, can use lines and marching with apparent marked effectiveness.

Organizing the lines. If the principal decides to use lines, and to have the pupils march into and out of the building in lines and to music, he needs to organize the whole line problem thoroughly. Its success should be marked from the first, and this calls for attention to the small details and an enthusiastic and vigorous organization at the start. Good psychology demands that the whole activity be transformed into mechanized routine as quickly as possible.

Where marching in line is to be the policy, the principal is responsible for assignment to position of each class in the lining up, order of march, etc. To be sure, he may call his teachers into conference and work out the details with them, or will propose a working plan and ask them to help refine it for him. The order of march should be arranged as far as possible so that the class having the farthest to go before reaching its room will get in first. It is well to arrange this order if possible so that it will be identical with that to be

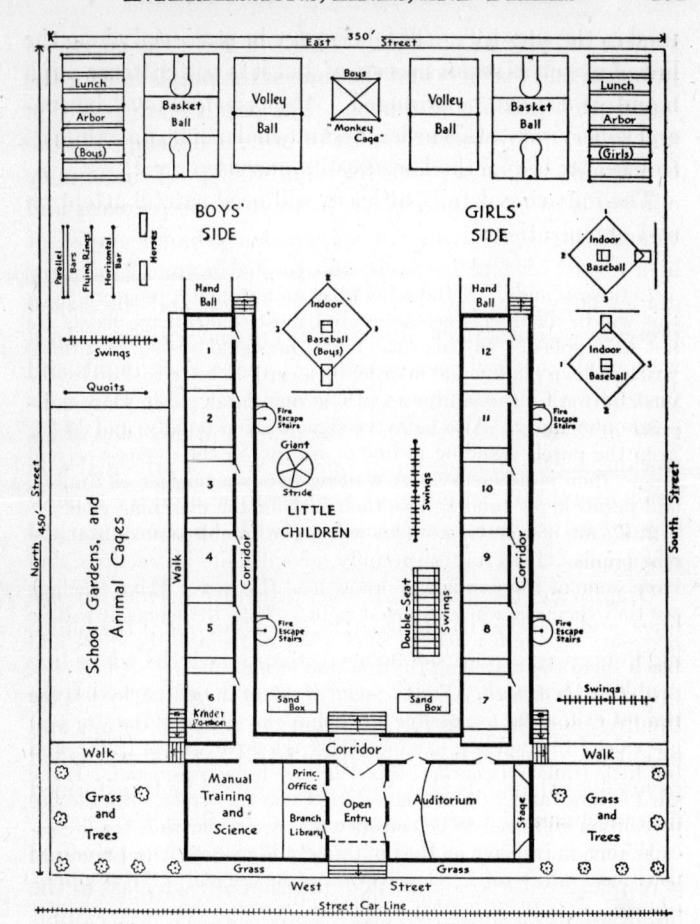

FIGURE 10. A MODERN-TYPE FIREPROOF CITY SCHOOL BUILDING

Located on a city block of approximately four acres. The school is two stories high, and has two covered wet- or hot-weather playgrounds on the roof. Toilets are located throughout the building, off the various rooms. The school has twenty-four regular classrooms, an auditorium, and special rooms for manual training, domestic science, music, drawing, and science. The carrying load of the school is 840 children. The school has a kindergarten and nine grades, the three highest being organized as a junior high school. This gives a ground space of 187 square feet per pupil, building included. The domestic science suite, and the art and music rooms are on the second floor at the front. The branch library, office, and auditorium may be reached without any other parts of the building being opened.

used in the fire-drill. Teachers may be stationed along the line of march as seems necessary, but it is better to use pupil monitors if it can be arranged. The principal must be general supervisor of this order, and much depends upon him as to whether the method secures its purpose or not.

The following details, at least, will need careful attention and organization:

1. Gong signals. If the school has an automatic program clock this will be all that is necessary, but most elementary schools are not so supplied. In this case, have the signal system and times written down plainly and in order on a card, to be tacked up by the push button for the janitor's use in giving the signals. Do not depend on memory. Also have the signals given rapidly, and do not keep the pupils standing in line or waiting in the rooms a second longer than is necessary. A waiting line is a breeder of trouble, and pupils kept standing lose their zest for the marching game.

2. Routes of marching. This will prove troublesome only to the new pupils. Plan routes carefully, give definite instructions, and have some of the pupils who know lead the way. Have teachers see that their classes get started right. With little ones it will be necessary for the teachers to start many of them in the steps, and teach them the marching rhythm and swing.

3. Exits to be used. For the sake of safety in case of fire use the nearest exit, as far as possible for each room. If there is a street on one side of the building in which there is a great deal of traffic, and but little traffic on another, this will have to be considered. If the yard is large and exits are not directly on the street, only the fire precaution will need to be considered. A circular slide for fire escape, such as is shown on the buildings of Figures 6, 7, and 8, can be used most effectively. Deprivation of its use will serve as a punishment, so popular is such a slide.

4. Double and single files. This will depend on the width of the halls. Pupils from different rooms may pass out in single parallel lines or join into double lines. Keep 18 inches between pupils if possible, but do not keep lines standing long.

5. Use of stairways. If very narrow or crooked, use single lines; if wider, double lines. On a very broad staircase, four-abreast may be managed. Always think of fire precautions and safety of descent.

INTERMISSIONS, LINES, AND DRILLS

6. Traffic in the streets. Insist that children stay on the sidewalks, if there is much traffic in the street. If one or more streets next the building are practically free from traffic at dismissal, allow children to use street if necessary to avoid congestion. Lines probably will not need to be maintained after reaching the sidewalk. The organization of a traffic squad of older pupils to police the streets will prove useful.

7. Signals for return. Three minutes before time for the close of play give a warning signal on gong, different from other signals. Three or four short-spaced rings will be good. This will be a warning signal only. Pupils can go on with play, get drinks, or gather up balls and wraps, and get ready. At the end of the three minutes give one long sharp signal. At this every pupil is to stop play and talking, and face the yard teachers or the school. The yard teachers or principal may now make announcements, or the principal may use a megaphone for the same purpose if he could not otherwise be heard. When ready to pass a signal is given on a whistle, at which the pupils move to their positions, form in lines, and pass into the building. If no announcement is to be made, give not less than five nor more than ten seconds before blowing the forward movement signal, to let the play exuberance quiet down somewhat and bring the school under control. The psychology of eliminating trouble in the lines lies largely in gaining this control.

8. Returning to rooms after recesses. Have the older pupils lead, and have the pupils return the way they marched out. Have teachers go with the primary pupils. Have all directed as to the place where lines form after recess.

9. Dismissing big and little children without interference. This will take care of itself if the time schedule is properly cared for. The rooms on the lower floor should pass out first, while the pupils from the upper rooms are coming down stairs. Good timing here is desirable.

10. Leaders for lines. These should always be selected from last year's pupils. Have the teachers pick dependable children at first; later the class may be permitted to choose, or leadership may be made an honor.

11. Music for marching. If available this is a potent aid to order and regularity. Drum or victrola or triangle will serve as a substitute if piano or orchestra is not to be had. If the school has an orchestra this is a good time to use it.

Have the teachers give these instructions to the pupils

as the need for them arises. It is poor planning to give a lot of instructions that are to be held in mind for execution at a remote time. Children will remember, if they do the thing when it is ordered, and just as it is ordered.

The argument against lines. The bearing of the method of movement in and out and about a building on the lives of the children outside the school needs also to be considered. There are many principals who oppose the use of lines and marching and contend that, since school should prepare for life by living life, and as adults do not line up and march into and out of buildings, shops, stores, churches, theaters, or public meetings of any kind, lines and marching in schools are unnatural life procedures and should be abandoned. The cry of progressive educators, they say, has been against the creation of an artificial schoolroom atmosphere and procedure, so why then should we create for the school an organized system entirely divorced from the usage of ordinary life. Pupils know where and how to go, they say, and would do so if left alone. Such principals allow their pupils to pass from rooms in any reasonably quiet manner, have no music or lines or marching, and bring the pupils into the building by one signal to stop play and stand just where they are, and another, immediately afterward, to move quietly to the proper entrance and walk to their rooms. The pupils move at their own rate, may talk and laugh in passing, and in every way conduct themselves as normally as possible. Some excellent training in self-control and self-direction no doubt is given in such schools, and a large amount of self-dependence is developed. Carried too far such schools become noisy and careless, the entry is a rough-and-tumble procedure, and the independence developed frequently exhibits its natural outcome in a lack of ability to act together in any united way.

Our national life calls for two types of self-discipline.

One type is the ability to care for one's self, and to direct one's own life. A too rigid insistence on lines and marching and quiet and policing naturally tends to defeat such independence in action. The other type of discipline called for demands that at times each subordinate himself to a common purpose, and at times yield up his independence in action and follow a leader. Both types of self-discipline are called for in the modern world, and a combination of the two is desirable in the school. The problem, then, that the school principal faces, is how to combine these two types of training and secure for his pupils the best in each.

Minimizing the marching procedure. Most principals would agree that, after the school has been organized, the principal and teachers established in control, the marching procedure learned for fire-drill and public-exercise needs, and the school reduced to order and system, then at least the principal and teachers might well set about the gradual elimination of all unnecessary formality and routine. The aim should then be to substitute individual control for mechanized routine in policed lines. To keep pupils marching in silent lines, to fife and drum, and with a teacher at every corner watching for offenders, not only does not develop self-control but is an almost certain breeder of disciplinary troubles. One of the strong arguments against lines and marching is that they are too prolific of cases of discipline. Not only is this true, but a situation is created in which teachers and principal do not show to advantage, and in consequence discipline is weakened.

It is possible gradually to change line organization from a routine to a judgment procedure, and to bring into it the educational elements of self-direction and self-control. This necessitates the gradual minimizing of lines and marching, and the limiting their use to those necessary occasions when such procedure is the obvious one to follow. Marching out in lines and order, a few times a week, is valuable as a matter of self-discipline, and as a preparation for such emergencies as the fire-drill. It is also useful as a phase of the work in physical training. To move a large number of children from their rooms to an assembly hall, in a short period of time, and to avoid congestion in entrance and seating, may also possibly call for dismissal by rooms and by orderly procedure. On the playground, special periods for marching exercises may be utilized, when all join in marching up and down, with music and flags, and as a pleasurable drill. The salute to the flag may be accompanied with a lining-up of the pupils in designated positions.

Building up self-control. A principal may allow rooms located near an exit to pass out quietly and quickly, without forming into lines. This liberty will be recognized as a privilege, and will serve to stimulate pupil control. By doing this, in some buildings, the pressure on central corridors may be so relieved that the others may then be allowed to pass out in the same informal way. In moving to assembly halls it may be arranged that pupils pass directly and without forming lines. A principal can easily find many opportunities to minimize routine and extend freedom, and in doing so save time and build up pupil self-dependence and control. This will tend to remove the cause of much petty discipline, relieve the teachers of an onerous duty, and train the pupils to respect the rights of others through rational self-control. By permitting the pupils to move freely and to converse while passing the school is extending to them, as fast as they can use it, a personal liberty that is important, and one which they may retain so long as the rights and privileges of others in the school are not molested.

As will be pointed out in a later chapter, such self-control can be greatly added to by organizing the school as a civic and social body, with departments of health, police, etc., and making the pupils feel that, subject to the necessary advice and guidance, it is their job to assume responsibility for control. To build up such a conception in some schools may require time, and in some foreign neighborhoods it may meet with opposition from the parents, but when it is once established the results in training for future living are large and school discipline is reduced in consequence to a minimum.

In conclusion, then, there is no one method that is best suited to all conditions and to all schools and seasons. At times a military procedure is desirable, and for certain purposes almost a necessity. At other times as large personal liberty as can be used intelligently is what is needed. In some types of buildings and neighborhoods marching in lines seems desirable; in other types of buildings and neighborhoods not. The principal must here be allowed a rather free hand so long as his method shows a definite plan and purpose and a reasonable degree of common sense. The danger lies in the two extremes — military precision and a disorderly procedure — rather than in a combined plan or on middle ground.

2. Fire-drills

Purpose of the drill. The laws of our different American States, and the rules and regulations of practically all city boards of education, alike require that the children in our schools be trained to leave the school building according to what is known as a fire-drill, so that, in case of a fire, the danger of loss of life may be minimized. The purpose of the drill is to make the exit of the pupils from the building as nearly automatic as possible. This drill takes precedence over every other school activity, and aims at the rapid and safe exit of every pupil and teacher from the school building. It is not to be taken as a joke, a race, or an exhibition, but is a serious undertaking intended to fasten a habit, so that panic danger in case of a real fire may be eliminated as far as possible.

Organizing the fire-drill. If the building of which the principal is in charge is a modern fireproof or largely fireproof structure, the inauguration of the fire-drill need not be taken up at once, unless the rules so require, but if the building is of wood or is a brick shell, or has poor stairways and exits, the matter of a fire-drill should receive attention not later than the second morning. In such cases the principal, at the teachers' meeting at the close of the first day's work, should give directions to the teachers that a fire-drill will be practiced the following morning, and should issue the rules that are to govern all signals and movements. The duty of the principal in the matter is to outline the best method for getting the children out of the building. If the principal is new to the school he will do well to confer with his teachers as to previous practices, and in any case to consider all suggestions they may offer as to the organization and conduct of the drills. After the details have been decided upon, and the teachers are conversant with the plan to be followed, it is then the duty of the teachers to carry out the plan and of the principal to see that they do so.

By way of illustration, the directions issued for the building shown in Figure 7, page 98, are reproduced here:

DIRECTIONS FOR FIRE-DRILL

1. *Fire signal.* One long and two short. Stop work and form in single files in aisles, teacher opens door, room captains lead, and pupils follow by rows and pass at once to street in order printed. Teacher last to leave room, except in kindergarten and first grade, where teachers will need to lead line until room captains arrive.
2. *Order of Passing.* Rooms 1 and 8, followed by 2 and 7, pass out north exit to street. If exit closed, then in reverse order

INTERMISSIONS, LINES, AND DRILLS

out of north side of rear exit to alley, and thence to position in north street.

Rooms 4 and 5, followed by 3 and 6, pass out south exit to street. If exit closed, then in reverse order out of south side of rear exit to alley, and thence to position in south street.

Second floor rooms 9, 10, 15, and 16 move by twos down north side of stairway to landing, and rooms 11, 12, 13, and 14 down south side of stairway to landing and join, and then descend main stairway by fours and pass directly out front door. If front door blocked, then divide by twos and pass out of north and south end exits and pass to position on west street via sidewalks.

3. *Regulations.* Move carefully, by twos. Do not try to hurry. Step quickly, but do not run. Keep step and speed with the line. Do not talk after leaving classroom until in position in street.

    Follow the captains, and look and listen for directions from captains or teachers. Follow any directions they may give.

    Do not move from your position in the street until directed to do so by teacher. In case of a real fire no pupil may leave the line except by permission of the teacher.

4. *Return Order.* When "fire out" signal (one long and two short whistles, given by principal) sounds, follow directions of teacher and lead of captains, and return to rooms in reverse order of exit.

Let us assume that the principal and teachers agree that the first practice drill is to be held at 9.45 the second morning. This will give the teachers time to explain the signals and procedure to the children, and to practice the little children in the movements. The signals and procedure for each room above the first grade should be placed on the blackboard by the teacher, and allowed to remain for a week or two, until the drill has been learned. In a school which has quite a permanent constituency much less time will be needed to learn the drill than in a school where many changes are taking place. The first time the drill is tried the pupils should be told that the fire signal will sound this morning, for a practice drill. When the signal sounds, the class should follow the directions just given, and should be told that they may be halted at the stairs or doorway for further instructions. No attempt at speed should be made. Under the leadership of the teacher the class should pass to the yard and to the designated position outside, where the class in the future will always line up. This is to be a fixed position for each class, so that, in case of a fire, parents will know where to find their children. There the class is to remain, under the care of the teacher, until the "fire-out" signal is sounded, when the class is to return with the teacher to the classroom.

To see that the pupils understand the plan, a second alarm might well be sounded immediately after the pupils are well in their seats, this time without warning. All future drills are also to be sounded without warning. During the first few weeks the drill should be sounded rather frequently. As soon as it is evident that the pupils have learned the drill, and such variations, such as blocked stairways, as the needs of the building seem to require, the frequency can be reduced to once in two or three weeks, or even once in four weeks later in the year, unless drills at stated intervals are required by the schoolboard regulations.

Cautions to be observed. The fire-drill, to be most effective, should be adapted to the conditions peculiar to the particular building. Unless building conditions are uniform, no one form of drill should be prescribed for the school system of a city. The special conditions within a building may make two, or possibly even three variations of the drill desirable, the one to be used being indicated by different signals or different forms of control. In an old frame building, with heating plant in the basement, the stairways might easily become blocked and other than the regular ways would then have to be used. Even the fire escapes might have to be employed. Because of the danger of confusion, however, the number of plans should be limited to the fewest possible, safety considered. A useful variety may be introduced by occasionally closing or roping-off certain exits or stairways, by having certain rooms use the fire escapes, or by planning the drill to empty all from the assembly hall.

In giving the practice drills, certain precautions need to be borne in mind by the principal. The time for the drill should be chosen with some care. For this reason it is better that the time for drills be determined by the principal, and he be held responsible for the use of good judgment as to when to call for them. In many cities it is customary for the superintendent to announce his presence by sounding the alarm, or for the city fire department officials to enter the building and give the signal. It is not a bad idea to have a member of the district fire department occasionally present to witness the drill, and to listen to any suggestions he may have to offer. In many other cities, on the contrary, the responsibility for fire-drills is placed solely with the principal. Parental complaint as to unseasonable alarms then comes directly to him.

A drill should not be sounded when it is raining, during or after a heavy snow and before walks have been cleared, or on cold, windy, raw days when the exposure of children from warm rooms might result in injury. For this reason the drill should be thoroughly learned early in the Autumn, so as not to need much practice in mid-winter. A large degree of common sense, too, must be used as to when to hold the practice. In general, morning is the best time, and immediately after lunch the poorest.

Special points to be looked after. The following special points should be observed in the organization and conduct of the fire-drill:

1. The signal. A special loud gong, located in the main hallway of each floor and basement, and not used for any other purpose, is desirable for fire-signal purposes. This should be so wired that all bells can be rung from any floor. It should be tested each morning to see that it is in order. If the building does not have a separate bell system, then a special signal, not used for any other purpose, should be employed. The signal should be sharp, and of a character to take the children out of their seats with a jump.

2. Exits. All doors should open outward, and be provided with panic bolts so adjusted that kindergarten children can by pressure open the doors. If panic bolts are not on, the doors must be kept unlocked while children are in the building. Certain older children should be chosen, from the upper rooms, to move to the various exits on the sounding of the alarm and see that all doors are open.

3. Leaders or captains. The most level-headed children should be chosen for leaders or captains of the lines. There should be two for each room, and they should be seated near the exit. Older captains from adjacent rooms should be ready to lead the kindergarten and first-grade children, so that the teacher may be the last to leave. Unless these little ones have a separate exit, or can easily get out first, they should wait until the last, as they are timid and panicky, and harder to keep moving.

4. Care for cripples. Children slightly crippled should go to rear of room line, and be looked after by some able child. In general they should pass out after the room has been cleared; they must not be allowed to impede the motion of the lines. For each seriously crippled child have two able pupils designated to make a hand saddle, and carry such from the building, following after the others.

5. Lines. Have an order for passing, with lead classes for each floor. Have children pass by twos, as this tends to prevent panic and gives each child a helper in case of a stumble. Some principals have each pair take hold of hands, though there are often personal objections to this, unless there is smoke in the building, or unless the stairs are crooked and dark. In general, lines from a floor above must halt at base of stairs if lines from below are using exit, though one line from above may step abreast of a line below and pass if exit is wide enough. Teachers direct such movements.

6. Order and speed. Safety first is the important principle. Give attention to this, and not primarily to speed. Do not emphasize the time element. If a building can be cleared in two and a half to three minutes, it is safe enough. Nothing is to be gained by hurrying the lines, as disorder and stumbling not only delay but tend to general panic. No talking, not necessary, should be the absolute

INTERMISSIONS, LINES, AND DRILLS

rule. Order and discipline in the lines should be made to seem very important to the children.

7. *Music and marching.* Some principals use music and marching, as tending to quiet a panic should one arise, but in general this is not desirable. There will be delay in waiting for the music, and in case of actual fire it might be lacking. Pupils trained to good and automatic response and possessed of a sound morale will move more rapidly without music.

8. *Clearing the rooms and floors.* Every one — children, cripples, teachers, and visitors — must leave the rooms and floors. In general, the room captains should lead and the teachers leave last, after all is clear; but, since the teacher should keep with her class, there should be floor captains to check up each room, cloakroom, and hallway, and report the floor clear to the principal below. Sometimes each teacher is responsible for her room and one teacher for the floor, these "clean-up" teachers reporting from the top floor downward and the basement upward to the principal, who should take his stand in the main lower hallway, help direct the passing, and leave the building last. Arrangements should be made with the telephone company, by the superintendent's office, that, in case of an actual fire in any building, a message will be telephoned to central that a certain school is on fire, and that the building has been cleared and every one is safe and under the care of teachers outside. Central can then answer all inquiries from parents.

9. *Stopping places.* A designated stopping place for each room must be determined upon, and never varied from. If not reached by the regular exit, a roundabout route to the designated place must be followed. These stopping places must be selected with reference to distance from danger, street traffic, fire-engine approaches, hydrants and hose-lines, etc. On arrival the pupils must stay placed, remain reasonably quiet, and the teacher must not leave them. In case of fire and bad weather the principal may direct their removal to some better place or shelter, leaving a room captain to direct parents. In no case should a teacher permit a child to leave the line to start home alone, but should hold them until the parents arrive, or until the principal authorizes their dismissal to go home. Only the principal should sound the "fire-out" or recall, and until this has been sounded the classes should not move to return.

10. *Books and wraps.* It is not the prime business of the drill to save property, but to get the children to safety. No attempt should be made to save books or wraps if the building presents

a bad fire hazard. Books should be left in any case, but in bad weather and in buildings that present no bad fire hazard (heating plant outside; not over two stories; good stairs; slow-burning construction) a separate signal may indicate that pupils should pass through cloakrooms and get and throw about them coats or wraps for protection. If wraps are taken, stop and adjust hastily before passing into the hallways, so that there may be no confusion in or stopping of the line once it gets started.

11. Fighting the fire. It is not primarily the business of the school to fight a fire, yet some effort should be made to hold a small fire in check until the fire department arrives. To this end a small number of chosen or elected older boys, probably best the clean-up floor captains, should remain with the principal and janitor to act as temporary firemen until the regular firemen arrive. Of this little group the principal should be commander-in-chief.

Carried out in this way, the fire-drill can be made educative to a high degree in any school.

QUESTIONS AND PROBLEMS

1. What is your judgment as to lines and marching, after reading the arguments on both sides, and what combination uses would you plan to employ:
    a. In a school in the best neighborhood of a residential city?
    b. In a poor neighborhood of a working-class city?
    c. In a negro ward school?
    d. In a school in a foreign quarter of the south and east of Europe types of parentage?
    e. In a good middle-class American small county-seat city?
2. Show how you would arrange the recess periods and the play spaces for each of the buildings shown in Figures 5 to 10.
3. Plan the fire drills for some one of the buildings shown in Figures 5 to 10, planning stairways and exits to be used, order of marching and exit, the stopping places outside of danger for each class, room and floor captains and their work, fire department signal in case of need, return order, and alternate routes and plans.

CHAPTER VII
YARD AND BUILDING ORGANIZATION
1. Yard organization

Varying problems. As was stated in the previous chapter, the size of grounds and school are very important limiting factors in determining not only recess periods, but schoolground organization as well. In a school such as the one shown in Figure 5, where a double recess is necessary, or the one shown in Figure 6, where a triple recess is advisable, and where there is actually much congestion at times before school in the morning and at noons, quite a different problem confronts the principal from that found in such schools as are shown in Figures 8, 9, and 10, where the playroom is ample for all. The lack of play apparatus in the school yards shown in Figures 5 and 6 also accentuates the problem, and the prohibition of street play by city ordinance in both cases adds still further to the difficulties which the principal must meet and solve as best he can.

One of the problems, then, which every principal faces the first few days of school, is that of the organization of his playground so as to get a maximum of results with a minimum of difficulties. The pupils will want to get the games started from the first, and it is important that they should be started early and started right. In crowded schools with small playgrounds this presents difficulties which require careful planning in advance. Fortunately, in most schools, the new principal will find established traditions and ways of doing things. These old ways should be followed at first, unless so fundamentally wrong as to warrant prohibiting them from the start, and changes should be made after there has been time for the school to settle down and fewer other matters are demanding attention.

The teachers and yard duty. In different schools one finds different practices as to teacher participation in the school-ground activities. In some schools every teacher is expected to pass to the playground, with her class, and be on playground duty during the recess period. This gives more supervision than is needed, is not liked by either teachers or pupils, leaves the building unattended, and is unnecessary. In most schools only a few of the teachers are expected to be on the playgrounds, the others being allowed to remain in their rooms or the building. This is much better, as it distributes the supervision over both building and grounds, gives teachers larger freedom, and tends toward freer yard play.

In determining the division of yard duty, one of two plans is usually followed. One plan is to select the number of teachers needed from among those who know the games best and like the playground work, leaving those who by reason of age or inaptitude are not useful for playground work free to remain in the building. This plan often pleases all around, but it is questionable if it is the better plan. The other is to divide the school into details, under which the teachers either take turns for one- to two-week periods, or for certain days each week, and from one third to one fourth of the teachers being on the playground at any one time.

For example, in the school yards shown in Figures 7 and 8, where the common recess would be used and where the play space is ample and plenty of apparatus for play at hand, 4 of the 16 teachers in building 7, and 5 of the 24 teachers in building 8 would probably be sufficient for any desirable playground supervision at any time. As a matter of fact, the school grounds shown in Figure 8 were supervised by four teachers, whose work was distributed as follows:

YARD AND BUILDING ORGANIZATION

Grades I and II — All teachers came out with classes, and then all but one returned to rooms. The three teachers alternated in supervision, each serving one day in three.

Grades III to VIII, girls — Five teachers, each taking supervision but one day a week.

Grades III and IV, boys — Three teachers, each taking supervision one day in three.

Grades V to VIII, boys — Under the principal, every day.

The other form of detail is where the teachers are given assignments for longer periods of time, and then are relieved for a time. Under this plan the assignments are made out a term in advance, the whole assignment being reduced to a table or a chart, copies of which can be given the teachers and one posted in the principal's office. Figure 11 (page 121) shows one such chart, the assignments here having been arranged on the basis of shifting the teachers from one play-period to another, and from one part of the playground to another, so that each teacher may come to know the different play groups and they her. While the theory underlying such rotating assignments is good, it might not be desirable in some schools to carry out the shifting of teachers so far as is indicated in Figure 11. Some teachers might work better with the boys than with the girls, or with the older children than with the little ones, and *vice versa*.

Instead of such a long-term program, or rather as a supplement to it, some principals who have office clerks go still further and give each teacher a Daily Program and Assignment Card, of which the following is a sample:

MONDAY, NOVEMBER 2, 1922

Duties:

In charge of halls . . . . Miss Wilson
In charge of left playground . . . . Miss Abercrombie
In charge of right playground . . . . Miss Danforth
In charge of lunchroom . . . . Miss Simmons

Meetings:

Group Conference, Grades III and IV . . . . . Office, 3.15
Meeting Music teachers, Central, Room 25 . . . . 4.00

Notices:
   November Science Outline begins.
   Monthly supply orders due Thursday.
   Monthly reports due Friday.

Whatever form of detail is employed, and notice of such given, there should be a few teachers on the playground, for emergency purposes, at all times. The more the yard and building organization can be handled by the older pupils the less there will be for the teachers to do. In schools where double or triple recess periods are needed, a larger number of teachers will naturally need to be given assignments each day than where a single recess is the rule.

Dividing off the play space. On a school ground that has been well organized and provided with play apparatus, a division of the grounds for groups and sexes will nearly always have been made. This is well shown for the grounds of Figures 7, 8, 9, and 10, where spaces for boys, girls, and little children have been marked off. In school grounds such as are shown in Figures 5 and 6, sides will have been assigned, but in the organization of play work on such grounds a mapping off of space will need to be made. Where the streets can be made use of they should be used for some of the games of the larger children, particularly the boys.

In dividing off the playgrounds it is best to provide for the separation of the sexes, above the second or at most the third grade, though in small schools there are some games, such as blackman, that may be played together. Folk dancing may also be joined in by both sexes. It is also a good plan to divide the grounds still further, where space will permit, making the division by ages or grades, because of certain differences in play needs that manifest themselves in children of different ages. These differences may be indicated roughly by the following groupings, and are also shown in the diagram on page 123.

YARD AND BUILDING ORGANIZATION

1. Abelson, Marie	1 L		4 L	3 L	2 L	1 B		4 B
2. Brown, Sadie	1 B		4 B	3 B	2 B	1 G		4 G
3. Carr, Jennie	1 G		4 G	3 G	2 G	1 L		4 L
4. Dougherty, Anna	2 L	1 L		4 L	3 L	2 B	1 B	
5. Faber, Caroline	2 B	1 B		4 B	3 B	2 G	1 G	
6. Hughes, Jeraldine	2 G	1 G		4 G	3 G	2 L	1 L	
7. Jamison, Mary	3 L	2 L	1 L		4 L	3 B	2 B	1 B
8. Koch, Gretchen	3 B	2 B	1 B		4 B	3 G	2 G	1 G
9. Lampson, Anabel	3 G	2 G	1 G		4 G	3 L	2 L	1 L
10. Murphy, Jennie	4 L	3 L	2 L	1 L			3 B	2 B
11. Olerich, Katrine	4 B	3 B	2 B	1 B			3 G	2 G
12. Peterson, Alma	4 G	3 G	2 G	1 G			3 L	2 L
13. Quigley, Blanche		4 L	3 L	2 L	1 L		4 G	3 B
14. Stevens, Elizabeth		4 G	3 G	2 G	1 G		4 L	3 G
15. Wilders, John		4 B	3 B	2 B	1 B		4 B	3 L
B = Boys Weeks	1 and 2	3 and 4	1 and 2	3 and 4	1 and 2	3 and 4	1 and 2	3 and 4
G = Girls Months	September		October		November		December	
L = Kn.,I,II Periods	1 = 8:30 to 9:00		2 = Morning Recess		3 = 12:30 to 1:00		4 = Afternoon Recess	

FIGURE 11. YARD DUTY ASSIGNMENTS FOR A
FIFTEEN-TEACHER SCHOOL

The playground here is managed by three teachers at each play period, assigned to definite times and stations. The principal gives general oversight, but may move about as seems desirable.

Ages 5 to 8 — Children good imitators, individualists, and with little ability to coöperate except under direction. Need suggestion and direction of teachers. Games involving largely individual action, such as sand box and building blocks, or slightly coöperative ring games under the direction of the teacher or an older pupil-leader, make most appeal. Imitation, impersonation, imagination, repetition, and singing strong elements in games.

Ages 8 to 10 — With girls the above characteristics last a little longer than with boys. By the third grade the boy has become a marked individualist, and games involving competition, daring others, choosing sides, climbing, jumping, and running, make strong appeals. The inclined ladder, swings, bars, ropes, the giant stride, and the slides are favorites with both sexes of these ages. Games involving muscular coördination such as rope jumping, and sense judging such as marbles and top spinning, are also popular. Handling children of this group is difficult, because they tend to scatter so, their competition being individual rather than group. It probably calls for more supervision and cheerfulness than any other period.

Ages 10 to 12 — The preceding characteristics continue, but tend to pass over more into group competition. Tug-of-war, crack-the-whip, wrestling, boxing, and other rough games tend to be rather prominent with the boys, and need some control, while the girls take on some of the rough-and-tumble plays as well.

Ages 12 to 16 or 17 — This is the early adolescent period and is marked, with both sexes, by the rise of an interest in team games under a leader, and coöperative group play involving rules and organization, with strong loyalty to sides. Games which develop and challenge courage, endurance, self-control, bravery, and similar virtues, are favorites now, and can be used by supervisors with large educational results. Football, indoor baseball, bat-ball, basket-ball, cricket, volley-ball, and tennis now begin to make a strong appeal, and individual stunts where a side's winnings are at stake are also of much importance. Group consciousness begins to arise, and a desire to manage things for themselves becomes evident.

Apportioning the grounds and apparatus. Applying the above to the grounds of the Figure 8 school, we find the first two grades, boys and girls, assigned to the space between the

YARD AND BUILDING ORGANIZATION

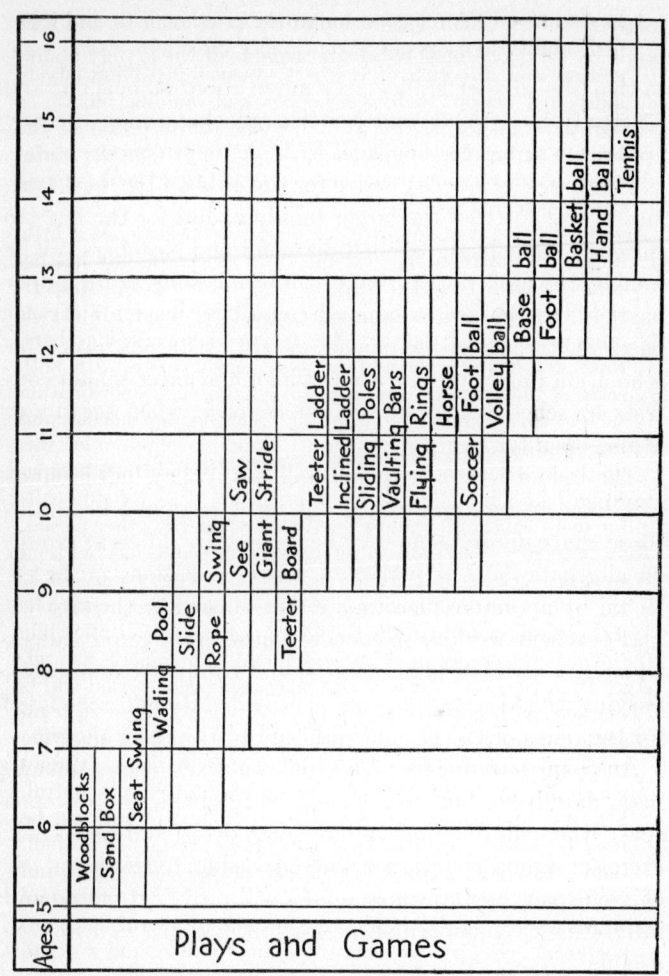

FIGURE 12. AGE-PERIODS FOR PLAYS AND GAMES

two buildings, and on the grass to the south side; the older girls to the north, on the west side; the smaller boys east of the buildings and along the driveway; and the larger boys further to the east. Interest can be kept at a little higher point by an occasional rotation of parts of these play spaces, so that the smaller grades may move about somewhat, and especially that third- and fourth-grade boys may use any apparatus suited to their age.

This gives a free play space for the girls on the west lawn and to the north of the larger building, and for the boys to the east. The large baseball diamond and bleachers can be used by the little boys for play at intermissions, or for indoor baseball, as the large diamond cannot be used for regular baseball, because of the danger, except at stated times after school, on holidays, and when school and inter-school contests are scheduled. The volley-ball space, when not in use, is also open for free play.

The indoor baseball, basket-ball, and volley-ball grounds will have to be apportioned out on a regular schedule to those who can use them, they being used by different groups on alternate days or periods. An organization can be effected by an active principal, either himself or through his play teachers, working in coöperation with the pupil leaders, whereby a series of plays, games, and competitive matches, varying with the seasons, can be provided for and scheduled for the parts of the grounds allotted to the older pupils.

An open space for free play by both sexes, such as blackman, dare base, tag, etc., should be retained, and an open space where all may join in marching, drills, and calisthenic exercises should be retained where possible. Occasional use of such space by the whole school will prove profitable and interesting. A smooth space for folk dancing is also very useful.

The small school grounds. When we pass from such large well-organized school grounds as are shown in Figures 7 to 10 to such small and unequipped grounds as are shown in Figures 5 and 6, where there is no play apparatus, where the play space is quite limited, and where, as in both cases, street play has been rather foolishly prohibited by city ordinance, the problem of providing for the needed play becomes a much more difficult one.

At the recess periods, the double or triple recess helps solve some of the difficulties, as the limited grounds can then be made to do double duty, but in the mornings, at noons, and after school serious difficulties present themselves. The basement play spaces and the inner first-floor hall can be used for some relief, and still further relief may have to be found by arranging different times for beginning and ending the sessions for parts of the school. If the city authorities could be induced to permit of roping off the streets at recesses and noons, and their use at such times for play spaces, it would remedy the matter somewhat. A traffic squad of older boys and girls could be organized to help protect those at play, if street play were permitted. In any case some space, for both boys and girls, should be set apart for playing the organized games of the older pupils, and where group matches may be prepared for and played. After this, the remaining space must be apportioned off as can best be done.

A satisfactory playground outfit. The provision of playground apparatus for a school ground seldom is made all at once. Usually the apparatus is obtained a piece at a time, and often pieces are made in the school shops and erected by the older pupils. We find playgrounds in all stages in the matter of equipment. Some of the playgrounds shown for the schools drawn in Figures 5 to 10 have even more equipment than is actually needed, while two of the schools have no equipment at all. As equipment usually comes a few pieces at a time, it may be well to list here the type of equipment an elementary school should aim to secure. This may be indicated as follows:

1. A sand court and shelter for the little ones.
2. A frame, carrying five or six swings.
3. Another frame, carrying five or six teeter ladders.
4. A single combination frame, or two or more shorter frames, carrying:
    Two inclined ladders,
    Two sliding poles,
    Two vaulting bars,
    One pair of flying rings,
    One hand swing,
    Two climbing poles.
5. Another frame, with four or five flying rings.
6. One or two giant strides.
7. One or two ladder-and-incline slides.
8. Two indoor-baseball diamonds.
9. One or two volley-ball courts.
10. One or two basket-ball courts.

A reference to Figure 12 will show the ages to which the different sports make their chief appeal, and will help somewhat in deciding what pieces of apparatus are most important when one cannot have all.

Supplies, and use of grounds. The needed play supplies, such as baseballs, bats, basket-balls, and footballs, are now rather commonly supplied on requisition by the school department, as are paper, ink, and books. Where this is not the case, and the board of education is not willing to assume the charge, the school may raise the needed funds by appeals to parents, citizens, athletic clubs, or by giving entertainments. Until such general provision can be made the pupils must be depended upon to furnish the needed equipment. This latter plan is a little less desirable, as thereby some pupils are prevented from playing some of the games they could and would like to play.

When supplies are furnished by the school department, or by the school itself, they must be kept under control in a special room or place, and checked out to the pupils or classes and checked back in return. This should not be a teacher's job, except possibly in a small school or at the start. Instead, pupil storekeepers should be developed and trained to accountability. To allot a sufficient supply of commonly used play supplies to each classroom is a good plan, as the bats, balls, etc., can be taken into the classroom by pupils at the end of each intermission and carried out again when the pupils pass out for play.

While it is not always possible of attainment, the ideal for school-ground use should be a neighborhood playground, open on school days from early morning until dark, on Saturdays at least, and on holidays and during the long summer vacation. The grounds should be open for play both before and after school for a definite time, the length of the time to be extended as pupil control is built up or special play teachers are provided. If play teachers are provided the grounds should also be open at certain hours on Sundays as well. The grounds where large enough should be the natural place for school and inter-school contests, and after school and on Saturdays is the natural time for such affairs.

Supervising the play. What is wanted on the playground, in having some teachers always on hand, is organization and proper supervision rather than any minute control. Policing of the playground by the teachers will create plenty of disciplinary cases for the school to handle. What is needed, instead, is only so much supervision of the play as is necessary to teach the pupils the games, organize the activities, start things off well, and keep them running freely and smoothly. Too much organization, like standing in line and marching to commands, tends to defeat its purpose. As much freedom in play as can be used safely and intelligently is the desideratum.

This supervision naturally differs somewhat with children

of different ages. With the little ones the teacher must initiate and assist and guide and keep interest going, and teach them how to play many simple games suited to their ages. The work will in great part consist in awakening a play spirit and developing a play habit. The middle groups are harder to handle, and must be allowed to follow much their own wishes, so long as this does not lead to what is harmful. The older pupils need starting and direction, but much less supervision, and the girls need more attention than do the boys. The teachers on duty need to be constantly on the watch to see that the play apparatus is not monopolized by a few, and that the games are kept open and inclusive and not confined to small groups to the exclusion of worthy pupils. When teams are formed in any game or group, they should receive no more of the teacher's time than an equal number of pupils not in the teams. This calls for tact and for a good understanding of human nature. Immorality, fighting, and too rough play of course call for interference.

Teachers who are to supervise play, and the principal in particular, need a sympathetic understanding of not only play and play possibilities, but also a quick and sympathetic insight into child character and motives. No better means for promoting good relationships with the pupils could be found than for the principal to attain the reputation of having a good understanding of plays and games, and of being a thoroughly good sport. For the same reason it is good for all teachers, on some days at least, to take part in the plays of their children.

While the principal will have some general supervision of the whole playground, and will at times give attention to the play of the pupils, his work will naturally center with the play and games of the older boys of the school. He needs especially their respect and good will, as in any form of pupil control or helpfulness he must depend largely on them for coöperation and support.

Advantages of good play organization. The building up among the pupils of the school of a good physical tone and a good school morale is one of the large returns that come from giving some attention to the organization of the play activities of the school grounds. Few other things do as much as these same activities to transform the yard bully into a useful school citizen, bring out the timid and backward pupils, limit accidents, create good feeling, assist discipline, teach pupil self-control, train the muscles and the eye to coördination, or awaken the best spirit of the pupils.

Indoor baseball and basket-ball and bat-ball, which are favorites among both boys and girls, are excellent developers of the qualities needed for good citizenship. In the establishment among the pupils of some such principles or rules of action as the following, formulated in the Seattle schools, the school playground is giving very valuable civic training. The Seattle school playground rules read as follows:

1. The rules are to be regarded as mutual agreements, the spirit or letter of which one should no sooner try to evade or break than one would any other agreement between gentlemen. The stealing of advantage in sport should be regarded in the same way as stealing of any other kind.
2. No action is to be taken nor course of conduct pursued which would seem ungentlemanly or dishonorable if known to one's opponent or the public.
3. No advantages are to be sought over others except those in which the game is understood to show superiority.
4. Officers and opponents are to be regarded and treated as honest in intention. When opponents are evidently not gentlemen, and officers are manifestly dishonest or incompetent, future relationships with them may be avoided.
5. Decisions of officials are to be abided by, even when they seem unfair.

6. Ungentlemanly and unfair means are not to be used even when they are used by opponents.
7. Good points in others should be appreciated and suitable recognition given.

The transformation that has taken place in recent years, in these games, through the influence of the school playground, is wonderful. The corner-lot baseball game of a decade ago, with its constant quarreling, profanity, and gang groupings, has given way on the playground to a game of law and order. In all the organized games a fine point of contact between principal and teachers and pupils is established, and the ancient antagonism of youth chafing against teacher restraint disappears. In the development of team and school spirit, and the preparation for and planning of contests, much fine feeling is awakened and much ugly disposition is worked off.

Supervision at the lunch hour. There is a phase of building and yard supervision, closely connected with the playground, that often is of much importance, and that is the supervision of the building and grounds during the time that the pupils are eating their lunch at noon. This is especially the case if many pupils eat their lunch at the building, and still more so if the school grounds have play apparatus. If not regulated, the tendency is for the pupils either to bolt down their lunch so as to get out early, or to take their lunch to a piece of play apparatus and then exercise the rights of squatter sovereignty on the piece of apparatus so preëmpted. The grounds are also likely to have lunch débris left scattered over them.

The proper supervision of the lunch hour calls for the detail of one or two teachers, the requirement that the pupils eat together, in one or two places, spend a definite time at their lunch, clean up all débris and put away their lunch boxes, and then pass to the playgrounds at a given signal. In

YARD AND BUILDING ORGANIZATION

schools such as those shown in Figures 5 and 6 there is nothing to do but use a couple of classrooms, or possibly the basement playrooms. In the schools shown in Figures 8 and 10, however, much better arrangements have been made. In the Figure 8 school a common out-of-doors lunch place has been provided between the buildings and under the trees, and in bad weather the domestic science and manual training rooms are used. Not many pupils at this school remain for lunch. In the Figure 10 school, which is in a city of some size and where a large number of pupils bring their lunch with them, two vine-covered arbors have been built in the yard for luncheon purposes in good weather, and in bad weather the auditorium is used. The roof playgrounds were used before the arbors were built by the boys, as a shop exercise.

In any case some such rules as the following should be enforced:

1. All who are to lunch at the building are to pass at dismissal to the lunching places.
2. No one is to leave until the teacher in charge gives the signal, which is only given after inspection to see that all débris has been gathered up and is ready for proper disposal. Use pupil monitors for the oversight where possible.
3. No one is to leave, even though through, except on permission for emergencies, until after twenty minutes have elapsed. This gives time to eat leisurely, tends to prevent bolting down the food, and gives all an equal opportunity at the play apparatus.

Where the school building is fortunate enough to have a school cafeteria, as some of our more recent buildings now do, the lunch problem can be handled in a still better way. Even where a cafeteria is not provided, and where no city lunch organization attempts to help the schools meet the lunch problem, the domestic science equipment can be used to provide at least one hot dish for those who remain for lunch at the building. This plan is being adopted by an increasing number of elementary schools. The school-lunch problem in its hygienic aspects is, after all, really a part of the school-health problem, and city school systems are beginning to take it up and deal with it on that basis.

In connection with the lunch hour, it might well be added here that it ought to be an unwritten rule of every school that the principal and all teachers who lunch at the building and are not required for duty be expected to lunch together. If everything is going well this may not be important, but it prevents the formation of little groups and the growth of clannishness, promotes friendliness and understanding and sociability, helps smooth out many a wrinkle, and, if anything arises in the school system over which there is likely to be a sharp division of opinion, the common lunch understanding will hold a group together that would otherwise break up into factions.

2. *Supervision of toilets and basements*

Toilets a strong influence. The maintenance of a good physical tone among the pupils, and keeping them interested in school affairs which call for action and coöperation, will do much to head off that peculiar and difficult type of trouble one encounters in connection with the use of the school toilets. If plays and games are made of but small importance, if the activities of the school are not emphasized, and if the pupils are allowed to stand around and loaf, trouble in the toilets is almost certain to develop, and trouble there is hard to handle. In such cases the toilets not infrequently become focal points for insubordination and vandalism, as well as for vulgarity, obscenity, smoking, and licentious practices. The proper supervision of the school toilets thus becomes an important feature of building supervision. In a well-organized school, supplied with proper and

YARD AND BUILDING ORGANIZATION

adequate sanitary appliances and in good condition, trouble from this source is much less common, but even here sporadic outbreaks are likely to occur.

Toilets are provided for a certain use, but not to become social centers for either sex. When so used, it is commonly the pupils whose morals are low and vulgar who hold forth. The toilets must be frequented by all, from the most modest to the most vulgar-minded, and it is part of the work of the school so to shape conditions and control that the toilets may be used only as they should and not become centers of moral contamination.

Shaping conditions. One of the things that a new principal should examine carefully, on taking charge of a school, is the toilet facilities of his school plant. These facilities should be as nearly adequate as possible, and in a clean and sanitary condition. Still more, they should be so built and finished that they may be kept in good condition easily, and if they are not, at the end of the year, in his lists of wants, he should request such reasonable changes as will make them easier to care for, both from a sanitary and a moral point of view. Good, light, well-ventilated rooms, supplied with a sufficient number of seats and urinals, and with plenty of toilet paper, towels, running water, and liquid soap, give far less trouble than do the inferior and inadequate equipment so commonly found in the older type of school buildings.

The toilets for the two sexes should, of course, be entirely separate, with no connecting passageway, and so set off that conversation will not carry over. The entrances should be from separate directions. The toilets should be light, well-ventilated, capable of being kept clean easily, and at some time of day should get sunshine. It is desirable that little children, those below Grade III, have separate places, but, as this is seldom provided, except in the newer and more modern-type buildings, it probably will be best that they have a separate time for general use of the toilets unless the facilities are quite ample for all. In any case, some lower seats or raised platforms might well be provided for their special use. In number there should be, for proper equipment, approximately one urinal for every twenty boys, and one toilet seat for every fifteen girls and twenty-five boys. These numbers are based on a common recess, and need not be quite so large where pupils mostly go home for lunch, or where the double or triple recess is necessitated by playground conditions. The supervision is much easier where the toilets and urinals are banked around the walls, with openings facing out to a large central room, than where a double row of toilets, back to back, run down the middle of the room. Dividing partitions should not be over five feet high, both for light and for supervision, and the toilet doors should be cut away ten inches at the bottom.

Use and supervision of the toilets. The free use of the toilets during school hours should be discouraged, where not necessitated by physical conditions, and teachers should, in general, not allow two pupils of the same sex to pass from the room to the toilets at the same time. Any long absence from the room should be noted by the teacher. In the first and second grades a greater freedom will have to be allowed. The recesses should be long enough, in good weather, to allow for both a full use of the toilets and a good play, and pupils should be encouraged to go to the toilets first and then pass to the playground. Some principals send their pupils first to the basements, for use of toilets and drinking fountains, and then to the grounds. This is a very good plan if the school is not large, and if the basement and toilet space are ample, but it is not applicable to crowded-building conditions.

A rapid inspection of the toilet rooms by the principal, preferably early in the morning, should be a part of his daily routine of building inspection. This should be made to see that the janitor has done his cleaning properly, that supplies of all kinds are at hand, and that the conditions are right for the day. An occasional entry of the boys' toilet during the day by the principal, and of the girls' toilet by some woman teacher, serves as a desirable check on conditions. The janitor, if a man, should have as one of his important functions the oversight of the boys' toilet room, and he should be on the quiet watch for the appearance of obscenity or vulgarity on the walls or about the room. Under the guise of brushing up, putting in supplies, and looking after sanitary conditions, an intelligent janitor can be of great help in preventing loitering, smoking, obscene talk, writing, or carving, and the moral contamination of the many by the few of vulgar nature and often of low intelligence as well. In a similar manner, the girls' toilet room needs a certain supervision. If there is a woman assistant to the janitor, she can assume the responsibility, but if not, some supervision by a rotation of the women teachers should be provided. The idea to be borne in mind is that of keeping the toilets clean and sanitary, with no associations connected therewith to direct attention to bad habits, or conditions that would stimulate their development.

Stopping trouble. The degree of trouble that will arise from toilet room sources will naturally vary much with the character of the neighborhood and the pupils, the degree of congestion, and the presence or lack of adequate facilities. In practically every school, though, some trouble will from time to time break out. While this is mostly confined to the boys between the third and seventh grades, and often comes from over-age pupils of lower mental ability, yet it is not wholly confined to these, nor to the boys alone. Sometimes serious trouble arises on the girls' side.

A plan of spying out and catching and punishing the culprits will hardly be effective. The more spying that is done, the more ordinarily there will be to do, though there are times when catching a culprit will have a beneficial effect. This usually is when the evidence points to an individual, or a small group of individuals, as being guilty of some particularly indecent happening. Often this can be accomplished best by the janitor, sometimes necessitating a checking up of suspects after each use of facilities. In all such supervision, however, care should be taken that such work is not overdone, to the extent of drawing general attention to it. The supervisory work should be done as quietly and unostentatiously as possible, and with as little publicity of results as can be done.

If a serious situation arises, with either sex, it is best to face the matter frankly at once. The principal can handle the boys, even though the principal be a woman, and some teacher, selected on the basis of wisdom and discretion, can take the situation in hand if it be with the girls. Call a meeting, without stating the purpose, and then face the issue quickly and frankly in a simple and direct talk. Tell them briefly the conditions that need remedying, that such conditions affect the reputation and standing of the whole school, that they would not want such conditions in their homes, and that the school is a big family and in a way a home. One may frankly state that it is not easy for the principal or teacher to watch for and catch the offenders, and that you do not intend to do so. That really it is up to them to stop it, and you appeal to their school pride and school morale not to tolerate such offenses from a few of their number. Accordingly you ask them to put a stop to it themselves, and that you will approve any reasonable punishment they see fit to inflict on those who continue to offend. One principal, of the writer's acquaintance, confronted by a series of particularly dirty incidents which he could not locate, told the boys that if they caught the offenders and gave them a pounding or hosing he would approve and protect them. Two boys stuck in a water trough, a few days later, ended the trouble.

Handling through school organization and teaching. Proper supervision and control, here as elsewhere, are closely linked with the creation of a wholesome pride in the school, the activities of the institution, and the proper care of both building and grounds. School spirit and school morale are as effective agents in handling toilets and basements as in handling building activities and playgrounds, and should be the object of constructive effort on the part of the principal. Emphasis on those things that build up school spirit, encouragement of healthful play on the part of all, and the development of a school pride in building and grounds, all tend to foster a school morale conducive to proper conduct elsewhere. In the teaching of hygiene, science, and civics, opportunities are presented for constructive work along sanitary lines.

The most effective means, though, lies in the development of a school civic league or coöperative pupil control, through which school and yard supervision is effected largely through the older pupils, and proper standards as to health, cleanliness, sanitation, and care of public property are built up. The supervision of toilets then would be but one specific example of this type of service. A committee of the boys and of the girls, or better still school police and school sanitary inspectors, can be organized to handle the whole problem in a quiet but effective manner. A word of warning from a pupil officer is far more effective than from a teacher. A strong social pressure, with a reasonable certainty of punishment for continued offense, is now set up to put an end to practices which the pupils themselves have come to condemn. As will be pointed out in a later chapter, some such form of organization, though requiring work to start and care in handling, is nevertheless one of the most effective means not only for control but for teaching a practical form of civics that can be devised. The pupils learn virtue and citizenship by practicing them.

The basement. Where there are basement playrooms for hot weather, wet weather, or winter play use, the same principles of play supervision would apply as for the grounds. Much depends on the space available, but ordinarily it will be too cramped to provide for a common recess or any games requiring much space. In hot weather the space may be used by the little children. For wet or cold weather, games which do not require much space, in which some can play and others watch, should be chosen. In schools such as are shown in Figure 10, where the entire roof is a covered playground, hot- and wet-weather conditions do not offer any particular difficulties.

Into the janitor's quarters, in the basement, the pupils should not go.

QUESTIONS AND PROBLEMS

1. What, in your judgment, is the best plan for yard supervision? Why do you think so?
2. Show how you would distribute your teachers for playground supervision, in the case of building 6, where a triple recess is necessary, and how many would you need to use at recesses and noons and mornings?
3. Do you think the arrangements made for yard duty, given for the school shown in Figure 9, were good?
4. Suppose that the school board furnished all play supplies, how would you arrange for their care, and for checking them in and out?
5. Arrange the play spaces for each of the schools shown in Figures 5 to 10, including double or triple recess periods and different times for beginning and closing schools for Figures 5 and 6.
6. What plans would you suggest for use of the toilets in the buildings shown in Figures 5 and 6? How would you supervise their use in these buildings?
7. Was it a good plan for the principal, described on page 109, to turn the discipline for toilet obscenity over to the pupils to handle? Why?

SELECTED REFERENCES

Ayres, M.; Williams, J. F.; and Wood, T. D. *Healthful Schools.* 292 pp., Boston, 1918.
Chapter XII good on physical training and recreation.

Bancroft, Jessie H. *Games for the Playground, Home, School, and Gymnasium.* 456 pp., New York, 1909.
A complete classification. No theory. Instructions for games in elementary and high schools, playgrounds, and camps. A valuable book.

Bowen, Wilbur P. *The Teaching of Play.* 114 pp., Springfield, Mass., 1913.
Good short descriptions of playground games, and how to organize them.

Curtis, Henry L. *The Practical Conduct of Play.* 330 pp., New York, 1915.
Deals with the organization, equipment, games, apparatus, and management of the playground. A very useful book.

Curtis, H. C. *School Grounds and Play.* 31 pp. Bul. 45, 1921, United States Bureau of Education, Washington.
A very good brief statement as to equipment and work.

Fisher, Katharine A. *The Lunch Hour at School.* 62 pp., illd. Health Bulletin No. 7, United States Bureau of Education, Washington, 1920.
A very useful description of the details of organization.

Hunt, Caroline B. *The Daily Meals of School Children.* 62 pp. Bulletin No. 3, 1919, United States Bureau of Education, Washington.

Johnson, Geo. E. *What to do at Recess.* 33 pp., Boston, 1910.
A good but brief outline of how to handle small groups.

Keene, Chas. H. *Manual of Physical Games and Mass Competition.* 124 pp., Yonkers, 1916.
Outlines work for each grade, 1 to 8, and tells how to play 67 suitable games.

Playground plans, designs, and blue prints. These may be obtained from:
Fred. Medart Manufacturing Co., St. Louis, Mo.
Narragansett Machine Co., Providence, R.I.
A. G. Spaulding Bros., Chicopee, Mass.

Reilly, F. J. *Rational Athletics for Boys.* 125 pp., Heath, Boston, 1915.
A little book which gives a plan for socializing public school athletics and gymnasium work, developed by the author in a New York City elementary school.

Williams, J. F. *The Organization and Administration of Physical Education.* New York, 1922.
Chapters 6 and 7 deal with playground supervision and physical education work.

CHAPTER VIII

THE CROWDED-BUILDING PROBLEM

The principal and the problem. A steady increase in the number of school children to be provided with seating accommodations is a common condition in our American cities. Often the increase in population is so rapid that the increase in school attendance comes faster than is expected or than buildings can be arranged for and built. Since the World War, and the general halt in schoolhouse construction occasioned thereby, hundreds of American cities find themselves with totally inadequate seating accommodations. In consequence, principals of schools, superintendents of instruction, and boards of education alike find themselves hard pressed to care for the needs of the pupils who present themselves for schooling, and all kinds of temporary makeshifts are employed to provide some semblance of schoolroom facilities.

Where the problem is a general one, facing a city as a whole, it is largely for the central school officers to solve rather than for the individual principal, but even then it is well for the school principal to have some ideas as to how he might handle the problem, and thus be able to work independently in case he is thrown on his own resources, by the central office, in the rush period of the opening days of school. Even though the central office should ultimately decide just what is to be done, it is well for the principal to have thought out what might be done and be able to offer some helpful and constructive suggestions. The superintendent and his assistants are almost certain to be extremely busy during the opening days of the school year, and any intelligent superintendent is glad to receive helpful suggestions for the solution of the practical problems which daily arise. Every superintendent knows the principal who dumps his problems at the superintendent's feet and offers no suggestions — often has no ideas — as to their solution. It is not his business to think them out; he exists only to execute orders. Such men are often exasperating, and such principals are seldom singled out for promotion. It is the man who studies the problems of his superiors and comes to know what they know, who, given the proper personality, is usually selected for advancement.

Solutions for the crowded-building problem. Fortunate indeed is the principal these days who has a building with a few extra rooms, as the constant increase in the number of pupils is one of the problems with which principals almost everywhere have to contend. A principal is wise, too, who anticipates not only an increase in numbers but also what grades will be most crowded, and who so arranges his room-distribution that he has a place ready for any overflow.

To illustrate, one principal of the author's acquaintance, who had two vacant rooms in his building, concluded from walking through his district a few days before school opened that the new families had mostly little children and that the crowding would be in the kindergarten and the first and second grades. He then so distributed his teachers that he left one vacant room near the first-grade room, and one near the second. The first morning 112 children came who were classified as first-graders. By temporarily putting two rather small upper grades together under one teacher, and using the teacher thus freed to help temporarily with the little ones, and himself helping, the situation was tided over until the afternoon, when a substitute teacher arrived, and thus to the next morning when a second teacher was obtained.

Most principals, though, have little or no space in which

to fit out new rooms, and, should the school be crowded on the opening day, they must resort to some one or other of the following plans:

1. Shift the district lines, with the consent of the superintendent, and transfer some pupils of the crowded grades to other schools having vacant seating space. This can often be done with the older pupils, who can walk longer distances, but is not a feasible plan for the little children.
2. Secure the so-called "portable buildings" and set them up in the schoolyard, or in adjoining vacant lots which the school department may lease.
3. Use vacant storerooms, or even residences, if any are available near by.
4. Use the auditorium or the gymnasium, if there be such, for classroom purposes.
5. Put the teachers of the younger children on a part-time plan — that is, give the first-grade and possibly the second-grade teacher two classes, one in the morning and one in the afternoon, such children attending school only half the day. Two different teachers may be provided instead, as the central office may decide.
6. Reorganize the instruction in the school in such a way that the building will be made to carry a larger load of children.

While any one of these plans naturally requires the consent of the superintendent of schools, the principal should nevertheless have considered what he might do and how he would do it in advance of the situation itself. He is not then taken off his feet by the condition which develops, as he has gone through such a problem already in his thinking and is ready with a solution as soon as it presents itself.

The advantage of securing a preliminary "Room and Grade Classification Report" (Chapter V) as early as possible in the morning will now be apparent. By ten o'clock the principal should know the exact nature of the problem he faces, and be ready to report it to the superintendent's office. If he can solve it himself without incurring any serious expense, seriously disturbing district lines, or without fundamentally reorganizing his school, he should go ahead and solve it and report his action afterward. Superintendents usually like men who can act independently. Marks of ex-

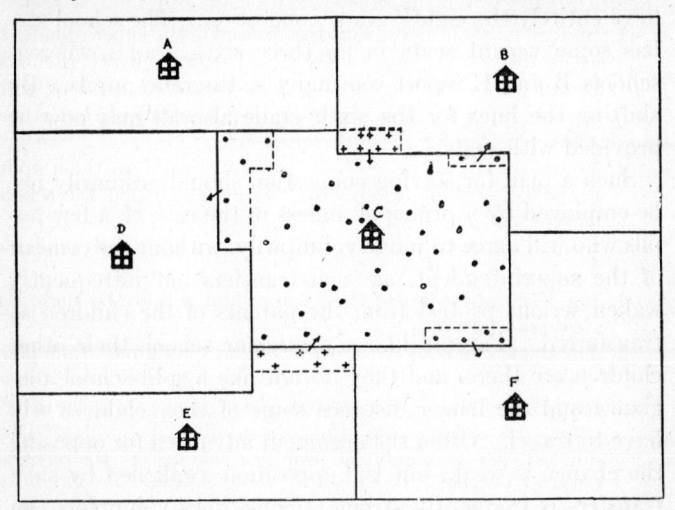

FIGURE 13. SHOWING HOW CONGESTION MAY BE RELIEVED BY MOVING DISTRICT LINES

School C, a large school, has two seventh grades and room for but one eighth, but there are forty-six eighth-grade pupils, indicated by dots, residing in the district. Schools B and E and F can each take a few more eighth-grade pupils. By drawing in the district lines for eighth-grade pupils, two will be transferred to school B, five to school D, and four to school F, thus reducing the number to thirty-five, which can be cared for. Similarly, the two sixth-grade rooms have some vacant seats, whereas the one sixth-grade in schools B and E have too many pupils. By expanding the district lines for sixth-grade pupils, seven sixth-grade pupils from district B, and six from E, indicated by crosses, may be provided with seats and instruction in school C.

ecutive capacity are insight into problems and the willingness to undertake their solution.

Shifting the district lines. The shifting of the district lines, with the consequent transfer of a few pupils to some neighboring school, is often an easy solution, as Figure 13 shows. This drawing shows a large school which has two seventh grades, and too many pupils for one eighth grade and not enough for two. By spotting the residences of the eighth-grade pupils on a street map of the district it is seen to be possible to move enough to adjacent schools, which telephonic inquiry had shown to have vacant seats, to relieve entirely the eighth-grade congestion. The school also has some vacant seats in its three sixth grades, whereas schools B and E report too many sixth-grade pupils. By shifting the lines for the sixth grade also all may now be provided with seats.

Such a plan for solving congestion should ordinarily not be employed by a principal, unless in the case of a few pupils who will agree to move voluntarily, without the consent of the superintendent, as such transfers not infrequently waken serious protest from the parents of the children so transferred. Parents like a particular school, their other children are there, and they do not like a split-school allegiance and the longer distance some of their children will have to travel. Often the argument advanced for opposing the change is weak, but the opposition awakened by such transfers is frequently strong. Sometimes volunteers can be found who will make the transfer, but often the transfers have to be made in the face of protests.

In making the transfers the principal and the teachers should take care to smooth out the situation as much as possible. Say little about the transfers in advance of taking action, and when action is taken carefully explain to the pupils the necessity for it, point out that the schools are city schools and that all the children of the city are to be considered, and ask them, as a matter of good citizenship and loyalty to public interest, to go and do their best to fit into the new school and be happy there. As school loyalty and athletic rivalry often enter as factors, say that the school regrets their loss, but that they will strengthen the teams of the schools to which they go, and if, in the new teams, they can come back and squarely defeat their old school, that the

CROWDED-BUILDING PROBLEM

school will be proud of them and will take its punishment without a whimper.

Using portables and renting rooms. Often such a shifting of lines cannot be accomplished, either due to popular opposition or to lack of room in other schools. In such a case some other expedient has to be adopted. A very common solution, in such a case, is to set up the so-called "portable buildings" in the school yard, or on some adjacent empty lot which can be leased, or to rent vacant storerooms or residences in the immediate neighborhood and fit up schoolrooms in them. The school is then reorganized to fit the new conditions, and the makeshift arrangement can usually be made to last a year. The portables, though, nearly always become permanent, and, if yard space permits, are added to from year to year. Figure 6 shows such a condition well, where a school yard having but 107 square feet per pupil has had a row of six portables installed in the yard, trees having been removed to make place for them. Sometimes an empty storeroom some distance away has to be rented, one or two classes of younger children installed, and a branch school established there. A number of problems, involving the employment of such expedients, are given at the close of this chapter.

The portable buildings, very often, are in their interior arrangements not particularly objectionable. They are built according to good schoolroom specifications, are thoroughly sanitary, and are well lighted and heated, though in warm weather they are likely to be hot and on very cold days cold. The chief objection to them is rather in their outward appearance, the space they take from the playground, and, if on vacant lots a little removed or across the street, in their separation from the other children of the school. It is best to use these portables for the little children, whose plays are different and who do not so much miss contact with other children, or else for special work, such as domestic science or manual training.

Part-time instruction. The provision of part-time instruction is another solution. It does not fill up the school yard with portables, but in other respects does not offer so satisfactory a solution. The essential idea of the plan is to put two classes, each attending only a half-day (three hours) in each classroom, and thus make each room so needed carry a double shift of pupils. Generally only the little children — first or first and second grades — are so arranged for, but in some of our crowded cities entire or almost entire schools are working on the part-time or half-day plan. The classes so divided come in two sections, one in the mornings from 9 to 12, and the other in the afternoons from 1 to 4. This can be made to answer fairly well for first-grade children, and tolerably well for second-grade pupils, but for the older children the school hours must be lengthened or the instruction is insufficient.

Quite commonly one teacher teaches both classes, and is given extra pay for the longer hours. It makes a long day, though, for the teacher, and is a hard nervous strain. If a teacher is provided for each shift it is much better, but school boards often object to the full double pay, and without full pay the teachers do not like the plan. This, however, is a detail that is settled at the superintendent's office, and which the principal must accept as it is.

There is usually little objection from the parents of the little children who can come in the morning section, but usually much from the parents of those who have to attend in the afternoon.

Other expedients to increase the carrying load. The use of the auditorium stage, the gymnasium, the school library room, and the fitting up of rooms in the basement for class use are other expedients not infrequently used to tide over situations. None of these is very satisfactory, but one is sometimes forced to employ them. The erection of portables offers a far more satisfactory solution than any of these expedients, because the portable is a room adapted to instruction, and the expedients mentioned above seldom are.

Another plan, which the tendencies of the past half century have been against, but which has begun to find some favor again since the building shortage has become so pronounced and the cost for schools has risen so markedly, is to increase the number of pupils per room by putting in more seats. Until recently the tendency has been to reduce classes to 30 or 35 pupils, but some recent studies have seemed to show that good teachers can carry classes of 40 to 45, if pupils are properly classified into working groups, with about as good results, measured in instruction, as though the classes were smaller. Some contend that it is more economical to employ good teachers at good salaries and increase the size of the classes up to 40 to 45 children for grades 2 to 6 inclusive, with a somewhat smaller number in first, seventh, and eighth grades. Where the size of the rooms and the quality of the teacher will permit, a classroom could be seated to carry $6 \times 7 = 42$ children, instead of $5 \times 6 = 30$, or $5 \times 7 = 35$. Some of our larger cities, in their recent building programs, have fixed on 40 to 42 children for their classrooms in grades 1 to 6 inclusive. The Batavia plan, of which much has been written by its few advocates, has been based on putting 50 to 75 children in a classroom, with a second capable teacher added whenever the number exceeds 50, and half the time being given to supervised pupil-study under the direction of the teacher or teachers.

Building reorganization to increase the carrying load. Another solution not infrequently employed, within recent years, is that of increasing the carrying load of the building by reorganizing the instruction, rather than by merely increasing the number of seats in the classrooms. This plan, where the character of the building makes its employment possible, is much to be preferred because it enables the building to carry a larger pupil load without increasing the burdens of the individual teacher. There are two main forms for this reorganization, one of which moves the teacher with her class and does not involve the specialization of teachers, and the other moves the classes from teacher to teacher, and involves more or less specialization of teaching work. Combinations of the two plans are possible to any degree desired, but only the two types will be considered here. The first form we will term the companion-class plan, in which both teacher and pupils move from room to room without specialization of teachers. The facilities for instruction are specialized, but the teachers are not. The second form, commonly known as the platoon school, involves the specialization of teachers as well as facilities for instruction.

The companion-class plan. This plan calls for the least specialization of facilities and the smallest withdrawal of classrooms from regular instruction to be fitted up as special rooms. The essentials of this form of school reorganization can be seen at a glance from the drawing given in Figure 14. In the first place a small number of the regular classrooms are withdrawn from regular class use and are fitted up as special rooms. Let us take the school shown in Figure 5 to illustrate the plan. This is a fourteen classroom old-style building, carrying the eight grades and organized on the straight grade plan. The building has two fairly satisfactory playrooms in the basement, and two buildings in the yard for domestic science and manual training. Of the fourteen classrooms we will need to take three for special purposes, to be fitted up for class work in drawing, music, and science. This leaves eleven classrooms, which may now be made to carry two separate schools of eleven classes each, which we will designate as an A school and a B school.

Period	A School	Time	B School	Period
1	Arithmetic	8.40–9.00		
2	Arithmetic	9.00–9.20		
3	Manl. Train. Draw- ing Manl. Train. Draw- ing Sci- ence	9.20–9.40	Arithmetic	1
4		9.40–10.00	Arithmetic	2
5	Physical Training	10.00–10.20	Supervised Study	3
6	Reading	10.20–10.40	Manl. Train. Draw- ing Manl. Train. Draw- ing Sci- ence	4
7	Spelling	10.40–11.00		5
8	Supervised Study	11.00–11.20	Physical Training	6
	Noon Intermission	11.20–11.40	Reading	7
		11.40–12.00	Spelling	8
		12.00–12.50	Noon Intermission	
9	Literature	12.50–1.10		
10	Geogr. Hist. Geogr. Hist. Geogr.	1.10–1.30		
11	Music Science Music Science Music	1.30–1.50	Literature	9
12	Supervised Play	1.50–2.10	Geogr. Hist. Geogr. Hist. Geogr.	10
13	Language	2.10–2.30	Music Science Music Science Music	11
14	Penmanship and Comp.	2.30–2.50	Supervised Play	12
	▨ In Classrooms	2.50–3.10	Language	13
	☐ Out of Classrooms	3.10–3.30	Penmanship and Comp.	14

FIGURE 14. A FIFTH-GRADE PROGRAM IN A COMPANION-CLASS SCHOOL
As carried out in one of our American cities using the plan.

By dividing the day into fourteen equal periods, and having the B school begin and close two periods later than the A school, it is possible to get the use of the eleven classrooms in the building, for each of the schools (A and B), for a total of nine of the fourteen periods of each day. Of the remaining five periods, three are spent in the special rooms, and the remaining two on the playground or in the indoor playrooms in supervised play. How this can be done is well shown in Figure 14, on page 149. Under such an arrangement, this building could be made to carry 22 classes instead of 14, or, at an average of 34 to the room as at present, 748 pupils instead of 475. The plan would also, by doing away with the common recess, put fewer pupils on the playground at any one time, a part of the noon hour excepted, than under the grade plan now in use.

Under the companion-class plan as commonly used there is a teacher for each class, or in this case there would be 22 teachers for the school, not counting manual training or domestic science teachers. Each of these teachers moves with her class, teaching the drill work in the regular classrooms, the special work in the special rooms, and the plays and games in the playrooms or on the playground. It is in reality a grade-school plan of organization, with a shift plan introduced to vacate the regular classrooms five fourteenths of the day, so as to make possible the addition of a second or B school to the building. A more detailed program for such a school will be given in the chapter which follows. If instead of such a straight-grade organization, as is described, we begin to specialize the teachers and the instruction, the plan shades into the platoon plan.

The platoon plan. The essentials of the platoon plan, as before, lie in the setting aside of a certain number of classrooms to be fitted up as special rooms, in which only instruction in the special subjects will be given, and the organization of a double school (A and B) for the building. If both schools begin and dismiss at the same time, morning, noon, and afternoon, a larger number of special rooms will need to be fitted up than if the hours are different, as shown in Figure 14 for the companion-class plan. The plan works best in a school where, after withdrawing rooms to be fitted up as special rooms, at least eight to ten classrooms are left for regular work with the A and B schools. There will ordinarily need to be special rooms for music, drawing, science, literature, manual training, and domestic science. If the beginning and closing hours are different, the literature room can be eliminated and this work done in the regular class periods, thus adding two more classes to the number the building may be made to carry. The auditorium is a very useful addition to the list of special rooms, and is a necessity in a good form of the platoon system. Two small indoor playrooms or gymnasia are also very desirable, to be used in place of the playground for supervised play and physical training in bad weather.

The school is then divided into two schools, which are perhaps best called the A and B schools, though X and Y schools, and Alpha and Beta schools are terms also used. The instruction is then so arranged that when one school is using the regular classrooms the other school is using the special rooms, laboratories, playgrounds, gymnasium, or the assembly hall, and these two schools alternate twice during the day in the use of the school facilities. The day is lengthened somewhat to give more time for the special instruction, though the time actually spent in the classrooms is decreased. Roughly the plan would be somewhat as follows:

Periods	A School	B School
8.30 to 10.00	Class work	Special work
10.00 to 11.30	Special work	Class work
11.30 to 12.30	Noon intermission	
12.30 to 2.00	Class work	Special work
2.00 to 3.30	Special work	Class work

Applying the platoon plan to an old-type building. How this plan of organizing the school into two platoons would increase the carrying load of a building may be illustrated by selecting three of the buildings shown in Figures 5 to 10.

We will first take the building shown in Figure 7. This building now has 16 classrooms on the two main floors, and two small indoor playrooms as well as two special rooms for manual training and domestic science in the basement. It has no assembly hall, however. The building now has seats for 560 children, or an average of 35 seats to a room. There are eight grades and a kindergarten in the building, there being three teachers for the first grade, two for each grade from second to sixth inclusive, and one each for the seventh and eighth grades. The work in the kindergarten and the first grade is well connected. The sixth, seventh, and eighth grades are organized on the departmental plan.

To reorganize this school to make the building carry a larger load we would first set off the kindergarten and the two first grades, since the work of the two is so well integrated, and in addition we would set off one more room to carry the additional first-grade pupils who would come in under the platoon plan. This leaves twelve classrooms. We would next take four more classrooms to be fitted up as rooms for special instruction — one each for drawing, music, science, and literature. In each of these rooms the ordinary furniture may be left, if necessary for economy, but it is much better to replace this by music racks, tables, and armchairs. In these rooms each class would be taught as one section. The school has no auditorium, so auditorium work could not be included. While it is possible to schedule the work without an auditorium, by increasing the number of classes at play, still, to show the plan better, we will assume that a regular "portable" is erected on the northeast corner of the school yard for use as an auditorium.

This leaves eight classrooms, which can now be made to

CROWDED-BUILDING PROBLEM

do double duty and carry two schools, an A school and a B school, which will alternate in the use of the classrooms. This would be 16 classes. Adding now the three first-grade rooms and the kindergarten, gives a total of 20 classes as against 16 before, or a gain of 140 pupils in the carrying load of the building secured by the platoon-type reorganization.

How program such a school. A detailed program for such a school will be given in the chapter which follows. Here we will merely indicate the general plan for such a reorganization. Roughly this would be, taking a fifth-grade class (see Table 3, p. 171) as an example:

PERIODS	A SCHOOL		B SCHOOL	
8.30 to 10.00	Class work	Reading Arithmetic Penmanship *Recess time*	Special work	Auditorium Supervised play { Drawing (2 days) { Music (3 days)
10.00 to 11.30	Special work	Auditorium Gymnasium { Drawing (2 days) { Music (3 days)	Class work	*Recess time* Reading Arithmetic Penmanship
		Noon intermission		
12.30 to 2.00	Class work	Reading Arithmetic Language Spelling *Recess time*	Special work	Literature { Geography (3 days) { Science (2 days) Manual training (B) Sewing (G)
2.00 to 3.30	Special work	Literature { Geography (3 days) { Science (2 days) Manual training (B) Sewing (G)	Class work	*Recess time* Reading Arithmetic Language Spelling

Other classes would have a somewhat similar program.

In carrying out such a plan two classes or rooms would be on the playground at once, and two in the playrooms. In the auditorium and literature rooms there would be one class each; one each, on alternate days, in the music or drawing room; and one in the science, or in the domestic science (girls) or manual training (boys) rooms.

The classes would then be distributed as follows, taking the first period of the day as an illustration:

A School	B School	
8 classrooms, at	Auditorium	35 pupils
35 pupils each = 280 pupils	Literature room	35 "
	Music or Drawing room	35 "
	Science or Arts room	35 "
	In playrooms for gymnastics	70 "
	On playgrounds for supervised play	70 "
	Total	280 "

If one more classroom were available, which might be secured by erecting another portable in the yard, each school (A and B) could be made to carry 9 classes, or a total of 18 instead of 16 classes, thus adding 70 more pupils to the school. This could be accomplished by sending two classes to the auditorium each period instead of one. Each school would then carry 9 classes and 315 pupils.

Applying the platoon plan to a modern building. If instead of taking the building shown in Figure 7, we take the much more modern building shown in Figure 9, the platoon plan is much easier of application.

Leaving out the kindergarten room and the two rooms for the first grades, we have nine regular classrooms. Whether the first grades shall be left out or included in the platoon plan depends much on the relation of their instruction to the kindergarten work below. If the connection is close they should be left out; if there is little connection they may be included. We will assume here that the connection is close and leave them out. The high basement already contains a gymnasium, and special rooms for manual training, science instruction, and domestic science. The school has a good auditorium on the first floor. Taking one of the classrooms for a music room, one for a drawing room, and one for

CROWDED-BUILDING PROBLEM

a literature room, and using the basement rooms as before, we have six regular classrooms left. Putting in an A and a B school gives 12 classes. With the kindergarten and the two first-grade classes this gives 15, as against 12 under the old plan. At 35 pupils to the class this is a clear gain of 105 pupils after providing well for special rooms. If the two first grades were included in the platoon plan, two additional classes could be accommodated, adding 70 pupils more.

The weekly distribution of classes then would be (see Table 7, p. 180) taking the first period of the day as an illustration:

A School	B School	
6 classrooms, at 35 pupils each Total 210 pupils	{ Science room (3 days) { Drawing room (2 days)	35 pupils
	Gymnasium	35 "
	Supervised play	35 "
	Literature room	35 "
	Auditorium	35 "
	{ Music room (3 days) { Manual training (B) (2 days) { Domestic science (G) (")	35 "
	Total	210 "

In such a building as is shown in Figure 10 the plan is still easier to carry out, as the building has more special rooms. Leaving four rooms for kindergarten and first grades, and one for an ungraded or special room, still leaves 19 regular classrooms. The school has an auditorium, two roof playgrounds for hot or wet weather use, and special rooms for manual training, domestic science, music, drawing and art, and science. Taking one more for a literature room leaves 18 regular classrooms. At 35 pupils to the room, the carrying load of the building with 24 classrooms is 840 children; under the platoon plan of 18 classes each, and 35 pupils to the class, the same building will have a carrying capacity of 1260 pupils, or 630 pupils in each of the two platoon schools.

Adding kindergarten and first grades, at the same number per room, will add 140 more pupils, or a total of 1400 pupils when organized as a platoon school, as against 840 as a grade-type school.

The distribution of classes in the Figure 10 school, when organized on the platoon plan, would be about as follows:

A School	B School	
18 classrooms at 35 pupils each = 630 pupils	Assembly room (3)	105 pupils
	On playground (4)	140 "
	On roof gymnasium (3)	105 "
	Music room (2)	70 "
	Drawing room (1)	35 "
	Science room (1)	35 "
	Literature room (2)	70 "
	Manual training (1)	35 "
	Domestic arts (1)	35 "
	Total (18)	630 "

Administrative details to be considered. In any platoon-plan form of organization certain administrative details need to be considered and provided for. These relate to cloakrooms, books, attendance, special rooms, recesses, and similar items.

In new buildings built for the platoon plan, special lockers and cloakracks are usually built in the basement or along the first-floor walls to provide space for the books and wraps of all pupils attending the school, but in old buildings this is usually an expense neither desirable or possible. Instead, either the existing cloakrooms are made to carry a double load of hooks and spaces for wraps, or racks are added in the hallways, if wide enough, or in basement space, to carry the extra pupil wraps. As for books, box racks having 70 to 80 spaces are usually erected in the classrooms, and each pupil then has a box space, with name on it, for his or her books and supplies.

Regular desk equipment can be used in the special rooms, but in buildings erected for platoon use special equipment is provided in the form of long music benches, tilted drawing stands, flat science tables, and armchairs for the literature room. While these are very nice, they are not a necessity.

The attendance of pupils is cared for in various ways, the most common plan being to have the first teacher of each main division of the school record attendance, both morning and afternoon.

Usually a short recess of ten minutes is given at the end or the beginning of each classroom period, but sometimes the play activities take the place of the regular recesses and only a short period (2–3 minutes) for passing is allowed. As will be seen from the detailed programs given in the following chapter, the recesses of the two schools do not come together.

The platoon plan provides a six-hour day, not counting the noon intermission, which is long for teachers, though usually considered as compensated for by the relief that comes from the specialization of work. In most of our large city schools using the plan the actual teaching work is reduced to five hours by the employment of so-called "relief teachers," one for every five regular classes, and these are then so assigned and move about as to give every regular teacher one free hour each day. In the program calculated out in the following chapter a still more liberal allowance is made by having each teacher teach but three of the four main periods of the day, or a total of four and a half hours. This requires the addition of one relief teacher for every four classes, or a number slightly higher than is usually provided. Under the 1 to 5 plan there is a slight saving in teachers; under the 1 to 4 plan, the same number of teachers is required as for grade work.

Educational advantages of the plan. Whether or not the platoon plan is to be applied to any school building involves questions of administrative policy which must be settled by the superintendent's office, but in some of our cities, not using the plan generally, individual principals have been permitted to experiment with the plan and to make the necessary reorganization of their schools. The educational advantages which the platoon school is believed to offer may be summarized briefly, as follows:

1. A larger carrying load for a given building.
2. A more constant use of the whole school plant, and particularly beneficial use of the assembly hall, gymnasia, and playgrounds.
3. Addition of specialized instruction in what are often regarded as extras — music, drawing, science, school gardening, domestic arts, manual training, shop work, and directed play — and without prohibitory costs.
4. The introduction of play and auditorium activities as integral parts of the course of study.
5. Special emphasis on the work in literature with a view to its cultural value.
6. Provision for pupils of a school day more varied, more intense, and more interesting. Experience shows that the pupils do not become as fatigued as when they sit in classrooms for long sessions.
7. The partial specialization of the work of the classroom teachers, and to a still greater extent the work of the special-activities teachers.
8. A great reduction in the need for special-subject supervisors.
9. Economies in the cost for building, and for general and special supervision.
10. The pupils gain from the different contacts, get the best from a number of teachers, and the exceptional child advances more easily.
11. The assembly-hall period can be made a distinct addition to the social side of school work, as will be shown in a later chapter. (Chapter XVII)
12. The opportunities for the socialization and Americanization of the pupils are greatly increased.
13. Physical training under direction and supervised play take the place of the old-fashioned pell-mell recess, with its congestion and its disciplinary problems.

CROWDED-BUILDING PROBLEM

14. Class discipline is easier because the pupils do not become restless from long sitting.

It is these advantages which have caused many thoughtful educators to give serious consideration recently to the platoon-type school.

QUESTIONS AND PROBLEMS

1. Suppose that the school shown in Figure 5 becomes badly crowded, there being 180 pupils beyond the seating capacity for the school. Assume also that it is possible to install six portables on a quarter of a block of rented ground to the east and rear, and that the congestion is solved in this manner. Show a distribution of classes in the school before, and after the increased enrollment has been cared for by the use of the six portables.
2. Make a grade-and-room distribution for the school shown in Figure 6, and show how you would rearrange matters if 60 pupils beyond capacity appeared, and the board gave you two more portables for use in the yard.
3. Suppose, in the above case, you had 100 excess pupils, no more portables were provided, and any reorganization of instruction did not seem advisable. Instead, part-time instruction became necessary. How would you then rearrange your school?
4. Under the same conditions as above, how would you rearrange your school in case the excess amounted to 200 pupils?
5. Instead of reorganizing the school shown in Figure 5 as a companion-class school, as described in the text, work out a platoon type of organization for it and show its possibilities, assuming the use of the lower central hall for assembly-hall purposes, the pupils either standing or sitting on the floor at assembly periods.
6. Instead of reorganizing the school shown in Figure 7 as a platoon-type school, as described in the text, reorganize it as a companion-class school after the plan of Figure 14. How would you then arrange it, and what would then be its carrying capacity?
7. Point out the many advantages of such a building as is shown in Figure 10, for any type of school organization.
8. What type of educational organization will use the building shown in Figure 7 to the best advantage? What form the building shown in Figure 10? Why, in each case?
9. Arrange the different types of school organization, discussed in this chapter, in the order of the degree of skill required to organize, administer, and supervise the instruction in the school, and give reasons for the order you indicate.
10. What type of educational organization is most likely to provide a rich and stimulating atmosphere in the school? Why?

SELECTED REFERENCES

(For this and the following chapter)

Bankes, W. J. "An Experiment with the Platoon-Type of School Organization in Akron, Ohio"; in *School and Society*, vol. 14, pp. 553–56. (December 10, 1921.)
>Description of the platoon organization, the curriculum, and a good statement of the advantages and disadvantages of the plan.

Bliss, Don C. "The Platoon School in Practice"; in *Elementary School Journal*, vol. 20, pp. 510–15.
>A description of the plan used in Montclair, New Jersey.

Brown, Sam W. "Some Experiments in Elementary School Organization"; in *Proceedings, National Education Association*, 1913, pp. 458–63.
>Deals with the requirements of a flexible program to permit of promotions by subjects instead of by grades.

Burris, Wm. P. *The Public Schools of Gary, Indiana.* Bul. No. 18, 1914, U.S. Bureau of Education.
>A brief description of the organization and work of the Gary schools.

Flexner, Abraham, and Bachman, Frank P. *The Gary Schools; a General Account.* 264 pp. General Education Board, New York, 1918.
>A general summary of the results of a survey of the Gary schools. A much more detailed account than 9, above.

Hartwell, S. O. *Overcrowded Schools and the Platoon Plan.* 77 pp. Cleveland, 1916.
>A volume in the Cleveland Educational Survey Series, describing the platoon plan in Kalamazoo, Michigan, and its applicability to the Cleveland problem.

Hughes, H. F. "Limited Departmentalization, Grades III to VI"; in *Elementary School Journal*, vol. 19, pp. 361–66. (January, 1919.)

Kennedy, John. "The Batavia Plan after Fourteen Years' Trial"; in *Elementary School Teacher*, vol. 12, pp. 449–59. (June, 1912.)
>A brief for the Batavia plan.

Kilpatrick, V. E. Departmental Teaching in Elementary Schools. 130 pp. New York, 1908.
>A good brief statement of the departmental plan of elementary-school organization.

Koos, L. V. "Plan of Organization of the Green Lake Elementary School"; in *Elementary School Journal*, vol. 20, pp. 435–48. (February, 1920.)
>Describes organization, based on the platoon plan, and reproduces a partial time-table of classes.

Spain, Chas. L. *The Platoon School in Detroit.* 108 pp. In *Detroit Educational Bulletin*, No. 2, 1920.
>The most comprehensive document in print on the platoon school, giving full details as to organization, programs, and teaching staff.

Spain, Chas. L., et al. *The Intermediate School in Detroit.* 39 pp. In *Detroit Educational Bulletin*, No. 6, 1921.
>An equally important document with the preceding, but dealing with the organization of the junior high school years.

Stevenson, P. R., and others. *Relation of Size of Class to School Efficiency.* Bulletin No. 10, Bureau of Educational Research, University of Illinois, 1922. 39 pp.
    A study of the problem, for both elementary and secondary schools.

Taylor, Jos. S. "The Duplicate School as an Educational Asset"; in *School and Society,* vol. 5, pp. 301–307. (March 17, 1917.)
    Describes work in New York City.

Washburne, C. W. "The Individual System in Winnetka"; in *Elementary School Journal,* vol. 21, pp. 52–68. (September, 1920.)
    Describes use of individual promotion plan, and results under it.

CHAPTER IX

PROGRAM–MAKING

Different types of programs. One of the problems of organization which every principal, old or new, must look after early in his work is that of the programs for daily work of the different teachers in his building. The extent to which he will need to give attention to this phase of school organization will be determined somewhat by the type of regulations as to time allotments and program-making in force in the city in which he is at work, and the type of educational organization found in his school. In many cities general regulations covering the details of program-making are issued for all grades, and these prescribe the maximum and the minimum time-allotments by grades and subjects. In a few cities quite uniform time-allotments and program-types are enforced. On the other hand, there are many cities which leave such matters largely to the judgment of the principal, recognizing that conditions vary much as between schools and even from time to time within the same school. If the principal is in a town school where there is no superintendent over him, he will then naturally have to formulate his own plans and make his own requirements.

The type of programs to be formulated for a school will vary somewhat not only with the character of the pupils and teachers and neighborhood, but also with the peculiar demands of the building and grounds. If a double or a triple recess is necessitated by conditions, the principal must plan his time schedules accordingly, and may even need to arrange his opening hour in the morning and at noon slightly differently for the different grades of pupils. If his school is crowded and he has part of the pupils on part-time, this will necessitate still different types of programs.

Still more, the types of programs the principal will need to use will vary with the type of educational organization existing in the school or the city. If the school is organized as a straight eight-grade elementary school, a quite simple type of program will be required. If the upper grades are organized on the departmental plan, a different type of program will need to be employed for these grades. If the school is organized on the 6–3 plan, a still different arrangement will need to be effected. If the school uses some special type of educational organization, such as the Batavia plan, the promotion-by-subjects plan, the companion-class plan, the platoon plan, or a highly organized Gary plan, still other types of programs will need to be employed. The more complex the plan of organization the more minutely will the principal need to supervise and approve the work of program-making.

Principles in program-making. In any case, though, the principal will need to look after the matter of the programs of his teachers if for no other purpose than to see that they conform with regulations, provide properly for the special work, and are properly organized and proportioned. He ought to do more than this, even in simple grade-type schools. He should be able to help his teachers to formulate their programs in more scientific form than many of the teachers would themselves be able alone to do. At the same time he must avoid rigid prescription in opposition to the judgment of a teacher, or any unreasonable insistence on what is after all only his own point of view.

In the first place, it is a good plan to let the more experienced teachers make their own room programs, the principal reserving his help at first chiefly for the new teachers. For beginners it probably will be best to provide them at the start with a prepared program to be used at least until they are able to make a better one. By the beginning of the second week of the term, or by its close at latest, every teacher should have determined on her daily program and submitted it to the principal for his files and his approval. In the case of experienced teachers programs should not be disapproved or changed except for good cause, and then only after consultation with the teacher concerned.

In the making of programs, or the approving of programs submitted, the principal should work with certain constructive ideas in mind. He must of course see that the allotted times figure out correctly, that the recesses and dismissals come as they should, that schedules do not conflict with assembly periods, that the maximum and minimum time allotments prescribed are not exceeded, that the work to be supervised by special teachers comes in proper rotation so far as is possible, and that the number of periods for each subject per week are as they should be. In addition the following principles ought to find embodiment, so far as can be done, in the permanent programs:

1. After the opening exercises should come one of the more difficult subjects, and preferably the one that is hardest for the teacher to teach.
2. Subjects similar in character, such as writing and drawing, phonics and word study, reading and literature, should not ordinarily follow one another.
3. Similarly, subjects in which the school is taught as a whole should not follow one another, some sectional subject coming in between.
4. Subjects requiring good muscular control, such as writing or drawing, should not immediately follow a recess period.
5. Class work in physical training should not either just precede or immediately follow a recess.
6. Subjects which require the use of special material, such as drawing or science, should come when such special material can be taken care of with the least waste of time. If special

rooms are to be used, then conflict between classes in the use of rooms must be avoided.
7. Something of a balance should be retained between the work of the morning and that of the afternoon, not all the easier subjects being placed in the afternoon, though the more exacting subjects may well come in the morning.
8. A heavy or an exacting subject, or one requiring physical activity, should not be placed immediately after lunch.
9. Subjects requiring close mental work should alternate, where possible, with subjects requiring motor activity.
10. Study periods with a teacher should not immediately precede recitation periods in that subject, as this plan tends to prevent the formation of habits of independent thought.
11. The number of subjects per day, and the time given each subject should vary with the grade periods, becoming longer as the children grow older. Recitation periods in the first grade should not ordinarily exceed fifteen minutes, in the second grade not over twenty minutes, in the third and fourth grades not over twenty-five minutes, in the fifth grade not over thirty minutes, in the sixth grade not over thirty-five minutes, and in the seventh and eighth grades not over forty-five to fifty minutes.
12. If the work of special teachers must be provided for, the subjects they supervise should be arranged, so far as can be done, that they can visit the classes in rotation on the days or half-days they visit the school for supervision, and thus avoid disarranging the school programs the days they visit the school.
13. The degree of flexibility and variability in a program may very properly vary with the experience and ability of the teacher concerned.

Special supervisors and the programs. The presence of supervisors of special subjects in the school system, who visit the schools at stated times for the purposes of supervision of the work of the regular teachers in their subjects, often offers difficulties in the matter of program-making to the principal of a school organized on the grade plan. While at first thought it would seem that an experienced teacher should be permitted to organize her program as she wished, if proper program standards were met, this cannot always be done if the traveling supervisors must be provided for so that they can do their work in the most economical manner possible. If there are three or four such special supervisors, the principal may have some difficulty in arranging satisfactory programs and at the same time satisfying his room teachers. The special teachers feel that their work is highly important, and resent it if their work is not properly arranged for. The regular teachers, on the other hand, have their preferences as to times and order of work. It is not possible for the special teachers to come at times that will best suit the room teachers, either, as they usually must confine their work to a half-day visit to the building.

Some concessions by the regular teachers will probably have to be made, and the principal will have to secure these on a give-and-take basis, and try to secure the best coöperation possible on the part of all concerned. He and his teachers must realize that the special supervisors have some rights in the matter, and the special supervisors must also recognize that the programs cannot be framed with their needs alone in mind. In grades organized on the departmental plan these difficulties largely disappear, while under the platoon type, where the special work is done by teachers in the school, the problem solves itself. Often no complete program arrangement satisfactory to all can be made, and the best plan will be to make programs that are satisfactory to the school, and then change them on the days when the special teachers come for their work.

Program standards. A number of studies of time allotments and distribution have been made in recent years, and these show very wide variations in the time given different school subjects. Other studies have revealed that excessive time given to a subject seldom gives returns in learning which warrant the longer time involved. Other studies of school fatigue have shown that the quantity and quality of work done by pupils at different times of the day vary much less than has been commonly supposed. Results at the close of afternoon sessions, under good conditions of school hygiene, have been about as good as in the morning. As a result of these studies there has been a growing tendency, within recent years, to approach more uniform standards in time allotments, and to give less attention to subject fatigue as related to time of day. Accordingly many of our school systems have recently issued maximum and minimum time schedules, or a common time schedule with maximum and minimum variations from this stated. On pages 168 and 169 we reproduce two pages of a time schedule arranged on the latter plan, as issued by one of our larger American cities, and which may be taken to represent good present-day practice in the matter of time distribution. The rules governing the use of these time-distribution tables are printed under them.

Using such tables as guides, teachers can work out programs for temporary use and, when refined, for approval by the principal. The eventual program should be made out on printed cards, about 8 × 9 inches in size, and somewhat after the form shown in Table III, one copy to be given to the principal for reference and filing in his office, and one copy to be fastened to the outside of the room door. A copy of the program should also be written on the room blackboard. As worked out for the fifth grade in a grade-teacher-system school, the program given on page 171 would result.

Departmental type programs. The time distribution by grades and the program just worked out for the fifth grade represent the simplest type of program to construct. With a time-distribution sheet as a guide, such programs, except in the case of beginners, should be left to the teachers to formulate, the work of the principal being supervisory to see that conflicts in the use of rooms or special facilities are

TABLE I. SUGGESTED TIME DISTRIBUTION FOR PRIMARY GRADES

Subject	Sections per Grade	Classes per Week	First Grade	Second Grade	Third Grade	Fourth Grade
Morning Opening Exercises...	1	5	50	25	25	25
Word Study	2	10	300	125	..	..
Spelling (½ time for study)...	1	5	..	..	25	25
Language Games	1	5	50	25	..	..
Language Work	2	10	50	..	..	..
" "	1	5	..	75	..	..
" "	1	4	..	..	100	100
Reading	2	20	240	340	..	..
"	2	10	..	..	240	240
Literature	1	5	75	80	..	..
"	1	3	..	..	100	100
History	1	1	20	25	25	25
Geography	1	4	..	..	100	100
Number Work	2	10	..	150	250	250
Drawing	1	3	60	75	75	75
Manual Arts	1	2	60	60	60	60
Nature Study	1	2	45	20	50	50
Writing	1	5	50	75	75	75
Music	1	5	75	75	75	75
Physical Training	1	10	50	50	50	50
Recess — Morning	1	5	75	75	75	75
" — Afternoon	1	5	..	75	75	75
Total minutes per week			1200	1350	1500	1500
Total minutes per day			240	270	300	300

RULES GOVERNING USE OF TABLES

1. The above time allotments have been worked out to cover the needs of the present course of study, and in schools having no exceptional conditions may be considered as approximately the proper proportional distribution.
2. Variations from the above may be permitted, to adjust to time schedules or to meet special conditions and needs, with the consent of the principal, to an extent of not over 25 per cent with short-period classes, and 20 per cent with long-period classes.
3. The recess periods must not be cut down, or the total school time lengthened. In schools in which the upper grades are organized on the departmental plan, two full hours of instruction in the afternoon will, however, be permitted for these grades.

TABLE II. SUGGESTED TIME DISTRIBUTION FOR GRAMMAR GRADES

Subject	Sections per Grade	Classes per Week	Fifth Grade	Sixth Grade	Seventh Grade	Eighth Grade
Morning Opening Exercises.	1	5	25	25	25	25
Reading and Literature....	2	10	250	250	250	250
Composition and Language.	2	10	200	200	200	200
Spelling and Word Study...	1	5	90	90	80	80
Penmanship	1	3	60	60	..	..
"	1	1	..	..	20	20
Hygiene and Civics........	1	2	40	40	40	40
Geography...............	2	8	160	160	..	..
History.................	1	2	40	40	..	..
"	2	8	..	..	200	200
Mathematics..............	2	8	200	200	200	200
Drawing.................	1	3	75	75	75	75
Science..................	1	2	50	50	50	50
Music	1	3	60	60	60	60
Manual Training (Boys)...	1 }	1	50	50	100	100
Household Arts (Girls).....	1 }					
Physical Training.........	1	10	50	50	50	50
Recess — Morning.........	1	5	75	75	75	75
" — Afternoon.......	1	5	75	75	75	75
Total minutes per week....			1500	1500	1500	1500
Total minutes per day.....			300	300	300	300

RULES GOVERNING USE OF TABLES — *Continued*

4. The opening morning exercises in the first grade should be used to put before the school the thought for the day, and in the other primary grades for a somewhat similar purpose. Talks, songs, poems, reports by pupils, or an experiment may be used. In the grammar grades the time may, with the consent of the principal, be used for other purposes.
5. In Word Study, Reading, Language in the first and grammar grades, Geography and History in the last two grades in which these subjects are taught, and in Mathematics, it is assumed that there will ordinarily be two sections or classes in each room. In other subjects the room will work as a whole.
6. In the common or one-section work, with mixed grades, take the work assigned to the higher section.
7. Boys in the grammar grades go to work in Manual Training at the same time that the girls go to their work in the Household Arts, so that both boys and girls have the full time indicated each week.

avoided, that time allotments are not exceeded, and that good principles in program-making are employed. This simple type of program would apply to such a simple school organization as is found in the building shown in Figure 5, which has only the eight grades, or in Figure 7, which has only a kindergarten and a straight eight-grade educational organization.

For the other buildings shown in Figures 5 to 10, a more complex educational organization exists and must be provided for. These will be:

Figure 9. Kindergarten; grades 1–5 on grade-organization plan; grades 6–8 on a departmental plan, but with special rooms sufficient to permit of the reorganization of the school as a platoon school.

Figures 6 and 8. Kindergarten; 6–3 plan, the three upper grades being organized as a junior high school.

Figure 10. Same, but so equipped with special rooms that it could be reorganized as a platoon school or as a full Gary-type school.

The building shown in Figure 9 will illustrate the departmental type of program. This building has twelve classrooms, all in use, an auditorium, gymnasium, and two specially equipped rooms in the basement. The classroom distribution for this building is: kindergarten; grades 1 to 5 on a grade form of organization, with seven teachers; and grades 6 to 8 organized on the departmental plan, with four teachers.

The seven grade-organization-type teachers will have programs of the simple grade types, as shown on page 171, and can arrange their periods with some freedom, but the four departmental teachers must rotate their pupils at the same times, and must also divide the teaching subjects between them. The departmental program must then be divided into four main periods, approximately equal in length for morning and for afternoon, at the end of each of which

TABLE III. PROGRAM FOR A FIFTH GRADE IN A GRADE-TYPE SCHOOL

(FIGURE 5 OR 7 TYPE OF SCHOOL)

Gwendolyn Jones......Teacher Longfellow......School
Grades (or Subjects)......5 A and 5 B Half year......First, 1922–23

TIME	MONDAY	TUESDAY	WEDNESDAY	THURSDAY	FRIDAY
9.00– 9.10 9.10– 9.35 9.35–10.00 10.00–10.25	Opening Exercises A Arithmetic B Arithmetic A Reading	Opening Exercises A Arithmetic B Arithmetic A Reading	Opening Exercises {Boys—Man'lTrain. {Girls—Sewing A Reading	Opening Exercises A Arithmetic B Arithmetic A Reading	Opening Exercises A Arithmetic B Arithmetic A Reading
10.25–10.40			Morning Recess		
10.40–11.05 11.05–11.30 11.30–11.40 11.40–12.00	B Reading Drawing Physical Training Music	B Reading Science Physical Training Music	B Reading Drawing Physical Training Music	B Reading Science Physical Training Music	B Reading Drawing Physical Training Music
12.00–1.00			Noon Intermission		
1.00– 1.20 1.20– 1.40 1.40– 2.00	A Geography B Geography Penmanship	A Geography B Geography Penmanship	A History B History Penmanship	A Geography B Geography Penmanship	A Geography B Geography Penmanship
2.00– 2.10			Afternoon Recess		
2.10– 2.30 2.30– 2.50 2.50– 3.00	A Comp. & Lang. B Comp. & Lang. Spelling	A Comp. & Lang. B Comp. & Lang. Spelling	A Comp. & Lang. B Comp. & Lang. Spelling	A Comp. & Lang. B. Comp. & Lang. Spelling	A Comp. & Lang. B Comp. & Lang. Spelling

the pupils move to another room and teacher, finally returning to their "home rooms" just before dismissal in the afternoon. The program must then be organized about these four major movements, and will be approximately as shown in Table IV, on the opposite page.

From this program it will be seen how the departmental plan specializes the work of the teachers. In this program each teacher looks after her opening exercises and gives the ten minutes of physical training required. Aside from these there is no common work. Teachers A and C divide the reading and literature between them; teacher A teaches the history and penmanship; teacher B the mathematics, drawing, and science; teacher C the geography, music, and the hygiene and civics; and teacher D the composition and language, and the spelling and work study. The manual training, domestic science, and sewing are taught by special teachers, who spend one day each week at the school.

Other special-type programs. The buildings shown in Figures 6 and 8 will call for much the same type of organization, the first six grades in each being organized on the straight grade plan, and grades 7 to 9 being organized on a departmental plan as a junior high school. If some differentiation in courses is allowed in the latter a somewhat more flexible program is called for, so as to permit of a choice between certain studies. Promotion in junior high schools, too, not infrequently takes place by subjects instead of by grades, and if this is to be done programs must also be arranged with possibilities for some choice or variation as to studies, without conflict as to time.

The common plan for dealing with elementary-school pupils who get ahead or behind in certain subjects in their grade is to employ the ungraded room, or the special coach teacher, either to bring the pupil up to the grade in the subject or subjects in which he is behind, or to prepare him for

TABLE IV. DEPARTMENTAL PROGRAM, GRADES 6-8
(FIGURE 9 TYPE OF SCHOOL)

PERIODS	TEACHER A HOME ROOM FOR 6 B GRADE	TEACHER B HOME ROOM FOR 6 A GRADE	TEACHER C HOME ROOM FOR 7TH GRADE	TEACHER D HOME ROOM FOR 8TH GRADE
First Period 9.00–10.25 85 minutes	*6 B Grade* Opening Exercises 5 min. Reading and Literature 50 " Physical Training 10 " History (2d) 20 " Penmanship (3d) 20 "	*6 A Grade* Opening Exercises 5 min. Mathematics 45 " Physical Training 10 " Drawing (3d) 25 " Science (2d) 25 "	*7th Grade* Opening Exercises 5 min. Reading and Literature 50 " Physical Training 10 " Music (3d) 20 " Hygiene and Civics (2d) 20 "	*8th Grade* Opening Exercises 5 min. Comp. & Language 40 " Physical Training 10 " Spell'g & W'd Study 20 " Manual Training (B) 80 min. Domestic Science (G) 80 " 1 day each week
10.25–10.40			Morning Recess	
Second Period 10.40–12 80 minutes	*6 A Grade* Reading and Literature 50 min. Study 10 " History (2d) 20 " Penmanship (3d) 20 "	*7th Grade* Mathematics 40 min. Study 15 " Drawing (3d) 25 " Science (2d) 25 "	*8th Grade* Reading and Literature 50 min. Music (3d) 30 " Hygiene and Civics (2d) 20 "	*6 B Grade* Comp. & Language 40 min. Study 20 " Spell'g & W'd Study 20 " Manual Training B) 80 min. Sewing (G) 80 " 1 day a week
12.00–1.00			Noon Intermission	
Third Period 1.00–2.00 60 minutes	*7th Grade* History 40 min. Penmanship (1d) 20 " Study (4d) 20 "	*8th Grade* Mathematics 40 min. Drawing (3d) 20 " Science (2d) 20 "	*6 B Grade* Geography 40 min. Music (3d) 20 " Hygiene and Civics (2d) 20 "	*6 A Grade* Comp. & Language 40 min. Spell'g & W'd Study 20 " Manual Training (B) 60 min. Sewing (G) 60 " 1 day a week
2.00–2.10			Afternoon Recess	
Fourth Period 2.10–3.10 60 minutes	*8th Grade* History 40 min. Penmanship (1d) 20 " Study (4d) 20 "	*6 B Grade* Mathematics 40 min. Drawing (3d) 20 " Science (2d) 20 "	*6 A Grade* Geography 40 min. Music (3d) 20 " Hygiene and Civics (2d) 20 "	*7th Grade* Comp. & Language 40 min. Spell'g & W'd Study 20 " Manual Training (B) 60 min. Domestic Science (G) 60 " 1 day a week

a special promotion to a higher grade. This carries pupils along rather uniformly, makes grade organization easier to handle from the administrative end, and makes the transfer of pupils from school to school easier of accomplishment. Occasionally, however, one finds an elementary-school principal, and sometimes even a school system, where the idea of individual progress is carried to the extreme of promotion throughout by individual subjects, with the resulting mixing of pupils for recitation purposes by sending them to recite, in each subject, to the grade where they most properly belong.

Such a plan calls for a common recitation time for all the important school subjects, such as language, arithmetic, history, geography, reading, and drawing, so that pupils may pass from room to room at the recitation periods, and recite in the grade to which they are assigned. Otherwise the programs are of the grade-room type.

The companion-class and the platoon-type programs. When we pass to these types of programs a much more complicated problem in program-making presents itself to the principal for solution. There are now two schools to be cared for, an A and a B school. The pupils now pass from room to room, and in consequence conflicts in the use of the school's facilities must be looked after with care. In the strictly companion-class type of organization, the teachers move with the classes from room to room and from room to playground. They are in reality moving class or grade teachers. The difficulty then that presents itself is that of keeping the classes from conflicting in the use of the special rooms. This type of organization is shown in Figure 14. As the arrangement of a schedule for the use of rooms and playground is so similar to that found in the platoon schools, we will pass directly to a consideration of the platoon-type programs.

In the platoon-type school, program-making becomes still more difficult. The teachers no longer move with their classes, in the pure platoon type, but are selected and classified for special types of work and their room distribution is relatively easy. Some overlapping of work and some "filling-in" teaching is almost inevitable, however, to provide for the needs of all the classes. One difficulty that presents itself lies in the proper scheduling of the work of the relief teachers, as any one teacher seldom teaches the whole of the six-hour day. The greatest difficulty lies in the scheduling of the use of the special rooms to avoid conflicts in the use of the special facilities. This calls for even more care in arranging the program when the two schools (A and B) begin and close at the same time than when different opening and closing hours are taken, as in the companion-class plan shown in Figure 14.

The chief difficulties encountered. The chief difficulties in platoon-type program-making can be illustrated by taking the school shown in Figure 9, and using the platoon organization for this school, as described in the preceding chapter (page 154). The platoon organization here involves grades 2 to 8 inclusive. Assuming that no teacher will be expected to teach more than three of the four major periods of the day ($4\frac{1}{2}$ of the 6 hours the school is in session), this will call for 8 classroom teachers and 8 special teachers, whose distribution will be shown in Table V. The first thing to be worked out, in preparing a program for such a school, is the class programs. These are given for the school in Table VI. At first these will have to be in tentative form, and must next be transferred onto a room-distribution program, as shown in Table VII, and the necessary adjustments and corrections made.

In making the room-distribution table (VII) care must be taken to keep the same relative order for the classes in the

TABLE V. TEACHER DISTRIBUTION FOR A 12-CLASS PLATOON-TYPE SCHOOL

(Based on the School shown in Figure 9)

TEACHER	9 to 10.15	10.30 to 12	1 to 2	
I. *Grade Teachers*				
Kindergarten....				
Receiving Class .				
Grade 1 B......				
Grade 1 A......				
	8.30 to 10	10 to 11.30	12.30 to 2	2 to 3.30
II. *Class Teachers*				
No. 1.........	2B	2A	2B	..
" 2.........	3B	..	3B	2A
" 3.........	..	3A	4B	3A
" 4.........	4B	4A	..	4A
" 5.........	5B	5A	5B	..
" 6.........	6B	..	6B	5A
" 7.........	7A–B	6A	7A–B	..
" 8.........	..	8A–B	Lit.	8A–B
III. *Special Teachers*				
1. Auditorium [1] ...				
2. Gymnastics and Play [2]				
3. Literature [3].....				
4. Drawing.......	++	++	++	++
5. Science and Geography ...	++	++	++	++
6. Music	++	++	++	++
7. Manual Training..........	++	++	++	++
8. Domestic Science and Sewing.......	++	++	++	++

[1] The Auditorium teacher is helped somewhat in preparing programs by the class teachers, and in the conduct of the work by the music teacher, who here has but about two thirds of a teaching load.

[2] The teacher of gymnastics is assisted in the mornings by the teacher of manual training, whose load here is light. If a play teacher were added, to assist and have charge of the playground after school hours, it would be better.

[3] The Literature teacher is relieved the third period by the class teacher No. 8.

++ In all these cases the work is scattered throughout the day, but averages about three periods of work.

different shifts, as may be seen by looking over the table given. In the literature-room assignments, for instance, the assignments for the auditorium periods are just reversed, morning going to afternoon, and *vice versa*. Next the three divisions of each main period are each changed in order in the same way; to get the gymnasium assignments, the gymnasium periods find their complement in science. Then one more change in order in each period and the combination shown in the drawing and music periods is produced, and this in turn is reversed to secure the assignments for manual training, sewing, and domestic science. The secret of making such a program is the following of a fixed order of assignments and changes; any guesswork placing will lead to conflict after conflict. The final results are shown in Tables V, VI, and VII. If the school were larger, as is the school shown in Figure 10, the plan would be much the same, except that two or more classes would now go to the auditorium, gymnasium, and play at once, instead of one, and more special teachers and rooms would be required. A complete program for the Figure 10 school, similar to one given for the Figure 9 school, could be constructed by following the plan just outlined.

In a platoon-type school the principal must be responsible for the organization of the school and the working out of the program. The class teachers merely work out their class period time-distributions, so as to provide for section work, recesses, and a proper distribution for each hour and a half period. This is a relatively easy thing to do. The program, too, must be ready in advance of the opening of school, and should be ready for distribution in printed form, at the preliminary teachers' meeting, so that each teacher may know the arrangement and distribution of her work.

The weekly class and room programs for the Figure 9 school are given on the following pages.

TABLE VI. WEEKLY CLASS PROGRAM OF A 12-CLASS PLATOON-TYPE SCHOOL, BY CLASSES

Based on the School shown in Figure 9.

Time for "Home Room" work given in minutes per week; each "activities" period is divided into three periods of 30 minutes each.

GRADE AND CLASS	DAY	8.30 TO 10.00		10.00 TO 11.30		12.30 TO 2.00		2.00 TO 3.30	
B 2—Class 1	M Tu W Th F	Opening Exercises Reading and Phonics Number Work Recess Time Total	25 min. 250 " 125 " 50 " 450	Science Drawing Science Drawing Science	Lit. " " " " " " " " " " " "	Play " " " " " " " " " " " "	Reading and Phonics Language Work Penmanship Unapportioned Recess Time Total	200 min. 100 " 75 " 50 " 25 " 450	Aud. " " " " " " " "	Gym. " " " " " " " "	Music Man. Av. Music Man. Av. Music	50 min. 200 " 100 " 75 " 25 " 450
A 2—Class 2	M Tu W Th F	Science Drawing Science Drawing Science	Play " " " " " " " " " " " "	Lit. " " " " " " " " " " " "	Recess Time Reading and Phonics Number Work Unapportioned Total	25 min. 250 " 125 " 50 " 450	Gym. " " " " " " " "	Music Man. Av. Music Man. Av. Music	Aud. " " " " " " " "	Recess Time Reading and Phonics Language Work Penmanship Unapportioned Total	50 min. 200 " 100 " 75 " 25 " 450
B 3—Class 3	M Tu W Th F	Opening Exercises Reading Arithmetic Penmanship Recess Time Total	25 min. 150 " 150 " 75 " 50 " 450	Science Drawing Science Drawing Science	Play " " " " " " " " " " " "	Lit. " " " " " " " " " " " "	Science Drawing Science Drawing Science	50 min. 150 " 150 " 75 " 25 " 450	Reading Language Spelling Unapportioned Recess Time Total	150 min. 150 " 25 " 75 " 50 " 450	Music Man. Av. Music Man. Av. Music	Aud. " " " " " " " "	Gym. " " " " " " " "
A 3—Class 4	M Tu W Th F	Play " " " " " " " " " " " "	Lit. " " " " " " " " " " " "	Recess Time Reading Arithmetic Penmanship Unapportioned Total	50 min. 150 " 150 " 75 " 25 " 450	Music Man. Av. Music Man. Av. Music	Aud. " " " " " " " "	Gym. " " " " " " " "	Recess Time Reading Language Spelling Unapportioned Total	50 min. 150 " 150 " 75 " 25 " 450
B 4—Class 5	M Tu W Th F	Opening Exercises Reading Arithmetic Geography (study) Recess Time Total	25 min. 150 " 175 " 50 " 50 " 450	Geogr. Science Geogr. Science Geogr.	Man. Av. Play Man. Av. Play Man. Av.	Lit. " " " " " " " " " " " "	Reading Language Spelling Penmanship Recess Time Total	100 min. 150 " 75 " 75 " 50 " 450	Aud. " " " " " " " "	Gym. " " " " " " " "	Drawing Music Drawing Music Drawing
A 4—Class 6	M Tu W Th F	Lit. " " " " " " " " " " " "	Science Geogr. Science Geogr. Geogr.	Man. Av. Play Man. Av. Play Man. Av.	Recess Time Reading Arithmetic Geography (study) Recess Time Total	50 min. 150 " 175 " 50 " 25 " 450	Aud. " " " " " " " "	Gym. " " " " " " " "	Drawing Music Drawing Music Drawing	Recess Time Reading Language Spelling Penmanship Total	50 min. 100 " 120 " 75 " 75 " 450

TABLE VI. WEEKLY CLASS PROGRAM OF A 12-CLASS PLATOON-TYPE SCHOOL, BY CLASSES — *continued*

GRADE AND CLASS	DAY	8.30 TO 10.00		10.00 TO 11.30		12.30 TO 2.00		2.00 TO 3.30	
B 5 — Class 7	M Tu W Th F	Opening Exercises Reading Arithmetic Penmanship Recess Time Total	25 min. 125 " 175 " 75 " 50 " 450 "	Aud. " " " "	Gym. " " " "	Drawing Music Drawing Music Drawing	Reading Arithmetic Language Spelling Recess Time Total	100 min. 100 " 125 " 75 " 50 " 450 "	Lit. " " " "	Geogr. Science Geogr. Science Geogr.	Man. Tr. (Sewing " " "
A 5 — Class 8	M Tu W Th F	Aud. " " " "	Gym. " " " "	Draw. Music Draw. Music Draw.	Recess Time Reading Arithmetic Penmanship Unapportioned Total	50 min. 125 " 175 " 75 " 25 " 450 "	Lit. " " " "	Geogr. Science Geogr. Science Geogr.	(Man. Tr. Sewing " " "	Recess Time Reading Arithmetic Spelling Total	50 min. 100 " 125 " 75 " 450 "
B 6 — Class 9	M Tu W Th F	Opening Exercises Reading Arithmetic Penmanship Recess Time Total	25 min. 125 " 175 " 75 " 50 " 450 "	Music Man. Tr. & Sewing Music Man. Tr. & Sewing Music	Aud. " Aud. " Aud.	Gym. " " " "	Reading Arithmetic Language Spelling Recess Time Total	100 min. 100 " 125 " 50 " 75 " 450 "	Drawing Science Drawing Science Drawing	Lit. " " " "	Geogr. " " " "
A 6 — Class 10	M Tu W Th F	Music Man. Tr. & Sewing Music Man. Tr. & Sewing Music	Aud. " Aud. " Aud.	Gym. " " " "	Recess Time Reading Arithmetic Penmanship Unapportioned Total	50 min. 125 " 175 " 75 " 25 " 450 "	Drawing Science Drawing Science Drawing	Lit. " " " "	Geogr. " " " "	Recess Time Reading Arithmetic Language Spelling Total	50 min. 100 " 100 " 125 " 75 " 450 "
7 B & A — Class 11	M Tu W Th F	Opening Exercises History Mathematics Recess Time Total	25 min. 175 " 200 " 50 " 450 "	Gym. " " " "	Music Science Music Science Music	And. " " " "	Reading Language Spelling & Word Study Penmanship Recess Time Total	150 min. 100 " 75 " 25 " 50 " 450 "	Drawing Man. Tr. & Dom. Sci. Drawing Man. Tr. & Dom. Sci. Drawing	Lit. " " " "
8 B & A — Class 12	M Tu W Th F	Gym. " " " "	Music Science Music Science Music	Aud. " " " "	Recess Time History Mathematics Total	50 min. 200 " 200 " 450 "	Drawing Man. Tr. & Dom. Sci. Drawing Man. Tr. & Dom. Sci. Drawing	Lit. " " " "	Recess Time Reading Language Spelling & Word Study Penmanship Total	50 min. 150 " 150 " 25 " 75 " 450 "

TABLE VII. WEEKLY ROOM PROGRAM OF A 12-CLASS PLATOON-TYPE SCHOOL, BY ROOMS

(Based on the School shown in Figure 9)

Room	Day	A. School 8:30–9	A. School 9–9:30	A. School 9:30–10	B. School 10–10:30	B. School 10:30–11	B. School 11–11:30	A. School 12:30–1	A. School 1–1:30	A. School 1:30–2	B. School 2–2:30	B. School 2:30–3	B. School 3–3:30
Auditorium	M Tu W Th F	5 A 5 A 5 A 5 A 5 A	6 A .. 6 A .. 6 A	8 A–B 8 A–B 8 A–B 8 A–B 8 A–B	5 B 5 B 5 B 5 B 5 B	6 B .. 6 B .. 6 B	7 A–B 7 A–B 7 A–B 7 A–B 7 A–B	4 A 4 A 4 A 4 A 4 A	3 A 3 A 3 A 3 A 3 A	2 A 2 A 2 A 2 A 2 A	2 B 2 B 2 B 2 B 2 B	3 B 3 B 3 B 3 B 3 B	4 B 4 B 4 B 4 B 4 B
Gymnasium (or Playground)	M Tu W Th F	8 A–B 8 A–B 8 A–B 8 A–B 8 A–B	5 A 5 A 5 A 5 A 5 A	6 A 6 A 6 A 6 A 6 A	7 A–B 7 A–B 7 A–B 7 A–B 7 A–B	5 B 5 B 5 B 5 B 5 B	6 B 6 B 6 B 6 B 6 B	2 A 2 A 2 A 2 A 2 A	4 A 4 A 4 A 4 A 4 A	3 A 3 A 3 A 3 A 3 A	4 B 4 B 4 B 4 B 4 B	2 B 2 B 2 B 2 B 2 B	3 B 3 B 3 B 3 B 3 B
Supervised Play	M Tu W Th F	3 A 3 A 3 A 3 A 3 A	2 A 2 A 2 A 2 A 2 A	4 A .. 4 A	3 B 3 B 3 B 3 B 3 B	4 B .. 4 B	2 B 2 B 2 B 2 B 2 B						
Drawing	M Tu W Th F	2 A .. 2 A	4 A Geog 4 A Geog 4 A Geog		2 B .. 2 B		5 B 3 B 5 B 3 B 5 B	6 A (M.A.) 3 A (M.A.) 6 A 3 A (M.A.) 6 A	2 A (M.A.) .. 2 A (M.A.)	4 A 4 A 4 A	3 B (M.A.) 6 B (M.A.) 3 B (M.A.) 6 B	4 B 4 B 4 B	2 B (M.A.) 2 B (M.A.)
Music	M Tu W Th F	6 A 6 A 6 A	8 A–B 8 A–B 8 A–B	5 A 5 A	6 B 6 B 6 B	7 A–B 7 A–B 7 A–B	5 B 5 B	3 A 3 A 3 A	2 A 2 A 2 A	4 A 4 A	3 B 3 B 3 B	4 B 4 B	2 B 2 B
Science and Geography	M Tu W Th F	2 A 2 A 2 A	4 A 8 A–B 4 A 8 A–B	3 A 3 A 3 A	4 B 4 B 4 B 4 B 4 B	2 B 7 A–B 2 B 7 A–B 2 B	3 B 3 B 3 B	6 A .. 6 A .. 6 A	5 A 5 A 5 A 5 A 5 A	6 A 6 A 6 A 6 A 6 A	6 B .. 6 B	5 B 5 B 5 B 5 B 5 B	6 B 6 B 6 B 6 B 6 B

TABLE VII. WEEKLY ROOM PROGRAM OF A 12-CLASS PLATOON-TYPE SCHOOL, BY ROOMS — *continued*

Room	Day	A. School 8:30–9	9–9:30	9:30–10	B. School 10–10:30	10:30–11	11–11:30	12:30–1	A. School 1–1:30	1:30–2	2–2:30	B. School 2:30–3	3–3:30
Literature......	M Tu W Th F	4 A 4 A 4 A 4 A 4 A	3 A 3 A 3 A 3 A 3 A	2 A 2 A 2 A 2 A 2 A	2 B 2 B 2 B 2 B 2 B	3 B 3 B 3 B 3 B 3 B	4 B 4 B 4 B 4 B 4 B	5 A 5 A 5 A 5 A 5 A	6 A 6 A 6 A 6 A 6 A	8 A–B 8 A–B 8 A–B 8 A–B 8 A–B	5 B 5 B 5 B 5 B 5 B	6 B 6 B 6 B 6 B 6 B	7 A–B 7 A–B 7 A–B 7 A–B 7 A–B
Man. Train. (Boys only,except in 4th grade Manual Arts & 7th & 8th grade Drawing)	M Tu W Th F	6 A — Man. Train. 6 A — Man. Train.		4 A (M.A.) 4 A (M.A.) 4 A (M.A.)	6 B — Man. Train. 6 B — Man. Train.	4 B (M.A.) 4 B (M.A.) 4 B (M.A.)		8 A–B — Drawing 8 A–B — Man. Tr. 8 A–B — Drawing 8 A–B — Man. Tr. 8 A–B — Drawing		5 A 5 A 5 A 5 A 5 A	7 A–B 7 A–B 7 A–B 7 A–B 7 A–B	5 B — Drawing 5 B — Man. Tr. 5 B — Drawing 5 B — Man. Tr. 5 B — Drawing	
Domestic Science & Sewing. (Girls only)	M Tu W Th F	6 A — Sewing 6 A — Sewing		.. ..	6 B — Sewing 6 B — Sewing	.. ..		8 A–B — Dom. Sci. 8 A–B — Dom. Sci.		5 A 5 A 5 A 5 A 5 A	7 A–B 7 A–B	7 A–B — Dom. Sci. 7 A–B — Dom. Sci.	
Regular Classrooms Classroom No. 1..... " No. 2..... " No. 3..... " No. 4..... " No. 5..... " No. 6.....			2 B 3 B 4 B 5 B 6 B 8 A–B			2 A 3 A 4 A 5 A 6 A 8 A–B			2 A 3 A 4 A 5 A 6 B 7 A–B			2 A 3 A 4 A 5 A 6 A 8 A–B	
" No. 9..... " No. 10..... " No. 11..... " No. 12.....						1 C 1 B 1 A Kindergarten			1 C 1 B 1 A ..				

QUESTIONS AND PROBLEMS

1. Assume, for the school shown in Figure 5, that the first two grades are part-time double-session grades, and that it is necessary to arrange matters so that the kindergarten and grades one and two, grades three to five, and grades six to eight shall have different recess periods. Show how you would arrange the program.
2. Using Tables I and II for seventh- and eighth-grade studies, and assuming mathematics, general science, English, and an option between a language and a vocational subject for the ninth-grade studies, construct a departmental-type program for grades seven to nine, or the junior high school, of the school shown in Figure 8, assuming four teachers for the three grades.
3. Using the same time schedules as are given in Tables I and II, and assuming a school managed on the promotion by subject plan, as described on page 174, show how you would arrange the school programs to carry out this idea, and to embrace as many of the principles stated on pages 164–165 as possible.
4. Calculate costs for the twelve-class platoon-type school shown in Figure 9, as described in this and the previous chapter, and show whether or not it will cost more or less to conduct the school as a platoon-type school than to care for an equal number of children under a grade-school type of organization. Estimate also the educational efficiency of the two types of school organization.
5. Outline a program for a platoon-type school in the building shown in Figure 10, calculating the number and types of teachers needed and work out a room and class distribution for this 36-class platoon-type school.
6. Calculate costs, as in problem 4, for the two types of schools for Figure 10, as indicated in problem 5.
7. Which type of school adapts itself best to the platoon type of educational organization, a large or a small school, and a school with few special rooms or with many?

SELECTED REFERENCES

(See end of preceding chapter.)

PART III
THE ADMINISTRATION OF A SCHOOL

CHAPTER X

BUSINESS ORGANIZATION AND ADMINISTRATION

1. *The office and its work*

The principal and office routine. In Chapter III (page 51) we gave a daily program which one principal worked out for his own guidance and emancipation, and pointed out a number of means for saving time and getting routine work done. It ought to be possible for any principal working without much clerical assistance, and in a city not afflicted with an excess of central-office regulations and red tape or an inordinate amount of report work, similarly to free himself from the pressure of office duties and gain time for the real work of school supervision. What was said there need not be repeated here, but instead certain additional points in business organization and management will be considered.

A certain amount of office work is inevitable and must be handled. This naturally will be greater in some school systems than in others, much depending on the type of administration imposed on the schools by the central office. The question is how to handle routine work expeditiously and satisfactorily. Much will depend on the principal himself, his habits of work, his conception of the position, his ability as an organizer and systematizer, his sense of proportion, his mastery of the details of his work, and his ability to work through others. His capacity for getting work done will also be in part determined by the facilities at his disposal to expedite his work, such as a satisfactory office, desks, filing cabinets, typewriter, duplicator, good signal system, good blank forms, and above all, if the system can afford it, a good office clerk.

System and the man. In the great majority of schools and school systems the principal must work without the assistance of an office clerk. If he then is to secure adequate time for the real purpose of his presence — that of high-grade professional supervision and school leadership — he must find ways of cutting through the administrative routine and getting done the many little time-consuming but after all mediocre tasks that come up for handling in every school. One often hears a principal say that he simply can't find time for supervision, helping his teachers, or keeping abreast of his profession, because of the pressure of administrative details that cannot wait, such as pupil cases, seeing parents, answering the telephone, discipline, records, supplies, reports, forms, and sundry routine matters, and without an office clerk to carry these duties real supervision is with him impossible.

These duties no doubt cut down greatly the time available for supervision, and if given encouragement will take all of it, but they are not insurmountable. The introduction of system will do much to help find time for the more important duties, but other factors are involved besides the lack of system. Some men, due to certain personal limitations, such as lack of a time-sense or a sense of values and proportion, could not operate a good system were it devised for them. A, for example, treats all cases as about of equal value, gives too much time to individuals, and is always behind in his work and his engagements. B has such an exaggerated idea as to form, neatness, promptness, and accuracy that the mechanical phases of his work keep him tied to his office desk. C feels so personally responsible for everything that he tries to do everything himself, and never clears the way for really big things. D, who could organize and do better, chafes so under the necessity of the mechanical work of his office that he spends his time and energy in condemnation of the system and wishing for different conditions, instead of working out a scheme of things that will lead to his emancipation. The trouble with E is that he is as yet so little the master of his work that he does not see beyond the minor and more pressing problems of his situation.

The school without an office clerk. In a school where the principal must handle all the office details himself, keep his own records, write his own letters, compile his own reports, care for the stock room, answer the telephone, and see pupils and parents, the task is hopeless without good system, if any real supervision is to be done. The principal must adopt some workable scheme for economizing time and working quickly. He must also expect to remain at his building and work after school hours. If he trusts to chance he is almost certain gradually to become an office principal and be forever busy with letters, reports, supplies, pupils, the telephone, and the minute details of his work.

The first thing to do then, as soon as the principal gets his school started in the autumn and sees the run of the work, assuming him to be new to the position, is to draw up a tentative working schedule of work, somewhat after the plan of the one given in Form 1, page 51. If the principal finds that the program cannot be followed, even when he conserves his time, he should readjust the program to a more workable basis. He must keep in mind, though, that the chief difficulty will lie in keeping to his program rather than in making it, and that if he is to save time for important work he must try hard to follow his program rather than readjust it. The more he allows the details and office work to run over their allotted time the more they will continue to run over. It is better to try to reorganize the work, and to find means of getting through the details more rapidly. It is true that any working schedule will be upset from time to time by unexpected happenings or special occasions. In such situations the schedule will of course have to be temporarily set aside. The merit of the schedule will be that as soon as the interruption passes the principal may turn to the thing that should be done next, rather than starting in in a haphazard manner on anything he may happen to think of, or wasting time trying to decide where to begin or what to do.

Classifying duties and organizing a working schedule. The duties of every principal naturally classify themselves under: — (1) regular duties, that is duties which must be looked after every day; and (2) those occasional duties which come up irregularly or only at stated intervals. These may be arranged, somewhat as follows:

I. REGULAR DUTIES.
  1. Early arrival at school building. (8.00)
  2. Morning inspection of building and grounds. This should be done early, before teachers and pupils arrive. (8.05 – 8.15)
  3. Hasty glance over office, desk, program for day's work, and any list of things to be done or attended to. Fill in time with any minor detail work at hand. (8.15 – 8.35)
  4. Teachers and pupils arriving, and possibly parents. Time best spent in the hallways or near front or office door, where cases can be attended to standing, and time saved. This is no time for the principal to go into his office with callers and sit down. Assembling of school. (8.35 – 9.00)
  5. Morning assembly of pupils, if there be an assembly hall that will accommodate the school. (9.00 – 9.10)
  6. Short period at office, seeing pupils sent there by teachers, receiving reports as to attendance, starting attendance officer on his work, doing necessary telephoning to central office, and glancing hastily over office mail for anything of special importance. (9.15 – 9.30)
  7. School supervision, giving the best hours of the day to the work. (9.30 – 11.45)
  8. Minor office work, — tardy reports, fill out and file supervision records. (11.45 – 12.00)

Noon Hour

9. Same as No. 4 in morning, moving about building and grounds, overseeing conditions, and settling minor matters with quick decisions. (12.40 – 1.00)
10. Short office period for pupil cases, "good-work" interviews, afternoon attendance records, attention to mail, and filling out reports and records demanded by system. (1.00 – 2.00)
11. School supervision; on stated days principals' meetings. (2.00 – 3.00)

    Note: Numbers 10 and 11 to alternate as necessary, so as to cover supervision of work from 1.00 – 2.00.

12. Office Hour, Mondays, Wednesdays, and Fridays. Announce office hours " from 3.00," so as to get business in promptly, and fill in all vacant time to 4.00 with routine work, such as records, reports, requisitions, letters, memoranda filings, etc. (3.00 – 4.00)

    Teachers' Meetings on alternate Tuesdays; Parent-Teacher Meetings on alternate Thursdays.

13. Clean up office work, arrange bulletin board, plan coming day's work, and leave by 4.15 to 4.30.

II. OCCASIONAL DUTIES.
1. Special conferences and disciplinary cases.
2. Checking up the supply room, and ordering supplies.
3. Special monthly and term reports.
4. Meetings of parent-teacher, pupil organizations, and neighborhood clubs.
5. Special problems in school organization and the supervision of instruction.

From such a list it will be seen that a working schedule can be prepared, once a school is under way, which will leave the principal, working without an office clerk, from three to three and a half hours, on most days of the week, for the work of school supervision and such other important duties in connection with the progress of pupils through the school as may need attention. A principal who has a good office clerk ought to find still more. By organization and system the principal who really wants to do so may shake himself partially free from the much magnified clerical and office demands, and be able to devote his powers, on most school days, to the educational problems connected with the instruction in his school. There will come times, naturally, when a principal may have to spend a half-day or even a whole day consecutively at his desk, because some important problem may need to be worked out before other matters dependent on it can proceed. Most big problems, though, should be thought out and planned away from the interruptions of the office.

Minor schemes for saving time. To carry out such a working schedule the principal must resolve to cut himself loose from clerical duties by minimizing their importance, attending to them after hours, and making time by cutting off all unnecessary wastes and drains on his time. Teachers should be asked and expected to do everything of a clerical nature pertaining to the work of their room or class that they can possibly do. Train teachers to assume responsibility, and to handle minor matters themselves. Notes from pupils' homes can be handled by the classroom teachers, when regular, and sent to the office only when office approval is needed and at times when the principal is likely to be there. Clear instructions given teachers, at the teachers' meetings early in the year, can be made to save much office time. Teachers should be trained not to expect to find the principal in his office except at the hours stated, and should not refer matters or pupils to the office except at these hours. In special emergencies a pupil may be sent to find the principal, or the signal for the principal may be sounded on the gong. The issuing of supplies and textbooks should take place only at stated times, or may be placed in charge of the janitor, who will file the charge and credit slips and see that they are properly made out.

A pull-gong signal system, by which a loud gong, **centrally** located, may be pulled to give signals, is a very desirable addition to a school's equipment, and can be made into a time-saver. By the gong should be a card giving the signal code, such as:

EMERGENCY SIGNALS

1 stroke, Janitor wanted
2 strokes, Principal wanted
3 strokes, Medical Officer (or School Nurse) arriving

Another good device is a bulletin board, upon which is placed the daily registration sheet for teachers, and all special and general notices of interest or importance to teachers. Notices which all teachers should read should be so indicated, a pencil on a string be near, and all teachers, on reading, be expected to pencil their initials beneath the notice. A mail box for each teacher and for the janitor, just outside the general office door, is also another good device. Into this all mail or instructions for teachers or janitor may be placed, including also circulars, report forms, returned pupils' notes, and any material to be distributed. Teachers may call for these, or the janitor or a pupil may distribute at some fixed time each day. Pupils in the manual training work can make the bulletin board and mail boxes if the school does not have them.

The school with an office clerk. Only the larger schools may be expected to be provided with an office clerk, but where such a helper is provided she can be made very useful. In a school of a dozen to fifteen teachers a clerk ought to be provided, beginning with those schools where there are principals who can use a clerk to the best advantage and gradually extending the plan. She can handle the supply room, deal with many pupil cases, get rid of callers the principal should not waste time on, answer the inquiries of many parents and make engagements for the principal with others, answer the telephone, reply to much of the mail, make and file records, fill out requisitions, compile many of the school reports, execute many directions from the principal as to work or people to call up and see, remind the principal of things to be done in case he forgets, and manage the office and answer inquiries in his absence. Of course the larger the school the more there will be to be done, but with a good clerk on the one hand and a principal who knows how to use helpers on the other, the principal ought on an average to give sixty per cent of the time the school is in session to educational and supervisory work.

Office hours. A principal needs to have some definite office hours to systematize the calls of parents. These hours can be posted in the lower hall where all can see, be printed on a little card to be enclosed in notes when a call is desired, be printed on his letter heads, and otherwise be made generally known. Some such plan as the following will be good for all but the larger schools:

```
Daily   — 8.40 to 9.00, (In hallways or office.)
  "     — 12.40 to 1.00, (In    "       "    ")
M.W.F.  — 3.00 to 4.00, (In office.)
```

In all conferences it is important that the principal meet parents pleasantly, but that he expedite business as much as possible. Some callers — for instance a wrathy parent — will have to be heard through, but most cases can and should be heard and decided quickly. How rapidly the principal can handle people will depend somewhat on the ways and habits of the community itself. In a city people are used to rapid action, but in small places, where time is worth less, people are not used to being handled rapidly and sometimes resent it if not permitted to talk themselves out. The principal then must learn to size up people and situations quickly and plan ways for getting through without giving offense. If there is an office clerk, make liberal use of her by giving directions, and having the parent explain details to her. If there are a number of people waiting, it may be wise to sort out the short cases first. If there is likely to be anything disagreeable in an interview, train the clerk, at a certain signal, to take notes of what is said. With a copy of the conversation, by a reliable witness, there is little danger of being caught in an unpleasant situation without adequate defense.

One of the most wasteful features of the office hour, to most young principals and to many older ones, is that of keeping busy when no visitors are about. It is relatively easy to spend the vacant time in musing, walking about, or looking out of the window. This is an unnecessary waste. A desk nearly always has something on it waiting for attention, and these odd minutes can be made very useful. One of the best devices is to jot down on a card work to be done, or have two or three classified cards, or a little note book, and then keep these before one as one works. Some days there may be little to do, and on other days a dozen or more little things. As each is attended to, scratch it off. When all are done throw away the card; if one or two remain, transfer to a new card and start over the next day. In this way it is relatively easy to utilize moments that would otherwise be lost. Such an organization of details helps immensely in office work as well. One cannot regulate the time of callers, but the plan should be to have plenty of fill-up work to put in time on. One can accomplish much in odd moments if he sorts out and saves up for them those little details and odd jobs which do not require careful or continuous thinking, and which may be dropped anywhere and taken up again easily.

2. Supplies and the storeroom

Types of supplies required. The rules and regulations of boards of education commonly hold the principal responsible for the ordering and care of the needed school supplies and the equipment of his school, and the superintendent's office, to a greater or lesser degree, holds him responsible for their proper and economical use. The supplies used about a school may be classified under a number of heads, somewhat as follows:

1. *Janitor's supplies.* These include cleaning compounds, soaps, towels, toilet paper, mops, brushes, floor oil, sweeping compounds, dusters, window brushes and driers, pails, dust pans, gas mantles, electric bulbs, thermometers, waste paper baskets, nails and screws, paints and oils, tools, ink, and similar material.
2. *Blank forms and office supplies.* These include the various blank forms used by principal, teachers, and janitor, and such office supplies as letter paper, envelopes, postage stamps, thumb tacks, mucilage, rubber stamps, and paper fasteners.
3. *Instructional supplies.* These include chalk, erasers, pointers, blank paper of all kinds, pencils, penholders and pens, writing pads, blotters, paste, twine, rulers, blank books, and similar material consumed in office work or classroom instruction.
4. *Textbooks and supplemental books.* These include the regular free textbooks supplied pupils, the free texts supplied indigents if free books are not supplied generally, the desk books supplied teachers, and the supplemental books supplied for instruction.
5. *Special supplies.* These include kindergarten material, special primary-grade material, and materials used in manual training, domestic science, sewing, art, and science instruction. They also include, if furnished by the school, all play material, such as balls, bats, nets, and similar equipment. Still further they may include such more-expensive, less-frequently-used, and more-easily-broken supplies, such as lantern slides, stereoscopes and views, maps, charts, pictures, knives, scissors, and special pieces of teaching apparatus.
6. *Health-work supplies.* These include all material needed in the first-aid cabinet, and special materials used by the nurses and health inspectors on their visits or in their clinics.
7. *Fuel.* Wood, coal, and kindling.

Ordering these supplies. Different school systems have

different methods for furnishing these supplies to schools, but the most common way is to provide the school with an initial supply in the autumn, and then deliver additional supplies each month, as requisitioned for by the school principal. Supplemental and reference books are supplied as needed, as are wood and coal, while orders for special material needed and not in the stock rooms are usually honored as received.

Different forms of requisition blanks are usually supplied schools on which to order the supplies needed. The janitor requisitions for his supplies as needed, the principal approving the requisition and forwarding it to the central office. The janitor usually telephones to the central office his needs as to wood and coal. The janitor also verifies, and signs and issues receipts for all coal, wood, and general supplies delivered at the school. He also issues orders for pay for removing each load of garbage or ashes, and often verifies the readings each month of the water, gas, and electric light meters. The principal or his clerk must keep up the stock of instructional supplies, office supplies, and blank forms by watching his supply room and ordering properly in advance, while the special teachers and the school nurse will be expected to make their requisitions to him, similarly, for the special supplies they need for their work. The regular textbooks and desk books are usually supplied not more than twice a year, and the indigent books and supplemental books as needed for instruction. Special orders need the oversight and approval of the principal. If the school has a small expense budget, small items needed in a hurry may be purchased in the neighborhood.

Toward the close of each year the principal is usually expected to give an estimate to the central office, based on the past requirements and the expected future increases, of the amount and kind of supplies needed by the school the coming year. At the close of the year he is usually expected to make out an inventory of all supplies and equipment on hand, and for this purpose he either gathers into the stockroom all instructional supplies from the rooms, or has each teacher give him an inventory of the supplies in each class or special room. The latter is the easier way, unless there is some special reason for gathering up the supplies. The special supplies are inventoried by the special teachers. The principal is also expected, before leaving for his vacation, to file a requisition for enough of all kinds of supplies to start the school in the autumn and carry it along the first month. In some school systems, or for some kinds of supplies, the requisition is for the half year. Then month by month, or term by term, the principal is expected to supply the central office, by a certain day, with requisitions for all additional supplies needed. These are then sent on certain days from the general storeroom, or by the dealers to the school, and the principal or janitor must inspect the delivery and receipt for the supplies.

Giving out the supplies. The janitor's supplies are kept in the janitor's storeroom, and used as needed. The principal merely has in his office a duplicate inventory and requisition record, from which he can check up the amount of each supply used. The blank forms will be stored in a cabinet or drawer in the principal's office, or in the adjacent storeroom. The office supplies and the instructional supplies will be kept in the general storeroom, and distributed to the rooms as needed. The special supplies needed in the kindergarten, primary grades, manual training, domestic science, and sewing will best be stored in the special rooms. The play equipment should be in the basement or the gymnasium, and some special pupil or teacher checking-in-and-out system devised for it. New equipment should go through the storeroom. All books not in use should be on the shelves of the storeroom.

To retain control of the supplies, and be able to check waste, a number of different plans are in use in different cities, and these plans run from the extreme of keeping everything under lock, and the principal carrying the keys, to an open storeroom where teachers may help themselves. The former is too wasteful a method to be tolerated, yet the writer once examined one large city school system where this plan was followed. Supplies were given out in doles, under a false idea of economy, and it was necessary to find the principal and have him unlock the door every time anything was needed. He became, in reality, "a hander out of chalk and paper." Of the two plans the open storeroom is preferable, as any waste in supplies is many times counterbalanced by the saving of the time of the most highly paid employee of the school.

If the principal has an office clerk she can handle the storeroom and oversee all income and outgo, but, if not, a plan somewhat after one of the following can be made to work easily and well.

If the schoolrooms are provided with a closet for room supplies, as most schoolrooms are, have placed in each room, at the beginning of school in the autumn, a reasonable quantity of materials, say enough to run five or six weeks. Train the teachers to anticipate their needs, as far as possible, and get new supplies at stated times once a month, or at most once each week. Hang the key to the storeroom in a known place in the office, so that special or unexpected needs may be attended to and charged by the teachers themselves. This plan places on the teacher the responsibility for accounting for what is taken. Another plan which centralizes responsibility on the janitor is to have him attend to all orders or wants of the teachers, taking their requisition slips to the storeroom, placing them on the file, and bringing back to the rooms the material needed. It is usually not advisable that pupils be sent to the general storeroom for supplies.

Keeping records and charging. No supplies should be taken or issued except on the filing of a simple requisition, or charge slip, dated, listing everything and the amount wanted or taken, and signed by the teacher desiring the supplies. All such charge slips are to be put on a file from which they will be taken, from time to time, by the principal or his clerk, for record and tabulation. If supplies are issued ordinarily only once a month, a monthly requisition can be made out by the teacher, and then charge slips are used only for special items. The trouble with any insistence on a monthly requisition is that it is hard for new teachers to anticipate needs and order enough and not too much, and the fixed plan tends to interfere with instructional needs. Teachers go without supplies, or borrow from one another, rather than ask the principal for more.

Some simple plan, such as one of the above, will prove satisfactory in nearly all schools, and will obviate the necessity for any elaborate requisition form, prior approval by principal, issuance of duplicate "I charge you" slips to be signed by the teacher, and the return of these slips to the office for record.

Nor need there be any elaborate bookkeeping. The charge slips form an account with each teacher, and from these once or twice a year a tabulation can be made and undue waste seen and checked. The record for instructional supplies need only contain date, item, quantity, and signature, as they are not expected to come back. Books, maps, globes, lantern slides, and apparatus are different — especially books. For these devise as simple a charging system as is definite and workable. A card, on which can be entered date and signature when taken and returned, answers for most pieces of supply. For books a charge card for each book or set of books may be kept, or, easier still, a large card can be thumb-tacked to a drawing board fastened on the door, and ruled so as to carry a complete record of all books in the school.

By some such simple means as the above the principal can so organize the supply problem that it will not cost him more than a couple of hours a month at most. With an office clerk to attend to the ordering, storing, and charging, it need require hardly any attention.

3. A small school budget

Need for and use of. The school department furnishes each school with a definite list of supplies, this being larger in some cities than in others. Often in cities the list previously given (page 194) of "5, Special Supplies," will be strictly limited, while "6, Health-Work Supplies," will not be furnished at all. In other cities, though these may be furnished, in whole or in part, it is difficult to get new or special items added to the list. Yet in the administration of every school building many little unforeseen and unclassified items of expense arise during the year that are legitimate school expenditures. Many of them are too trivial, and many of them are of too irregular a nature to bring before the central office or board of education on requisition, and as a result the principal either pays for them or the school goes without what are often minor necessities. Some principals shoulder the burden uncomplainingly, while others refuse to provide many small expense items that would minister to the smooth and efficient administration of the school.

In many school systems an attempt has been made to meet this by authorizing entertainments to raise funds for special school purposes, or by allowing the principal a small budget for minor miscellaneous expenses, or, still better, by both. Money raised by entertainments is best used for special purposes, such as the purchase of playground equipment, a phonograph, a lantern, pictures, or some analogous expenditure. The budget for minor miscellaneous expenses can be made to cover a host of needs, such as express on exhibits, telegrams, toll telephone calls, car tickets for messengers, pupils sent home because of illness or accident, taxi fares for the same purpose, printing of school programs, postage, decorations for special occasions, copies of playlets to be put on, renting of costumes for free entertainments, ribbon, pennants, Christmas tree, display material, crêpe paper, drayage, supplies for the first-aid cabinet, folk-dance music, baseballs and bats, basket balls and volley balls, minor expenses of speakers or musicians, emergency janitor or teacher supplies, some little change about the building, etc.

Apportionment and accounting. The common plan is either to allow the principal a definite amount per half-year, generally about $50.00, or a definite amount per pupil enrolled for each half year, such as 10 cents per pupil. This amount the principal is allowed to pay out, and from time to time is reimbursed by check on the submission of an itemized petty-fund account. Money raised by special entertainments within the school is likewise to be spent under the direction or requisition of the principal, though when any large item is to be bought it is best to purchase it through the school purchasing department.

The school principal is a business manager as well as an educator, managing a $20,000 to $50,000 a year business, and he should be allowed what business superintendents generally are allowed — a small petty-expense fund for contingencies and minor miscellaneous purchases. To keep a record of receipts and expenses is simple and will require but little time. If the principal has an office clerk she can attend to it all. The whole record can be kept on a card, or a sheet of ledger paper.

Another special budget item sometimes granted, and one which is best done quietly, is one for the purchase of milk, eggs, butter, soups, cereals, etc., for the special school feeding of the children of poor and often ignorant parents, many of whom are undernourished, anæmic, or tubercular. A special budget of $50.00 per half year for this purpose would add greatly to the efficiency of the instruction given such children in many a school.

4. *Blank forms and reports*

Blanks for pupils and parents. In the office of the principal of every school, large or small, quite a number of blank forms must be kept on hand, and a certain number of required reports must be made to the central office. The making of certain statistical reports to the central office is a necessity, though the matter is often overdone. Not infrequently reporting is made more time-consuming than necessary because the report forms from teachers to principal and from principal to the central office do not have the items arranged in similar order. On the other hand, the more printed forms available for charging, requisitions, notices to pupils and parents, and for sending information to the central office the better. These forms require only the filling in of a name or a brief statement of facts, and the signature of the teacher or principal. It is quite important, though, that these printed forms be couched in good language, and that the information they contain as to pupil conduct or studies be so stated as to elicit coöperation instead of awakening resentment. While the blanks used by any city are determined by the central authorities, and the principal must use what is given him, yet he always has a chance, in principals' meeting or in personal conferences, to suggest improvements.

A list of some of the more commonly used blanks relating to pupils will serve to indicate the nature of the forms a principal may expect to find in use in the administration of his school.

I. Forms needed especially at the beginning of each term.
  1. General printed statement as to conditions of admission to school, to be given to parents, and containing the school calendar and the more important regulations relating to attendance, books, etc.
  2. New-pupil assignment cards.
  *3. Pupil registration cards, giving pupil and home data.
  *4. List of books to buy, if free books are not furnished.
  5. Notice as to tuition dues, for non-resident pupils admitted.
  *6. Vaccination notice.
  7. Pupil cumulative record cards.

II. Forms needed at close of each term.
  †1. Promotion cards.
  †2. Pupil term reports (also often monthly forms).
  3. Application blank for summer-school privileges.
  4. Age and schooling certificate.
  5. Work permit.
  6. Reports on pupils and work.

III. Forms needed at any time.
  1. Transfer cards.
  *2. Principal's tardy and absence notice for parents.
  *3. Excuse form for 2.
  *4. Inquiry form as to absence from school.
  †5. Notice of pupil failure in studies.
  †6. Notice of pupil delinquency.
  7. Notice of suspension of a pupil.
  8. Notice of expulsion of a pupil.
  9. Transfer to special class.
  10. Transfer to disciplinary class.
  11. Transfer to parental school.
  †12. Extra-promotion form.
  *13. Request to parent to call and see teacher (or principal) regarding pupil's work or conduct.
  †14. Notice as to lack of cleanliness.

* Means that this blank can be filled out and sent or used by teachers.

† Means that this blank may be filled out by the teacher, but not to be sent home or used without consent of principal.

15. Notice as to exclusion from school.
16. Notice as to physical defects needing attention.
17. Accident-record cards.

Other blanks and forms used in the school. In addition to the above for use with pupils and parents, there are numerous other blanks and report forms commonly used in schools, which may be listed here. Not all are used in every school system, and often two or more are combined in one. These are:

I. Janitor's forms.
  1. Monthly report form.
  §2. Annual report and estimate form.
  §3. Inventory form.
  4. Requisition for supplies.
  5. Request for repairs.
  6. Coal receipt record.
  7. Ashes and garbage disposal record.

II. Special forms.
  1. Manual training.
  2. Domestic science.
  3. Drawing and art.
  4. Health department.
      a. Pupil records, examination reports, parent notices, etc.
      b. Nurse information, records, reports, quarantine reports, etc.
  5. Home visiting-teacher form.
  6. Attendance officer forms.

III. Teachers' forms, for reporting to office of principal.
  1. Daily reports on absences and tardies, for attendance department information.
  ‡2. Special reports on a pupil's work.
  3. Discipline report. (Used usually only in large cities.)
  4. Weekly outline of work.
  5. Seating diagrams.
  6. Program cards.
  ‡7. Directory data cards.

§ To be filled out as called for by the central office.
‡ To be filled out as called for by the principal.

8. Requisition for supplies.
9. Monthly report form.
10. Term report form.
11. Semiannual class promotion sheet.
12. Semiannual class record sheet.
13. Annual term report form.
14. Annual inventory form.
15. Summer addresses of teachers and principal.

IV. Teacher's pupil-and-room records.
1. School register.
2. Special record cards, as needed.

V. Forms used by the principal in reporting to the central office.
1. Room and grade classification sheet. (Numbers, and vacant seats.)
2. Age and grade classification sheet.
3. Order for books for indigents.
4. Report on tuition pupils enrolled.
5. General and special requisition forms.
6. General monthly report form.
7. Monthly report on pupils leaving school.
8. Monthly report on moneys collected, and expended.
9. Monthly report on attendance and tardiness of teachers.
10. Monthly pay roll for teachers and janitor.
11. Monthly requisition for supplies and equipment.
12. Monthly report on disciplinary cases.
13. Monthly report on use of building.
14. Monthly report on special promotions.
15. Semiannual promotion sheet.
16. Semiannual report on 6A, 8A, or 9A graduates. (Varying with the type of school.)
17. Semiannual estimate as to classes the following term.
18. Report on work of substitute teachers.
19. Report on work of special teachers.
20. Report on work of classroom teachers.
21. General annual report form.
22. Annual report on seats, and condition of building.
23. Annual inventory form.
24. Annual book records and report.
25. Annual report on building needs.
26. Annual estimate of supplies needed for following year.

VI. Office record forms.
1. Pupil continuous record cards.

2. Various cumulative records, for a series of years.

(A *Record Book for Elementary School Principals*, such as the one by that title devised by Strayer and Englehardt, and published by C. F. Williams and Son, Inc., Albany, New York, gives the principal a choice of a large number of records, which may be kept for a series of years and in good form for easy reference.)

5. *Relations with the central office*

Punctuality and proper form. Promptness, punctuality, courtesy, and respect for authority are prime essentials in a successful principal. In the matter of reports and requisitions certain principals are almost always late, while certain others can be counted on to get their reports in on time or a little ahead of time. The same is true of teachers in the matter of their reports to the principal. The supply clerk cannot combine requisitions and place orders, the superintendent of schools cannot complete his statistical report for the board of education, and the principal cannot complete his report for the superintendent of schools because some one person along the line is late. An occasional failure, due to illness or overwork, can be passed over, but the delay becomes exasperating when caused month by month by the same small group of unbusinesslike teachers and principals.

The delay is usually wholly unnecessary. The thing for the principal to do is to anticipate his work, and see to it that his teachers do the same. Often he must anticipate it for them. The same principles so frequently mentioned as means of saving time and expediting work, applied to reports, will produce similar results.

Courtesy and respect for authority too are essential. The superintendent of schools, business manager, attendance officer, and health officer may all be inferior to the principal in education, knowledge of their work, or in culture and refinement, yet they hold certain positions which represent authority and in such should be given the same respect that the principal would like to have extended to him as head of his school. One can be friendly without being familiar, respectful without being obsequious, and can accept decisions and carry them out without kow-tow-ing. In addressing communications to his superiors in office, a polite acknowledgment of relationships is an evidence of good breeding. At the heading of the letter and on the envelope, of all official communications, put the officer's official title. Do not address the letter or the envelope to "John Jones," or to "Supt. John Jones," or to "John Jones, Supt. of Schs.," but take time to spell out the words and to address your communication to "Mr. John Jones, Superintendent of City Schools," and head your letter "Dear Sir," or "Dear Superintendent Jones," according to the nature of the communication and the extent of your acquaintance. Besides being in proper form, and evidencing a gentleman, such little courtesies actually pay in the long run. The same is true of the other officers connected with the school system.

QUESTIONS AND PROBLEMS

1. Can you characterize principals you have known who represent different types from those described under A to E, on page 186? If so, do so.
2. Plan a working schedule, similar to Form 1, page 51, for the last month of school.
3. Have you anything to add to or to change in the tentative daily Program for the principal, given on pages 188–89?
4. Most people waste an inordinate amount of time in purposeless talk and inability to state quickly a problem or an issue. This human characteristic will cause a principal to waste much valuable time from his five valuable school-session hours if he is not careful. Suggest other means, than those mentioned in the text, for preventing waste of time in this way, and at the same time without giving offense to parents or teachers.
5. In establishing such office hours as those given on page 192, should a new principal hold rigidly to them at first, or should he gradually train people to know and to follow them? Why?

BUSINESS ORGANIZATION

6. How will a principal's ability to establish such hours vary with:
    a. The character of the neighborhood?
    b. The size of the school?
    c. The presence or lack of an office clerk?
    d. The traditions and habits of the community?
7. Outline a simple plan by which a principal could make a semi-annual per-pupil check of instructional supplies used by each teacher in his building.
8. Should the principal know the actual and relative consumption of fuel by his janitor? Why?
9. Make up a single charge-and-credit slip, for use by teachers in securing or returning:
    a. Instructional supplies.
    b. Special supplies.
    c. Desk and reference books.
    d. Supplemental readers.
10. Prepare a monthly account statement, for the superintendent's office, showing status of and expenditures from:
    a. The petty school budget.
    b. The special pupil-feeding fund.
11. The Superintendent of Schools has, by general letter, asked all principals in the city to make a brief report to him, in writing, as to the difficulties now experienced, if any, in the matter of pupils securing their textbooks promptly, and whether, in the judgment of the principals, the difficulties encountered are such as would warrant the Board of Education in supplying free textbooks, in whole or in part.

    Prepare your report on the matter, in proper form, for forwarding to the superintendent's office.

SELECTED REFERENCES

Ayres, May, Williams, J. F., and Wood, T. D. *Healthful Schools.* 292 pp., Illustrated, Boston, 1919.
> A very useful book. Contains good chapters on school housekeeping, the work of the school janitor, and heating and ventilation.

Boggs, J. "School Board Regulations concerning the Elementary School Principal"; in *Elementary School Journal*, vol. 20, pp. 730–39. (June, 1920.)
> Tabulates for thirty cities; quotes sample rules; and compares with Reavis' study, and Nutt's study. Classifies duties.

Finney, R. L., and Schafer, A. L. *The Administration of Village and Consolidated Schools.* 298 pp., New York, 1920.
> Part IV, Chapters XIII–XV, deals with the material equipment of a school, school housekeeping, records, accounts, and reports. Chapter XV reproduces many blank forms used.

Nelson, B. E. "How can the Ward School Principal be of Most Service?" in *Proceedings*, National Education Association, 1909, pp. 324–26.
> Good on the administrative and supervisory work of a school principal.

Nutt, H. W. "The Duties of an Elementary School Principal"; in *Elementary School Journal*, vol. 19, pp. 174–97. (November, 1918.)

Perry, A. C., Jr. *The Management of a City School.* 434 pp., 2d ed., New York, 1919.
> Chapter III, on the Principal and the Public, is good on interviews, notes to the home, and correspondence with parents. Chapter VI deals with heating, lighting, supplies, and work of janitor.

Reavis, W. C. "Duties of the Supervising Principal"; in *Elementary School Journal*, vol. 19, pp. 279–84. (December, 1918.)

Strayer, G. D., and Englehardt, N. L. *Record Book for Elementary School Principals.* C. F. Williams & Son, Albany, 1918.
> A useful loose-leaf book of forms for record keeping.

CHAPTER XI

THE SCHOOL JANITOR AND HIS WORK

The position, and janitorial types. It is often and quite truthfully said that the most important individual about any large school building, after the principal, is the school janitor. Outside of the principal, no one has more influence over the physical well-being of the children in the school than has the janitor. It is he who under-heats or over-heats the classrooms, controls the ventilation, cleans the building properly or does not, and keeps the toilet facilities in proper order if they are so kept. He is often a potent influence in the discipline of the school; he knows the good and the poor teachers of the school as few other persons do; and he is often an influential factor in the formation of neighborhood opinion as to the school and the principal.

Important as the position appears to be, he is the only official in the school who is not required to have any training for his work. Despite the marked improvement in janitor service which has taken place in the past quarter-century, in few of our cities is there as yet any adequate conception of the importance of the position, or any standards for the man's selection. Sometimes, when the salary paid is low, any one who will apply will be taken. Sometimes, even when the salary is satisfactory, the long hours and the numerous "bosses" keep good men from seeking the appointment. Sometimes one finds cities where the place is a political sinecure, and the janitor a powerful personality in the politics of his district. The writer has been told of two cases in which janitors have been elected to the school board, and one in which the janitor was elected as a member of the city council, a body which in that city fixed the school department annual budget. Occasionally, in the smaller cities, one finds the janitors are political pensioners, and in such a case the principal often is compelled not to see too much or to expect too much.

In most cases, though, the janitor, man or woman, is just an ordinary individual, unskilled in any line of work, ignorant of sanitary standards and educational needs, sometimes grouchy, sometimes pig-headed, but usually quite human, amenable to kind treatment, and willing to do about what seems to him as fair and reasonable for the pay he receives, and not much more.

If one could choose his janitor he would set up as standards such qualities as good moral character, cleanly personal habits and speech, reasonably good English, an interest in and a right attitude toward children, and a willingness to be useful and to learn. This last is more important than initial skill. A young man is usually better than an old man, and a married man than one who is single. The kind of work he has been engaged in before is often indicative of the type of janitor the person will make. The best three janitors the writer has known, two men and a woman, had previously been a carpenter, a pastor of a little church, and a nurse with inadequate preparation.

Varied nature of the janitor's work. The school janitor who is efficient and useful has a varied task, with at times hard work and long hours, and under modern conditions he is expected to manage complicated processes and do technical work for which he seldom has any preparation. In a modern school building to-day there are complicated heating and ventilating plants, electric switches, vacuum cleaning equipment, electric motors, and, in dirty cities, expensive airwashing machines. The building, too, has special rooms, equipped with expensive and often delicate apparatus. The work calls for a combination of a good housekeeper, a sanitary expert, a carpenter, a plumber, an electrician, and an engineer. There is as yet, though, scarcely anywhere any training given for the work, even to those in service.

Janitors, especially men janitors, certainly are not born, but must be made. This task devolves on the principal, and it is for him to get satisfactory service from unskilled and often unintelligent labor, and to develop some pride in good work in a man of no perspective. The janitor usually does his work by rule of thumb, and often sees no reason for many of the things he is required to do. Particularly does he usually fail to appreciate the sanitary aspect of his work, and considers many of the requirements as sheer nonsense. Fresh air and sunlight he often seems afraid of, and dust usually has no terrors for him.

In winter the janitor must be on hand before daylight to get the fires started and the building warm. He must shovel coal, ashes, and snow, and dispose of dirt, paper waste, and garbage. He must clean the building daily and in a sanitary manner. He must act as general repair man, doing bits of carpenter work, plumbing, painting, wiring, and oiling. Doors, seats, hinges, sidewalks, tree-protection frames, and loose things generally call for his attention. He is under obligations to afford police protection to his building and grounds. He receives supplies as delivered, keeps an eye on strangers, admits workmen to the building and keeps an account of their labor, and answers the doorbell when the building is closed. It is his duty to assist the principal with discipline, especially as it relates to the basement and toilets. If he understands children he can be very helpful. He is a sort of chore boy for all the teachers. They call upon him to bring them supplies, hang pictures, open windows, put up shelves, oil rusty locks and hinges, fill ink wells, and adjust seats as directed. He must work in the dirt of the basement, and yet, if summoned to a teacher's room or to the principal's office, he is expected to present a reasonably good appearance. Though teachers and principal at times are tired and peevish and fussy, he is expected to be always polite and good natured when asked to do something. The position is not an easy one to fill satisfactorily, the janitor often receives little education or training from the principal, and all in all is probably more often maligned than understood.

The task of the school principal. One measure of the success of a school principal and of his fitness for the position should be his ability to give any willing and reasonably intelligent janitor a large conception of his job, and to help him to see how important in the lives of children is the work he has to do. He must help the janitor to evaluate his work, establish in him standards of accomplishment, and must appreciate and encourage and protect him as long as he exhibits a willingness to try to render satisfactory service.

The principal going to a new position will do well to get acquainted with his janitor early, and take his measure well. It is good psychology to have the janitor show a new principal over the building, and explain things to the newcomer. A good janitor will nearly always show an interest and a helpful spirit, but if the principal finds a man who is secretive, grouchy, on the defensive from the start, and inclined to stand on his rights, it is best to ignore these qualities at first and try to warm him up a bit. Most janitors have too much to do, all are human, and almost all are sensitive to little courtesies and expressions of appreciation, as well as to criticism and attempts to drive them, or to impose on them what seem to them to be unreasonable requirements. It is well to understand these things and act accordingly. Perhaps the janitor is overworked and underpaid; perhaps he and the last principal did not get along well; perhaps the teachers are fussy and the pupils careless; perhaps he has troubles at home; perhaps his defensive attitude is merely that exhibition of bad manners and an "I'm as good as you" pose not infrequently shown by poorly educated working people toward those who wear better clothes and have better manners than they.

It may be just his way of showing you his conception of democracy. The probabilities, though, are that the principal is facing a situation in which ultimately he will need to know how far his authority will be supported when the test comes as to who is in control. If the janitor happens to be a janitress, the task may be still more unpleasant under such conditions. Even though this should be the case, little can be accomplished by posting rules and regulations, laying down the law prematurely, or nagging or scolding. The janitor may be lazy, incompetent when judged by fair standards, uncouth and rude, and even at times discourteous, and still one may have to get along with him for years to come. He certainly will be a trial, but he may not be entirely hopeless. Possibly the teachers in the school may exhibit some of the same characteristics; they may even be the characteristic traits of the people of the neighborhood. If so, here is a fine opportunity for a kindly, considerate gentleman to teach by example, even though at times he boils within. On the other hand the man may be ugly by nature and be trying out the new principal, and things may come to a crisis rapidly. If the test really comes the principal must possess power to deal with the janitor in a brief and pointed manner. The relation between principal and janitor is so close that friction between them soon impairs the efficiency of both, and when it does arise it is better to try a new janitor — or principal.

Administrative principles in dealing with the janitor. In nine cases out of ten, however, the principal will find instead a well-meaning janitor, possessed of ordinary average intelligence, and willing to try to please if he understands what is wanted and does not have what he considers unreasonable demands made upon him. The task of the principal is to get as good results as possible under such conditions. The problem presented is as varied as human nature itself, but there are certain administrative principles which underlie the relations between principal and janitor, and teachers and janitor, which should be observed. Briefly stated, these are:

1. Make your janitor feel that you are open to suggestions, and will welcome any ideas as to procedure that he may offer. If they are good, thank him and tell him so; if you cannot use them, explain to him why. The janitor often knows pupils and teachers well, and in addition possesses a fund of practical experience that can be made to contribute to the efficiency of the school.
2. The principal should stand ready to make the janitor's work as light as reasonably good service permits. To this end he should insist that he be provided with as good quarters and as good supplies as possible. Do not expect him to do good work with poor brooms and brushes and cleaning materials.
3. Keep in mind that his hours are long, and that he gets tired and sleepy just as other people do. Try to help him to adjust his work to a good schedule so as to lighten it when possible, and do not allow teachers to delay him unnecessarily in his work or make it difficult for him to do.
4. Protect him as far as possible from the fussy teachers of the building. Some women are never pleased with anything a man does, particularly in the line of housekeeping. Ask them not to find fault with him, especially in the presence of their pupils, but to bring their complaints to you.
5. Do not address him as "Janitor," or "George," but as "Mr. Strowbridge," and ask your teachers to do the same. When you give him instructions, do not say "Do so and so," but rather "Will you please do so and so." Don't forget to say "Good morning" to him, and if he tells you that his wife or baby is sick, ask him occasionally how they are getting along. If he works well and is attentive to little things, express appreciation from time to time. A "that's fine," or "I'm glad

THE SCHOOL JANITOR

you thought of that," helps very much. Have the teachers say such things to him, too, once in a while. In showing visitors about the building, do not ignore him, but ask him to explain things, though you might easily do it yourself.

6. Cultivate in him a feeling of ownership in the building and grounds, and occasionally take orders from him. You can afford to let him be a little important and officious provided he is rendering efficient service. Occasionally ask him if everything is all right, if he needs anything, how the furnace is working to-day, or "how much coal was burned last month," and how that compares with a year ago. Teach him to read the meters, if he does not know, and to figure out something as to maintenance costs. Occasionally give him an article relating to his work, as in the *School Board Journal*, or show him a picture of some new school or school appliance.

7. Cultivate in him a pride in doing his work, and help him to find better and more economical ways of doing things. Sometimes the suggestion that you will furnish the paint or varnish for some little job will start a regular clean-up about the building. If he is interested in having some flowers in the yard let him put them out, and if necessary train the pupils to let them alone.

8. Train pupils and teachers to help him in his work by keeping loose paper off floor and yard, by clearing desks in the afternoon, and by turning the seats ready for sweeping. It is much easier for forty pupils to pick up loose paper than for one man alone, and for four hundred boys and girls to learn to scrape their muddy feet than for one man to gather the dirt from the floors and stairs of the building. Such little courtesies are appreciated, and are besides good training in decent living procedure for boys and girls — especially for the boys. An assembly talk on the janitor and his work might be given once each year or two.

9. If the janitor has a grievance, let him tell it to you; if it is a reasonable one, remedy it if it relates to the school work. He is a human being and an American citizen, and as such has his rights. Many teachers are unreasonable and inconsiderate, and a janitor can often tell you things it is good for you to know. He has many opportunities for observing teacher's methods of class control.

10. It pays well in service, if the teachers and principal and janitor can work harmoniously together, to show the janitor some

little courtesies occasionally that come as the joint thoughtfulness of teachers and principal. A turkey at Thanksgiving, a box of cigars or some piece of wearing apparel at Christmas, and when the fine spring days come and there are no fires to keep up, a few days off until late afternoon to go fishing or to set out his garden, and the saving of some refreshments for him when these are served at the school, are little attentions that are much appreciated and pay big dividends.

Placing responsibility for service. Such a policy in handling a school janitor and getting work out of him does not mean that he is to be coddled to get him to do his work, or that he is to be given an exaggerated opinion of his own importance. Neither does it mean that he is to be allowed to dictate or to choose his own methods, duties, or hours. Such a policy does mean, however, that the principal is to take pains to get the janitor's viewpoint, to encourage suggestions, to give orders and directions to him in a tactful manner, to help soothe irritated feelings caused by thoughtless teachers with sharp tongues, and to endeavor to awaken in him ideals for his work and a pride in the appearance of his school.

At the same time have fixed standards of work and responsibility, and see that these are met. The rules and regulations of the school board usually cover most important points, and frequently there are supplemental instructions from the superintendent's office. Do not ostentatiously tack these up in his quarters, but inquire if he has a copy, or hand him any new instructions received. Assume that he reads and will follow these, but if they seem too unreasonable, in view of his other work, try to lighten his load. Have perfectly attainable standards, adapted to different types of days — clear and dry, rainy and muddy, snow and cold, parent-teacher days, entertainment-night days — and help him plan and shift his work so as to get along reasonably satisfactorily under different or vexatious conditions.

THE SCHOOL JANITOR

The janitor should know just what he is to do each day and week and month. He and the principal must agree upon what is a reasonable basis for judging the quality of the work, in case the principal is not satisfied with the way it is done. There are many degrees of "good" in the way a room may be swept, but it must be clearly understood what kind of sweeping will be accepted and what will not. After a definite understanding has been arrived at, if an understanding becomes necessary, the principal must see that the requirements are met, as any let-up in the case of an unsatisfactory janitor will be regarded as a chance to slight the work.

Reasonable standards for work. The question as to what are reasonable standards for work will vary somewhat in different cities, in different types of school buildings, in different seasons and conditions of weather, and somewhat also according to the size of the building and the amount of janitor assistance provided. The following at least, with sufficient service provided, seem reasonable standards upon which to insist:

1. That wooden floors in classrooms and main hallways should be thoroughly waxed or oiled twice a year, and cleaned once each day. Some hallways may need cleaning still oftener in bad weather.
2. That dampened sawdust or a sweeping compound should be used, and that dry sweeping or sprinkling floors should be prohibited.
3. That feather dusters should not be used, but dust cloths should be employed and the dust shaken out outside the building.
4. After sweeping the desks are to be wiped off, and the curtains left up so that the room may get all the sunlight possible.
5. Blackboards are to be cleaned each night.
6. Erasers and chalk troughs must be clept clean. If the school has a vacuum cleaning plant, the erasers may be cleaned by it in the basement; if not, then out of doors and away from the building.

7. Windows and doors are to be kept in repair, and windows cleaned on a schedule to be determined by local atmospheric conditions.
8. Electric light and gas fixtures are to be kept clean, and broken bulbs and gas mantles replaced.
9. Waste paper baskets to be emptied and contents burned daily.
10. Foot mats at entrances, steps, and hallways to be kept clean, shaking and brushing up as often as necessary.
11. Fire fighting apparatus to be inspected at stated periods, these being determined somewhat by the nature of the building.
12. Waste paper and trash never to be allowed to accumulate in basement or near furnace. Oiled rags to be hung up in the open air, and never kept in a closet or box.
13. Temperature to be as directed by principal, and fires to be started early enough to secure it by the time pupils begin to arrive.
14. Toilets to be inspected after each intermission, to see that they are clean and flushing properly.
15. Drinking fountains to be kept in repair.
16. Ventilating furnace for toilets, if there be one, to be kept running at all times during school hours.
17. Vacuum cleaning apparatus, where provided, to be used daily, as this obviates most of the dusting.

In the carrying out of these and other desirable regulations, leave as much discretion and choice of time to the janitor as service will permit. Whether he shall clean the schoolroom floors in the morning before teachers and pupils arrive or in the evening after they leave is immaterial, so long as they are in order when wanted. What is true of the sweeping is true of many other phases of the janitor's work.

Have the janitor responsible to but one person, and that person the principal. Teachers may of course ask him for little favors, but the constant giving of directions by too many people ultimately leads to friction and is not desirable. When teachers want things done that call for time and labor, it will be best if they make their requests through the principal, or at least ask the principal about it before speaking to the janitor. While hard and fast rules in such matters are not desirable, especially in small schools, it is well that the principal at least should first know of and approve of any special requests for janitorial service.

Estimating the janitor's work. While the above seem reasonable standards, they may be impossible of fulfillment at times due to extra work or unexpected happenings, or they may be impossible of fulfillment at all because the janitorial service provided is inadequate for the size of the building and the character of the work. It is important that the principal come to know just what the janitor has to do each day and week, and how long it takes him to keep the building in good condition. Careful observation of his work for a while will give the principal a basis for judging. Reasonable allowances must be made for bad weather conditions and extra occasions, and for the furnace work in winter. If the janitor is overworked, the principal should plead his cause with the superintendent or business office.

In time we shall doubtless have good rating cards for janitorial service, but as yet the cards devised leave much to be desired. One worked out a few years ago for Rockford, Illinois, tried to provide a quantitative measure of a janitor's work and standardize it on the basis of one man for an eight-classroom and office building. This gave 100 points for this size of building, distributed 75 on care of building and the heating plant, 15 on care of grounds, and 10 on coöperation with principal and teachers. The one recently worked out by the National Association of School Business and Accounting Officers, which is typical of most attempts to construct a rating card, neglects building size and conditions entirely, and rates the janitor on a number of items as superior, above average, average, below average, poor. Following the standards stated in this chapter, with adjustments and allowances for conditions, the principal can evaluate the work his janitor is expected to do and performs. The value of a rating sheet is that it provides a somewhat objective measure of efficiency that at times may be valuable.

The daily building inspection. Even assuming a good janitor the principal should never take chances on things being properly done, but should make a daily building inspection. As has been said before, the best time for this is on arrival in the morning, before teachers or pupils arrive. If the janitor knows that all his work, from cellar to roof, is to be inspected by the principal, he will tend to do his work better. Any manager of a business or an industrial plant will tell you that systematic inspection is one of the surest remedies known to cure inattention to duties. A janitor, fair or good, needs the tonic that comes from inspection as much as a teacher or a principal does. Every good housekeeper, too, finds constant supervision of servants indispensable to good results. In a few minutes, if things are as they should be, the principal can walk through the building and hastily note its condition. If things are not satisfactory he must first consider whether conditions and the amount of work to be done has made better work impossible. If the principal feels that the work ought to have been done, then he should ask the janitor the reason; if the excuse is unsatisfactory, he may ask the janitor to go and give immediate attention to what is wrong. In general this latter is not a wise plan, as it savors too much of the arbitrary exercise of authority, but there are occasions when failure to follow it would be a mistake.

The items to be looked after on this hasty building inspection include:

1. Condition of the classrooms — floors, desks, blackboards, erasers, chalk troughs, books, cloakrooms, etc.
2. The special rooms — office, teachers, lunch, emergency, music, drawing, manual training, domestic science, assembly hall — similarly examined.

3. The toilet rooms for conditions, lewd pictures, writing, toilet paper, towels, soap, cleanliness of wash bowls, etc.
4. The basement for cleanliness, the furnaces for general condition and the small ventilating furnace, where such is a part of the equipment, to see that it is in use.
5. The halls and stairways, for cleanliness and general appearance.
6. Small repairs needed, any over-night damage to building or grounds.
7. The playgrounds, play apparatus, shrubbery, walks, fences, etc.

It is well also to pass into the toilet rooms occasionally during the day, to see that all continues well. In time a principal becomes so sensitive to conditions that he notices things that are wrong when he would not have noticed them if right.

As the pupils come, and as the principal passes about the building later in the day, he should also note:

8. The general "atmosphere" of the rooms as shown by teacher, pupils, written work, cleanliness, ventilation, etc.

The janitor as a helper. A good janitor, who is interested in children and who understands them, can be of much assistance to the principal in the matter of the discipline of the school. He ought to be on reasonably good terms with the boys, yet he must at times help supervise them. One janitor whom the writer knew was so up on games that he was continually called on by the boys to act as starter and umpire; another taught the boys new games; another (the former pastor) attended to all injuries on the grounds and looked after the youngsters generally. Such help in school management is a valuable addition. Often a little encouragement will bring out the janitor's good qualities, and when the boys take to him they will do much to lighten his load. Often the principal, by a word now and then, can help develop such a situation.

On the other hand, some janitors by their ways and talk bring down ridicule on themselves, and sometimes even annoyance from the children. Unless the matter goes beyond the point of innocent fun it is not advisable to interfere, even though the janitor complain. Perhaps the best attitude to take in case of difficulty between janitor and pupils is that of mediator. Usually a little smoothing of the ruffled feelings of the janitor, a little timely advice as to why they annoy him, and suggestions as to how to get along in the future and avoid further trouble will solve his side of the problem, while a frank discussion of the difficulty with the class containing the mischievous ones will handle the boy end.

QUESTIONS AND PROBLEMS

1. Would you add anything more to the ten administrative principles for dealing with the janitor, stated on pages 214–16, and if so, what? Do you take exception to any of the ten, and if so what ones, and why?
2. Would you add anything more to the seventeen standards for work stated on pages 217–18, and if so, what? Do any of these statements appear to you to be too exacting?
3. Do you agree that requests for service from the janitor should, in all important matters, first be approved by the principal? If not, why?
4. What sort of records should the janitor keep?
5. If there is too much for the janitor to do, and he has no helpers or insufficient help, what work may he best be permitted to neglect? What must he not neglect?
6. Assume that your new janitor is willing, faithful, and ignorant; outline a plan for his gradual education.
7. What ought a good janitor to know regarding his job?

SELECTED REFERENCES

Ayres, May, Williams, J. F., and Wood, T. D. *Healthful Schools.* 292 pp., Boston, 1919.
   Chapter X good on the work of the school janitor.

Dresslar, F. B. *School Hygiene.* 369 pp., New York, 1913.
   Chapters XIV and XV good on cleaning the schoolhouse and the work of the school janitor.

CHAPTER XII

HEALTH AND SANITARY CONTROL

A principal's work in health matters. While the work of school sanitation, health supervision, health teaching, physical education, and child hygiene each represents a special field, for which in large school systems expert service is usually provided, there is nevertheless a certain amount of knowledge as to each subject that is common and of which the principal should be cognizant. There are also certain measures that he should take to improve the health conditions in his school, even though some expert professional health supervision is provided by the school department or by the health department of the city. In many schools in the smaller cities and towns, however, no professional health supervision will be provided, and in such schools whatever is done to care for and to improve the health conditions surrounding the children in his school must be planned by the principal himself. The position of principal offers large opportunities for useful constructive work along lines of health conservation, as much can be done independently of professional assistance, but the position is not one in which a person holding Christian Science ideas as to health work can render much service.

There are five divisions of educational hygiene concerning which a principal should have some knowledge, and on each of which he should have at least one good book in his library for occasional reading and consultation. These are:

1. Play and physical education.
2. School sanitation.
3. Child hygiene.
4. Health teaching, including first-aid work.
5. Health supervision, including the work of the school nurse.

By familiarizing himself with their contents, and using good judgment as to what he is to do and what to let alone, a principal ought to be able to look after the health work in his school with a reasonable degree of satisfaction, even though he be without expert scientific assistance.

Something as to the nature and problems of play was indicated in Chapter VIII, and in the chapter just preceding this one the work of school sanitation was dealt with as it relates to the work of the school janitor. In this chapter, then, we shall treat briefly only the three other aspects of educational hygiene not previously considered.

Child hygiene. The need here, on the part of the principal, is for good general knowledge of the problems involved and possible lines of remedial treatment, to guide him in the many problems of school work that concern the hygiene of instruction. It is necessary that both principal and teachers take a biological point of view in dealing with the educational process, and relate their school work to the laws of physical growth. For an understanding of childhood this biological point of view is essential. A defect of the school through all the ages has been the tendency to regard the child as exempt from the laws of physical nature, to judge the child by adult standards, and to forget that much that is best in education is, after all, wisely guided natural growth. There is an order of physiological development of which education must take cognizance, and the close connection between mental and physiological growth needs to be kept clearly in mind. Some knowledge of the principles of child hygiene will do much to correct wrong points of emphasis in the education of children.

It is not necessary here to do more than indicate the general field of educational hygiene, though it is one that the principal needs to master to help guide and shape his educational philosophy. Without a clear understanding of its

HEALTH AND SANITARY CONTROL

importance his school is likely to be a subject-matter school, and not a real educational institution. Briefly, then, the knowledge of educational hygiene that a principal needs lies along the following lines:

1. The physical basis of education.
2. The general laws of growth.
    a. Growth rate and disease resistance.
    b. Relations between physical and mental growth.
3. Factors influencing growth.
4. Physiological characteristics of children.
5. Educational significance of physiological age.
    a. Contrast between this and mental age.
6. Disorders of growth.
    a. Chief defects, and their causes.
    b. The hygiene of posture.
7. Malnutrition in school children.
    a. School feeding; children's dietaries.
8. The school and tuberculosis.
    a. Proper regimen.
    b. Open-air schools.
9. The physiology of ventilation.
    a. Respiration, air currents, temperature, humidity.
10. Skin diseases.
    a. Impetigo; itch; ringworm.
11. Common children's diseases.
    a. Chicken pox; measles; scarlet fever.
12. The teeth of school children.
13. The nose and throat.
14. Defects and hygiene of the ear.
15. The hygiene of vision.
16. Speech defects and possible treatment.
    a. Stammering, stuttering, lisping.
    b. Hygiene of the voice.
17. The sleep of school children.
    a. Amount; conditions of.
18. Children's headaches.
19. The hygiene of instruction.
20. Preventive mental hygiene.
    a. The nervous child.
    b. Education of the nervous child.

    c. Common neuroses of development.
21. Evil effects of school life.

Terman's *Hygiene of the School Child* is the best single book for the principal's use along the lines of educational hygiene.

Health teaching. In the matter of hygiene teaching much will be outlined in any city course of study, and some "Health Primer" or series of "Health Readers" probably will be available for school use. In addition, the principal has constant opportunities to stimulate the teaching of proper health ideas and the formation of proper habits of health by the children.

During the first six years of school life the formation of proper health habits is perhaps the most important thing to be looked after, and this involves right ideas as to cleanliness and personal care. In addition to such general instruction as may be provided for in the course of study, and which may come from a primer or reader, one good plan for teaching proper health habits is the gradual inauguration of a daily personal inspection by the pupils themselves, the teacher guiding the work. This may well include:

1. Did you sleep with your windows open last night?
2. Did you brush your teeth last night and this morning?
3. Did you wash your face, hands, neck, and ears before coming to school?
4. Are your finger nails clean?
5. Did you go without tea and coffee yesterday?
6. Did you play at least one game yesterday?
7. Did you practice at least three physical-training exercises yesterday?
8. Did you try to sit, stand, and walk correctly yesterday?
9. Did you keep your desk and surroundings in good order yesterday?
10. Did you do at least one helpful deed yesterday?

The morning is the best time for this inspection. It may be a rapid checking-up by the teacher, or it may be made one of the functions of a school health club, in which the children are inspected by health officers of their own election. The latter plan is the more effective. The inspection ought also, after it is once fully inaugurated, to go further than the above ten items, and include questions as to diet, sleep, and exercise. The gradual introduction of a health scale, such as is given in Oppen's *Teaching Health* (p. 7) will add much to the concreteness and effectiveness of the instruction.

In the upper grades the instruction should center about bodily care, health rather than disease, and should pass over into practical studies involving health conditions on the playground, about the school, in the home, the city streets and alleys, and such places as a bakery, a market, a dairy, a mill, or a factory. The principal can do much to direct the health teaching along practical lines, and keep it from becoming bookish and ineffective.

What any school may do. In most of our schools the great burden for proper health work will still rest with the principal and teachers, and for the simple reason that the community has not as yet seen fit to make any provision for special service. Despite this lack of provision a principal and teachers who are interested can do much that is valuable, working alone. Some of the simple means at hand may well be indicated.

As a beginning, the school might well take time to make a health and nutrition survey, to find what are the actual existing conditions in the school and among the pupils. This may well include the sanitary conditions in the school building, toilets, and rooms; the play activities and possibilities; the heating, lighting, and ventilation of the building; the recess periods, study periods, and the home work; what type of instruction in health is given; how effective is the instruction in cooking and physical training, as measured by the health habits of the pupils; what foods the children eat; what kind of lunches they bring to school and eat; how they live and sleep, and how much they sleep; what their health habits are; etc. On the basis of the summarized results of such a study the instruction given in hygiene can usually be materially improved, better lessons on proper diet and bodily care given, and many features of the school work and school regimen changed.

A next step is to determine the physical condition of the children themselves. There should be a pair of scales, with height measuring rod, in every school, though this is not usually found. Often a Parent-Teacher Association will supply this, if the board of education will not. If not, height can easily be determined, and a pair of scales can be located in town where children may weigh themselves, or be weighed. Tables of normal height and weight can be found in many easily available books, and classroom weight records, like the one opposite, can be obtained on cards $12\frac{1}{2} \times 20''$ in size, as indicated. With these aids the undernourished pupils can be singled out for attention, those falling 7 per cent or more below normal being considered as undernourished. A medical examination for these is desirable, if obtainable, to locate the causes for the malnutrition, and if possible secure their removal. No school, though, should hesitate to make the beginnings indicated because it has no physician and no funds for examinations. The resulting improvement in the health instruction will in itself pay for the labor of the survey.

A campaign of health education. Based on the results of the survey, a campaign of health education can now be inaugurated. This will call more for enthusiasm than for technical knowledge. To enlist the leaders of the school in a health campaign calls for some of the same type of imparted enthusiasm as the selling of liberty bonds, tickets for a

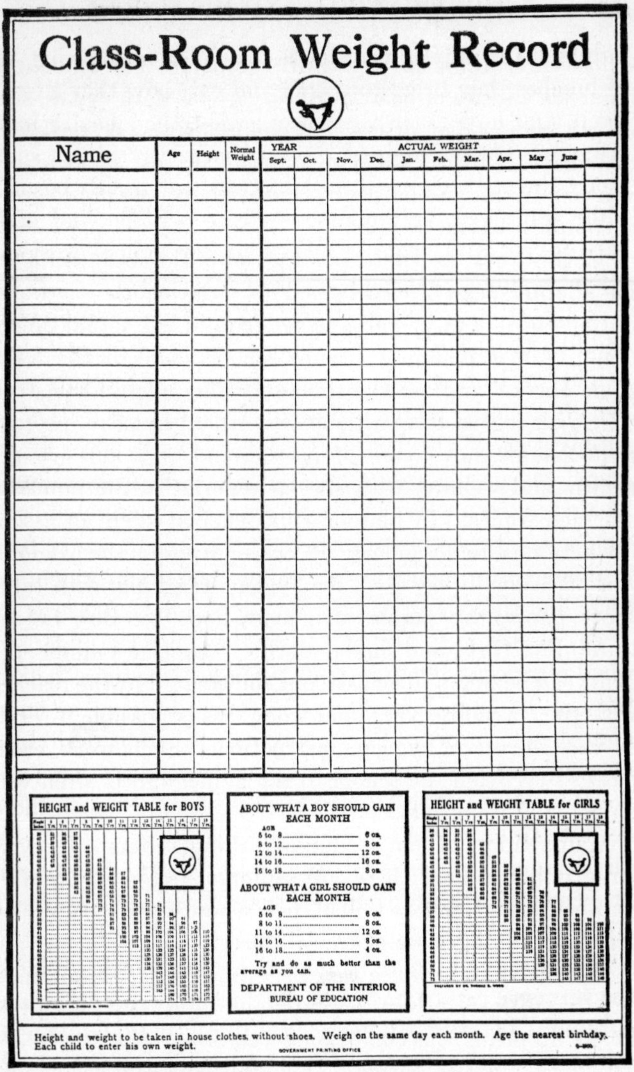

FIGURE 15. A CLASSROOM WEIGHT RECORD

(Reduced in size.) These may be obtained, printed on cards 12½ x 20 inches in size, of the Government Printing Office, Washington, D.C. Single copies, 5 cents; each additional copy, one cent. Each card holds the record for a school year of a class of forty pupils.

school entertainment, or a thrift campaign. The school that launches a series of health drives, care-of-teeth drives, sleep drives, proper-diet drives, anti-coffee drives, better-breakfast drives, no-sweets-between-meals drives, accident-prevention drives, and be-strong-and-well drives will be sure to accomplish lasting results.

All this work, as will be pointed out in this and the following chapters, can be closely tied up with the other activities of the school, and in consequence require less actual time in doing than in planning. Some schools have regular "Hygiene Days," and use the time very effectively for instruction with regard to questions of personal hygiene, posture, remedial measures, care of person, and questions of civic health and welfare, with special reports by the pupils on assigned topics. In platoon-type schools, where an assembly period is used regularly for class purposes, the assembly can occasionally be used for hygiene teaching, with talks, short papers by pupils, demonstrations by Boy Scouts, Camp Fire Girls, and similar work. Sometimes minor accidents can be taken to a classroom and treated by the teacher, with the class observing, and when this is possible it serves as very effective hygiene instruction. Such work easily passes over from the school to the home, and is often very valuable in its results.

Malnutrition, school feeding, fresh-air rooms. In every large public school there are children, frequently quite a number, who do not do well in their school work because they are cold, or hungry, or sick, or all three. These a health and nutrition survey at once reveals. In schools having many children of foreign-born parents, and especially South and East Europeans, this condition is very likely to exist. Poor, with large families, earning a low yearly wage, relatively ignorant, living in cramped quarters, and careless as to clothing and feeding and the laws of health, the children of these families come to school in a poorly clothed or nourished condition, and not infrequently evidence the beginnings of tuberculosis. The marvel is that they are able to get along as well as they do. When the father is without work the children come to school without breakfast, or with a breakfast of only coffee and bread, and sometimes get no lunch, or at best buy a few pennies' worth of food from a push cart or a neighboring grocery.

Often the school can do nothing to remedy this condition. The people have not been educated to appreciate the need, they are too poor to act even if they did understand, and the sentiment of the school board and the community would be against any public attempt to alleviate this condition. Still, it is a sheer waste of good money to pay good salaries to good teachers to try to teach such children, as the instruction is seldom fifty per cent effective. Here is a problem for a principal to see if something cannot be done to remedy the condition and inaugurate a limited school feeding. Often, when the facts are presented to a Parent-Teacher Association, they will interest themselves and contribute both money and food to solve the problem. A number of instances where this has been done have been described. Sometimes boards of education can be interested, and a small appropriation for the work made. Sometimes school entertainments have been given to raise funds, but this is objectionable because of the publicity it gives to what is being done. Sometimes the principal is allowed to use part of his small school budget, or petty expense fund, for this purpose, the fund being increased to cover the added costs.

The amount needed is not large — a little goes a long way and renders real service. The details of such work have been described, and do not need repetition here. The work requires some supervision, and records as to its cost and effectiveness and as to weight growth should be kept. Care must be taken that the food value of what is served is high. Eggs, milk, hot soup, cereals, and fruit are among the best things to use. For all children seven per cent or more under weight a mid-morning lunch should be served, at 10.00. For this bread or graham crackers and butter, with a half pint of milk, is very satisfactory.

Even with children of low mentality some change is observable with this extra feeding, but near-normal children show a change of attitude toward school work that often is striking. The discipline work with these children largely disappears, they become mentally much more alert, their appearance is better, they increase in weight and height and chest expansion, they take a new interest in play, their school work materially improves, and the percentage of non-promotions among them is very materially reduced. Measured by the cost for repeaters in the school, the school feeding gives large returns.

In schools having regular open-air schoolrooms, these, coupled with studied school feeding, often render large service with children of tubercular tendencies. In warm climates, such as Florida and Southern California, the open-air or partially open-air room usually gives good results for all children. Recent experiments, though, seem to cast much doubt on the value of open-air rooms in cold climates, and rather emphasize the importance of well-ventilated and properly-heated schoolrooms of the ordinary type.

First-aid work. Other lines of health work than those indicated above may be carried on by a principal and a body of interested teachers, without the aid of professional health service, or even a school nurse. One of the easiest of these lines is that of first-aid work, in the care of accidents.

A school without accidents would indeed be a curiosity. Accidents are constantly happening about every school — small cuts of fingers, usually done in the manual training

HEALTH AND SANITARY CONTROL

rooms or in the elementary sloyd work; burns, in the cooking room; scratches and bruises of head, arms, hands, and feet on the playground; stubbed toes; bumped and bleeding noses; toothache; fainting; chills; frozen ears, fingers, and feet; serious jolts or cuts, made by ball bats, or in falls from the apparatus; and occasional broken bones and epileptic fits.

To care for such accidents and illness every school should have some provision for caring for the injuries of the pupils. There should be a rest room, fitted with a plain rattan or leather couch, on which a sick teacher or pupil may be laid. There should also be blankets, hot water bottles, and granite iron basins for use. Hot water, or a quick means of heating water, should also be at hand. If the building has no such room, and old buildings usually do not, then the principal's office should be so arranged that it can be made use of for the purpose.

In addition there should be in every school at least one first-aid cabinet or case, in which are to be found needed supplies for first-aid and emergency work. Many schools have one on each floor, easily reached, as well as one in the rest or nurse's room. Partial supplies are also often found in the manual training shop, to care for minor accidents there on the spot. If the school department does not and will not provide such equipment, then the principal, through health teaching, Boy and Girl Scouts, and Parent-Teacher meetings, should awaken enough interest in having these things that they will be provided by gifts or obtained by purchase from the proceeds of entertainments given for the purpose.

The first-aid case. With the spread of the industrial-accident insurance idea by reason of state legislation, the first-aid case can now easily be bought complete. Usually, for school use, it is better to have it made and organized at the school, under the direction of the school nurse or some teacher. The pupils can then be made to understand why the different things are included, and how to prepare a somewhat similar kit for home use. The first-aid case should contain at least the following:

1. Rolls of absorbent cotton.
2. Rolls of sterile gauze.
3. Several bandages, of assorted sizes, triangular and roll.
4. Spools of surgeon's zinc-oxide adhesive tape, of different widths.
5. Bottle of alcohol (not wood alcohol).
6. " " flexible collodion.
7. " " Pond's Extract.
8. " " 10 per cent carbolic acid.
9. " " vaseline.
10. " " tincture of iodine.
11. " " aromatic spirits of ammonia.
12. " " Bernay's bi-chloride of mercury tablets.
13. " " oil of cloves, or oil of cloves and chloroform mixed.
14. Package of toothache plasters.
15. Pair of scissors.
16. Pair of dressing forceps.
17. Safety pins, of assorted sizes.
18. A few tourniquets.
19. Tongue depressors, and swabbing sticks.
20. A book on emergency treatments, such as Morrow's *Immediate Care of the Injured*, or the American Red Cross *Text Book on First Aid and Relief*.

The emergency books will give the necessary routine that can be studied and followed at once. In addition, the principal should have on a card on the case door the telephone calls of the nearest doctors who will respond to such cases, and the nearest ambulance, in case either should be needed. The telephone call of the school nurse and school physician, where such are not stationed at the school, and of the city health department when it performs such services, should also be at hand. It is also a good idea to have four or five eighth-grade pupils trained as assistants for emergency work, who should respond to calls and:

1. Notify the home, if this should be done.
2. Call doctor or nurse, as needed.
3. Stay with the pupil, and assist.
4. Make up card data of accident for principal's records.
5. Accompany a sick or injured pupil home.

First-aid teaching in the school. Training for emergency work and accident prevention should begin by the fifth grade, and should continue on up through the grades. The purpose is not only to care for simple accidents at once, but also to teach hygienic practices and procedure in the most effective manner. Demonstration first-aid work should be given in all rooms each year from the fifth grade up, and the pupils may well have explained to them the make-up and use of each article in the first-aid kit. One main idea is to have the principles of good health service carry over into the homes and stay by the pupils for life. Where this work is well done it is not uncommon, as a result of what the children carry home, for parents to ask that the school nurse, or some teacher, give a demonstration at a Parent-Teacher meeting.

The following suggestions will prove of value in the conduct of the work in a school.

1. Begin by taking precaution against injury. Teach with a view to accident and disease prevention. A recent little book, *Hygiene for the Worker*, offers the material for good instruction.
2. Emphasize the safety-first idea, and make definite use of the Boy and Girl Scouts along this line, as well as in first-aid work.
3. Emphasize good posture, and its relation to good health.
4. Have the school nurse, or if there be none some teacher, give demonstrations in first-aid methods, including bandaging, in each grade from the fifth up, each year. Later have the Boy Scouts give demonstrations.

5. Train the older pupils to clean bruises and cuts and simple injuries, and to bandage them.
6. If in a river or seaport town, train in resuscitation from drowning.
7. Emphasize everywhere the proper care of cuts, bruises, bleeding of the nose, fainting, toothache, etc., and the importance of attention to minor injuries.
8. Make the school nurse serviceable, but see that she works under definite rules, not too restrictive in type, but clearly specifying her field of work.
9. While treating minor injuries and cases of illness, be careful to exclude the serious ones. For these call a physician at once and get in touch with the home. If a child is not in need of immediate medication, as in case of fits, call an ambulance or taxi, and send the child home. Usually the police ambulance can be summoned and used without cost.

Keep a card or book record of all cases handled, the same to include name, date, time, nature of case, treatment, and disposition of. This data can be filled out quickly, often by pupils, on printed forms or cards which should be provided. Such a record may be useful in case of trouble, and a study of cases may help to reveal causes of the more frequent accidents, and means for preventing some of them. As an example of such a study and instruction, one of our larger school systems (Detroit) was able in one year to reduce its accidents as follows:

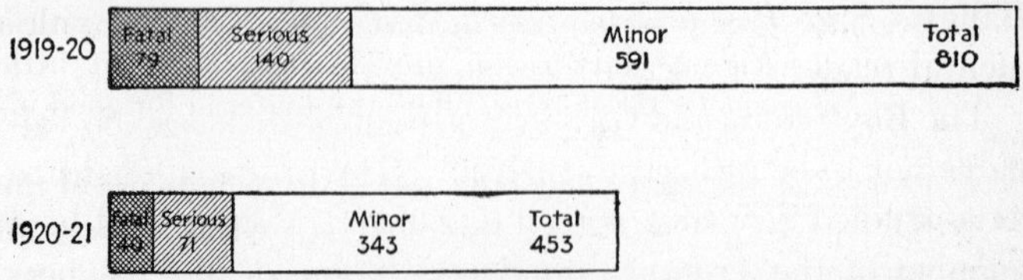

1919-20 | Fatal 79 | Serious 140 | Minor 591 | Total 810

1920-21 | Fatal 40 | Serious 71 | Minor 343 | Total 453

FIGURE 16. RESULTS FROM ACCIDENT-PREVENTION INSTRUCTION IN DETROIT

Reductions: Fatal, 79 to 40; serious, 140 to 71; minor, 591 to 343.

Such a record means that by accident-prevention instruction, and notwithstanding a rapid increase in the total number of children enrolled and the number of automobiles registered, the number of fatal and serious accidents in the city was cut in half, and the minor ones reduced two fifths. Stated otherwise it means that 39 more children were alive at the end of the year than would have been the case if the accident teaching had not been undertaken, 69 children were saved from confinement to bed and possibly a crippled existence, and 249 were saved from minor injuries and resultant shock.

Utilizing the Scouts. The Boy Scouts and Girl Scouts (or Camp Fire Girls) organizations can be made very useful in teaching hygiene, personal care, first-aid work, and accident prevention, and in helping care for those who are sick or have been hurt. By proper management these Scouts can be trained to help in teaching the use of the playground apparatus; to point out the dangers and danger line for swings, rings, bars, teeters, etc.; and to be a strong influence for order and fair play on the playground, with a view to reducing crowding, roughness, and accidents. They can also be used to advantage in taking care of the sick and injured, attending to some of the first-aid work, keeping records, and in accompanying the sick or injured home. Demonstrations of accident-prevention, safety-first work, and first-aid methods given before a school or class are excellent. Bailey's *Sure Pop and the Safety Scouts* is a good supplemental reader for use with the lower grades.

The Boy Scouts and Girl Scouts organizations are too valuable not to be utilized to the full. The principal ought to have studied Scouting, served as a Scout Master, and be a member of the Troup Committee. Some of the teachers ought to have had equivalent experience with the girls. The members of these organizations should then be utilized to assist the teachers and the principal in organizing safety patrols, whose duties would be to guard street intersections when children are passing or at play; to rope off the streets and direct traffic at mornings, noons, and recesses, when this is permitted by the city authorities; to help smaller children at crossings; to help organize the pupils for coöperation in safety-first and first-aid work; to coöperate in the fire drills; to report any dangerous conditions anywhere to the principal; to help remove or guard injurious obstructions, or protruding nails, or open manholes; and to make reports of accidents to the principal.

The "Big Brother" and "Big Sister" idea can also be made helpful in securing easy supervision of the little children by the older ones. This can be handled so as to be made an effective teaching instrument, and yet so that no one will lose any of the joy and freedom of spontaneous play.

Organization of a school health department. The same idea is carried out in some schools through the organization of the school into departments, such as police, judicial, health, etc. The health department then takes partial charge of the health, cleanliness, sanitation, accident prevention and care, and similar functions about the school and playground and streets. There is a chief health officer, selected from the highest grade, with assistants for playgrounds, toilets, streets, and building service. There are also room health officers, from the third or fourth grade up, to look after the morning inspection and to assist the teacher in her health work. The whole department is under the supervision of some one teacher, who keeps an eye on what is being done, advises and suggests, stimulates enthusiasm, receives reports, and handles cases requiring special attention.

In the morning room inspections, directions from the room health officer to go to the washroom and clean hands, comb hair, or wash the face are received and acted on much better than if given by the teacher. Still more, the pupil-work is so effective in results that there is soon little to attend to. Children who have "temperature" and look sick are segregated by the teacher, and taken to the nurse or principal by the room health officer. Children absent and reported ill are looked up by the health officer, and reported to the nurse or principal. In case of a child being cut, bruised, or hurt while at play or about the building, or if he becomes ill, one of the health department officers has him brought to the rest room for treatment by the teacher in charge. After treatment, the injured or sick child is often taken home by this same officer.

The children in such schools are very proud of being selected for office in the health department. Election to this board can be made both an honor and a reward for proficiency in health work. The idea, like that of the Scouts, can be made to contribute much to teaching health habits, the idea of "service," and to the development of an excellent school spirit.

Junior Health Leagues. In some of our school systems excellent results have been obtained by the organization of what are known as Junior Health Leagues in each of the elementary schoolrooms.

Once each week the pupils of each room elect a health officer from among their number for the following week. This officer wears a badge, showing his authority. It is his duty during the week to look after the general health conditions of the rooms, halls, and grounds. A blank report sheet is furnished which is filled out at the close of the week, and copies of this filled-out report are placed in the hands of the principal and the city or school health officer. On this blank, among other items, the junior health officer for each room reports the following: The temperature of the room, taken three times a day; the cleanliness of floors and walls in room and halls; the quality and method of dusting by the janitor; the lighting of the room; the ventilation; condition of the drinking facilities; condition of toilets and grounds; and possibly a few other items. A record of absentees is also kept for the week, and, in cases of sickness and disease, an accurate report is given, noting especially the prevalence of any contagious disease. That part of the report relating to absentees may be given to the attendance department, and that on health to the health department. The janitor is also furnished a copy as it relates to his work.

The reports in themselves may not be of much value, but the chief benefit in the plan is the training it gives the children, and through them the home, in forming habits of observing and correcting unsanitary conditions. Another benefit is that it causes the teacher to be conscious of general conditions. The school health officer can handle the ventilation, working under general rules, usually better than the teachers will attend to it. In attending to the duties of instruction she frequently neglects to give proper attention to health conditions.

Not the least of the advantages of the plan is that it enables a follow-up system to be carried on by the health and truancy officers. The children usually delight in acting as active junior health officers, and take an interest in the work It frequently leads to an improvement of both attendance and health conditions that the teachers alone would not be able to secure. The fact that these officers are given some authority, and are encouraged to exercise initiative in the performance of their duties, furnishes an opportunity for no mean training in itself. The pupils often get results with ease that a principal would find difficulty in securing.

The Junior Red Cross. The Junior Red Cross is another excellent organization that principals and teachers should make use of in the work of the school. Realizing that the hope of the future lies with the children, the American Red Cross has organized the Junior Division, so that school

HEALTH AND SANITARY CONTROL

children may be trained early in health ideas and in the habit of service. When school children are given an opportunity to understand how other children live, to learn what is their proper share of the world's work, and to coöperate in large plans for a better and happier childhood the world over, they have taken a long step toward good citizenship and toward world peace and good will.

Through coöperation in constructive undertakings, mutual service, helpful community work, clean-up campaigns, promotion of health knowledge, enforcement of health regulations, participation in civic and patriotic movements, making toys and hospital equipment for distribution at home and abroad, and in helping to clothe, feed, nurse, and educate thousands of suffering children in Europe and Asia, this organization of children is rendering a service that will do much to give the children a world outlook of large possibilities, develop higher ideals of citizenship, do much to alleviate suffering and eradicate disease, and carry American altruistic service to new heights.

The Junior Red Cross did very important service during the World War, but in places has lost its importance since the close of the struggle. Where the school has focused its efforts anew on some home undertaking its importance has on the contrary increased. No better form of "project teaching" could be devised than some of the coöperative home work done by this organization. One of the best of the many which have recently been described has been the work of the children of Spokane, Washington, working in coöperation, by schools. There a clinic and five-bed hospital for the care of children suffering from remediable defects and too poor to pay, was first established and supported. The removal of adenoids and tonsils were the main operations. Much of the fitting up of the hospital was done by the boys in their manual training and the girls in their sewing. The next addition, a year later, was the provision of a full-time nurse for nutrition work among the children. A year after this, when the Supreme Court forbade the expenditure of school money for a dental clinic, the children took this over and employed a full-time dentist to care for the children's teeth. That the work has made a strong appeal to the children is evidenced by an increase in membership, in the four years following the War, of from 48 per cent to 75.6 per cent of the enrollment of children in the public schools of the city. Such work has very large values in teaching coöperation and service and in training for citizenship, wholly aside from its large value as health work.

Every school could well be enrolled as a Junior Red Cross Auxiliary, and receive and make use of, in teaching history, geography, English, and civics, the *Junior Red Cross News* which comes with membership in the organization. Full information as to this can be obtained from the American Red Cross, Department of Junior Red Cross, Washington, D.C., or from local state and county directors.

The school nurse and health supervision. Every large school should have the services of a part-time or full-time nurse, and the partial services of a school physician as well. This, though, many cities and towns do not provide, and in many smaller cities no health service is furnished. Sometimes even a first-aid case is refused. In such cities the Parent-Teacher Association is a good center with which the principal may begin a propaganda for some form of health service. In some of the larger cities having "Visiting Nurse Associations," or "Health Centers," or "Out-Patient Dispensaries," a nurse can be obtained for part-time school service. If so, this service is an excellent one to utilize when the school department does not provide the needed aid.

If but little can be had at first, it is better to start with the partial services of a school nurse. In making routine schoolroom inspection, in the detection of contagious diseases in the early stages, in looking after minor injuries, in assisting in the direction of any school feeding, and in giving instruction to teachers and children in first-aid work, the school nurse has repeatedly proved her high efficiency. One very good explanation for this is that a school nurse probably meets with more cases of whooping cough, measles, mumps, and cut fingers and heads in a good-sized school in two or three months than an ordinary practicing physician would deal with in a decade. Much contagious disease is detected in its very beginnings, and excluded before much harm has been done; cases of malnutrition can be looked after; help given in physical examinations; homes can be visited and advised and follow-up work done; and many health defects can be attended to, both in the school and followed up in the home. To influence parents to provide medical attention for their children is usually no small task. Often the parents are poor and object to the expense. Many have strong prejudices against glasses for their children. Many resent being told that they do not feed or clothe their children properly. Much time and tact and patience often are required to get results. This home work is very important, though, as almost every extreme disciplinary case is found to have some serious physical defect back of it, and after correction of such defect marked improvement usually results.

A professional school health service. In school systems where a professional school health service is provided the principal can turn over to it many of the problems that in a school less well equipped he must look after largely alone. If this health work is to render its greatest service, those directing it should have passed in their thinking beyond the stage of mere disease detection, though this will always remain an important feature of the work; and beyond mere physical examinations, though these should be given; and should conceive of the service as preventive more than remedial, and should lay the emphasis on the preservation of health even more than on the elimination of disease. Such a service calls for:

1. The detection of incipient disease, and especially contagious disease.
2. Careful physical examinations yearly, to detect hidden defects.
3. The establishment of free medical and dental service for those unable to provide such.
4. Systematic instruction throughout the grades in matters of health and bodily care.
5. Some attention to play activities and athletics.
6. Some instruction to teachers in health matters.
7. Improvement of the janitorial service, with special reference to heating, lighting, ventilation, and school housekeeping.
8. School feeding.
9. Some attention to speech defects.
10. Organized extension work, through nurses, designed to improve conditions surrounding children in their homes

School health work of this larger type goes far beyond what is commonly thought of under "medical inspection," and may well be termed "health and development supervision." Its aim is to focus attention not only on the prevention of disease, but also on the development of as high a degree of physical efficiency as possible. A principal who has the assistance of such a complete health service is fortunate indeed, and he should coöperate loyally in the carrying out of such a health policy.

QUESTIONS AND PROBLEMS

1. Explain what is meant by saying that teachers should "take a biological view of child life"?
2. State, and characterize, each of the five divisions of educational hygiene.

HEALTH AND SANITARY CONTROL

3. Explain the difference between physiological and mental age.
4. State the progressive change in the character of health instruction as children grow older.
5. Outline a general plan for a "Hygiene Day" for a school.
6. Show how malnutrition is primarily a problem for the school to handle.
7. Draw up a simple card form for Accident Record use.
8. Indicate the importance of the attitude of the principal toward all health and development work.
9. Would you consider that the psychological advantages gained, in the matter of health instruction, from the organization of Junior Red Cross, Health Leagues, and similar organizations compensated for the time involved in their organization?
10. How would you connect up the noon lunch supervision with the school-feeding idea.

SELECTED REFERENCES

Ayres, Williams, and Wood. *Healthful Schools.* 292 pp., Boston, 1919.
   Contains good chapters on medical inspection and school feeding.

Bancroft, Jessie H. *The Posture of School Children.* 327 pp., Illustrated, New York, 1913.
   Clear explanations and concrete suggestions, with many excellent pictures.

Brown, Maud A. "Health Program in the Kansas City Schools"; in *Elementary School Journal*, vol. 22, pp. 132–39. (October, 1921.)
   Describes outline of work proposed, which is simple enough to be carried out by grade teachers and without help of nurse or physician.

Collier, Lucy W. *Child Health Program for Parent-Teacher Associations and Women's Clubs.* Health Education Bulletin No. 5, United States Bureau of Education. Washington, 1920.
   Contains good descriptive bibliographies on health teaching, school lunches, nutrition classes, correction of physical defects, play, teachers' health, and school sanitation.

Finney, and Schafer. *Administration of Village and Consolidated Schools.* 298 pp., New York, 1920.
   Chapter X brief but good on health work with school children.

Gaylor, G. W. "An Experiment with School Lunches"; in *School and Society*, vol. 2, pp. 169–70.
   Describes work in ward schools of Canton, Illinois.

Hoag, E. B., and Terman, L. M. *Health Work in the Schools.* 321 pp., Illustrated, Boston, 1914.
   A very useful book on the whole field of health supervision and control. Contains two chapters (V and VI) on the health-grading of children that every teacher ought to know.

Hoefler, Carolyn. "Methods in Health Instruction in Public Schools"; in *Elementary School Journal*, vol. 22.

Increasing efficiency, pp. 31–43 (September, 1921);
In 2d and 3d grades, pp. 212–22 (November, 1921);

In 4th and 5th grades, pp. 361–71 (January, 1922);
In 6th grade, pp. 535–43 (March, 1922).
> Good suggestions, methods of work, and bibliography of books and articles suitable to use with children.

Hoefler, Carolyn. "Health Program in the Public Schools of Joliet, Illinois"; in *Elementary School Journal*, vol. 22, pp. 764–65. (June, 1922.)
> An illustrated descriptive article of important work done.

Howe, Wm. A. "Efficiency in School Health Service"; in *Educational Review*, vol. 64, pp. 52–63. (June, 1922.)
> A good general article on the work that needs to be done.

Hunt, Caroline L. *The Daily Meals of School Children.* 62 pp. Bulletin No. 3, 1919, United States Bureau of Education, Washington.

Oppen, Lucy. *Teaching Health.* Health Education Bulletin No. 4, of the United States Bureau of Education. Washington, 1919.
> One of a series of eight useful little booklets on health education that a principal ought to have.

Payne, E. G., and others. *Education in Accident Prevention.* Illustrated. Lyons and Carnahan, Chicago, 1918.

Payne, E. G., and others. *Education in Health.* 253 pp., Illustrated. Lyons and Carnahan, Chicago, 1921.
> Two very useful books containing new, well-organized, and very concrete subject matter, with new social objectives in mind. Prepared by the faculty of the Harris Teachers College and the Wyman Observation School at St. Louis.

Payne, E. G. *A Program of Education in Accident Prevention, with Methods and Results.* 54 pp. Bulletin No. 32, 1922, United States Bureau of Education, Washington.
> An important document, with a good bibliography.

Roberts, Lydia. "Malnutrition, the School's Problem"; in *Elementary School Journal*, vol. 22, pp. 456–57. (February, 1922.)
> Outlines problem, and gives plan of procedure for schools desirous of undertaking school nutrition work.

Strayer, G. D., and Englehardt, N. L. *The Classroom Teacher.* 400 pp., New York, 1920.
> Chapter XI good on the health of school children.

Terman, L. M. *The Hygiene of the School Child.* 417 pp., Illustrated, Boston, 1914.
> One of those books that every teacher should know, and one that principals ought to master.

United States Public Health Service, Washington, D. C., and your State Department of Health can usually send valuable bulletins of use to schools, and are glad to do so on request.

Wile, Ira S. "The Cost of Educating the Underfed"; in *School and Society*, vol. 4, pp. 973–76. (No. 105.)

CHAPTER XIII

THE ATTENDANCE OF PUPILS

A universal problem. The problem of securing good and prompt attendance in school on the part of the pupils is one with which every principal has to deal. Much of the ease or difficulty of the problem will of course be determined by the nature of the community in which the school is located and by the character of the people who form the patrons of the school. In some places the sentiment for education is strong, and the parents readily and fully support the principal and teachers in their efforts to have the pupils in school on time each day. In such communities the task of regulating attendance is easy. In other communities no such sentiment is general, and the task of the principal and teachers is one that calls for continual vigilance and at times an appeal to authority.

Because irregular attendance is such an important cause of retardation and ultimate elimination from school, because the irregular pupil becomes such a drag on the class on account of what he has missed, and because truancy and tardiness are bad habits and tend to undermine the discipline and morals of a school, it is important that the principal give careful attention to the matter of attendance. It is a problem upon which he may easily be led to spend much time; therefore it is important that he systematize his procedure so as to handle the work both expeditiously and effectively.

Causes of irregular attendance. While the poverty of parents, sickness, and a desire to put children to work are common causes of absence from school, these are, after all, not the serious causes. They can generally be easily removed or controlled. Among the children of foreign-born parents ignorance of the law is often a cause, but when the law and its penalties are once made clear to them this class usually makes little trouble thereafter. Irregular attendance commonly comes from a relatively small number of families, and much more trouble from both tardiness and irregular attendance is usually experienced from the children of native-born families than from the children of the foreign-born.

While in some cases the prime cause of the trouble lies in the home, the great source of irregular attendance, though, lies rather in the school itself. Statistical studies have clearly shown that the majority of pupils leaving the school before completing its work do so because of a lack of interest in the school itself. Neither they nor their parents feel that the school is of much value for them. Studies of truancy show the same reasons. To the truant the school work lacks interest and vitality, the companionship found in the school and on the playground does not appeal, and often the upper-grade work at least is not well adapted to his needs.

It is perhaps not too much to say that the holding and drawing power of a school is one of the measurable standards by which its efficiency may be judged. Many things, though, contribute to the creation of a strong holding and drawing power. Some of these are external to the particular school itself, such as the character of the community, its attitude toward education, the nature of the school census, the compulsory attendance law, and the character of the compulsory attendance service. Others are characteristic of the school system as a whole, such as the organization of the instruction, the types of school work offered, the emphasis placed on different aspects of the instruction, and the types of teachers employed. Still others lie wholly within the school itself, such as attention given to the problem, motivation of the school work, and the development of a

THE ATTENDANCE OF PUPILS

school spirit, and for these the principal must be held responsible.

Handling the problem. Plans in use for handling the attendance problem vary somewhat from city to city, depending in part on the size and character of the city and in part on the conception of the attendance problem held by the state and city educational authorities. In a general way they vary from lax to strict enforcement, and from an emphasis on compulsion from without to motivation from within. Every principal will naturally have to adjust himself somewhat to the regulations and plans in force in the state and city in which he works, so that any description as to desirable methods can only be applied where the principal is given a rather free hand. Assuming that the principal is allowed a certain amount of initiative, the suggestions which follow ought to prove helpful.

To secure a quick and effective handling of the problem by the use of commonplace methods, the principal needs some simple device for securing, sorting, reporting, and recording information. This will involve checking the school census at the beginning of the year, a daily classroom check, good relations with the compulsory-attendance officer, and teacher and pupil relations.

Checking the school census. In handling the school attendance problem it is quite important to get as early a start on it as is possible. If the city has an even fairly accurate school census it is possible to get a good check of all pupils the first week of school. If a school can get the children started properly in September, non-attendance can be kept down throughout the year.

Schools to-day are usually supplied with a "Census List" of the pupils who reside within the school district lines. Sometimes this is in card form, in which case the cards are easily sorted, and sometimes the names occur on slips, or sheet lists. If the principal has been in the school before and knows his district, a preliminary survey of it in the days just preceding the opening of the school will be helpful by way of noting new families in the district.

The first day of school a registration card should be filled out by or for each pupil, giving name, age, grade, parent, and residence, and, if new to the school, school last attended, in city or elsewhere. These ought to be checked up the first night against the school census lists. In doing so the principal will find his cards falling into three piles, or classes.

1. Children whose names are on the census lists and who are in school.
2. Children whose names are on the census list but who are not in school.
3. Children whose names are not on the census list but who are in school.

Class 2 will include children whose parents have left the city or have moved to some other school district in the city, children who have gone to the high school, children who have not as yet returned from their summer vacation, and children who are staying out of school and need looking up. Class 3 will include children whose parents have moved into the city or the district, and children belonging to some other district who are trying to "sneak" into the school. For new children census cards should be made out for filing in the school records, and for reporting to the attendance office.

Locating the missing ones. After school on the first Wednesday afternoon the principals of all schools in the city should meet to check up their new and missing children. Where children are found to have moved during the summer, and have hence entered the school in their proper district, permanent record cards are exchanged. Where children are attempting to get into another school outside their district, without transfer or permission from the superintendent, their names are exchanged and the children are sent to their proper school the next morning. Children in the high school are checked off all lists. This leaves on each list the names of those children who have either left town or have failed to enter school. These names the principal takes back to his school and divides among his teachers and himself to be investigated. This does not give any one person a very large number of names, and by the end of the week every child of compulsory school-attendance age on the census list can be accounted for in some way. The telephone may be used in some cases. Pupils from the same street may give useful information. A call often reveals a legitimate excuse. Sometimes the parents merely need to have the law explained to them. New families should also be looked after and checked. The teachers and principals, by persuasion or mention of the law, thus get the most of those out of school but still in the city back into school. Those who have moved into another school district and are not in school are reported to the principal of that school. Those who have moved out of the city are struck off the census list. Those who have gone to a private or a parochial school are so checked, and the attendance officer deals with such schools thereafter for the attendance of these children.

The names of those whom the principal and teachers find should be in school and who fail to appear by the following Monday morning, as well as all for whom information is lacking or uncertain, are then given to the attendance officer to round up. Usually there are but few cases left to be investigated, and the attendance officer gets the difficult cases to handle right at the start. This is a great advantage over the plan of reporting all cases to him and causing him to waste days in investigating simple cases, while the really hard ones are not reached for weeks. Under this plan the principal and teachers handle the easy ones, and the second week the attendance officer can reach the difficult ones. By the end of the second week the docket is cleared, and the officer is ready to go after the first cases of truancy and non-attendance reported from the schools.

The daily classroom check. Having located the children thus early, a rapid, simple, and effective means for checking absences each day and half-day throughout the year is now desirable. One means, commonly used, is to have each teacher send to the office of the principal a printed slip form, on which the teacher writes the names of pupils absent and any information she may have as to the cause for the absence. These slips then have to be tabulated onto cards, and the names sorted out under the headings of probably tardy, probably truant, sick, and unclassified. While this can be done rather rapidly, and if the principal has an office clerk it can be attended to by her, it is still more complicated than need be.

The simplest form which the writer has ever seen, and at the same time the most effective, is the one given on the opposite page. For this plan the school needs printed cards, $8\frac{1}{2} \times 11$ inches in size, printed on good cardboard. There is a card for each room in the school, and each card is used for a month. The cards are placed on the teachers' desks daily before 9.00 and 1.00, by a monitor, who goes to the principal's office for them, they being placed regularly in a definite box or place for him. Each teacher pencils in on the cards the absentees, and room monitors take them back to the principal's office by or before 9.15 and 1.15 daily. The teachers write on the front or back of the card only with a pencil, and the principal only with ink. One card thus covers all cases of tardiness or absence for each room for a month, and at the end of the month is filed in a letter-file case. As a labor-saving device this monthly attendance rec-

Room...14 [98—8—22—3 M.] MONTHLY ROOM ATTENDANCE RECORD Month......April
Grade...6B   Teacher......Mary Jones

		Monday	Tuesday	Wednesday	Thursday	Friday
First Week	A.M.	Smith, John X Sunderson, Mary Wessels, Harry S	Sunderson, Mary (Measles — Be out about 2 weeks)			
	P.M.	Sunderson, Mary Wessels, Harry S		Day, Sherman Villa, Sam. T		
Second Week	A.M.		Murphy, Eva T		Anderson, Sam, Humphreys, Will, } Truant *Yes — Penalized* ? Ellis, Howard	
	P.M.		Murphy, Eva T *Mother promises*	Day, Sherman *Mother promises not to detain again*		Vargas, Serafina X
Third Week	A.M.	Benson, Mary			Ellis, Howard *Mother let sell Sat. Eve. Post. Promises not to allow again*	
	P.M.	Benson, Mary T†,* Westover, Alice X*				
Fourth Week	A.M.		Frata, Mary X			Donovan, Jimmie } Religious Frata, Mary } Festival Lopez, Mannel } at St. O'Toole, Sarah } Gregory's? Silva, Mary } *Yes*
	P.M.					

Markings to be used on sheet.

Name only = Absent ; S = Reported sick ; T = Came in tardy ; Tru. = Truant ; X = Excused ; Tr. = Transferred elsewhere.

Notes and explanations on back of sheet. Teacher write only with pencil; principal only with ink. (Ink indicated above by Italics.)

FORM 2. A MONTHLY ATTENDANCE RECORD SHEET

ord is excellent, and for a principal without an office clerk it is by far the simplest form to use. One of its special merits is that everything for a month is before one and may be seen at a glance, without the necessity of sorting out slips or hunting up cards. Individual cumulative record cards may be made up from this record form, at any time, as desired.

All of this, with blanks and a little system, requires less time to handle than it takes to describe it, and makes the administration of the attendance records quick and automatic and easy for all concerned. Transfers, removals, truancy, and sickness are easily discovered, with the result that records are kept more accurately and non-attendance is decreased.

Some principles to be followed. In the absence of specific rules directing otherwise, the following plan will be found to be workable.

1. Each teacher is to keep a record of the daily attendance of each pupil, in a register provided for that purpose.
2. Each teacher is to handle cases of tardiness, subject to such oversight as the principal sees fit to give.
3. There is ordinarily little reason for requiring a tardy pupil to go first to the principal's office and wait for his permission before coming to his room. Get the pupil into class and at work as quickly as possible, and attend to excuses afterward.
4. Pupils not present at a designated time are to be reported on slips or cards, to the office, as outlined above.
5. In reporting pupils absent, teachers should give an opinion or guess, if illness or truancy is suspected.
6. Teachers should make an effort to find out from others why pupils are absent, and when found out, state reasons on subsequent reports.
7. Teachers should avoid making so much of the evil of tardiness that a pupil, especially in the lower grades, will go back home rather than be tardy.
8. Excuse those from work missed on account of sickness only until they shall have had time to make it up, and those absent without a satisfactory excuse must make up the work lost out-

side of hours. Those excused may be helped on back work; those not excused to receive a zero on the time lost.
9. Excuses for tardiness and absence should first go to the teacher, and may be referred to the principal later, if she thinks it desirable or necessary. In the case of absences caused by truancy, or some form of pupil negligence, it often has a very wholesome effect if the pupil has to take the excuse to the principal and secure his approval. This should be done, though, at his office periods, or at intermissions.
10. When new pupils enter, or pupils leave or are transferred, the attendance officer should be notified accordingly.
11. Keep in mind that the machinery of attendance is only a means to an end, and that results often depend more on the attitude toward promptness and regularity assumed by the principal and teachers than upon compulsory enforcement.
12. It is well to establish helpful relations with the police as regards attendance. If pupils inclined to play truant know that a number of persons in authority are likely to be looking for them, they will be more careful about their absences.

It must be remembered that the prime purpose of all regulations and machinery for attendance-enforcement is to try to establish habits of punctuality and regularity in attendance at school. This is done more for the future value of such habits to the pupil than for bringing up the average attendance, desirable as this may be. Something can be accomplished by using certain devices to stimulate attendance, much by building up a school spirit that will make pupils want to come to school promptly and regularly, and in a few cases something by an impartial and effective enforcement of the compulsory education law.

Devices for stimulating attendance. The main idea underlying the use of all devices for stimulating attendance is that of placing a premium on regularity rather than the penalizing of delinquency. An attempt is made to render a motive from within more effective than a danger from without. To this end numerous devices are used by schools, among which should be mentioned:

1. The placing and keeping of lists of pupils on the blackboards of the different rooms, with a star for each month or week in which the pupils have been neither absent nor tardy. Diagrams and charts which compare the room records with other rooms, and the school with other schools, are often useful.
2. The use of banners or pennants, one to be awarded to each room having a perfect-attendance score for the week or month, and a champion-room pennant to be held for a month by the room having the best attendance for the preceding month. A similar champion-school pennant may be used, to be flown from the flagpole by the school in the city having the highest attendance score, month by month. If the awarding and hanging of these banners or pennants are administered by a student organization, added interest in attendance is awakened.
3. The publication of lists, in the local papers, at the end of each term or year, of all pupils who have not been absent or tardy during the designated period.
4. Having student officers, such as the health officer or the police officer, take the attendance for the rooms from third or fourth grade up; make out the "missing lists," subject to the approval of the teacher; and have them find out, so far as can be done, why pupils are tardy or absent. Student pressure to keep up a room average is often far more effective than any other kind. When this plan is coupled with pennants, and perfect attendance is made much of by the school authorities, these student organizations often effectively round up most of the habitual cases. Sometimes the school has even to interpose to prevent the offender from being too severely handled by the other boys.
5. Sometimes very effective results can be obtained by making attendance officers of some of the offending pupils, thus placing responsibility directly on them.
6. Where credits for home work are given, these should be made dependent upon the attendance record.
7. Pupils arriving tardy are required to remain after dismissal in the afternoon to make up all time lost — sometimes time and a half or double time is required.
8. Some schools give an early dismissal once a month, and some even a partial holiday to those pupils or rooms having a perfect or nearly perfect score. This plan is open to rather serious educational objections, however. A much better plan is

to permit the substitution of something unusual to the qualifying rooms, such as a special school "movie," a school excursion to some point of special interest, or a nature study trip, in place of part or all of the last Friday afternoon's work.
9. Interesting opening exercises are often very useful. Reading a good story serially, having pupils take part in the exercises, singing songs which the children like, the use of the victrola, and selections by the orchestra are some of the other means which may be employed. In schools having an assembly hall the assembly period can be made very attractive.

Most of these devices, while working well with the majority of the children, often fail to reach the calloused, habitual offenders. In plans where the pupils of a room or school become interested collectively in the attendance problem, because of an awakened school pride or to win some prize or to secure some reward, the children themselves often find some means of rounding up and bringing in these habitual offenders. To assign to such persons some distinctive duty which requires regularity, such as putting up the school flag, ringing the bells, playing in the orchestra, inspecting and reporting on the toilets and playground, reporting the room attendance, or some form of service or monitorial duty, usually acts as a very effective stimulant.

In most cases where habitual truancy occurs, a careful health examination should be made; often bad physical conditions will be found which may largely explain the delinquency. Wherever physical examinations of habitual truants have been made a surprisingly large percentage of remediable defects, such as nasal obstructions, defective eyesight, bad tonsils, and similar disorders, have been found to exist. Sometimes improper or deficient feeding is the cause of the trouble.

Principal and teachers and the home. Along with all such devices the principal and teachers should stand for a positive policy as to the importance of punctuality and regularity as life habits, without which the pupils can hardly hope to succeed in the business world. This conception will often have to be extended to the homes. To require excuses in writing, and, when the validity of the excuse is doubtful, to impress upon pupil and parent that irregular attendance is certain to interfere with the child's progress and chances for promotion will be necessary in many cases. A talk on this subject to the Parent-Teacher meeting, illustrated by charts and figures giving the results of studies of irregularity in attendance on promotions and school progress, will often prove helpful.

All possible coöperation between the school and the home should be established, leading as it does to better results and the avoidance of friction. In the matter of enforcing attendance a common method is to notify the attendance officer the first day a pupil is absent, and he then goes to the home and finds the reason for the absence. Possibly the child is sick, possibly there is sickness in the family, possibly he has been kept at home to render some service which seemed important, and possibly it is a real case of "playing hookey." Whatever the cause, the home often resents the visit and a feeling of antagonism is engendered. Not infrequently the home comes to take the attitude that the school is meddling in matters that are none of its business, and that to be able to outwit the school is quite legitimate. The pupil thus acquires an attitude from the home that is anti-social and vicious.

On the other hand, if the principal and teachers try to know something of the home, and show a genuine interest in the children and in the family as a whole, in most cases they win the family as well as the children and make of all loyal supporters of the school. In many places, to-day, principals and teachers and nurses are making an effort to know every home that sends a child to the school. When such relations have been established and a pupil is absent, instead of sending an officer to the door, the principal or teacher can often handle the case by an inquiry through some pupil, or by a personal call. The latter can in most cases be made as the exhibition of a friendly interest, and will be appreciated where the visit of an officer would be resented. Often both parent and child may be won by such methods not only to reasonably satisfactory attendance, but also as supporters of the social order for which the school really stands.

This does not mean the substitution of easy or slip shod methods for definite records and follow-up methods in attendance matters. It merely means the use of gentle methods first without making a display of all the authority of the school.

The visiting teacher. There has recently been introduced into our school organization a new type of helper with the difficult cases, intermediate between the teacher on the one hand and the social worker on the other, and known as the Visiting Teacher. Beginning in 1906–07, in three of our American cities, and as yet confined to some fifty or sixty of the larger ones, the services rendered have proved so useful and helpful that it is not unreasonable to expect that in time such a personage will be found connected with each small city school system, and with groups of schools or large individual schools in our larger cities.

Such a teacher has an office and office hours, in the school building or at the central office, according to the scope of the service rendered, and to her are referred, for investigation and handling, the difficult pupil-cases the school work reveals. Children irregular in attendance, children unable to make necessary social adjustments in the school, children deficient in scholarship, cases of probable home neglect or underfeeding, cases involving moral delinquency or serious discipline, and sometimes the cases of precocious children, are referred to the visiting teacher for special investigation and report. For each case a card is made out, the visiting teacher sees the child and talks with the teacher, visits the home, sees the parent, analyzes the case, tries to gain the family confidence, when necessary secures the coöperation of other social agencies in the community, represents the school in relations with the home and the home in relations with the school, suggests readjustments or changes in school work, follows up the case much as does the visiting nurse her cases, and occasionally enforces the law to protect the child. Visiting teachers thus come into such close and intimate relations with the homes that not infrequently, at office hours, the visiting teacher finds awaiting her, for further help, some mother whom she once advised in a case that has been "closed."

Such a visiting teacher, connected with a school or a group of schools, such as a supervisory group, can be of very large assistance to teachers and principal in helping them to handle their most difficult and most time-consuming problems, thus saving their time for the more important work of instruction. Such a teacher, in part due to training, special personal qualifications, a specialization of functions, and more and better home visiting, can develop a technique of social-case work not possible to the class teacher and to but few principals. Each irregular or difficult case becomes a special case for individual study and adjustment, and the causes underlying the trouble are ascertained and so far as possible removed. In smaller cities, and in many schools in cities of any size, the work, at least in its beginnings, might well be and often is combined with the functions of the school or visiting nurse.

The spirit of the school and attendance. Where no such special help is available, which will be in the large majority of schools for some time to come, the regularity of attend-

THE ATTENDANCE OF PUPILS

ance will have to depend largely on the attitude and personality of the principal and teachers who handle the problem. The machinery provided by law and by the school board for enforcing attendance may be good, but the professional skill of the instructing staff will mainly determine its effectiveness. A notable falling off in attendance in any one room during the early days of the school should be a notice to the principal to examine the instruction and general attitude of the teacher of that room.

There is too much of a tendency to consider the attendance problem chiefly from the standpoint of a rigid enforcement of the attendance laws. This idea rests in great part on a belief that children and parents should be made to feel the dignity of the law and fear the penalty of its violation, and in part on a feeling that looking up children who fail to come to school is not the teacher's business. In specific dealing with attendance cases the principal and teachers must consider irregularity in attendance the serious matter that it is, and must possess the knack of talking to the pupils in such a way as to make them also so consider it. In passing about in the rooms the principal will do well to evince his interest in the problem by complimenting rooms in which the attendance is perfect, or especially good in view of bad weather conditions or community distractions.

Children, however, ordinarily like to go to school and like the companionship of the other pupils. In most cases they await with impatience the day they can start to school, and they enjoy the feelings of friendship and interest manifested by the principal and teachers of their school. If they later lose this feeling for the school, may not the school itself be largely to blame? The school work must be made interesting and vital, and the pupils must be made to like their school and to believe in the value for them of what it has to give. Making the school work really vital through motivation and intelligent supervision of instruction, attention to the play periods, the building up of a strong school spirit, making the building and grounds as attractive as possible, enlisting the coöperation of parents whenever practicable, all coupled with a quick and energetic handling of the first cases of irregularity that occur, will do much to reduce the problem to its lowest terms for any particular school. In the absence of an attendance officer it often has a wholesome effect on a school if the principal will go out and quickly round up a few cases of "hookey," and bring the youngsters in.

Use of stronger methods. There will still be some cases, both of pupils and homes, which cannot be reached by any of the above gentler methods. These, once they are clearly segregated, should be dealt with promptly and vigorously by the attendance officer. But even he should show a humane attitude in dealing with the homes. Often he will find poverty, sickness in the home, and lack of proper clothing at bottom the real cause. He and the principal should be in touch with relief organizations that can render help when needed. The school nurse and the visiting teacher often need to be called in for help. Only the stubborn parent should be made to feel the weight of the law.

The work of enforcing attendance will be made much easier for all concerned if the school system has some special schools for handling both the incipient and the more stubborn cases. Otherwise the enforcement of attendance will bring into the classroom many children who gain little of value from the school and who often become a nuisance. The result is an increase in corporal punishment and retardation, and a failure, from the citizenship point of view, of the school to attain the ends for which the school really stands. Without such special classes and schools, expulsion is all that is left for those who cannot be brought under control.

THE ATTENDANCE OF PUPILS

The first of these special schools is the disciplinary class. One of these rooms should be attached to a number of the elementary schools of the city, and to this class principals should be permitted to send pupils who are breaking from the ordinary classroom control, the purpose being, if possible, to check the first tendencies to waywardness and to return the pupil in time to his regular classroom. The second special school is the parental school, to which those who cannot be controlled in the disciplinary class may next be sent. The purpose here is to hold the pupil to a routine impossible in the home from which he comes, and to try to discover upon what interests the building of his character may be begun. A third type of school is the central or industrial school, a school which disregards grading and courses of study and leads toward instruction in the trade or industry or occupation in which the pupil may find himself.

QUESTIONS AND PROBLEMS

1. Suppose that, the first week of school in the autumn, a new principal finds that eight boys from two sixth grades are not in school some nice afternoon. What would you suggest that the principal do about it, assuming that the school employs no attendance officer?
2. How do you explain the greater irregularity of attendance of children from good-stock native-born families than from among the foreign born?
3. Do you know of any better plan for checking the school census, early in the school term, than the one given on pages 249–51?
4. Suppose that the city does not employ an attendance officer; what plan would then be followed after the preliminary checking of the school census?
5. Do you take exception to any of the principles stated on pages 254–55, and if so to what ones, and why? Would you add any to the list, and if so, what new ones?
6. Can you suggest any additional devices, to those listed on pages 256–57, for stimulating attendance?
7. Does the strict attitude of the school toward attendance tend to develop an anti-social and non-coöperative attitude on the part of the parents? If so, are there ways of preventing this?
8. What penalties would you impose for playing hookey, and what aim would you have in mind in imposing each?

SELECTED REFERENCES

Gleim, S. G. *The Visiting Teacher.* 23 pp. Bulletin 10, 1921, United States Bureau of Education, Washington.
A brief summary of development in the United States up to 1920. Good bibliography.

Gray, R. F. "The Home Teacher in California"; in *School and Society*, vol. 12, pp. 330–34. (October 16, 1920.)
Describes the California law of 1915 for and the work of the Visiting Teacher.

Hiatt, Jas. S. *The Truant Problem and the Parental School.* 35 pp. Bulletin 29, 1915, United States Bureau of Education, Washington.

Holley, Chas. E. "Relationship between Persistence in School and Home Conditions"; in *Fifteenth Yearbook of the National Society for the Study of Education*, Part II, 1916.
A consideration of the different home factors involved.

Maxwell, Wm. H. "The Attitude of the American Parent toward Education"; in *Educational Review*, vol. 45, pp. 167–85. (February, 1913.)

McAndrew, Wm. "Parens Iratus; his Cause and Cure"; in *School Review*, vol. 19, pp. 1–12. (January, 1911.)
Offers some good advice on causes for and management of the irate parent.

National Association of Visiting Teachers. *The Visiting Teacher in the United States.* 64 pp. Public Education Association of City of New York, 1921. 20 cents.
The best available statement of development and work of this new type of teacher.

Snedden, D. S. "The Public School and Juvenile Delinquency"; in *Educational Review*, vol. 33, pp. 374–85. (April, 1907.)
An excellent article on the handling of juvenile delinquents, and the place and work of the public schools in the process.

CHAPTER XIV
DISCIPLINE AND CONTROL

Inheriting an unruly school. If irregular attendance and an occasional case of "hookey" were all the disciplinary disturbances coming in to interfere with the work of a principal, his lot would be an easy one. Unfortunately he will frequently have much more serious troubles. Even in the best of schools there will be mischief, line trouble, snowballing, fighting, petty thefts, and obscenity to deal with, while in a school which has become unruly and is largely out of control the problem may at first call for an inordinate amount of time and attention. While some neighborhoods will, by their nature, call for more disciplinary control than will others, a school in any neighborhood which has been subjected to a harsh and unsympathetic treatment, or to the other extreme of indulgence and weakness, will cause a new principal disciplinary difficulty until he can bring it under control. His problem then will be to transform an unruly into a well-governed school, and this may require some time.

There are many causes for an unruly school, though the two most common are those stated above. A third common cause is consistently poor teaching and a type of instruction lacking spirit and vitality. Disciplinary weakness on the part of the teachers, arising from unfitness for their work, lack of sympathy with young people on the part of either teachers or principal, vacillation in control, want of tact, procrastination in handling cases, an unimpressive personality, lack of administrative force, failure to mechanize the routine elements in management and control — these are other causes which combine to create a school that is hard to handle. The transformation of this type of school into a school of spirit, proud of its ability to do things, and desirous of the approbation of principal and teachers, calls for a good understanding of human nature and no false moves on the part of the principal.

Transforming an unruly school. The principal must first of all understand boys, as most of the trouble comes from them. If the boys assume the right attitude the girls usually cause little concern. He needs a saving sense of humor, a spirit of frankness and fairness, the ability to make boys feel that he is square and a good sport, and also the ability to act quickly and certainly when action is the needed virtue. On the other hand he must not be an unsympathetic old man in his attitude, nor must he exhibit a certain "swagger of authority" if he wishes to gain and hold control. He must not see or hear too much, must not try to regulate everything at once, and must make but few rules and only such as will be easy of enforcement because of their evident fairness and justice.

The transformation of an unruly school must be accomplished largely by other means than rules and coercion, though these may have to be used. The awakening of a strong school pride and spirit, particular attention to playground organization, the stimulation of group responsibility, individual assignment for duty, snap and spirit in the school management, and a raising all along the line of the quality of the school work are all excellent helps. Order, system, a good regimen of work, and plenty of good play have a strong tonic effect on any school.

These are the methods of "peaceful penetration" that in time accomplish large results, and are the methods a principal should strive to use as much as possible. They are far more effective than force and punishment, yet there are times and schools where mild means must be temporarily set aside and force applied. A school in rebellion will regard a teacher or principal as weak who does not act then. Willful disobedience or mischief, insolence and insult, and bullying and maltreating of pupils usually call for discipline of a severe type. In such cases, if force is the thing to use, the action should be swift, unerring, and certain.

Few would care to be principal in a school where corporal punishment was forbidden under all circumstances. There are times in a school, as in a home, where its use is a means of saving grace. This is particularly true in dealing with boys. While the days of corporal punishment are passing, there still remain youths from certain types of homes to whom it alone will appeal. It must, however, be used sparingly, and should always be regarded as an emergency and transition remedy to be dispensed with as soon as milder methods can be made to work. With individuals and schools one strives to pass upward from the plane of imposed force, through indirect and constructive control, to smooth-running self-control, which is the best preparation for social life.

To prepare young people for proper social participation is one of America's most difficult problems. The securing of order in a conglomerate democracy such as ours is obviously a far more subtle and difficult problem than the maintenance of order in such a homogeneous and docile country as Germany. To strike a golden mean between iron-clad autocracy on the one hand and disorder and anarchy on the other, while preserving a respect for the individuality of the pupils under his control, is a neat problem for any principal to solve. It is clear to any one who is exposed to the bad manners of many school children, and to the general irresponsibility, slovenliness, and trouble-making capacity of many classes, that the problem of adequate government is far from solved in this country. Yet the welfare of our country demands that the school lead in finding a solution. Fortunately most of life is a succession of small things rather than a few big ones, and it is in the handling of these smaller difficulties where lie the main opportunities for constructive service. What a few of these smaller and common disciplinary troubles are we shall now consider.

Minor disorders in the school. In addition to truancy, described in the preceding chapter, and which is in most cases easily controlled, the principal of every school encounters many cases of pure mischief, which display only an exuberance of youthful spirits, induced perhaps by too rigid regulations, by teachers unsympathetic with children, or by those who see and hear too much. For example, pushing in line is a common cause of trouble. Some teachers are always nagging their children when in line. Some principals hold that lines and marching cause more cases of discipline than any other single thing. Still others have abandoned lines entirely and let pupils move as they wish, so long as there is no marked rudeness. Probably the trouble lies in an insistence on too perfect order in lines. Except in fire-drills, where the safety of the group may be imperiled by the inattention or disobedience of one, a certain amount of innocent foolishness from children just from the playground ought to be overlooked.

This same attitude may be best, also, regarding quite an amount of the harmless and perfectly natural and normal mischief and "monkey shines" that take place about a school building or in a classroom. Many a boy is haled before a class and punished by a teacher when what he has done should be ignored, smiled at, gently interfered with, laughed at, or the whole proceeding adroitly turned against him and he be made to appear ridiculous. A lack of understanding of child nature, a lack of sympathy with boys, a lack of love for and interest in teaching, and a lack of a saving sense of humor cause unhappy experiences to many a teacher and pupil. Such a condition is usually evidence of poor teaching, and cannot be remedied merely by instruction in classroom control.

Snowballing is often a source of trouble, and repressive measures, while holding it largely in check on the grounds, still give the principal plenty to do. A frank talk about the matter before the snow comes, and an understanding as to what is fair and right, will do much to prevent trouble. If possible, a part of the grounds or the street may be made free for the sport, and the regulation of it be given to the older pupils. Often a code can be set up under which immunity for pupils going to and from school may be largely guaranteed; other relations can be established with the police which will help to enforce the guarantee. If the sport must be prohibited on the school grounds, because of their small size and the attendant danger, the reasons for so doing ought to be made clear to the pupils.

Fighting among pupils. Fighting is another common cause of trouble in every school. Among boys from the ages of ten to twelve fighting is more common than among either the older or the younger children. At this age the instinct for fighting seems to be at its height. Boys appear to fight from the love of the game. Girls seldom fight, and when they do it is usually more distressing than serious. Boys on the whole fight fairly, and frequently a fight between two boys clears the atmosphere and makes friends of the combatants as nothing else could do. If the mothers of the boys can be kept from taking too active a part in the affair it usually has no bad results.

When two boys, fairly evenly matched, between whom trouble has long been brewing finally "get at it," it is a good plan for the principal not to be in any great hurry to arrive and stop the fight. Sometimes it is a good plan to let hostilities proceed until there are signs of slackening, and then step up and tell the boys they would better stop now and go in and wash up. The case can be investigated afterward. If the case was one where a mutual settlement was inevitable, and would have taken place outside if it had not happened on the school ground, and if it seems that a satisfactory settlement has now been arrived at, it is usually best not to inflict punishment at all.

In one such case as this, a principal of the writer's acquaintance merely told the boys that she hoped, now that they had the matter settled, there would be no further difficulty. She then gave the boys open excuses to their teacher for being tardy, stating that they "had been detained on important business," and sent them to their rooms. This made them grin, settled the matter, and the boys afterwards became good friends. It takes some courage to do this, when indignant mothers send notes denouncing the moral standard of a school which allows fighting, but practically no protests ever come from the fathers on this score.

Such fights are fights with a real cause, and the boys' way of looking at the matter must not be lost sight of. Adults are prone to think lightly of the troubles of children, but they are very real to them. Women particularly often fail to understand a boy's code of honor, and frequently regard such affairs as uncalled for and meriting severe punishment. Adults too often forget that the use of fists long ruled mankind, that intellect and the moral sense are comparatively recent developments, and that there are situations when a keen sense of his personal honor is a man's best capital. Not many boys are "too proud to fight." On the other hand it is undoubtedly a duty of the school to teach young people how to rise to a higher level, and how to settle disputes by an appeal to reason rather than to brute force.

After treatment for fighting. There can be no set procedure for handling fighting, and a principal should have no set rules regarding it. Fights are individual, and do not go

DISCIPLINE AND CONTROL

by rule. Some are childish, and may be classed as mere "scraps" without an apparent cause. Calling each other names is one of this class, and probably starts more school fights than any other one thing. It is usually confined to the younger boys and girls, and especially to those in grades four to six. One school known to the author broke these fights up by having a stock punishment for such affairs, consisting of requiring the contestants to sit together in one armchair for an hour, before the class, with their arms around one another. Sometimes such scraps develop into real fights when older boys are concerned, and usually arise out of a "kidding match." Finally one boy makes a jibe that goes beneath the skin, and a fight is on. In such cases little or no punishment is needed, but the silliness of such a fight needs to be adroitly brought out by the principal. Sometimes it is a school bully who picks on the wrong boy, or pushes some mild-mannered boy too far and gets a well-deserved thrashing. In such a case it is wise to let him get it, and then tell him that he got only what he merited.

As to how to take hold of an affair, once it is brought to the attention of the principal, depends on the circumstances involved. In the majority of cases it is fortunate if such things are not referred to him, for such notice merely serves to lend dignity to them. The writer knows a principal, and a very successful one, who simply lets the little fellows fight it out. Then it is settled. If a fight starts on the playground, among the younger boys, he steps over and insists that they settle the issue. As a matter of fact, the instigator becomes weak in the presence of authority and the affair speedily terminates. A fight among the older boys is somewhat different.

When two "scrappers" put in an appearance at the office with fighting as the cause, a good plan is to permit the boys to "sweat" a while. This permits their tempers to cool down a bit, and they are then more amenable to reason. Once they are in this frame of mind they must not be further aroused by undue severity from the principal. A friendly, kindly, and often a jolly attitude, and a refusal to take their difficulty seriously often suffices to make the boys feel foolish and accomplishes results, if the fight is about a trivial matter. On the other hand, when both combatants feel keenly the justice of their stand, quite a different method must obtain. The matter now deserves careful consideration, and the boys must be made to feel that they are going to get a square deal. Nothing less will suffice. Then by a course of mediation the breach may be healed. It must not, however, be forced. A principal is compelled to deal with human nature as he finds it. He may endeavor to remedy the situation; he may condemn the fighting; but he must not, by sheer authority, compel an external acquiescence to the judgment passed. This does not inspire respect for the principal's decision or fairness, and forced apologies are worthless and leave a lingering sense of injustice which may easily cause the trouble to break out again.

Sometimes talking the situation over with each offender individually, and then bringing them together and repeating the story will straighten out the trouble. The boys may be led to feel silly or ashamed, or to see the lack of good sportsmanship in their action. Where one is clearly the aggressor the other may be excused, even commended for defending himself if the aggression was unwarranted, and the aggressor punished or deprived of some privilege he values.

The school bully: promoted fights: gang fights. These are the more serious cases, and call for a different type of treatment. The school bully, who imposes on smaller pupils, is usually a coward, and a thorough whipping on the first clear-cut case will usually stop him. The bully is commonly a product of inadequate play facilities, and schools

DISCIPLINE AND CONTROL

with good playgrounds usually have few bullies to deal with. Making the bully an assistant play director often cures him by giving him a new and better occupation. Sometimes, on the contrary, he is merely low in mentality and vicious by nature, and needs to be sent to a special school.

Promoted fights, that is fights instigated by older boys, who by telling different lies to each of the principals finally get two boys to fighting, are hard kinds of fights to handle. At times these will be worked up and pulled off after school. The first knowledge a principal may have of them is when an indignant parent brings a battered-up boy to school the next morning and complains. It is best to proceed slowly here, and to be sure to have the instigators located before acting. The boys who have been led to do the fighting can usually be cured by showing them what fools the leaders have made of them. Sometimes, also, privileges that count will have to be withheld from them for a time. The promoters, when finally located, who in nearly all cases are older boys, need to be dealt with in such a manner as will effectively stop further fight promoting. The more a spectacle the fight was made the more severely they should be dealt with. The principal must make it clear to the school that, while he does not prohibit fighting when the provocation is great, fight-promoting he will not tolerate.

Gang fights are perhaps the hardest of all to handle. If the two gangs are from different schools it is a little easier, as school pride comes in to help. Little can be accomplished here by threats or punishments. The commonness of the gang spirit and the loyalty of the gang must be recognized. Usually the best avenue of approach lies in a pleasant smile and a "Well, boys, who won?" type of question. This will usually bring out all the little details, especially from the winners. Then the problem is rather to repair damages and try to prevent future gang fights. The ordinary good-natured town-boy gang does not need punishment so much as a deflection of its energy in better directions; the depraved village-tough type of gang calls for more severe measures. The principal must exercise common sense in such matters, and be able to distinguish between cases that can be partially or wholly overlooked and those calling for vigorous action.

Fighting, of course, must be condemned, but the principal should not make the mistake of trying to prohibit it entirely. Every case which comes up is worthy of more or less attention, and should be dealt with so as to try to teach the participants that arbitration, compromise, and often toleration are better than war. The lesson should be made as convincing as possible without savoring of the sanctimonious. The principal stands in the capacity of referee, and in this capacity he must measure up to a boy's conception of a square deal. He must be able to see the boy's point of view in the affair, and all his decisions must ring true. In the settlement of these "affairs of honor" the principal has an opportunity to do much to build up among the boys a reputation for fairness and justice. This is one of his most valuable assets as a principal. He has also a fine opportunity to do constructive work that will tend to establish better methods of settling disputes than by fighting them out. He may thus be able to make his discipline pay in social training all that it costs in time.

Lying and stealing. Lying varies in character and seriousness to such a degree that few rules can be laid down for dealing with cases of it. The causes for it are hard to find. With little children a vivid imagination may be responsible, and when this is true very mild correctives should be employed. Some children lie from fear to tell the truth; a premium on truth-telling and the sympathy of the teacher may

DISCIPLINE AND CONTROL

be helpful in such cases. On the other hand, unruly boys who want to accomplish some mischief through lying need much firmer handling. Some of the most baffling cases are with girls, for which little excuse is evident. It is best not to give public prominence to the cases, but to handle each as far as possible quietly. Often the lies are unpremeditated, do not indicate depravity, and do not warrant severe censure. Any attitude that provokes stubbornness on the part of the pupil will be fatal if the truth is desired. To tell a child caught in a lie that you will never believe him again is a great mistake. You may feel that way, but refrain from saying so.

Stealing is a much more serious matter, especially if the article stolen is of value. One must proceed slowly and be quite sure of the facts before acting. If very little stealing is done it is best not to warn the pupils about the safety of their belongings, as it leads to speculation and works against the morale of the school. When the offender has been located, the mode of approach will depend much on the nature of the child. It is best to take the matter up with the child and if possible settle it there. Sometimes it is best to call in the parents. In dealing with offenders, ask your questions so the pupil will feel that you know. To ask the pupil *if* he took the article is less satisfactory than asking him *why* he took it. Vigorous measures are less effective, except in the case of old offenders, than gentle measures.

Not infrequently one finds, too, a child not by nature bad but who by environment has come to consider deceit and theft something of an art, and who feels some pride in his or her success in this line. Many such children are classed as bad when in reality they are only ignorant. They frequently respond in a surprising way to kind treatment, to an appeal to a sense of honor, and to a new conception of standards and values in life which a principal or a teacher may give them. Harsh treatment of such children would probably lead to moral ruin.

The principal will do well in dealing with all such cases to emphasize the idea that neither lying nor stealing really pay. Our whole social and civic life is built up around the sanctity of one's word and the inviolability of private property. This can be pointed out, and that to repudiate these standards is always in the long run a losing game — loss of friendships, loss of self-respect, loss of position, failure to get on in the world, and ultimately the payment of a severe penalty. Honesty, as a mere practical proposition, is always the best policy, and wrongdoing never pays in the long run because the present-day world has set its face against it. Cases in real life that escape penalty for long are very rare, and the course can never be one of permanent profit. The child will grasp the idea more quickly if reduced from moral to practical standards. The causes back of these two offenses — lying and stealing — still remain to be dealt with, and they are delicate matters upon which to approach parents. Still, if tactfully done, nearly all parents will respond in the proper spirit when they see that the object in appealing to them is the good of the child. The chronic case, the habitual liar and thief, is another matter entirely. Such pupils should be isolated, if firm dealing with proves ineffective, or turned over to the juvenile court to handle.

Vulgarity and obscenity. This has been considered before, in Chapter VII. Most of the vulgarity and obscenity manifested about a school building — obscene writing and pictures on blackboards, walls, and in toilets, and foul talk — are closely associated with the reproductive instinct, and indicate not only an unwholesome state of mind but also a lack of enough good hard play to turn the attention into other channels.

In case of a proved piece of obscenity a plain frank talk

DISCIPLINE AND CONTROL

with the pupil may be effective, or a conference with the parents may seem desirable. To have the father or mother brought face to face with the child for such a transgression usually has a salutary result. To get the pupil busy in play activities also has a good tonic effect.

The principal as judge. Most of the cases with which the principal has to deal will be cases which arise on the playground, in the hallways or basement, or on the way to and from school. These may be classified as the general cases. Regardless of how good the corps of teachers may be, there will always be a few cases which arise in the rooms, in the handling of which the assistance of the principal is desirable. In most such cases it is better if the pupil has to go to the principal for a hearing. Usually this will be by prearrangement with the teacher, but sometimes a crisis will come so suddenly that this is impossible. It should be understood that a pupil so sent is virtually suspended from the room, and can only be reinstated by the principal after a hearing of the case. During this time the pupil should remain isolated, receive no favors, and be allowed no privileges.

In all such hearings the principal should choose his own time, and should adopt a system that will enable him to handle the cases rather rapidly. A few general rules may be useful.

1. Do not deal with an angry pupil. **Give him time to cool off** and think it over.
2. In the beginning, state the **complaint clearly and fairly** to the pupil, and listen to his defense.
3. If the case is a rather evident one, lead the pupil by questioning to see that he has convicted himself.
4. Show no feeling against the pupil while listening to his case. Avoid any personal feeling; be judicial; try to get the pupil to talk freely; get the facts.
5. Try to get at the motive behind the offense as well as the facts, and evaluate this in terms of the principles of organized society.

Having arrived at the facts and the motive, the principal must now determine what is to be done about it. He should not work by fixed rules, but should consider the offense, the motive, the provocation, and particularly the age, understanding, and general attitude of the pupil. He should remember that the purpose of all discipline is constructive and not penal, reformative and not retributive. There must first be order in a school that the school may do its work, but behind the requirement of order lies the end for which order is sought and enforced. In most cases the bad effect of such conduct on the society in which the pupil lives can be made clear, and how soon that society would go to pieces if all assumed such liberties pointed out. The difference between liberty and license, and the fact that one person's rights end when they interfere with another's liberties, may be brought out.

In determining what is to be done, the principal as judge should keep in mind certain principles of control.

1. The punishment should be adjusted to the offense, the motive behind it, and the pupil.
2. It should seem fair and just to a reasonable pupil, and be closely associated with the offense.
3. Unless a frank talk and an admonition are considered sufficient, which may be the case with certain first offenders, the punishment ought to cause the pupil some real discomfort.
4. Avoid using threats, school tasks, taking away earned marks, personal indignities, sarcasm, ridicule, or inordinate punishment as penalties.
5. Among desirable means are deprivation of privileges, isolation, restitution, public apology, appeal to public opinion, reports to parents, assignment to a special class, corporal punishment, suspension, and in extreme cases expulsion.
6. Do not give any decision or administer any punishment impulsively. The attitude toward the offender is important. Punishments should be impersonal, distinct, deliberate, and decisive. In case of corporal punishment it is best to have a witness present, and to keep a record of the action.

If the pupil has damaged or taken property, a willingness to repair or restore it is good, provided he actually does it; if he has wrongfully taken the time of a class, he may be asked to forfeit some of his own; if he has committed an offense against a class, he may apologize for it, and if against a teacher, to her. In certain types of offenses the punishment may be left to the class to consider and determine. A period of probation, if an old offender, may reasonably be insisted upon. A fundamental principle to be insisted on is that the amends or apology should be made before the group or person before whom the breach was made. If the offense was a public one the apology should be public; otherwise the pupils may think the offender "got away with it."

Making discipline productive. One often hears it said that discipline is worth its cost in the chance it gives for teaching life lessons of value. Handled rightly, every outbreak in a classroom or school offers an excellent opportunity to train young people for social control. Every fight, every gang scrap, every petty theft or piece of mischief, every truancy, and every offense against order or decency or law offers a constructive opportunity to teachers and principal to place the control of the school in the future on a little higher plane. A skillful principal will seize upon these situations and set them right before young people. He will gradually bring the pupils to see that conduct in a school is after all the same in principle as conduct in a home or in society.

The idea should be continually emphasized in handling cases that offenses are not offenses against the principal or teachers, but against the class or school, and that the class or school has some right to protection and in saying what shall be done with offenders against their rights. The analogy to society should be kept clear. The more thoroughly this idea can be developed in a school the more likely is the discipline to become easier and productive.

Young people usually have a strong sense of justice and fair play, know the meaning of a square deal, and appreciate being dealt with as though they possessed some manhood and were worthy of some respect and confidence. Dealt with on this plane they will accept punishment without bitterness, as the records of our juvenile courts well reveal. Wherever possible, it is on this plane that the principal should handle his cases. Take pains to get the pupils' point of view, try to look at the matter as they did at the time, find and bring out the weakness in their conception of their rights, deal with the case without passion, keep an eye for the humor of the situation, and test your decision before announcing it to see if it will appeal to the pupils as fair and just. Often it pays to be in no hurry about a decision; often it is a good plan to set the case clearly before the pupil and let him think out what ought to be done about it; and sometimes it is wise, after all the facts are in, to put the problem before the pupils of the offender's room and let them discuss it and decide by vote upon it. It is, after all, not so much a question as to what the principal or teacher will do about any particular breach of discipline as to what the pupil will do, and where the training in thinking out what ought to be done can well be extended to a group it is good to do so. It is often quite a revelation to a pupil to be told by his classmates that he was wrong, and, if he does not mend his ways, that the class does not wish him longer as a member. If this is to be done, however, teachers and principal must permit pupils to discuss the occurrence freely, and must at times accept decisions which are not quite what they would have made for themselves.

Decreasing discipline by prevention. The end and aim of school management and control should be to build up in the school such an interest in work and good order that discipline, as such, will be largely unnecessary. To shift

DISCIPLINE AND CONTROL

young people's ideals, by proper handling, from malicious mischief and general bad conduct to constructive work for a common good and purpose, and to make them feel that what they are doing is very important, is a wonderful service to them. It also contributes much to making a school easier to control. Constructive discipline, plenty of motivated school work, good teaching, good playground organization and inter-school games, organized pupil activities, a good grading and promotional plan, wise use of the assembly period, employment of the pupils as leaders, the awakening of a school pride and loyal spirit, the development of some type of community service, and the impress of the ideals and personality of strong teachers and a capable principal — all these contribute as preventive measures to decrease the necessity for much attention to discipline.

It is the business of the school to try to find and bring out the good that is in young people, and to turn youthful energy and spirit into useful channels. Unruly boys and girls can often be almost completely changed in character by awakening their pride, making them feel that they are of real help and use, and filling them with a desire to become somebody worth while in this world. The school offers an alert principal and body of teachers plenty of constructive opportunities, both in the school and in the neighborhood, for training pupils for useful participation in civic life. To open up these possibilities for service and turn the energies of the young people into new and useful directions constitute important means for reducing disciplinary troubles, and for shifting the disciplinary problem to higher levels.

QUESTIONS AND PROBLEMS

1. Point out the tonic effect on a school of plenty of play, good system, a good regimen of work, and spirit and snap in what is done.
2. Assuming that you keep lines and marching, what rules as to order in line would you insist upon?

3. Point out the opportunity for useful instruction in having pupils see the difference in order that must be insisted upon in a fire-drill.
4. Show how the bullying tendency may be made useful in helpful control of children, and what transformation to a higher level in thinking this produces in the boy.
5. Suppose two boys, in play. One makes some statement, the other flares up and calls him a liar, gets slapped in the face, and a fight is on. What would you do about it?
6. Suppose two girls, for no real provocation other than personal dislike of one another, get into a scrap with hair-pulling and kicking, when you stop the affair. What would you do about it?
7. A somewhat ugly and spoiled boy in a classroom refuses to do something a teacher tells him to do, and when she puts her hand on him to urge him along, he turns and kicks her on the shin. Without attempting to handle him further, she sends him to you. What would you do about this case?
8. You tell a big boy, on the playground, to do some simple thing; he does not move or say anything: you tell him again, and he tells you, "Go to Hell." What would you do in this case?
9. Half a dozen eighth-grade boys frame up a promoted fight, after school and off the school grounds, between two sixth-grade boys in your school, and before an audience of thirty or forty of your boys. They are fairly evenly matched, and both are badly bruised. The first you know of it is the next morning, when the mothers of the two boys arrive to complain to you of the affair. What procedure would you follow, and what would you do?
10. You set a trap and catch a twelve-year-old girl, at a recess period, taking small change from the pockets of wraps of other girls. The girl is from a reasonably good home, and there is no reason why she should steal. Map out two or three possible lines of action. Suppose the girl to be from a poor, ignorant, foreign-born home and, similarly, map out your lines of action.
11. Show the large opportunities that come, both in management and instruction, in bringing to pupils the conception that honesty actually pays.
12. How may a school, through discipline and control, promote the idea, often advanced, of nations finding a peaceful moral substitute for war?

SELECTED REFERENCES

(For this and the following chapter)

Bagley, W. C. *School Discipline.* 259 pp., New York, 1914.
    Very sane and helpful for either principal or teacher.

Barclay, L. W. "Educational Work of the Boy Scouts," pp. 663–77.

Crouson, B. *Pupil Self-Government.* 100 pp., New York, 1907.
    Somewhat elaborate self-government plans, based on the author's experience as a principal in New York.

DISCIPLINE AND CONTROL

Curtis, H. S. "The Boy Scouts"; in *Educational Review*, vol. 50. 495–508. (December, 1915.)

Low, Juliette. "Girl Scouts as an Educational Force," pp. 677–83.
> Two good brief articles in volume 1 of *Biennial Survey of Education*, United States Bureau of Education, Washington, 1921.

Morehouse, F. M. *The Discipline of the School.* 342 pp., Boston, 1914.
> A helpful consideration of the problem. Contains a good chapter on assisting a teacher with disciplinary troubles, with concrete suggestions.

Perry, A. C., Jr. *Discipline as a School Problem.* 273 pp., Boston, 1915.
> A good practical treatise on discipline as an individual problem, as a class problem, and as a school problem. Part III deals specifically with discipline as a school problem.

Puffer, J. A. *The Boy and His Gang.* 188 pp., Boston, 1912.
> A very good book for principals and teachers to read.

Reudiger, W. C., and Strayer, G. D. "The Qualities of Merit in Teachers"; in *Journal Educational Psychology*, vol. 1, pp. 272–78. (August, 1910.)
> A study of the ranking of 204 teachers by their principals. The study shows the most important element entering to be disciplinary ability.

Sears, J. B. *Classroom Organization and Control.* 300 pp., Boston, 1918.
> An excellent treatment of the subject from the teacher's end of the process. Part II deals with attendance, punishments, and incentives.

Smith, W. R. *An Introduction to Educational Sociology.* 412 pp., Boston, 1917.
> Chapter 13 contains an important discussion of the social aspects of school discipline.

Strayer, G. D., and Englehardt, N. L. *The Classroom Teacher*, 400 pp.
> Chapter VI, on Training for Citizenship, good on the disciplinary problem.

True, Ruth S. *Boyhood and Lawlessness; The Neglected Girl.* 358 pp., New York, 1919.
> Two studies in one volume. Valuable reading for the city teacher.

Waddle, C. W. *Introduction to Child Psychology.* 317 pp., Boston, 1918.
> A valuable book, summarizing the results of a quarter-century of work in child study. Contains very good chapters on the play of children, child morality, and juvenile delinquency.

CHAPTER XV

THE TEACHER AND GOVERNMENT

Relation of principal and teachers. While the principal must of necessity handle most of the general and more serious cases of discipline that arise on the playground and about the school, he must not be expected to do the entire disciplinary work. The infractions of order and the breaches of discipline which occur in the classrooms and in the presence of the teacher elsewhere should be handled largely by the teachers themselves, and without bothering the principal about it or taking him away from more important service. Just as the efficiency of a principal is to be in part measured by how few cases of discipline he sends to the superintendent's office, so the efficiency of a teacher must in part be determined by how well she handles her room and how few disciplinary cases she sends to the principal.

This does not mean that a teacher should not consult the principal about disciplinary cases, or seek his professional advice as to handling them. On the contrary, this is often very desirable. Serious cases he certainly ought to know about, whether he comes in touch with the case or not. The corporal punishment of the school would best be administered by him alone, but with the teacher or the janitor as a witness. It simply means that teachers should try, with advice as needed, to handle as many of the cases of discipline that arise under their jurisdiction as they can, and that sending a pupil to the principal's office ought to be in the nature of a last resort. More, naturally, can be expected of some teachers in this matter than of others, and full allowance for natural difficulties of new and inexperienced teachers must be made. These differences the principal should take into consideration, and he should accordingly lay down few general rules as to when he should and should not be called upon.

Different classes of teachers. Not infrequently a new principal will inherit a school, not unruly as a whole, but a school in which a few rooms are unruly. Again a principal who has brought a school under good control will find new teachers frequently have to be "broken in" and fitted into the organization. A principal in any large school will also usually find that he has three or four different types of teachers, considered from the point of view of classroom control, and different degrees of obligation will rest upon him, in the matter of helping in discipline, with these different classes. There will be at least the able and helpful teacher, who has little disciplinary trouble, and who seldom needs any assistance from the principal; the military disciplinarian, who secures order, but without the best results; the beginner, who needs help but can learn or is learning; and the beginner who lacks the personality and the understanding requisite, and who probably never will learn to be effective.

Any principal is fortunate if he has a majority of experienced teachers who are both able teachers and able disciplinarians. The better the teacher usually the better the disciplinarian, the two abilities being closely related. Often the best teachers seem to have no discipline to handle, and often they are unable to tell how such happens to be the case. These teachers will constitute the older, better trained, more discerning, and more experienced corps of the school, and will call for little help or advice in disciplinary matters from the principal.

Probably not all the older and more experienced teachers will belong to this first class, for one often finds among the older teachers one or more who handle problems of discipline alone and keep a certain kind of order, but whose ideal in discipline is fundamentally wrong. They are the martinets of the building, and the pupils usually resent their strictness and the military type of control which they impose. The effect of the discipline of such a teacher on the spirit of the school is not good. Sometimes a suggestion to her, as one who has perfect order and hence is in a position to allow more freedom and more spontaneity, will bring the desired results. Sometimes a teachers'-meeting consideration of the problems of child control will act as an entering wedge, and stimulate the teacher to read some good book on classroom organization and control. Often the principal can render a real service in enlarging the teacher's viewpoint and modifying the military aspect of her schoolroom control. Probably just as often, on the other hand, little or nothing can be done to change conditions.

It is with the beginners and the less experienced teachers that the principal's chief work in forming disciplinary habits must be done. These will fall rather quickly into at least two classes. The first class will be the teachers of promise who are anxious to be helped and to learn, and the second will be those for whom one can do little other than preventing anarchy before the year is over. Most beginners, however, belong to the first class. The second class will not often appear in school systems where evidence of professional training and competency are made prerequisite for employment.

An alert principal will discover the characteristics of his teaching force very early in their work together, and will seek to help those in need and to apply preventive measures before the situation gets beyond control.

Shaping conditions to be of service. The first thing a principal must do, in the process of helping a teacher in trouble with her discipline, is to diagnose the situation and locate the cause of the weakness. When that has been done, corrective treatment may follow. By first analyzing the problem the principal can determine if the teacher has the proper ideal of what good order is; if not, how he can impart this to her; if she has the right ideal, what is preventing her from realizing it; and what devices and line of procedure will enable him to help her most easily and surely. A careful analysis of the breaches of discipline occurring in her room may reveal the sources of weakness, and indicate the best type of remedial treatment to follow. The difficulty may arise chiefly in the passing in and out, or in the confusion caused by passing material. It may be that the trouble is caused by one or two pupils who are not classified properly, or whose loyalty is yet to be won. It may be that the pupils are not kept busy, or that the instruction does not call for activity in doing or thinking on their part. It may be that the difficulty arises from the teacher trying to teach some subject in which she is not competent.

Another necessary prerequisite to aiding a teacher is the establishment of sympathetic and helpful relations with her. She must be made to feel that the principal is interested in her success and really wants to assist her. Between teachers and principal there is not infrequently a lack of the right personal attitude. In cities where the board of education expects the principal each year to find teachers to dismiss, an attitude of fear and suspicion is almost certain to exist. An office-chair principal, who is primarily an executive, may awaken the same suspicious attitude on the part of the teachers. A not uncommon position for teachers to take toward a principal, until he disarms suspicion by service, is that he is a detective, a boss, a driver. Often in addition there is the feeling that, after all, he really does not know. Men principals probably are more often regarded in this light than are women.

A prerequisite to any large helpfulness, then, is that such

suspicions be allayed. If this can be done, and the teachers put in the right attitude toward the principal, the road in the future is much easier. Some principals do not try to do much in helping teachers until the right personal relations have been established — until the teachers have come to see that the principal wants to be a guide and leader and helper, and not a driver and boss and spy. A principal needs the friendship, confidence, and trust of his teachers, and they must feel that he can and will help them if they will give him the chance. It will be worth much to a principal to spend time and effort in establishing such relationships.

The situation having been diagnosed, and some sort of helpful relationships having been established, the principal is ready to proceed in assisting his teachers with their classroom problems.

Strengthening the teacher in government. Those most in need of help are usually the young and inexperienced teachers. What they need is advice as to how to strengthen their control. This must be given through observation and suggestion, but not by doing the governing for them. Above all, the principal must refrain from doing anything that may give the pupils the idea that he considers the teacher lacking in governing ability. From the start the teacher must realize that her problem must, after all, be solved by herself, and the principal should try to give her confidence in her ability to succeed. A great element in success is the feeling that one can "swing" what one undertakes to do. Usually a little encouragement, appreciation of what is well done, helpful suggestions, and an appeal to her self-reliance will be the best tonic for a live and capable girl that a principal can give. In addition, he may employ the following devices by way of helping her to put herself in control and to develop the necessary confidence in herself.

THE TEACHER AND GOVERNMENT

1. Give her very practical suggestions for improvement, out of your own experience as a teacher.
2. Caution her to make few rules, but having made a rule to insist upon a reasonable compliance with it.
3. Caution her against making rules involving definite punishments for misbehavior. The pupils may decide that the fun is worth the pain. Punishments should come as surprises.
4. Caution her to say what she means and to mean what she says. Do not try to discipline a school with a continual volley of Don'ts. Do not tell pupils twice. Do not try to bluff the American boy, and do not be bluffed by him.
5. Do not let her start out either too severely or too easily. One direction leads to the martinet, and the other to the easy, mushy, "golden-ruler," who soon forms an easy mark for the mischievous and unruly pupils. If she learns from the first to keep cool, to be sympathetic, but to temper her kindness and sympathy with firmness, and at times with the exhibition of a little "nerve," few pupils will care to bother her long.
6. Try to keep the beginner from worry and despondency; she needs all her energy for her teaching problems.
7. When you visit the room be careful to let the pupils see that you continually defer to her as in control. Never criticize her before the pupils.
8. Use your influence to build up in her class a kind of pride in the success of that particular class. Stress the fact that class comparisons are made, and show them what they need to do to bring their room up. The pupils will usually respond.
9. Show her that her strongest ally is public opinion within the schoolroom itself. If she assumes that the offender is on one side against the other pupils and herself, this alignment is likely to be a strong factor in her favor.
10. Remember that a well-taught school is usually an orderly school, and strive most of all to build up the teacher in teaching skill. In particular, show her how to strengthen the mechanized routine of the school. Have her grasp the idea that she is there primarily as a teacher, and that if she teaches well the discipline will be reduced to a minimum.
11. Locate the weak points in her control, and give her magazine articles or a book to read which will be helpful to her.
12. Give her a few half days for visiting, and let her see other teachers at work who do not have her defects. If there is a

"demonstration teacher" or a "training teacher" employed by the school system, arrange for her to visit the teacher and offer help.

The teacher must be brought to see that good control involves the recognition of the fact that different cases call for different types of treatment. Sensitive pupils sometimes offend against group well-being, and for these a reminder is enough. Stupid or thick-skinned obstructionists may need more vigorous handling. The worst type of trouble maker may sometimes be cured by securing from him acceptance of some responsibility; frequently "live wires" make trouble for lack of something better to do. Imposed trust may successfully challenge this type to higher action. Sympathy, humorous appreciation of the childish point of view, and ability to turn a clever jest — these sometimes relieve a situation for a group and call down on the offender the laughter of the class. In but few cases will there be those for whom the only effective treatment is through the cuticle.

If the principal has been so unfortunate as to draw a teacher who cannot learn methods of control, though he has exhausted all efforts to help her, he has one of two courses which he can follow. The first is to transfer the more unruly pupils to other teachers and reduce the size of her class, and the other, and probably the more effective of the two courses, is to tell her that you have done all you can to help her and that the responsibility for control must in the future rest with her. Thus thrown on her own resources, she must learn to carry the responsibility if she is to survive to the end of the year.

Causes of poor control. Poor control in a classroom usually is evidence either of a weak personality, one lacking in force, or of faulty organizing and instructing ability, or both. Native managerial ability plays an important part in classroom control. The teacher's general make-up may arouse hostility. A poor high-keyed voice, a high-strung nervous manner, peculiar dress, constant nagging, sarcastic remarks, and a lack of patience and sympathy with children may easily stir up a room to disorder. Unfairness in attitude toward children, and an easy manner one day and a cross one the next will not do. When such defects are evident, the principal must frankly tell the teacher the causes of her troubles and suggest corrective procedure. Many of these mannerisms and bad habits, once the teacher becomes conscious of the handicap they impose, may be eliminated by her personal attention to them. If the teacher has no real sympathy with and interest in children, tell her that she must at least assume these attitudes for the sake of her influence with them.

Inferior organizing ability and lack of system also cause much poor classroom control. The children feel the want of the smooth-running organization that evidences mastery. The room and the pupils often reveal these characteristics of the teacher. Things are helter-skelter, the room is often in confusion, often little is accomplished in the recitation time, and a poor start in the morning carries over through the whole day. The pupils fail to experience the pleasure that comes from thorough systematic work, and mischief and disorder arise. The principal must, little by little, train such teachers in order and system and organization. This he cannot do, though, if he does not possess such habits himself.

Poor teaching method is a prolific cause of poor classroom control. Poor methods of presentation, poor recitation technique, poor preparation and assignment, lack of content in the instruction, too much talking on the part of the teacher and too little work by the pupils, all are very conducive to disorder in a classroom, and the handling of this disorder inevitably degrades further the quality of the teaching. The close relation between a busy, contented school and good teaching technique and ease in control should be pointed out and illustrated by the principal. To teach the class for her, give her helpful constructive criticism on what she does, and send her to visit other classes with a definite purpose in mind, are all good correctives. Select some helpful book on classroom technique, such as Bagley's or Morehouse's *School Discipline*, or Sears' *Classroom Organization and Control*, for her to read.

What a new principal may find. A new principal, on taking charge of a building, may find that the teachers have in the past been in the habit of depending largely on the principal to handle the discipline of the school. His predecessor may have been more of an office type of principal, and may have not only enjoyed the disciplinary aspect of his work but may also have been remarkably efficient in it. In such a situation the new principal would best lay his plans to change the procedure. Helping children to overcome disciplinary ills and to develop into self-directing and useful citizens is a part of a teacher's work, and the problem of discipline can be made as productive in the classroom as in the principal's office. Still more, there is likely to be much more discipline to handle when the pupils see that the teacher does not or can not handle it.

The subject may be a very fruitful one for consideration at the teachers' meetings which the principal will hold. If so, he must approach the problem from the point of view of the pupils' best interests, rather than from a desire to be relieved from the work himself. While standing ready at all times to help his teachers with their discipline, he must nevertheless encourage them to study the problem and use their own resources with a view to becoming more self-reliant. Gradually he must more and more deal with his teach-

THE TEACHER AND GOVERNMENT

ers in the way described above for new teachers, and more and more push back upon them the greater part of the work of handling pupils and training them to overcome their objectionable habits and develop into useful citizens.

The principal should gradually come to an understanding with his teachers as to just what kind of disciplinary cases they are to refer to him, and what types they are to handle themselves. This will vary somewhat with different teachers, for reasons previously stated, though certain types of cases may be expected to be handled by all teachers alone. The principal should work to strengthen his teachers by resigning to them just as much control as they can learn to handle. The teacher knows the child and the offense better than any one else, and where she can handle it alone or deal with the parents about it alone she should be permitted to do so.

Supporting the teacher in government. The first real try-out of a new principal, in so far as the teachers of his building are concerned, will come the first time one of his staff sends an unruly boy to his office for discipline. Much of the principal's future success in the school will be determined by the wisdom with which he handles this first case. If he does not handle it well; if he is weak or vacillating; if he palliates the offense or sides with the pupil; and if he does not impose a punishment or require an amend suitable for the pupil and the offense, he will lose not only the confidence of the teacher sending the pupil but probably that of the whole force as well. News that the new principal is weak and will not back up the teacher spreads rapidly throughout the building, and it may take a good principal a long time to regain the confidence lost on a first case.

One of the greatest helps toward good discipline that a teacher, new or old, can have in her school work is the support of the principal in what she tries to do. The principal's attitude toward her, both in and outside the classroom, counts for much. She should be made to feel that the principal will stand behind her in all just treatment of pupils for purposes of control.

While the principal should stand behind his teachers and be ready to take over cases formally referred to him, on the other hand he should not be expected to settle every little perplexing case arising in a classroom. Teachers who begin that way should be gently given to understand that they must learn to handle the cases that are within their ability to handle. A principal who pursues any other course is not doing his duty by his teachers. Instead of building them up in classroom control he is leading them toward failure. The pupils sense the situation, the rooms become more and more unruly, and the boys and girls take a chance with the principal for the fun of worrying the teacher who cannot control them.

On the other hand, teachers are at times "run over" by the momentum of a disorderly school, where the real fault lies in the weak personality or lack of support of the principal. Not only must the general morale of the school be insured, but a teacher is strengthened by knowing that disciplinary cases which she sends from her classroom will be settled with decision in the office, or that her own rulings, if within the pale of justice and reason, will be promptly and vigorously sustained by her superior in case of an appeal. Given this assurance of solid backing from the principal, it is the teacher's next move to avail herself of it as little as is possible and to handle her own difficulties as long as she can.

Supporting the teacher when wrong. Even though the teacher may have imposed a punishment that is pedagogically wrong, or have gone a little too far, from the legal or politic point of view, if a new teacher and not knowing better the principal ought to stand by her. He should, of course, under such circumstances explain to her why he would not have done it that way, and why what she has done is pedagogically or even legally wrong, but assure her that this time he will stand behind her as fully as he can and help pull her through. Only when she has violated known rules can he fail to support her.

If, for example, she has punished a pupil by assigning him a lesson to study or a poem to memorize, enforce her authority and see that the pupil does it, but make her see that this is not a proper punishment because pedagogically it leads to bad results. Defend her as far as possible from irate parents, even though you may feel that she has not acted very wisely. The beginning teacher cannot be expected to possess the same sound judgment and pedagogical skill as an experienced principal. One of the reasons for the principal being in the position he is, is that he may guide and direct and help educate the new and younger employees in the teaching service.

The teachers must come to understand, however, that while advice and full support will be given them in handling their troublesome cases, and that while a strong arm will be ready in last resort to uphold their authority, still, for their own good and for the good of their children, they must feel that the final responsibility for good order rests with them. This is necessary for a teacher's best development, that she may in time learn to walk alone. Teachers must also be made to see that poor teaching organization and technique lies at the bottom of most disciplinary troubles. A busy school is a contented school.

Protecting the teacher. A principal can do much toward making a teacher's lot easier and winning her full coöperation by protecting her from over-strain and annoyances, that she may do her work under good conditions and in peace. He must possess tact and understanding, and be willing to shunt off from her all the worry and trouble he can. This is a part of what he is there for.

Teaching is a hard nervous strain to most women, and a young teacher often wears under it badly. When signs of nervous over-strain appear the principal should try to ward off trouble by assuming some of the teacher's burden, or by relieving her of her class at an hour when the class seems particularly troublesome. It is always desirable that the children should not detect any evidence that the class is too much for the teacher. An hour in the rest room at times has kept many a nervous girl from becoming discouraged and losing her hold. Sometimes an older and well-established teacher can be materially helped in a similar manner.

The complaining parent. Another form of protection of teachers that the principal ought to assume is that of dealing with parents who write or come to complain. It is probably best that teachers be instructed to turn over all complaining and fault-finding notes to the principal for reply, and it adds force and dignity to the reply when the parent sees that the teacher has taken the matter to the principal, and that the reply comes from him. His reply is more effective, too, if it is on official letter paper, is written on a typewriter, and is properly and formally addressed and signed.

Parents not infrequently send hasty and angry notes to teachers on the biased and incompetent evidence of their own children. It is best for the principal to assume the duty of answering all such notes, and his letter of reply should be dignified, brief, non-argumentative, should assume the parent's interest in the welfare of the child, and usually should be conclusive and not of a type to invite further argument. Where the letter is typewritten, it is well to retain a carbon copy for evidence, and this the teacher should be permitted to read.

The irate parent who comes to the school. A complaining

or irate parent coming to the school should in all cases be taken over by the principal. Notices in the hallway should direct the parent to the principal's office, and the rules should forbid a complaining parent going to the teacher's classroom. Should the parent do so, as is frequently the case, the teacher may talk with him or her if the school is not in session. If it is, she should politely but firmly refer the parent to the principal, and not permit the time of the class to be taken up in listening to a complaint. The teacher should be protected in this action by this being made a school rule. A pupil may be sent with the parent to find the principal, or to show the way to the office. The principal should then take over the case and handle it for the teacher.

A first rule in such an interview is to keep cool and collected and to let the parent do most of the talking. Talk is an excellent safety valve. Do not interrupt except to ask necessary questions. Assume throughout that the parent is reasonable and rational and deeply interested in the welfare of the child, even though you think otherwise. When you finally come to a decision, give it quietly and judicially. The fact that you have listened and have kept cool gives you the advantage that calmness always has over anger. Perhaps after all it is only some little misunderstanding caused by some child's tale, and a few calm, tactful, and reasonable words will set it right. If you think this will not be sufficient you may take the case under advisement, or, if you wish to secure further information, ask the parent to leave the matter with you and to call again. It is sometimes good psychology not to be in any hurry to make your decision. While giving each case a just settlement do not worry over the difficulty, and try to deal with each case as it is likely to look to you a month afterward.

Sometimes it may seem best to arrange for an interview

on the matter between the parent and the teacher. If it is after all a trifling matter, easily explained, it will be good for the teacher and the parent to talk it over. This meeting may be arranged for at the close of school, and may be left to the teacher to handle. If the parent is likely to be unreasonable, then it would best be in the principal's office, and the principal would do well to remain or to be within call. If matters become unpleasant, the principal should come to the rescue of the teacher and take charge of the interview. Such protection and defense of a teacher is just and right, and will do much to give tone and character to the management of a school.

Many of the complaints which come to a principal at his office he should handle and settle without saying anything to the teacher about them. If the teacher is right, as she usually is, he should protect her from the annoyance and worry incident to the complaint. It is part of the principal's business to shield his teachers as much as possible that they may do their teaching in peace and under the most favorable conditions.

Improving relations with parents. Much is now done by our schools to bring parents, teachers, and the public into better understanding and closer coöperation, and to promote harmonious relations generally. Parent-teacher associations, the visiting nurse and teacher, and organized school publicity are all new efforts to establish better understandings. These new developments are all very useful and, even in small school systems, can be made quite effective. Despite all that can be done, though, to keep parents in touch and sympathy with what the school is trying to do for their children, the difficult or unreasonable parent will from time to time appear. Both the principal and the teacher are likely to encounter him or her. While the number of such parents is relatively small, and if the school

THE TEACHER AND GOVERNMENT

stands well in the community they need not be taken very seriously, yet there exist a number of varieties of this species of parent, and these different varieties have to be dealt with in somewhat different ways. One principal has made the following classification:

1. Parents who listen to all the childish grievances, and develop unreasonable prejudices against the teacher.
2. Parents who incite their children to take revenge by petty annoyances for fancied grievances.
3. Faddists along some line, such as some school subject, vocational work, over-study, open-air classes, outdoor work, or religious education.
4. Parents who try to form the lives of their children, without considering abilities or aptitudes.
5. Parents who regard the teachers as servants, and claim special rights as taxpayers.
6. Parents who enforce no discipline at home, and object to the school having any.
7. Parents who expect the school to do for their children what their abilities will not permit of being done.
8. Sensitive parents, easily offended over nothing.
9. Egotistical parents, very sure of themselves and of their children.
10. Ignorant parents.

A safe method in dealing with all these cases lies in getting acquainted with the parents, learning their point of view, meeting them on the common and perfectly safe ground of mutual interest in the child's welfare, talking little and listening much, a plentiful use of tact, impartiality, and an effort to educate them as to their child's best interests by giving them new points of view. In case of necessity the principal can fall back on the perfectly safe ground that the superintendent and the board of education have so ordered, and that he is held responsible for certain results; that his teachers and he have better technical knowledge as to what ought to be done than has the parent; and that no one is more interested in the child's best welfare than are his teachers and himself. The handling of each case should be carried through in a calm, judicial manner, and should evidence the same dignified tone expressed in the principal's letters to the parents. The principal may be called upon to defend the school and his teachers. In so doing he should appear to maintain an impartial attitude and base all his reasonings and decisions on the real welfare of the child.

Many of the cases coming to a principal's office, generalized and made impersonal, form excellent material for discussion at general meetings at which parents are present. So utilized, tactfully and without fault-finding, they give a principal good opportunities to inform his community as to the work of his teachers and his school, and to contribute to the building up of a sentiment which will increase coöperation and decrease complaints.

QUESTIONS AND PROBLEMS

1. The first day of school, in the autumn, you enter the room of a beginning teacher and find it all in confusion. Throughout the first week the teacher seems to gain little in organization or control. What would you do, and why?
2. Suppose, in your building, of two beginning teachers in the lower grades, you finally come to the conclusion that one is of promise and anxious to learn, but very young and high-strung, while the other is heavy, slow, and probably hopeless. Give some lines of procedure for each.
3. Assume for the first one, and list, eight mistakes she constantly makes in control, and suggest a remedial line of treatment for each.
4. List half a dozen devices you would employ, in either case, to lead the pupils to think you look up to the teacher and respect her authority.
5. List, also, half a dozen mistakes a principal might make in such a room and with such teachers.
6. Show the connection between good health, a good time sense, good organization, a good sense of humor, good teaching technique, and good easy discipline and control.
7. Suppose a new but experienced teacher comes to your building, and from the first sends nearly all disciplinary cases to you to handle. Just what will you do about it?
8. Formulate, for your school, a line of demarkation to separate types of

cases teachers should handle for themselves and cases that should be sent to you. Would this vary in the different school buildings and under the conditions indicated for the six schools drawn in Figures 5 and 10? Why?

9. The first week you act as principal in charge of a school an old teacher in the building has an altercation with an upper-grade pupil. It seems to you to have arisen largely from the teacher having been hasty and not understanding the pupil, new to her room. She orders him to stand in a corner until dismissal time, and, when he refuses to obey, sends him to your office for punishment. What will you do about it?

10. Suppose a teacher in your building slaps a boy over the ears, contrary to the rule of the board of education, and the mother comes to you about it, quite angry, demanding redress under pain of carrying the case higher. What would you do?

11. Suppose, in the case of the boy in Question 7 of the preceding chapter, you temporarily suspend him, sending him home with a note requesting the mother to call. Your investigation leads you to conclude that the boy was wholly in the wrong. The mother calls, is very indignant, and defends her boy. She demands a transfer for him to another school. What would you do in this case?

12. A parent sends the following note to a teacher:

> Miss Eldridge:
> My boy is a good boy, and I don't like the way you pick on him and favor other boys. I told him not to stay in for you after school, so don't try to keep him again for trivial matters. If you do I shall be forced to carry the matter to the principal.
> Yours truly,
> (Mrs.) S. J. McCurdy

The teacher refers the letter to you. Just what reply (draft letter) will you send the mother?

13. Outline in syllabus form the main points in a talk you would give on "School and Home Coöperation," if asked to speak on such a subject to the Parent-Teacher Association of your school. How long would you plan to talk?

SELECTED REFERENCES

(See end of preceding chapter.)

CHAPTER XVI

BUILDING UP A SCHOOL SPIRIT

The school without spirit. The presence of any large amount of trouble with attendance and discipline in a school is generally indicative of something fundamentally wrong in the organization and administration of the school itself. Such a school probably stands as an organized institution, fulfilling the letter of the law, but without having developed that spirit which gives life to an institution and attaches children and parents to it. One still finds many such schools, though they are less common to-day than they were a decade ago. Where they do exist one generally finds that neither principal nor teachers have become conscious of any large social purpose in their work. In consequence, the school they control fails to measure up to its possibilities as a social institution, training young people for life. The pupils accordingly show toward the school little of that loyalty which they give to their outside interests; they disregard its regulations when it seems reasonably safe to do so; and they absent themselves from its instruction for trifling reasons. The school, in turn, falls back upon a stricter discipline and a more rigid enforcement of the compulsory attendance law, and a vicious circle is formed which prevents the possibility of improvement.

There are many explanations for such a situation, the chief of which has just been stated. In the end all explanations go back to a failure of the school to grasp the social significance of its work, to see the importance of taking pains with young people, enlisting their interests, and making the school seem vital and important and real to them. A principal and a body of teachers who regard such labor as too much trouble, who feel that they are not paid for work outside of school hours, or who have become afflicted with labor-union conceptions of the teaching service will quickly produce such a condition. One of the most unruly and socially most inefficient school systems with which the writer ever came into close touch was one in which the teachers had formed a teachers' union, the purposes of which were stated to be "to shorten the hours of labor, increase the compensation, and advance the professional interests of all." The first two purposes were the important ones. In five minutes after the schools closed in the afternoon one could seldom find a principal or teacher about a building. It was often a good wager as to whether the principal, teachers, or children would get away first. There was much truancy and many occasions for discipline, the instruction was lifeless and socially ineffective, the parents seldom visited the schools except when sent for or to complain, the private and parochial schools in the community were flourishing, and the community interest in public education was low. Yet in school systems of this type one occasionally finds a school or two, and more frequently rooms here and there, where quite a different attitude is evident and where that something called school spirit pervades the work.

What is school spirit? Every school, naturally, has some kind of a school spirit. There may be a spirit of insubordination or of indifference, or an anti-social attitude. These types, though, are not what is usually meant by the term. Instead, we have gradually come to use it as signifying something better and more social — a certain subtle something which motivates and gives purpose and life to the work of the school. Using a term made common in the World War, it might well be described as school *morale*.

It is not an easy matter to define what is meant by the right kind of school spirit, though its absence in a school is easily recognized. When absent, its lack is noticed at once by the experienced observer. When present, it stimulates and energizes all. Its influence is felt in every department of the school's activity — in the classrooms, on the playgrounds, about the building, and on the streets. It is responsible to a large degree for the good feeling, cheerful manner, school loyalty, and team work in evidence on every hand. Often, too, it expresses itself in a spirit of healthy pride, and in friendly rivalry with other schools. The discipline is materially decreased, the cases are simpler and more easily handled, truancy and tardiness are greatly diminished, while corporal punishment and the expulsion of pupils practically disappear. The principal is less often called upon for disciplinary service and consequently has more time to think and plan and supervise, while the superintendent's office gives but little thought to the school. School spirit is a contagious something, and soon spreads throughout a group from the one infected with it.

The principal creates this spirit. Probably in no single aspect of the organization and administration of a school is the statement that "as is the principal, so is the school" more true than in the creation and maintenance of a good, strong, healthy school spirit. If the principal loves his work, if he is adapted to the service, if he is possessed of a good working philosophy for the educational process, if he thinks and plans well, if he believes in young people, if he has energy and executive capacity, if he possesses that ability to fire others with his own enthusiasm for ideals and service, he can usually make over a school according to his own desires. If he lacks some of these qualities he should try to cultivate them, for nothing will help him more in his work, attach parents and pupils to him more closely, or do more to transform his school into a constructive agent for ministering to the social needs of a modern world than will the awakening among his pupils of a strong, healthy school loyalty and spirit.

How he goes about doing this is of the utmost importance. He may know perfectly well just what kind of a school spirit he would like to develop in his school, but by proceeding along wrong lines he may utterly fail to create it. In few places in his work will a practical knowledge of child psychology stand him in better stead. To talk to the pupils and tell them that they have no school spirit, that they ought to do this way and not to do that way, that they ought to be ashamed of their actions or of themselves, that some other school has so much more spirit than have they — these are sure ways to kill what little good spirit may exist. It cannot be stimulated that way. On the contrary, little talks about school spirit, and an emphasis on the constructive work which tends to awaken and develop spirit and ideals will be the most effective means a principal can use. He must create it by getting the pupils interested and busy rather than by too much talking about it, though a certain kind of talking, as we shall point out in the following chapter, is very valuable.

What means to use. Just what means a principal should use in the work of creating a strong school spirit for his building will vary somewhat with conditions which he may inherit, the character of his teaching force, the presence or absence of an assembly room, and the stage in development in which he finds his school. We shall briefly enumerate certain means which may be used, placing them somewhat in the order in which probably they will be most serviceable.

1. Make the instruction good. As has been previously pointed out, the improvement of teaching technique is one of the best means for improving order and discipline. A busy school is almost sure to be an interested and an easily-controlled school. If the teachers are not very capable, it is especially important that the principal give careful attention to this first of all. He must so arrange whatever else he has to do as to find much time to give to the supervision of instruction and the improvement of classroom technique. Through helpful suggestions, teachers' meetings, and selected reading, he must gradually build up not only the technical skill of his teachers but a professional pride in what they are doing as well. On the side of discipline they should be shown how to mechanize the routine work of a classroom so as to handle it rapidly and effectively, using pupils as helpers whenever pupils can assist advantageously. On the side of general conduct some attention should be given to good manners, and to the general human relationships expressed in the usages of society. On the side of the instruction itself, much attention should be given to the motivation of the course of study and to means for promoting effectiveness. Many opportunities come in history, literature, civics, and geography which an alert teacher can use to good advantage in giving to the pupils proper social and civic ideas. Good teaching, interested teachers and pupils, and well-motivated instruction lie at the very foundation of school spirit of the right kind.

2. Monitorial service. To make use of the surplus energy of the pupils, and especially of the more troublesome ones, in performing all kinds of little services about the school is a step toward building up school spirit and warding off trouble. A number of such services have been suggested in the preceding chapters, such as having pupils assist the teachers in various minor ways about the rooms — distributing and collecting papers and supplies, opening windows, cleaning blackboards, recording thermometer readings, collecting waste paper, etc. — and as room attendance officers, room and playground health officers, fire-drill officers, school flag details, managing the signals, street-control traffic police, managing the school bulletin board, oversight of the little ones on the playground, an accident squad, and similar forms of pupil activities. All such means require a little time at the start to interest the pupils and train them for the service, but the time is well spent, as it in turn relieves the principal and teachers from routine work. The pupils enjoy looking after such matters and regard their selection as an honor.

3. The playground games. Athletics offer large opportunities to a principal and teachers to organize the older pupils, both boys and girls, into groups and squads in a way that will do much to develop leadership. Often an incipient school tough may be made into a useful school citizen by making him an assistant playground director. In the games which are played, and especially the inter-school games, many opportunities for the development and expression of a school spirit and school loyalty are provided. To work off the surplus energies of a school in hard active play is a good way to shunt off trouble.

There ought to be in each school some teacher who would be willing to help the girls, and another the boys, in the matter of organizing and helping to direct the play and games of the pupils. The principal will find it time well spent occasionally to give part of his Saturdays to the games of his pupils, and to help them prepare for inter-school contests. To be selected to umpire a ball game or to referee a contest is an honor he should be glad to accept. It is a concrete expression of the pupils' belief in his good judgment and fairness, and is worth much to him in the daily work of the school. One main reason why discerning parents to-day pay large tuition fees to private schools for the supervision of the education of their boys is that the private schools make a strong point of giving to their pupils just this type of activity supervision and leadership training.

4. Organization of group activities. There are numerous other group activities which it is desirable to organize within or about a school. In the conduct of these the different teachers can render much service, as one teacher can take charge of the development of one group activity, another teacher of another, etc. Some of the possible activities of this group type are a school orchestra, a musical club to attempt more difficult work than the regular classwork provides, singing clubs for learning familiar songs for the pure enjoyment of it and also to entertain at assemblies, sewing clubs, cooking clubs, canning clubs, gardening clubs, bird (Audubon Society) clubs, nature-study clubs, hiking clubs, story-telling clubs, civic clubs, health leagues, etc. Such organizations often mean the adopting and transforming of the gang spirit. School gardening can often be made a very important spring undertaking, the work being done after school hours, and if an exhibit and prizes and ribbons can be added, it awakens much interest.

Which of these activities to organize will depend largely on the interests and abilities of the teachers and on the local environment, as well as somewhat on the season of the year. Do not attempt to organize more than one or two at a time. In connection with these various activities a school picnic may be given, once a year in the spring, in which the different clubs take charge of the arrangements and entertaining.

5. Scouts and Leagues. The Boy Scout and Camp Fire Girls or the Girl Scout organizations ought to find a place in each school, and some teachers ought to be interested enough to train themselves as Scout Masters and take charge. If the principal should have done this at some time and become a member of the Advisory Council it will be good. Whether a man or woman principal, few things are likely to give him or her a better hold on the boys and girls than to be familiar with and interested in the Scout work.

Another useful organization of a similar type is the Girl Reserves, an organization affiliated with the Y.M.C.A. The opportunities for enlisting service, building up a school morale, and toning up the whole school through the help of these organizations, are many and should not be neglected.

Pupils of the Scout age are easily enlisted in service, and service is a prime feature of the Scouts. A Scout is a friend to all. He is a big brother to every other Scout. To introduce such a spirit on the school grounds and about the building is most important. There is a spirit of adventure and romance in the Scout organization. There is a lesson to be learned and the Scouts are usually eager to learn that lesson, whether it be a lesson in nature-study, first-aid, kindness to animals, courtesy, or what not. There is an appeal in the drills and the "hikes" and the required accomplishments, and in these boys participate with enthusiasm. The girls have equivalent lessons which they take pleasure in learning. One of the reasons for the strong spirit of the Scout organizations to-day is that they teach their members to feel that there is a strong relation existing between them and society in general — that their organizations foster manliness, self-reliance, personal honor, truthfulness, helpfulness, service, and similar civic and social virtues.

There are certain other forms of service-organizations that can be made to present a strong appeal if properly carried on, though they are not so easy to put on a running basis as are the Scouts. The Junior Red Cross, school health leagues, and school civic leagues for the study and enforcement of local regulations have been made valuable adjuncts to school work in many places. The Junior Red Cross is doing good work generally; in one city known to the author a local school health league coöperated with the city health officer to clean up and make sanitary the dirty part of the city in which the school was located; in another city the pupils organized their school as a city, for school governmental ends; in still another city, the children of the whole city coöperate, by paper sales, service, entertainments, etc., to help maintain a free dental clinic for the children of the city.

6. *School entertainments.* School entertainments, while requiring work, are generally worth their cost in time and effort in building up a school loyalty and spirit, and in interesting parents in what their children are doing. Entertainments, in which many organizations participate, may be given to raise money for things the school may need, such as play apparatus, a projection lantern, a moving-picture machine, a Victrola and records, school pictures, etc. Keep the entertainments simple and representative. Have the pupils, not a few but many, prominent on the program. Try to do something that the pupils like to do and the parents like to see, and which will be somewhat representative of the school work. An annual school fair, or exhibit of work, to which the parents are invited and at which the pupils act as hosts, is another device sometimes used in building up school spirit among both pupils and parents.

7. *The school assembly.* Not many elementary schools possess a school assembly room large enough to seat all the pupils at one time, but where such does exist it is a school gain to take a quarter of an hour at the beginning of each day for a school assembly, if the school is organized as a grade school. Group work can be made much more effective than can the individual room exercises. If, on the contrary, the school is organized as a platoon-type or Gary-type school, neither the opening assembly nor opening room exercises will be needed, as the regular use of an assembly room by groups of classes throughout the day is provided for in such a type of school program. The assembly work then becomes one of the activity subjects of the school.

Even under these conditions a weekly school assembly is desirable, as school spirit rather than group spirit is built up here.

The assembly is so important and so useful, both in developing a school morale and as a teaching institution, that the subject will be considered more at length in the chapter which follows.

8. The school savings bank. The institution of the school savings bank has usually been found a very useful adjunct in developing school spirit. While the main idea is to teach thrift and the value of money, it also, if the idea gains momentum in a school, becomes another means of developing that form of healthy rivalry which contributes to the formation of a school spirit. Instead of the teacher doing all the work, it is a good plan to use eighth-grade pupils for the clerical work. It gives them practical experience and a sense of pride in their own importance. The pupils are likewise proud to be the possessors of a bank book.

9. Outside influences that help. In addition to all the influences within the school which have been enumerated as helping in the creation and maintenance of a school spirit, much valuable assistance can also be obtained by gradually enlisting the coöperation of certain forces without the school, as will be described more at length in Part V of this book. Chief among these are the Parent-Teacher organizations, any School Improvement League that may exist, and the press if the city be small.

The pupil-government idea. Another method of building up a school spirit that at times is made to work well, but which has to be approached very carefully and dealt with very intelligently, is that of using the pupils in a somewhat formal way as participants in the school government. Full school government in an elementary school seldom works even reasonably well, due to the youth and extreme individuality of the pupils. There is a tendency, too, to concentrate attention on the elections and then to leave to the officers the whole matter of the school government. Certain elements in the pupil self-government idea, however, are capable of application in the control of an elementary school. These cannot be inaugurated all at once, but year by year, as pupils and parents become accustomed to the idea of that individual self-control toward which any adaptation of the idea tends, the responsibilities for order can be shifted more and more from the paid employees of the school board to the pupils themselves.

Notwithstanding what has just been said, very elaborate plans for pupil government have been worked out and used with apparent success by a few principals here and there. The Jane Brownlee plan, worked out a few years ago at Toledo, and widely advertised, is a good example. The success of all such plans depends ultimately upon the principal and teachers behind the plan. Any successful plan for self-government in an elementary school requires stronger disciplinary skill on the part of the authorities than does the ordinary type of school control. A young principal in particular should be very sure of his ability to control a school and secure good conduct from the pupils under ordinary conditions before experimenting with any elaborate plan for self-government by the pupils themselves.

Partial plans and adaptations. A number of simple and partial adaptations of the pupil-government idea have already been described, such as pupil control and direction of the playground games, pupil attendance officers, pupil police, pupil health and first-aid officers, use of the Scouts, student handling of assemblies, and, in certain types of cases, student determination of punishments to be imposed. Often it is best to stop with these features as being about all that the peculiar conditions within the school and the neighborhood seem to make desirable or possible. Sometimes, on the contrary, it is perfectly safe to go further.

One simple plan, used here and there very effectively, is that of making the eighth-grade class feel a certain responsibility in the conduct of the school. The suggestion is given them that they set a pattern and establish an atmosphere, somewhat as do seniors in the high school or in a college. The principal and the teacher of the class make them feel that they consider them as anxious as they themselves are to maintain the best possible school spirit, and they and the other teachers also encourage the younger classes to make themselves ready for their responsibilities when it shall come their time to serve. Confidence in this class is shown by sharing with it many little duties and honors, and by making its members feel that they are of much importance in the management of the school.

The school council. Another simple plan, which certain principals have made work rather effectively, is that of creating a student council and using it to give pupil support to good ideas in school control. One plan used was to have each room, above the second, elect a boy and a girl to the student council of the school. Another was to have each room above the second elect but one person, boy or girl as they might decide, and then have also on the council the president or head of each registered organization (the council to determine the registration, according to rules), such as athletic clubs, music clubs, Scouts, Audubon Society, etc., as *ex-officio* members. This plan naturally brings to the council the leaders and framers of opinion of the school. Sometimes the pupils also select one or two teachers to be on the council with them. It is usually best that this be done. In any case the principal is a member *ex officio* and the guiding genius of the council.

This council meets once a week to consider school affairs

and problems, and all general regulations for the school as a whole are first approved by it. Such problems as yard control, care of building, throwing papers, conduct in the basements, Halloween control, annoying neighbors, snowballing, lines, drills, special entertainments and programs, and athletic events are talked over, and any needed rules concerning them made. Much valuable elementary training in parliamentary procedure can be given in such an organization. What the council considers is actually in large part what the principal and teachers have previously planned, and the council can nearly always be brought to decide as the school authorities wish. The pupils, though, think that they are making the decisions and promulgating the regulations, and in consequence enforce what they have decided upon. Still more, at assemblies or in class, what has been talked over and decided is reported and explained, and often student sentiment on a proposal may be polled, or enlisted by the class leaders.

Handled carefully, this type of organization can be made a very effective means for creating and maintaining a good helpful school spirit. If some other school does something good or wins some special recognition, the pupils begin at once to plan to do something better. As everything done can easily be made subject to keeping up the class work and having a good attendance record, the organization becomes a leverage for good school work as well.

The school-captains plan. Another adaptation of the pupil-control idea, which one principal known to the writer has carried on very successfully for years, consists of the appointing by the principal and teachers of one boy and one girl, each half year, from the eighth grade, to act as captains general for the boys and for the girls. These pupils then appoint, from among the older pupils, as many assistants, known as captains, as they deem necessary. These captains, under the direction of the captains general, take over the supervision of the building and grounds, from 8.15 to 4.00. The captains general assume full responsibility, and are the only ones the teachers or principal consult in case of any irregularity.

Captains are assigned for duty to handle the hallways, basements, toilets, playgrounds, ring the bells, care for apparatus, look after the lines, supervise the games, collect any information asked for by the principal, take the attendance records and look up absentees, collect fines, and protect property from damage. Each captain is given authority to impose discipline as in his or her judgment the case may require, reporting to the captain general. Any pupil or parent may appeal to the principal, who may be seen by any one with a grievance. He may confirm or reverse a decision. The regulations enforced are those of the school, though the captains may propose new regulations or the modification of existing ones, and these become effective if approved by the principal.

The School Congress idea. Another adaptation, sometimes used effectively, is the School Congress idea, in which a constitution is adopted by an elected Congress, somewhat after the model of our national Congress. This School Congress works through committees, a committee being appointed for each of the main activities of the school, such as school-ground control, playground supervision, attendance, discipline, complaints, color guard, games, field days, thrift, health work, special entertainments, speakers, etc. The purpose here is civic training, as well as school control, the plan being to make every pupil feel that he is an interested and responsible member of the school community, and that what he does is of importance in helping to create a good school spirit and a school of which all may be proud.

Results of such pupil-control plans. Such plans, when

they can be inaugurated under good conditions and be backed by the right school spirit, are very valuable aids in control and do much to teach young people to govern for themselves. They do not relieve the principal and teachers of the duties of oversight nor of the holding of control in the background, but they do change his work and that of his teachers from that of detectives to advisers, and greatly decrease the necessity for classroom and school-ground control. Such systems tend to break up gangs, decrease jealousy and bitterness between pupils, and do away with the spirit of trying to beat the teachers at a game of wits. They introduce the "Big Brother" idea into control, and relieve principal and teachers of any immediate building and yard supervision. They tend to promote frankness and honesty and a new attitude toward law and order.

Need for this work in our modern society. The great social and industrial changes in the past three-quarters of a century, with the accompanying development of city life, have thrown a new responsibility upon the school for the proper education of the young in much that makes for useful and successful living in organized society. The home has undergone great changes in nature and spirit and purpose, while both life and education have become specialized. In consequence, the home to-day leaves to the school a large amount of training which once formed no part of the function or purpose of the school. The modern city is essentially a center of trade and industry, and home life and home conditions must inevitably be determined by this fact. The city, too, emphasizes education through the eye and the ear, but gives little through actual doing. Children under the older home conditions, too, were taught reverence, courtesy, respect, proper demeanor, obedience, honesty, fidelity, virtue, and useful employments much more than they are to-day. The coming to our cities of large numbers of foreign-born children, and especially those from the south of Europe, has further complicated the educational problem.

To remedy some of these defects of our modern city life, to give pupils some useful education through doing, to create for them good standards and habits, to awaken the spirit of fair play, good sportsmanship, and high ideals of honor and righteousness in the social and civic life, are new opportunities and obligations of the modern school. Our school organization and instruction cannot be divorced from these essentials without the loss of valuable possibilities. The cultivation of a strong and healthy and loyal school spirit, by some such means as are indicated above, helps greatly not only in control, but, even more important, in preparation for civic usefulness and social participation.

Difficulties the principal will meet. This spirit of loyalty and idealism and service is not easily built up. Teachers often lack sympathy with the idea, and consider the time and effort required as completely beyond the benefits derived. Sometimes petty jealousies and animosities among the teachers undermine it, or prevent its creation. The pupils are at first shy of such organizations, and have to be dealt with carefully. Sometimes the parents think it is all nonsense and object. It has to be nurtured patiently year after year through its period of infancy, until a feeling of pride in the school because of what it does for one can be built up, and then transformed into a feeling of pride in one's self and a willingness to be of service to one's fellows. Such a spirit, once built up and carried along, often persists after principal and teachers have departed and the spirit of the school has changed. As evidence of this, one not infrequently reads, in our cities, of a meeting and banquet of the "old grads" of some grammar school, thus bearing witness to a spirit that once existed and to a leader no longer there.

Sometimes, on the other hand, it takes the form of a testimonial of affection to some principal, retiring after a quarter-century or more of service in one particular school.

In all this work the personality of the principal and the wisdom of his guidance are of much importance. A school, as well as any other human institution, moves forward or backward according to the quality of its leadership. It is the principal who must conceive the problem in its larger aspects, he who must think it through, he who must secure for it the sympathetic interest and coöperation of his teachers, and he who must guide and guard it in its development. Often he can do this best if he thinks his plan through and then outlines it to his teachers but slowly, making his moves one at a time. Teachers are easily frightened if they think their burdens are to be materially increased. As the different pupil agencies are developed the principal and his teachers must set aside time for the purpose of keeping in touch with the work they do, and the pupils must be made to feel their real interest in what is accomplished. A principal and teachers who have faith in children and in their power to govern themselves, and who train their pupils to have confidence in themselves and in their ability to do so, are the ones who make a system of pupil-government successful.

QUESTIONS AND PROBLEMS

1. Will such conditions as are described on page 303 almost inevitably follow such an attitude on the part of the teaching force?
2. What is the effect on the spirit of a school (or a class) of lecturing or scolding those present for the faults of those absent, or the many for the actions of the few? Under what conditions may this plan still be useful?
3. In the school buildings shown in Figures 5 to 10, in what ones would it be easiest and in what ones most difficult to develop a good school spirit, assuming teachers and pupils to be the same? Why?
4. In assuming charge of a school which has but little good school spirit, and in attempting to build it up, would it pay to take the time from classroom supervision which this new work would for some time demand? Why?

BUILDING UP A SCHOOL SPIRIT

5. Assuming that you decide to inaugurate a number of group activities to develop a better school spirit, as described in 3 to 6, pages 307-10, indicate how you would like to use your teachers for service in such a building as is drawn in Figure 7, page 98.
6. Suppose that your teachers have no special ability in any of these lines, and while not unwilling are not interested. What means would you take to get them into service?
7. Show the large values in citizenship training of health leagues, Junior Red Cross, Scouts, school civic leagues, and the school savings bank.
8. Why is the group assembly, in a grade-type school, so much better than individual room exercises?
9. Some teachers and principals object to assemblies of the whole school each morning as (a) a waste of time, and (b) likely to promote disorder. What of these objections?
10. Why is it a good idea to give special importance and position to the highest class in the school?
11. Why, in a school council, is it desirable to bring in the natural leaders of the school? In starting such an organization it may bring in the leading school toughs. Would this be harmful?
12. Suppose an old couple, living near the school, complain to you about the annoyance and discourtesy they are subjected to by the pupils of your school. What would you do, assuming it to be a legitimate case for complaint, (a) if you have no pupil organizations for control, and (b) if you have a school council or school captain plan in working order.
13. In a certain city known to the writer a group of men, between the ages of forty-five and sixty, meet once a year for a dinner and to tell stories of their school days. The group is known as the "old boys" of the Lincoln (elementary) School. What conclusions do you draw from this?
14. When labor strikes occur much lawlessness frequently results. Do you see any connection between this and the type of imposed discipline usually found in our schools?

SELECTED REFERENCES

(See end of the following chapter.)

CHAPTER XVII

USE OF THE ASSEMBLY PERIOD

Arranging for school assemblies. Another very important means for assisting in building up a school spirit which will materially aid in the elimination of tardiness, truancy, and disorder is the proper use of the school assembly. Many elementary schools, unfortunately, do not have an assembly room in which all or even half the pupils can meet together. Where this condition exists, the principal must resort to various expedients to try to obtain for his school the advantages that come from assembly periods. Sometimes this can be done, in good weather, by more or less frequent exercises in front of the school or in the yard. As the pupils must of necessity stand, these periods should be short, held only in good weather, and must be carried through with more snap and go than would be needed were the pupils seated in an assembly hall. If bleachers, such as are shown in the Figure 8 school, exist, they may also be used for good weather meetings of parts of the school. A larger lower central hallway, such as is shown in the Figure 5 school, may also be used for group assemblies. Basement playrooms may be utilized at times.

Where there is an assembly hall in the building the principal should utilize it for general meetings. Sometimes all the school should meet together, and in some schools it may seem desirable that this plan be followed regularly. Perhaps most of the time, however, the little ones, say the kindergarten and grades I to III, should meet separately from the grades from IV up. One suggestion as to meetings would be:

Wednesday   General meeting of all pupils.
Monday, Thursday   Kindergarten and Grades I–III.
Tuesday, Friday   Grades IV–VIII.

Another plan, though not so good, would be to have separate assemblies as the regular thing, on alternate days or at different times of the day, and joint assemblies only on such special occasions as Thanksgiving, Christmas exercises, February 12 and 22, Arbor Day, Longfellow Day, etc. The time given to the meetings, when the assembly hall is used, should be about fifteen minutes, with the time extended possibly once a week to twenty-five or thirty minutes, if something especially interesting is put on.

Importance of the assembly period. The value of an assembly period in unifying the work of a school and in giving tone and spirit to what is done is not fully appreciated by many principals and most teachers. Too frequently the principal carries it on largely because it is prescribed, or because in a general way it is thought to be a good thing to get the pupils together, while the teachers look upon it as a waste of teaching time. On the contrary, if rightly used, it is one of the most important periods of the day. A live principal can use this period as a means of getting a firm grasp on his whole school. Others may do much of the work, and the better he has it organized the more this will be the case, but he must keep in touch with all that is done and through it all stamp his personality on the work of the school.

The assembly, rightly used, offers a splendid opportunity for the awakening of that intangible but highly desirable asset called school spirit. It is here that the principal and his teachers and his pupil aids may create and build up that school spirit which is so useful for effective school control and for united effort. A school which can have assemblies, and which does not stress the importance of this period, loses a great opportunity to arouse school loyalty and an ambition to be useful and to succeed.

The principal and the assembly period. Too often the assembly period fails of usefulness because it is misused and mismanaged. Dry ceremonial, listless routine, a religious atmosphere or too much emphasis on religious observances, and an insistence on perfect order on entering and while there, invariably fail to produce results. The assembly, too, must not be a cut-and-dried affair. If the pupils know the nature and order of the exercises, and about what songs will be sung, the assembly will not make any strong appeal. Neither should the time be used for collective scolding and fault finding. Anything of this nature, as well as "sermonizing" by the principal, are certain to be fatal to school spirit. Not much time, either, should be taken for announcements. If announcements are to be made, do it with a clear decisive voice, in a businesslike manner, and with dispatch. If a bulletin board, or the classroom, or the school recess after-whistle period would serve better, do not use the assembly time. Nor should a principal use the assembly period often as his time for talking. There must be variety, and what is done must appeal to the interests of the children and be suited to their needs and capacities.

Yet at times the principal should take the assembly in hand and talk, using the period to fix more firmly his grasp on his school. For such times he must make preparation, and know just what he is going to do and how he is going to do it. For a young principal to go before the assembled pupils without detailed plans is most unwise. It is to him that the young people naturally look as the leader and final arbiter of the school. They recognize in him the head of affairs, and he ought by his assembly manner and speech to fix their faith in him and to awaken their admiration for the way he does things. It will not be possible for a principal to fix their faith or win their admiration if he fails to measure up to their ideas of him at these important times. If he conducts the assemblies as though they were a bore to him, if he seems weak and forceless, if he is unnecessarily stern and severe, or if his conduct as the pupils observe it does not square with his talks, he will awaken instead their disrespect — secret it may be, but none the less forceful. Hesitancy, weakness, vacillation, a fault-finding attitude, an excess of seriousness, lack of a sense of humor, or an exaggerated idea of his own importance may spoil the whole effect. Whatever the principal does should call for his best effort.

"Heart-to-heart" talks. If the right kind of relations have been established between the principal and his pupils, he can at times use the assembly period most effectively to appeal to the best side of the young people. The children of the early adolescent period are idealistic to a high degree, and are easy to set afire with enthusiasm for good things. The principal is the one to supply the spark. Rightly used, the principal can make these little talks, once good relations have been established, one of the strongest disciplinary agents in his school. He must be forceful, quick, good-natured, appreciative, and constructive to be effective.

At times the principal will need to talk directly to the pupils regarding some misconduct on the part of the school, or some needed change in the direction of school activities. Then he must be very clear in his own mind as to what he wants to accomplish and the means he must use, and he must be very concrete and talk in terms the pupils will understand. By making practical application to the needs of the moment he can, if he uses tact and skill, develop loyalty, ideals, appreciation, patriotism, and other virtues of a well-managed school. By occasional intimate talks on matters of school control, the general attitude and discipline of a school can be materially improved, and the school property protected instead of destroyed. By making the youngsters see that after all the school is their school, and that only foolish people destroy their own property, school depredations can be replaced by school protection. By talking simply but concretely and effectively on questions of civic responsibility, human relationships, morals, ambitions, and ideals, by skillfully seizing an opportunity presented to drive home great life lessons, and by talking with enthusiasm but not sanctimoniously, the principal may leave a lasting impression for good with the young people under his control.

Types of assemblies. A number of types of assemblies may be conducted with advantage, and quite a little variety in type is desirable. At times, as has just been described, the principal may use the assembly period to "put over" some idea he wants the pupils to get. Sometimes a teacher may present the program for the day, or some citizen be asked to speak. The assembly may at times be used for imparting information of general interest to the school, or for showing the place of the school in work or in competitive events with other schools of the city. In all these types the principal and his teachers conduct the assembly and present their points of view. Within limits, this type of assembly can be made very effective.

Another type is that in which the pupils as a whole participate, as in chorus singing, and in expressions of school loyalty and spirit. Mass singing is a very attractive and effective means for developing school spirit. Some schools use a song, often selected by the pupils, as the first number of every assembly. Some teacher who can lead well and put vim into the singing should take charge. It is important that there be some swing and go to the affair. On certain days special "song assemblies" may be found desirable. School loyalty and spirit demand opportunity for expression, and at times the assembly can well be given over to an

USE OF THE ASSEMBLY PERIOD

enthusiastic outburst of it. An occasional "booster assembly" has its place and use.

Most of the assembly periods, though, should be given over to the work of the pupils themselves. The assemblies will be much more potent influences in developing school spirit if the principal and teachers remain somewhat in the background. In the case of divided assemblies, the smaller pupils will naturally need more help than will the older pupils, but even here the little ones can be led to take part and do much that is interesting to them. To the extent that pupils can be trained to feel that the responsibility for interesting, helpful exercises is theirs, will the assembly period achieve its maximum usefulness. To enlist the activity of the pupils in the programs, and to have this activity shared by as many as possible, is a wise procedure. To use organizations within the school, such as classes, leagues, scouts, and clubs, is better than singling out individuals.

A good principle to keep in mind is that the exercises the pupils present should have an element of instruction in them, and should be of a character likely to affect favorably their ideas and aspirations. Another good rule is that nothing presented by the pupils should partake of the nature of a big "performance." The aim should be social and educational, and the pupil offerings should be largely summaries of projects actually growing out of the everyday classroom work, given for the purpose of entertaining or instructing others. The exercises should also be short enough to hold the attention of the youngest pupils present.

When this type of assembly program is being presented it is best for the principal and teachers to remain off the platform, leaving to the pupils the explanations and presentation of their program. Occasional questions asked by the principal or teachers or pupils may be helpful rather than otherwise, but any interruption should be very brief. Let the older classes select their own presiding officer, master of ceremonies, or stage manager, announce their numbers, and present their program. This adds to the interest, teaches proper procedure, emphasizes the importance of clear enunciation, develops self-confidence, awakens a sense of responsibility, and trains pupils to work in coöperation. Do not expect perfect order and quiet in this type of assembly, as there is bound to be a certain amount of disturbance, but it is usually of the harmless kind.

Types of assembly programs. Many different types of assembly programs, using the pupils, may be thought out and made to work successfully by an interested group of teachers and a principal directing the activities of the pupils. A few typical ones will be cited here.

1. Musical assemblies. At these a short musical program would be presented. There may be part-singing, folk-songs and dancing, patriotic songs, chorus work, orchestra assembly, victrola days, or some person from outside the school may sing or play for the entertainment and instruction of the pupils.

2. Literary exercises. Reading old poems, telling of stories, dramatization of stories, and pantomimes are examples.

3. Demonstration assemblies. Work of the Boy Scouts and the Girl Scouts. Demonstrations of simple experiments or of useful information.

4. Historical and geographical. Talks on other lands and peoples, often illustrated by lantern slides or other means. A talk on a foreign country by some one who once lived there or who has visited there may prove interesting at times.

5. Health work. Talks and demonstrations regarding health matters can be made very interesting and instructive. Food, exercise, sleep, care of one's body, accident prevention, germ carriers, importance of a clean water supply, milk inspection, work of the health department, cleaning of the streets, disposal of garbage, work of the visiting nurse, and work of the Junior Red Cross are all types of subjects.

6. *Civic talks.* Good relations with the city officials can be made useful here. A brief talk by the mayor, a juvenile court judge, the superintendent of parks and streets, the health officer, a police officer or fireman in uniform, the treasurer of the city, or the superintendent of schools, on their work for the city, can be made helpful, and makes friends for the school. This is not possible in large cities, but in smaller places such talks can usually be arranged.

7. *Talks by citizens.* Short talks by alumni of the school who see the value of their education, and by successful business men and citizens who know how to "get over" a short message to young people. Sometimes these talks will seem interesting to the children and will serve to make friends for the school without being especially good in themselves. Banking, thrift, success in business, selecting a career, and qualities that make for success in life are types of subjects for such talks.

8. *Special-day assemblies.* Brief programs for such days as Longfellow day, Lincoln day, Arbor day, Fire-Prevention day, Thanksgiving, and similar occasions. Such special-day programs might be a little longer than the usual assembly program.

9. *Special "movie" programs.* If the school has a moving picture booth and machine, some special programs of an educational type may be presented, once a week or so. These may come at the morning assembly or, possibly better still, at a special, voluntary-attendance assembly of thirty minutes or so at the close of school in the afternoon. Such films as making steel, the whaling industry, a coal mine, the city beautiful, birds of the southern coast, California, plant or animal life, the Yellowstone Park, health films, automobile

manufacture, etc., are interesting and instructive. The Pathé weekly news films are also good.

Class responsibility for programs. On pupil assembly days it is a good idea to have the various classes (and teachers) assume responsibility for the program. With the suggestion and guidance of the teacher the class chooses the type of work it will present, organizes the program, and carries it through. The assembly period thus serves as a stimulus to clear thinking, good organization, and distinct enunciation, as the children soon learn that unless they have something to say and say it in an interesting way they will not be able to command the attention of the school when they stand before it. Divided up in this way classes are not called on for programs very often, and have plenty of opportunities to think out, prepare, and try to excel in what they do. In a sixteen-room school having one common assembly a class would not be called on for a program oftener than once a month.

The pupils should be encouraged to present things that are interesting to them — experiences they have had, things they have seen or studied, or classroom successes they have made. Folk dances, rhythmic games and drills, good singing, science demonstrations, dramatization of a story, reading of a poem or story, results of some study — these are types of what a class may present. Dramatization of historical events, Greek myths, Indian legends, and simple stories furnish excellent material. Dramatization and class programs are particularly useful for such occasions, and may well be especially encouraged. In such work each child has a part to perform, and in the effort to carry it through in such a way as will be acceptable to the audience and fit in with the work of his classmates certain desirable results are certain to be achieved. The ability to coöperate is stimulated in a way that mere classroom instruction could not do, and self-

USE OF THE ASSEMBLY PERIOD

confidence and the acceptance of responsibility naturally result.

An aim in all such work to be kept in mind by principal and teachers is that of arousing in the children the feeling that they are all members of a single school family, and as such have certain duties and obligations which make for the pleasure and profit of all. This leads directly into good citizenship.

The period should be one to which the children will look forward. Interest must not be allowed to lag, or the activities be allowed to settle down into a rut. It should be the period when some kind of a surprise may be expected by the children at almost any time.

A month's program. To illustrate the possibilities of the assembly period, a month's program, as worked out by one school, may be given as a type.

FIRST WEEK
- Monday   The Kindergarten — Activity selected by the teacher.
- Tuesday   Seventh Grade — Germ carriers. Illustrated by lantern slides, two pupils explaining.
- Wednesday   A graduate of the school — Talk on "The Work of a Life Saver."
- Thursday   Chorus songs — Two sixth grades.
- Friday   Eighth-Grade debate — Boys against girls. Question: — Resolved, that the automobile has been more useful to mankind than the horse.

SECOND WEEK
- Monday   Victrola concert. Selections by pupil vote.
- Tuesday   First Grade — Dramatization of Little Red Riding Hood.
- Wednesday   The principal — Readings from Eugene Field.
- Thursday   Fifth Grade — Stories told by three children.
- Friday   Second Grade — Folk dancing.

THIRD WEEK
- Monday   Third Grade — Dramatization of story from Reader.
- Tuesday   Boy Scouts — Demonstration of safety-first work.

Wednesday City Traffic Officer — Talk on regulating city traffic.
Thursday Girl Scouts — Demonstration of ideas as to personal helpfulness.
Friday Fourth Grade — Dramatization of story from Reader.

FOURTH WEEK
Monday Performance by the school orchestra.
Tuesday The Audubon Club — Bird protection.
Wednesday The principal — Pictures from Fairchild's book on moral training, with brief comments.
Thursday Seventh Grade — Accident prevention.
Friday Flag Day — History; salute; singing of national songs.

Similar programs, bringing in an almost endless variety of topics, could be planned and carried on from month to month and from year to year. One good feature is to open one assembly each week, or the weekly assembly where only one general meeting is held, with the flag salute. Have one boy act as color bearer, and one as color guard, the latter giving the commands, "Attention," "Salute," etc.

The platoon school or Gary-type assembly. With the development of the platoon school and the Gary-type school a somewhat different type of assembly program now becomes possible, though the types described above may be continued with smaller groups. As will be remembered from the descriptions given of this class of schools in Chapter IX, the assembly now comes in as a regularly scheduled school exercise, just as does reading, arithmetic, play, or science, and is in charge of a teacher. The assembly room, too, while it may be large enough to accommodate the school as a whole, can now be used when so small as to hold but two or three classes at one time. Even assuming a large assembly hall, where the entire school can meet together on occasions, the major use of the assembly period will still be by small

USE OF THE ASSEMBLY PERIOD

groups. From two to four classes (see programs, pp. 154–56) now meet together, with one or more teachers in charge, and carry through a series of programs, day after day. The purpose, in addition to the acquirement of knowledge, is to train in self-confidence, expression, parliamentary procedure, coöperation, the assumption of responsibility, and the development of leadership. The assembly period being longer, usually about thirty minutes, the programs can be longer, and the emphasis need not be placed so strongly on quick work and snap in the proceedings.

It is rather common to develop a formal organization. The groups may elect a president and a secretary who conduct the meetings, and often keep written minutes, and a more consecutive program may now be carried out. Not uncommonly a week is given to a topic by the older grades. The following program, carried out in a Gary-type school by two seventh grades, may be taken as illustrative.

FIRST WEEK — General topic — Safety First.
    Monday   The increase in the number of accidents.
    Tuesday   Safety first on the streets.
    Wednesday Decreasing street car and automobile accidents.
    Thursday   Accidents and injuries about the home.
    Friday   Drowning and resuscitation

SECOND WEEK — General topic — Sanitary precautions.
    Monday   Our city water supply.
    Tuesday   Our sewer system.
    Wednesday Plumbing inspection.
    Thursday   Cleaning the city streets.
    Friday   Work of the health officer.

THIRD WEEK — General topic — Great sanitary undertakings.
    Monday   Cleaning up Cuba.
    Tuesday   Same, continued.
    Wednesday General Gorgas and the Panama Canal.
    Thursday   Health work in the Philippines.
    Friday   Same, continued.

Fourth Week — General topic — Some enemies to health.
  Monday   The house fly — lantern slides.
  Tuesday   The garbage pail.
  Wednesday The mosquito — lantern slides.
  Thursday   Street dust dangers.
  Friday   Meat shops and food stores.

Each program in this school occupied thirty minutes. Each month a president and a secretary were elected to manage the assemblies, and a committee on program worked with the teachers and assigned parts. Each meeting was called to order by the president, the minutes for the preceding day were read and corrected, and the program, usually consisting of about three five-minute papers or talks, with occasional lantern slides shown and explained by the pupils, was presented. Some general discussion often followed, and the meeting was properly adjourned at the end of the period. Judged by adult standards the programs and the procedure were at times not very good, but the children thought they were all right and entered into them with zest. To them they had a sense of reality and importance which was after all one of their best features.

Other values of the school assembly. As a means of eliminating tardiness and reducing absence a good school assembly organization is worth more than an attendance officer. If the programs are short, full of variety, and interesting, about the only cases of tardiness are those with perfectly satisfactory excuses. The author knows of one large-city school where the introduction of such assembly periods as have been described reduced the tardiness from near three hundred cases a month to almost nothing.

The discipline is also made much easier, in part by reason of the new interest created, and in part because problems of school control can be discussed with ease before all, and the best side of the pupils' nature appealed to. Little intimate

USE OF THE ASSEMBLY PERIOD

talks on matters of school control, as the need for them arises, will do much to give pupils right conceptions and to bring about the right reactions.

The athletic life of the school can be in large part controlled through the school assembly. Occasional athletic assemblies may be held, before some inter-school contest or after some big victory, in which the pupils will formulate their conduct and explain team work. Praise for sportsmanlike conduct and for gameness and fairness in play, rather than for victories won, goes a long way in creating proper attitudes.

As a means for motivating the classwork, awakening a healthful school spirit, increasing the interest and working capacity of the pupils, training for bearing responsibility, imparting useful knowledge and ideas, forming life ambitions, and stimulating to self-activity, the assembly is probably worth more in results than any other fifteen minutes of the whole school day. In arousing a good school spirit on the part of the pupils that in turn finds expression in an interest on the part of the parents, the assembly also has a value which is well worth acquiring.

QUESTIONS AND PROBLEMS

1. What possibilities would there be for holding an assembly in the case of any one of the schools shown in Figures 5 to 8?
2. Could any type of assembly desired be held in the schools shown in Figures 9 and 10?
3. Do you agree with the importance of the assembly, as stated in this text? Why?
4. Suppose an inter-school athletic contest is to be held on Saturday, and an athletic "booster assembly" is to take place on Friday morning. The young people have not yet caught the spirit of fair play and sportsmanship. The principal has three minutes to speak, along with the captains and leaders, and he chooses to use his time to urge fine sportsmanship and clean play, regardless of victory. Outline, or write out, his three-minute speech.
5. Outline a month's assembly program, similar in form to the one on page 329, for the school shown in Figure 10, assuming it to be conducted as a grade school?

6. Indicate some possible types of assembly programs for each group or grade in the platoon-type program given on pages 178–80.
7. Show how the assembly work may be used to motivate the classroom work in a few lines of study.

SELECTED REFERENCES

(For this and the preceding chapter)

Bourne, R. S.   *The Gary Schools.*   200 pp., Illustrated, Boston, 1916.

A good description of the work done, in classes, shops, and assemblies.

Bowman, M. E.   "The School Savings Bank"; in *School and Society,* vol. 16, pp. 309–16.   (September 16, 1922.)

A summary of results of an important study of the subject.

Curtis, H. S.   "The Boy Scouts"; in *Educational Review,* vol. 50, pp. 495–508.   (December, 1915.)

Gilbert, C. B.   *The School and its Life.*   259 pp., Boston, 1906.

Contains two chapters on the morale of the school which are very sound and wholesome reading.

Lincoln School.   *The Student Councils.*   36 pp.   The Lincoln School of Teachers College, New York, 1922.

Lincoln School.   *Some Uses of School Assemblies.*   69 pp.   The Lincoln School of Teachers College, New York, 1922.

Two important studies of work actually done.

Kendall, C. N., and Mirick, G. A.   *How to Teach the Special Subjects.*   310 pp., Boston, 1918.

Chapter I deals with opening exercises and programs for special occasions.

Oberholtzer, Sarah L.   *School Savings Banks.*   Bulletin No. 46, 1914, United States Bureau of Education.   34 pp., Washington.

The savings bank movement, statistics, and methods.

Parker, Francis W., School.   *The Morning Exercise as a Socializing Influence.*   Studies in Education, vol. 2.   Published by the School, Chicago, 1921.

A monograph, prepared by the faculty of the School, to show how to use the daily school assembly. Reports some exercises, and gives a typical list of suitable ones.

Perry, C. A.   *Wider Use of the School Plant.*   417 pp., New York, 1911.

An illustrated description of many possible uses.

Peterson, Alice.   "The Dundee School Improvement Club"; in *First Yearbook, Department Elementary School Principals, National Education Association,* 1922, pp. 123–26.

Describes an organization of elementary school pupils formed, in an Omaha school, to stop destruction of property, beautify the school grounds, promote safety, and train the pupils to assume and carry responsibility by means of parliamentary organization.

Russell, J. E.   "Scouting Education"; in *Educational Review,* vol. 54, pp. 1–13.   (June, 1917.)

A good article on the significance of the Boy Scouts Movement.

Sindelar, Jos.   *Morning Exercises for all the Year.*

PART IV
THE SUPERVISION OF INSTRUCTION

CHAPTER XVIII

KNOWING THE SCHOOL

Preparing the way for supervision. While the list of organizing and administrative duties so far given may seem quite formidable to one who has never been a principal of an elementary school, the list, after all, need alarm no one. In the first place, the organization duties, as outlined in Part II, will very largely have to be anticipated before the opening of school in the Autumn, or be mostly attended to during the first week of school, and thereafter will require watching and minor adjustments to keep things running smoothly rather than long periods of attention. The administrative duties, outlined in Part III, will in part require daily or weekly attention, though, if the work is properly programmed and the help of teachers is used, no inordinate amount of time will be required on any one day, always barring some unexpected trouble or "flare-up." Quite a large part of what has been outlined, too, can be tied onto and made a portion of the work of school supervision, to be outlined in this section of the book. This will be especially true of the health supervision, strengthening the teacher in government, the assembly-period work, and in part also of the work in building up a good school spirit. Organization, system, and careful planning beforehand can do much to decrease the time needed for administrative duties, and to increase that left free for school supervision.

As was said in the beginning, in Chapter III, the prime importance of the supervisory function cannot be gainsaid. It ought to be made the great constructive service of the head of the school. All that he does in organization and administration should look toward bringing teachers and pupils together under conditions most likely to be conducive to good instruction, which he, by his superior knowledge and skill, may then labor to make still more effective. To do this the principal must first come to know his school, as it relates to the pupils and the instructional organization; must know what the courses of study and the plans of the superintendent call for, and then lay his plans for as liberal an interpretation of these as is permissible and possible; must design his supervision carefully, so as to secure maximum results for the time he puts in on it; must measure and evaluate the instruction and the progress made under it; and must be able to interpret his aims and conceptions and the results of their work to the class teachers themselves. The first step in such a program is for the principal to know his school thoroughly. This calls for a knowledge of his community, his teachers, his pupils, and the parents.

Knowing his community. The character of the city itself — residential, manufacturing, agricultural, and trading, predominately native American or foreign-born, relative wealth, general character and tone, and conception of the importance of education — will somewhat determine the types of schools found in the city as a whole. In every city of any size, however, the character of the individual schools varies greatly in different parts of the city, and different educational problems present themselves to different principals for solution. The principal must accordingly know much as to the nationality, racial elements, occupations, home life, culture, relative wealth, belief in the school, and general character of the people whose children attend his school. The relative patronage of private or parochial schools by the people of his district is another element of importance to know.

Much of this information he will sense during the first week or two of his work as a principal. An exploratory

KNOWING THE SCHOOL

trip through his district will reveal much as to the character of the homes, and a tabulation of the school census cards or the pupil enrollment cards, for nationality, occupations, children per family, and similar data, will give him still more accurate information which it will be good for him to know. All this, though, is merely preliminary, relatively easily obtained, and requires but little interpretation. The more important knowledge relates to the children in the school — their position, advancement, intelligence, and needs.

The census reports and his school. Another type of somewhat general information which a principal ought to have and use is information as to the drawing and holding power of his school. This can be obtained from a study of the school census cards and the records of his school. It is a type of information to be compiled as he or his clerk has time. In some cities it is compiled at and provided by the central office, and as a phase of the research activities of the school department. If not so provided, the principal ought to compile it himself, doing it a little at a time as he finds leisure from other duties. It would be a good Saturday job.

This information ought to include such items as:

1. Percentage of the school census of his district, for the ages represented by his school, enrolled in his school, over a period of years.
    a. If low, how explain the large number not in?
    b. Is the percentage increasing, or not?
2. What is the drawing power of his school, as shown by:
    a. The regularity of school attendance?
    b. Attendance from his district at private and parochial schools?
    c. Is the drawing power increasing, or not?
    d. Use of the compulsory attendance officer.
3. What is the holding power of his school, as represented by:
    a. Average membership and attendance, based on enrollment?
    b. Children who remain beyond the compulsory-age limit?

c. Children who complete the highest grade in the school?
   d. Children who go to high school?
4. Plot a curve for his school, showing the relation of his enrollment and attendance, by grades, with the total possible enrollment, and also with the percentages for the city as a whole.

All this information, when collected, makes good chart material, useful both at teachers' meetings and at Parent-Teacher meetings, and often is good material to display in the office. With a view to its use for such purposes it ought to be charted on cardboard or heavy paper, large enough to be seen across a room when hung up. The regulation cardboard, $22\frac{1}{2}'' \times 28\frac{1}{2}''$, makes good charts. With paster hangers, set with eyelets, which may be purchased and attached to the charts, they may then be hung on a frame to stand in the office, or be moved from place to place. Such a frame can be made in the manual training rooms. The next best material after cardboard is heavy manila paper, or muslin, cut to some standard size. As a principal ought to prepare many such charts, to show graphically the work of his school, it is well to plan from the start for some standard form and method for display.

The age-and-grade distribution sheet. A still more important type of statistical data that every principal should collect early in the year is that showing, by rooms, by grades, and for the school as a whole, the age-and-grade distribution of the children in his school. To this end each teacher should turn in to him, quite early in each school

---

NOTE TO TABLE VIII (opposite). Enclosed within the heavy lines are the children who are of the normal chronological age for the grade, allowing three months' leeway at each end of the grade, or a year and a half for each full year. Children above the heavy line are accelerated, and those below the heavy line are retarded. The dotted line, below the lower heavy line, marks off those who are one year over age. All cases below the dotted line should be investigated.

TABLE VIII. AN AGE-GRADE SCHOOL DISTRIBUTION TABLE

(Constructed for the school shown in Figure 7, page 98, having 560 pupils, distributed through a kindergarten and eight grades. See note at foot of page 340.)

AGES (in years and months)	KINDER-GARTEN	GRADE I B	GRADE I A	GRADE II B	GRADE II A	GRADE III B	GRADE III A	GRADE IV B	GRADE IV A	GRADE V B	GRADE V A	GRADE VI B	GRADE VI A	GRADE VII B	GRADE VII A	GRADE VIII B	GRADE VIII A	TOTALS BY AGES
4 yrs. 9 mos.– 5 yrs. 3 mos.	6																	6
5 " 3 " – 5 " 9 "	17																	17
5 " 9 " – 6 " 3 "	11	18	1															30
6 " 3 " – 6 " 9 "	2	16	16	1	1	1												36
6 " 9 " – 7 " 3 "		10	15	11	1	2	1											38
7 " 3 " – 7 " 9 "		5	10	13	12	10	1											43
7 " 9 " – 8 " 3 "		2	3	9	13	12	11											39
8 " 3 " – 8 " 9 "				5	10	12	12	1										38
8 " 9 " – 9 " 3 "				3	3	6	7	9	2									35
9 " 3 " – 9 " 9 "					1	4	3	10	7	2								31
9 " 9 " – 10 " 3 "					1	3	2	8	9	9	1	1						35
10 " 3 " – 10 " 9 "						1	1	5	7	10	7	2	1					34
10 " 9 " – 11 " 3 "						1	1	2	5	5	8	7	7	1	1			31
11 " 3 " – 11 " 9 "								2	2	3	5	6	6	1	2			28
11 " 9 " – 12 " 3 "								1	1	2	6	5	4	6	5	3		30
12 " 3 " – 12 " 9 "									1	1	2	2	3	6	6	5	1	28
12 " 9 " – 13 " 3 "									1	1	2	2	2	2	2	4	2	24
13 " 3 " – 13 " 9 "									1	1	1	1	3		1	1	4	13...
13 " 9 " – 14 " 3 "									1	1	1	1	1				4	—
14 " 3 " – 14 " 9 "										1	1	1					1	—
14 " 9 " – 15 " 3 "											1							5
15 " 3 " – 15 " 9 "																		2
TOTALS	36	51	45	42	42	40	39	38	36	35	33	34	29	18	17	13	12	560
		96		84		79		74		68		63		35		25		

year (or term), an age-and-grade distribution sheet for the pupils in her room. These will show room distributions, and the data can be combined for grades and for the school as a whole. A principal who has been in a building for a number of years may be presumed to know fairly well the nature of the distribution existing in his school, though many do not, but for a principal new to a school such an age-and-grade distribution sheet is most important, should be made up early, and the results should be given careful study. On page 341, a school distribution sheet is shown for an elementary school of 560 pupils, which we may assume is for the school shown in Figure 7, page 98. This school has a kindergarten and eight grades, the upper three being organized on the departmental plan.

This table (VIII) has been made up on the assumption that semiannual promotions are in use in the school, and on the basis of what are probably the best age-limits to use. The plan employed is to count children as of normal age who range from three months too young to three months over the strict age-limits for the grade. Taking the first grade, for example, children would be considered of normal age for the lower division (1B) who range from 5 years 9 months to 6 years 9 months in age, and for the upper division (1A) who range from 6 years 3 months to 7 years 3 months. This allows a leeway of three months in each direction for each half-grade, or grade, or, stated another way, a range of eighteen months for each year grade. Such tables are frequently made up where this leeway at the bottom is not allowed in counting, though children lacking two or three months of full age are commonly permitted to enter in September or February. In such tables the age-limits for each grade begin with the even year, as 6 years for the first grade, 7 years for the second year, etc. Such tables, on the other hand, commonly allow from one and a half to two years for the grade limits, by ranging only upward from the basal age. Thus, for first grade, the range would be from 6 to 7½ years, or from 6 to 8 years. A better plan, it seems to the writer, is the one used in Table VIII, which allows a year for each half of a grade, and a year and a half for the whole grade, but with a leeway of three months in both directions instead of all at the upper end.

The two heavy lines seen on Table VIII then enclose the children who are of normal age for the grade by this method of calculation. The children indicated by numbers above

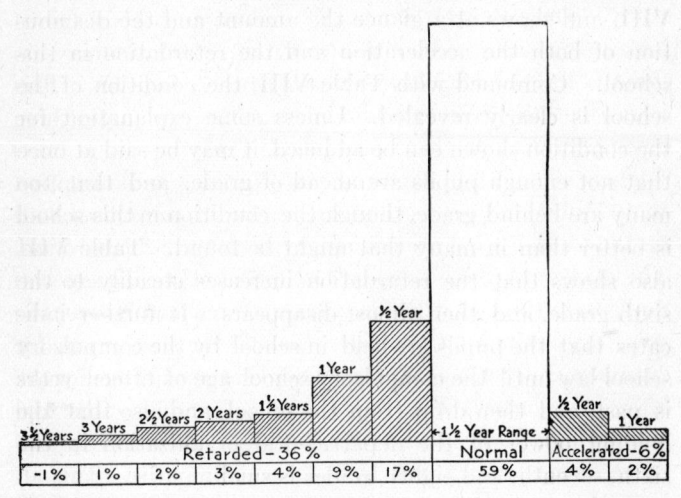

3½ Years	3 Years	2½ Years	2 Years	1½ Years	1 Year	½ Year		½ Year	1 Year
			Retarded − 36%				Normal	Accelerated − 6%	
−1%	1%	2%	3%	4%	9%	17%	59%	4%	2%

FIGURE 17. ACCELERATION AND RETARDATION SHOWN GRAPHICALLY

A pupil distribution for the school (Figure 7) shown in Table VIII, page 341. A similar distribution chart could be made for any school grade, or room.

the upper heavy line are those who are ahead — the accelerated; those below the lower heavy line are those who are not up to grade for their age — the retarded. The dotted line, below the lower heavy line, marks off those who are less than one year over-age for the grade from those who are more than one year over-age. The cases above the dotted line may not be important; those below should be investigated to determine causes for their low position in school. Acceleration and retardation can then be measured in terms of the number of years the pupil is under-age or over-age for the grade, and the percentage of acceleration and retardation in a school may be determined in yearly or half-yearly divisions. Making such a calculation from Table VIII we get the results shown in Figure 17.

The type of school revealed. Figure 17 gives the distribution of the pupils for the whole school, given in Table VIII, and shows at a glance the amount and the distribution of both the acceleration and the retardation in this school. Combined with Table VIII, the condition of the school is clearly revealed. Unless some explanation for the condition shown can be adduced, it may be said at once that not enough pupils are ahead of grade, and that too many are behind grade, though the condition in this school is better than in many that might be found. Table VIII also shows that the retardation increases steadily to the sixth grade, and then almost disappears. It further indicates that the pupils are held in school by the compulsory school law until the compulsory school age of fifteen years is past, and then drop from the school, and also that the holding power of the departmental organization in the sixth, seventh, and eighth grades is small.

While many schools would show a worse age-and-grade distribution than does this school, still the small number of accelerated pupils, and the much larger number of retarded pupils, ought to call for some inquiry as to the reasons therefor. If we assume intelligence to be about evenly distributed, as Terman's studies indicate that it is, and that there are approximately as many bright children as dull children, then the number accelerated after the second or third grade ought approximately to balance the number retarded, unless there is some special explanation for the situation in this school. A glance at Table VIII shows that late entrance to school has not been much of a factor in the retardation, as most 1B children have entered school in their sixth-age year.

Causes for this condition. To find the reasons and the remedies for such a condition may require some time. If the retardation is especially heavy in a school, and no particular attention has been given to it in past years by principal or teachers, a concentration of effort on the problem will, in time, give positive results of value. In one school of which the writer knows, a five-year study of acceleration and retardation furnished the results shown in Figure 18. Many

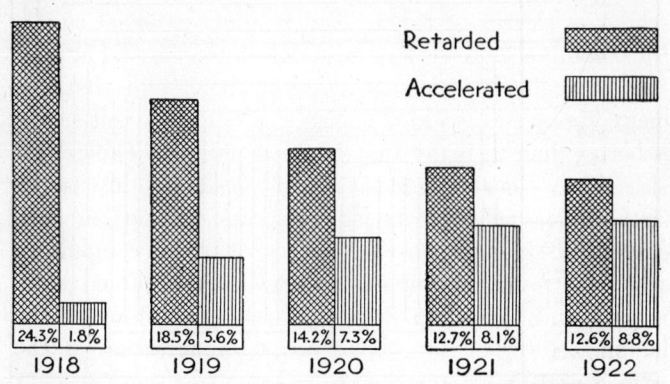

FIGURE 18. RESULTS OF A FIVE-YEAR STUDY OF PUPIL PROGRESS IN ONE SCHOOL

Percentages calculated from Age-and-Grade Distribution Sheets prepared after the opening of school each Autumn.

schools, in which no continued study of age-and-grade distribution tables has been carried on, would present conditions similar to those existing in this school in 1917, when the new principal took charge. Teachers tend constantly, as Terman has so well shown, to hold back the bright children who ought to go on, while the dull ones, by reason of failures in promotion and lack of special attention, tend to mire down deeper and deeper in the grades.

Room and pupil studies will reveal the cases and the causes of much retardation, and on the basis of such study individual promotions and readjustments may be made. An example of such room-and-pupil charting is given in Figure 19, which shows the conditions existing in the 5B grade

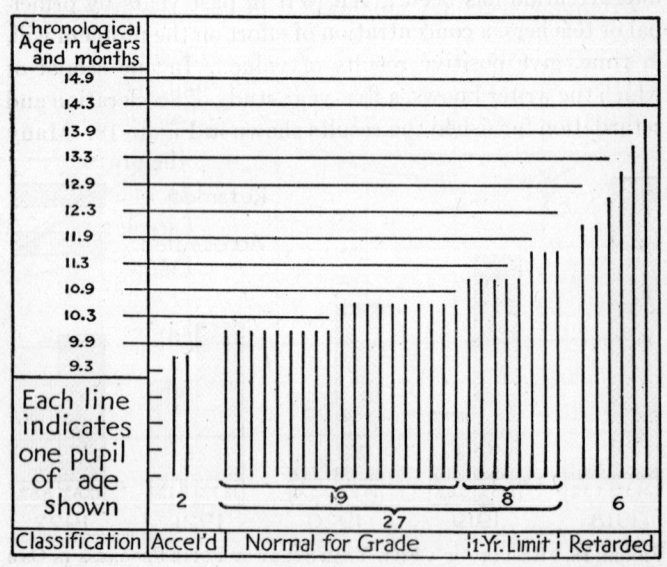

FIGURE 19. AGE-DISTRIBUTION OF THE PUPILS OF GRADE 5B
TABLE VIII, SCHOOL

In this room of thirty-five pupils are nineteen normal for the grade, eight one year or less over-age, two ahead of the grade for their age, and six so retarded that they probably ought to be removed to special classes. Each case of the six should be given individual attention.

of the school of Table VIII. On such a chart the pupil name corresponding with each line can be written in, and the chart then is a pupil age-chart for the room or grade.

The good results arising from making a reduction of retardation one of the major objectives in such a school, as was indicated in Chapter III to be desirable, and holding to the idea for a five-year period, is well shown in Figure 18. It will be seen from this figure that for this school, at least, the principal has now fully reached what the economist calls "the point of diminishing returns." His problem from now on will be to see that he holds things about as they are, and that the old conditions do not reassert themselves.

Promotional-failure studies. Another way of studying

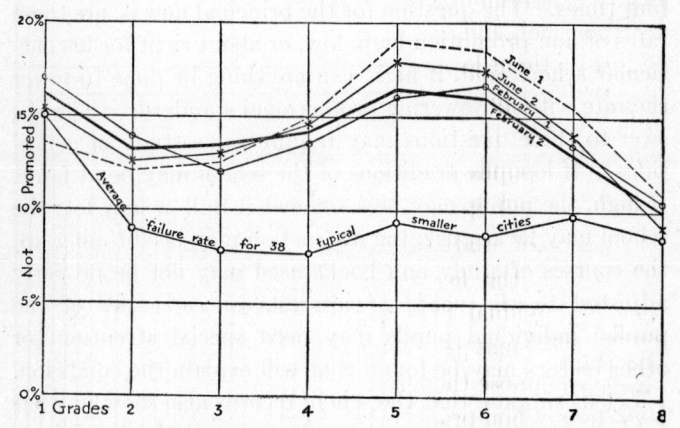

FIGURE 20. PERCENTAGE OF PUPILS IN EACH GRADE NOT PROMOTED AT LAST FOUR SEMI-ANNUAL PROMOTIONS

Assumed percentages for Figure 7, Table VIII, School, based on promotional failure rate for Cleveland as revealed by the School Survey there. Average failure rate for thirty-eight cities from a recent study by Deffenbaugh, covering 100,000 children.

the problem of retardation is that of finding the rate of non-promotion by grades, and the chief causes for non-promotion by grades and by subjects. Suppose that a tabulation is made of the failures in promotion by grades, and the results are charted, for this same school, for the last four semi-annual promotions, and suppose that the conditions shown in Figure 20 are revealed.

Such a result would be about what might be expected in

such a school as is charted in Table VIII. After a certain amount of holding back in the first grade, promotions go along rather evenly for the second and third grades. Then non-promotion begins to mount in the fourth grade, and climbs high in the fifth and sixth grades. The pupils who persist to the seventh and eighth grades are promoted rather well at the end of these grades. About the same rate of promotion has apparently prevailed in each grade for the past four times. The question for the principal now is, are these rates of non-promotion high, low, or about right for his particular school, and, if high, can anything be done to lower the rate without lowering promotional standards. The answer to these questions may require some study of conditions. If low, the traditions of the school may be at fault. If high, the pupils may be a somewhat dull or lazy lot; the school may lack spirit; the instruction may need toning up; the courses of study and books used may not be properly adjusted to the needs or interests or capacities of the pupils; individual pupils may need special attention; or other factors may be found that will explain the condition.

Let us suppose that the school records also show in what subjects the non-promoted pupils were adjudged deficient, and that the principal tabulates these records to see if they throw any light on the retardation problem. The results he obtains by tabulating are as given in Table IX. This table shows at once how a few subjects bulk large in holding pupils back, and indicate clearly where courses-of-study adjustments, change in emphasis, or the improvement of the instruction are needed.

A new aid in pupil classification. Enough has been shown by the tables and drawings so far used in this chapter to indicate clearly the wide age-differences that exist among our public school pupils, as one usually finds them distributed through the grades of our elementary schools. The

TABLE IX. CAUSES OF NON-PROMOTION, BY SUBJECTS AND GRADES

(Stated in percentage of the total number of failures occurring which are chargeable to each subject.)

SUBJECTS	END OF GRADE							
	1	2	3	4	5	6	7	8
Reading.............	100	72	35	15	5	3	..	..
Literature...........	..	..	..	..	..	3	6	10
Language............	..	6	10	21	26	24	14	18
Spelling.............	..	..	7	11	7	5	3	4
Arithmetic...........	..	22	48	47	41	35	29	28
Geography...........	..	..	..	6	20	18	12	10
History.............	..	..	..	..	..	5	27	23
Science..............	..	..	..	..	..	2	4	4
Manual Arts.........	..	..	..	..	0	0	0	0
Domestic Science.....	..	..	..	..	0	0	0	0
Drawing and Art.....	..	..	..	0	1	3	4	3
Music...............	..	..	..	..	..	2	1	0
Totals..........	100	100	100	100	100	100	100	100

number of pupils one still finds who are markedly over-age for their grade is large, despite recent efforts to reduce retardation, and also despite the rather common tendency of teachers and principals to promote pupils somewhat on the basis of their age and physical size.

Largely within the past decade an entirely new aid in the determination of the proper placement of school children has been given us in the form of the newly devised intelligence tests. Coming first as individual tests, and during the World War expanded into group tests, we to-day have well-standardized instruments for use in determining the mental capacity of school children, both individually and in groups. The group tests enable one to test a group or class at a time, and their chief value lies in the rapidity with which the group or class may be given a first sorting to determine the intelligence of the different pupils composing it. The individual tests have their chief use as a means of verification and for a still finer determination of what the group test has revealed.

Of the tests we have for use at present, the following probably are to be recommended as best to use for testing pupils of the different grades and ages indicated.

Individual Tests

Stanford-Binet, as revised by Terman, for all grades and ages.

Group Tests

Kindergarten — The Detroit Kindergarten Intelligence Test.
Grade 1 — The Detroit First Grade Intelligence Test.
Grades 2–3 — Haggerty Intelligence Test, Delta 1.
Grades 4–6 — National Intelligence Tests.
Grades 7–12 — Terman Group Test of Mental Ability.

Use of intelligence testing. The ability to give intelligence tests to pupils, and to interpret the results, may by now be said to have become a necessary part of the equipment of every elementary school principal. Even in cities which provide special service for such work, it is important that the school principal be familiar with and be able to supplement the work done. So important has intelligence testing become, in the handling and proper placement of pupils, that it is no exaggeration to say that what the blood count is to physical diagnosis the mental test now is to educational diagnosis.

By means of intelligence tests it is now possible to determine, with accuracy, the mental age of any pupil, as distinct from the chronological age. With this new device we have not only found that children of the same chronological age differ widely as to mental age, but that, taking large groups of unselected children, there are approximately as many

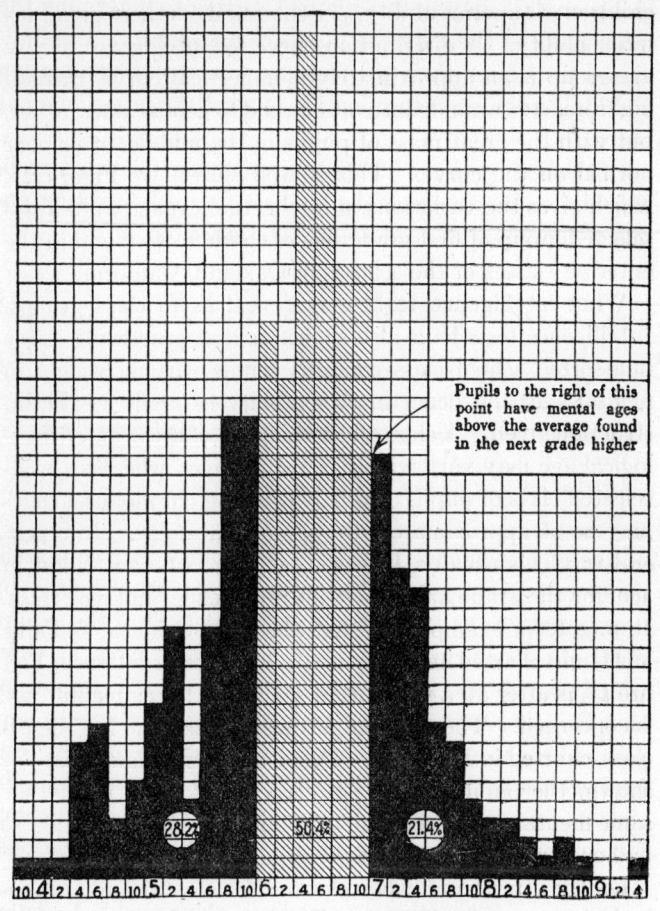

MENTAL AGE IN YEARS AND MONTHS.

(Each square □ in the above diagram represents one pupil.)

FIGURE 21. RESULTS OF THE BINET INTELLIGENCE TEST AS APPLIED TO 397 ENTERING (1B) PUPILS, OAKLAND, CALIFORNIA

City median, 6 years, 4 months. About ninety per cent of the pupils below six years of age mentally will fail in the 1B work; many of these over seven years of age mentally may be accelerated early in their course in school.

children of superior ability, per thousand, as there are of inferior ability. A distribution curve for intelligence of any age-group is an approximately symmetrical curve, extending from feeble-mindedness at one end to genius at the other, but with the great mass of pupils in the middle, at or near normal on the curve. This is well shown by Figure 21, which gives the variations in intellectual capacity of an unselected group of first grade school children, as found in the entering classes of the schools of Oakland, California.

What intelligence tests may reveal as to class groups. Intelligence tests have also shown us that practically every unassorted school class contains pupils varying widely in mental age, and hence in their ability to profit by the instruction given. A class all of which are of the same chronological age may vary widely in mental ages, whereas a well-selected class of pupils of widely differing chronological ages may be of approximately the same mental age. In a general way it is usually the case that those who are oldest in age for the grade are lowest in intelligence, and *vice versa*. It might, for example, be that the school shown in Table VIII, and charted as to acceleration and retardation in Figure 17, is after all a well-sorted school, so far as mental age is concerned. The same might possibly be true for the 5B class, charted in Figure 19. Despite the wide age variations shown, the pupils of this 5B class might be of nearly the same mental age, and the situation in consequence not be so bad as it appears at first sight.

On the other hand, when charted for mental and chronological age, grade 5B might possibly reveal such conditions as are shown in Figure 22. A class of school pupils showing such wide variation in mental and chronological ages calls for careful study and for some reclassification. A glance at Figure 22 shows at once that such a group of children cannot be expected to do average grade work, even under a very good teacher. There are at least five children so deficient in mental ability that they could not be expected to do average grade work anywhere, while at least three others are probably also so deficient in intelligence that the entire eight

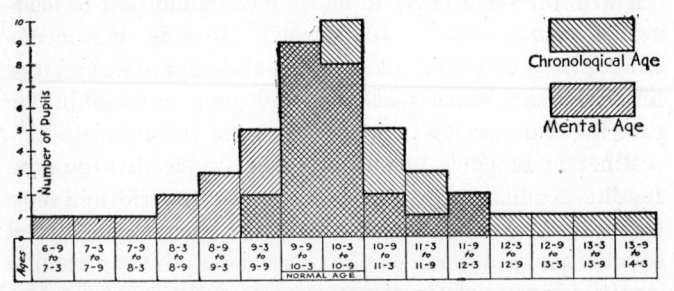

FIGURE 22. CHRONOLOGICAL AND MENTAL AGE COMPARED FOR THE PUPILS OF GRADE 5B, TABLE VIII, SCHOOL

This shows a class of 35 pupils ranging in mental age from 6 years, 9 months, to 12 years, 3 months, and in chronological age from 9 years, 3 months, to 14 years, 3 months. Such a class could hardly be expected to do even average grade work, even under the best of teachers, and needs reclassification.

ought to be sent to special classes. On the other hand, three pupils at least ought to be given an opportunity for promotion elsewhere. Such a group may look fairly well sorted to the casual visitor, but anything approaching the conditions shown in Figure 22, when charted, reveals the impossibility of school success with such an ill-assorted group.

Once the mental age of each child is known, the principal can now construct a Mental-Age-Grade School Distribution Sheet, following the same form as Table VIII, except that the numbers of pupils in each space on the table will now show the number of pupils in each grade of each mental-age group, instead of the chronological ages as in Table VIII. The two tables, then placed side by side, will present an interesting comparison, and reveal at a glance the capacity-character of the school. A series of detailed room studies, similar to the one given in Figure 22 for the 5B grade of

Table VIII school, will show the individual capacity-character of the different rooms. Such room studies as Figure 22 can be made quickly with a pencil on cross-section paper, and erasures and additions made as pupils come and go.

Importance of graphic methods and of the new psychological tools for the school principal. It is by such means as have been indicated that a principal should come to know his school as a whole, and each grade and class in it. The time taken in making the tabulations will well repay the investment. It is only by means of such studies that the true conditions and needs of a school can be ascertained, and only by means of intelligence tests that the true character and possibilities of a school can be determined. The principles involved in the construction of age-grade distribution tables and the charting of ordinary statistical data can easily be mastered. Charts are too valuable as a means for displaying facts to be neglected in the administration of a school. The results, though, are for the information of the school, and should be given to parents but rarely. The results of the intelligence tests should almost never be given to parents, and never by teachers. In the hands of parents such information leads to talking, criticism, bragging, and comparisons which often lead to serious trouble.

Intelligence testing calls for a somewhat special type of skill — a type of skill that requires some instruction to become proficient in using. Yet the educational significance of the results obtained from measuring the intelligence of the children of a school are so important that the work cannot be neglected much longer. If the city does not provide a psychological expert to do the testing, or if some teacher in the building is not skilled in the work, then the principal must learn how to do it himself. As a means for determining accurately the ability and needs of entering pupils the intelligence test is unsurpassed, as Figure 21 shows at a glance. More than all other forms of data combined, the intelligence test gives the necessary information from which a pupil's possibilities can best be foretold, and his further education be most profitably directed. The many questions, too, that arise in a school relating to grading, promotions, choice of studies, delinquency, vocational guidance, and the handling of sub-normals on the one hand and gifted children on the other, can all be handled far more intelligently when working with the results of intelligence tests at hand. In the handling of all peculiar or irregular cases the intelligence test has now become a matter of necessary routine which the principal of a school should know how to employ.

QUESTIONS AND PROBLEMS

1. Show that the plan used in determining normal age for a grade is in keeping with our usual method of counting pupils as of normal age who enter the first grade at six, and pass to the high school at fourteen.
2. On the above basis of counting, are not the pupils shown on Table VIII, between the lower heavy line and the dotted line, actually retarded pupils, though by a common method of counting they are not considered as so?
3. Would acceleration and retardation approximately balance one another in a well-graded school? Why?
4. What effect would late entrance to first grade make on an age-grade distribution table? For how long?
5. If the reduction of retardation were made a major objective for a number of years in a school, what checks could be introduced to prevent too rapid promotions, with the result that the upper grades would come to be filled with unprepared pupils? Is this a real danger?
6. What specific defects in a school might the promotional results given in Table IX indicate?
7. It is often stated that the ability to read and understand what is read is the best single basis for the classification of children, because so many different school activities depend on its acquisition. Do you accept this? Does Table IX indicate that it was accepted by that particular school?
8. Explain the tendency to promote over-age and "nice" pupils, and to hold back young but bright pupils.
9. What does Figure 20 indicate as to promotional bases?
10. Outline a procedure for dealing with such a situation as is indicated in Figure 22.

11. Explain why, in the different schools of most cities, the intelligence curve for the children tends to be skewed toward one end or the other of the curve, instead of being a symmetrical distribution.
12. Make up an age-grade distribution chart, as in Table VIII, for the school shown in Figure 8, page 99, assuming retardation to be at about the same rate as in Table VIII.

SELECTED REFERENCES

Berry, C. S. "Classification by Test of Intelligence of 10,000 First-Grade Children"; in *Journal of Educational Research*, vol. 6, pp. 185–203. (October, 1922.)
   Describes work done and results obtained in Detroit.

Doughton, Isaac. "Elimination of Pupils in a Small City"; in *American School Board Journal*, vol. 61, pp. 42–44. (September, 1920.)
   A long-term study of elimination in Phœnixville, Pennsylvania.

Hoke, K. L. *Placement of Children in the Elementary Grades.* Bulletin 3, 1916, United States Bureau of Education, Washington.
   A study of retardation and acceleration in the schools of Richmond, Virginia.

Kyte, G. C. "An Experiment in the Education of Gifted Children in the First Grade"; in *First Yearbook, Department Elementary School Principals, National Education Association*, 1922, pp. 71–81.
   A report on an interesting experiment in the schools of Berkeley, California.

Mitchell, D. "Psychological Examination of Pre-School-Age Children"; in *School and Society*, vol. 15, pp. 561–68. (May 20, 1922.)
   Gives the results of intelligence examinations of one thousand entering children in eight New York City elementary schools in September, 1921.

Rugg, H. O. *A Primer of Statistics.* Boston, 1923.
   A very simple and useful manual of statistical procedure and interpretation.

Stevens, H. C. "A Survey of Retarded School Children"; in *School Review*, vol. 24, pp. 450–61. (June, 1916.)
   A report on an investigation in a town in northern Minnesota.

Strayer, G. D., and Englehardt, N. L. *The Classroom Teacher.* New York, 1920.
   Chapter 8 contains a number of tables showing how to sort and classify the school.

Strayer, G. D., and Englehardt, N. L. *Record Book for Elementary School Principals.* C. F. Williams and Son, Albany, 1918.
   A useful loose-leaf book of record forms.

Terman, L. M. *The Intelligence of School Children.* 317 pp., Boston, 1919.
   A very interesting description of how children differ in ability, the use of intelligence tests in grading them, and the proper education of exceptional children.

Terman, L. M. *The Measurement of Intelligence.* 362 pp., Boston, 1916.
   A description and practical guide to the use of the Stanford revision of the Binet intelligence tests.

Uhrbrock, R. S. "The Retarded Girl in the Fifth Grade"; in *School and Society*, vol. 12, pp. 563–64. (December 4, 1920.)
   Results of a study in one Philadelphia school.

Williams, J. H. *Graphic Methods in Education and the Social Sciences.* Boston, 1923.
   A very useful book for one who desires to learn how to make charts and graphs and letter them, and the different types to use for different kinds of data.

Zirkle, H. W. "Caring for the Gifted Child"; in *First Yearbook of the Department of Elementary School Principals, National Education Association,* 1922, pp. 81–86.
   A report on work done in the Whittier School, Denver.

Zornow, Th. A., and Pechstein, L. A. "An Experiment in the Classification of First-Grade Children through the use of Mental Tests"; in *Elementary School Journal,* vol. 23, pp. 136–46. (October, 1922.)
   A study made in an Italian school in Rochester, New York, and the conditions revealed.

CHAPTER XIX

CLASSIFYING AND PROMOTING THE PUPILS

The principal and promotional procedure. In but few school systems into which a principal may go will he find himself at liberty at once to make changes in the system of classification and promotion of pupils. Such matters are usually settled for him, in advance, by rules and regulations applicable to the school system as a whole. His work will be rather to carry out the plan as it exists, though generally he has power, or will be given power as he convinces those in authority that he knows how to use it, to modify the plan in minor particulars in so far as it relates to the administration of his school.

Still, despite the fact that the system of classification and promotion for a city school system usually is settled in its main essentials for the school system as a whole, and not by individual schools, the reverse is sometimes the case. In some cities superintendents are willing to permit intelligent and enterprising principals, on a proper showing of reasons therefor, to modify the existing system and to experiment with some different plan. In any case, though, the work of classifying and promoting the pupils is of such fundamental importance to the successful administration of a school and to the proper progress of the children through the grades, that a principal should be familiar with the best principles of procedure in use, generally, as well as with those in use in the particular school system in which he works.

Type plans for school classification. While many small schools still promote their pupils but once a year, and hence have their pupils classified into year grades, the most general plan now in use is that of semiannual promotions. This divides each school grade into two sections or sub-grades, a B and an A. While the nomenclature is not uniform, still by far the most common plan is to designate the lower or beginning section as the B, and the more advanced or upper section as the A. This nomenclature will be used throughout this volume. Thus a pupil would enter the elementary school in grade 1B, and leave it at the end of grade 8A. Since there is such difference in practice in different school systems, and one must always learn whether B or A means low, it would be well if the use of B and A were abandoned, in school systems not following a differentiated type of course of study (see Figure 24, page 361) and L and H substituted in their stead.

In the parallel-course school system, shown in Figure 23,

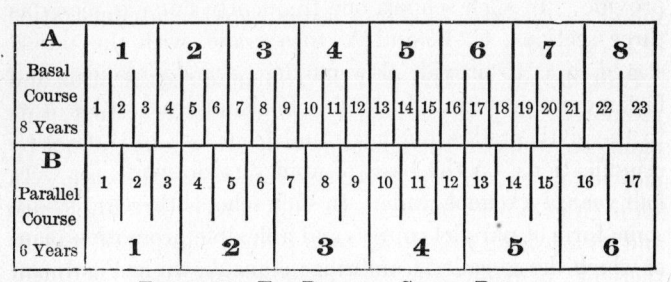

A Basal Course 8 Years	**1**			**2**			**3**			**4**			**5**			**6**			**7**			**8**	
	1	2	3	4	5	6	7	8	9	10	11	12	13	14	15	16	17	18	19	20	21	22	23
B Parallel Course 6 Years	1	2	3	4	5	6	7	8	9	10		11	12	13		14	15		16			17	
	1			**2**			**3**				**4**				**5**				**6**				

FIGURE 23. THE PARALLEL-COURSE PLAN

Two parallel elementary-school courses, with one third more work assigned for each year in Course B than in Course A. Pupils may be transferred from one course to the other at any of the five main junction points, or, with slight coaching or slight loss, at ten other points.

all except the last year of each course is divided into three sections, C, B, and A, each one third of a year apart. In a few large city schools a further subdivision is made into four sections, D, C, B, and A, with promotions but ten weeks apart. This latter plan, however, is not very common, and is not feasible except in quite large buildings. Under the semiannual promotion plan an eight-room building, with a school grade to each room, would have an A and a B section in each room, and a sixteen- to eighteen-room building could still further specialize the work by giving each teacher only a B or an A section of a grade, and this, for recitation and study purposes, could be still further subdivided into two sections.

In all the above described plans the different sections may be moving along at a somewhat uniform rate over a common course of study. This is the most common plan. On the other hand, and especially in the larger buildings, there may be instead some differentiation in the instruction, and the pupils in the different sections may be sorted so as to put them into more homogeneous working groups than any grouping on the basis of age or advancement alone can ever provide. In such schools one frequently finds as many as three sections, C, B, and A, to a grade, with the pupils sorted so as to provide slow-moving, average-moving, and fast-moving groups. In large schools, at least in the first to the sixth grades, one may find from two to three such classifications, on the basis of ability to do work, for each half year of a school grade. In such schools there is usually some form of parallel courses and a flexible promotion plan, of which the so-called Cambridge plan, shown in Figure 23, is a type. Almost all other parallel course and flexible promotion plans are more or less a variation of this plan. Under such plans the time a pupil spends in the elementary school may vary from six to eight or more years, depending upon ability and school progress.

Again, in still other schools, though a much smaller number, the classification of pupils during the first six grades is made on a different basis. For each grade, or half grade, there are three groups, C, B, and A, the pupils being sorted into these groups on the basis of intellectual capacity and working power, and the three groups then work along side

CLASSIFICATION AND PROMOTION

by side and at the same yearly rate, but following minimum, average, and maximum courses of study. Such an arrangement represents a second main type plan of grading and promotion. The common form taken is well shown in Figure 24, which is typical of all such differentiated-course plans for grading and promotion. While practically all pupils here take six years for the elementary school course, there may easily be transfers from group to group within a grade, as progress or lack of progress may seem to warrant, and even some special promotions to higher grades. This plan attempts to keep each pupil working where he belongs and up to full capacity.

Special plans sometimes used. Here and there one also finds such a special form of pupil classification as grading and promotion by subjects. Under such a plan the pupils are placed in the room nearest their natural stage of advancement, as for example 4A or 6B, but they may pass to some other room, either higher or lower, to recite in some one or more subjects

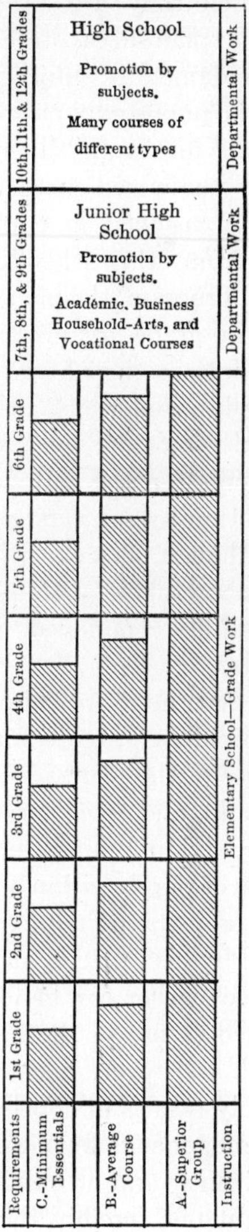

FIGURE 24. THE DIFFERENTIATED-COURSE PLAN

Often called the Santa Barbara plan, from it having first been worked out there. There are virtually three courses of study for the three groups.

in which they are either ahead of or behind the class. Such a plan necessitates a common school program for all fundamental subjects, at least from 3B to 6A, so that the pupils may pass from room to room for instruction, and calls for careful supervision on the part of the principal. Due to the mixed character of the progress made, the difficulty occasioned in transferring pupils to and receiving them from other schools, and the objections to a common school program, the plan has so far found but small acceptance in grade-organization schools. Subdivision of the grade into sections based largely on working capacity, flexibility in promotions, and the provision of a special or ungraded room, are felt by most principals to make better provision for the individual adjustments for which the promotion-by-subjects plan attempts to provide. The idea, though, as we shall point out later on, is in modified form a useful one with over-age children. It has also been successfully employed in Gary-type and platoon-type schools.

An even more special plan, still occasionally used, is that of individual progress and promotion, following the main outlines of the plan worked out many years ago at Pueblo, Colorado, and often termed the Pueblo plan. Under this plan individual pupils, or more generally four or five small groups of pupils within a room, make individual progress in each subject, the advancement of any pupil being determined by his capacity and willingness to work. Only a very capable teacher can handle such a plan. It is much better adapted to use in the high school than in the elementary school, and where tried wholesale in the grades almost inevitably results in hopeless confusion.

Homogeneous working groups. All our studies as to the intelligence and working capacity of school pupils have brought out forcibly the great differences existing among children of the same age, in these two important respects. Figures 17 and 19 show the age differences that commonly exist among pupils of the same school grades, and Figures 21 and 22 bring out even more strikingly not only the wide distribution in the amount of intellectual endowment possessed by pupils of the same age, but also the wide variations existing between mental and chronological age.

What is wanted, in each working group, is a fair balance between the work to be done and the capacity of the pupils to do it. Even a few ill-assorted cases, at either end of the scale, interfere tremendously with the ability of a teacher to render good service to a group, and such pupils ought to be placed in groups elsewhere where the work is nearer their needs and capacities. Each pupil, we know, has a certain inherited capacity for thinking, and this inherited capacity we know from intelligence testing varies widely with different pupils of the same age groups. In addition, each pupil has a certain ability to do, lower than his actual inherited capacity, and this also varies with pupils of the same inherited capacity. This difference is due to the effects of or the lack of certain specific training which pupils have or have not had. There is, still further, the actual performance of the pupils, which may be and in many cases is still lower than their actual ability to do. This difference between ability to do and actual performance may be due to low physical tone, bad sanitary conditions, laziness, lack of intellectual stimulus, or other somewhat similar causes. Whatever the cause, it should be one of the purposes of the school to diminish this difference between ability to do and actual performance by removing obstacles to progress and stimulating to activity.

The work of the principal then, as it relates to grading and promotion, is to see that the pupils are sorted into working groups which are as homogeneous in intellectual capacity and working power as is possible with the school organization at his command. He must study his problem and, if necessary, try to reshape or expand his working organization with a view to improving its usefulness to the pupils of his particular school. Often this can be done as needs can be proven; sometimes financial limitations or administrative rigidity will prevent any changes or expansions being made.

Means for obtaining homogeneous working groups. To secure and maintain working groups throughout his school as homogeneous as possible, the principal must so use whatever plan or plans he may be permitted to employ as to obtain the maximum possible results in the placing and progress of the children under his control. While different plans or systems for grading and promotion may prove helpful, in different ways, he must not forget that in employing these the most important single guiding tool at his command will be the intelligence test. It is on the basis of intellectual capacity, rather than on age or size or effort, or even the judgment of teachers, that the rate of advancement of individual pupils must largely be determined. He must also not forget that the important thing for a pupil is that he be placed where his ability to work will be most deeply challenged, and that frequently, as shown by educational tests, there is little difference in the achievement of pupils in grades one or two years apart. What a pupil loses by skipping a grade is frequently much more than compensated for by placing him where he will work to better advantage.

There are four main situations in which a principal may find himself in the matter of the grading and promotion of his pupils. Under perhaps the simplest of conditions he will find a uniform course of study and an annual or semiannual promotional plan in force, and with no special rooms or coaching teachers provided. Under such a plan he will have to make his adjustments wholly by means of special promotions, and such variations in the course of study as are permissible. A somewhat better condition will be that in which, in addition, he will be provided with one or more special or ungraded teachers and rooms to assist him in making pupil adjustments and transfers to other classes. Again he may find himself in a school having parallel courses of study, with pupils traveling at different rates and perhaps with one or more special teachers and rooms to facilitate adjustments. In a fourth situation, he may be working in a school with differentiated courses of study, the different groups doing different quantities and qualities of work.

The first is probably the more common situation, chief reliance being placed on special promotions for preserving somewhat homogeneous working groups. As yet but a relatively small percentage of our elementary schools are provided with special rooms and teachers to whom children may be sent for special help. Ungraded rooms, opportunity rooms, rooms for sub-normals, and disciplinary rooms represent special means for sorting and helping irregular or peculiar pupils, who do not do well under ordinary classroom conditions. While such special rooms and teachers are of much value and are highly desirable additions to school organization, greatly increasing the efficiency of the classroom teacher, nevertheless much can be done without them by working through the regular classroom organization, provided as much flexibility as can be advantageously used be introduced into the sorting and grading and promoting of the pupils. A few of the means for introducing this flexibility will be considered.

Promotional rules. Taking the first situation described above, the problem of the principal is to so handle his semi-annual promotions and the irregular promotions as to obtain the best results for the individual pupils concerned. The majority of the pupils, if the school is an average and not an exceptional one, one way or the other, will progress regularly and normally from grade to grade at the regular promotion times. The cases that will need watching are the ones at either end of the scale, as well as cases that are troublesome, from any cause. In a general way the following rules as to promotion should prevail:

1. Utilize the teacher's judgment as to promotion, as much as possible, but keep in mind that at times it is quite unreliable. If convinced that the teacher is wrong, make a trial promotion to see.
2. All promotions, regular or otherwise, should be *viséd* by the principal. It is one of his important means for supervising instruction.
3. All pupils whom the teacher considers as unquestionably ready for promotion should ordinarily go ahead.
4. In all doubtful cases, the educational importance of the subjects in which deficiencies exist should be considered. Different subjects have different promotional values in the different grades, and promotion, subject to a deficiency being made up, may at times well be made.
5. Promotions should not be based on the results of final tests. Instead, daily class work should be the main factor. A pupil may make a low mark in a written test in one or more subjects, and yet for his own good ought to go on.
6. Ability to do the work of the grade ahead is more important than the passing out of that just completed.
7. Any pupil not promoted at a regular promotional time should have the right of appeal to the principal, and objective tests should then be used to settle the question.
8. Only in very exceptional cases — many experienced principals would say never — should a pupil be held back at a regular promotional time because of misconduct. Often the best cure for troublesome cases is a promotion to work that will challenge larger effort. Especially is this the case with children of superior ability.
9. With pupils of average intelligence, a year of advanced work is worth more than repeating a grade. Failures in school offer

CLASSIFICATION AND PROMOTION

good preparation for failure in life. Teachers may object to a promotion, and the principal must decide what is best to do.

10. Where no special rooms or differentiated courses exist for handling pupils of low intelligence it is better to promote them, after reasonable trial in a grade, and then not expect full work of them, rather than to keep them back where they "mire down" deeper and deeper. After one repetition of a grade they will almost always absorb more that is useful for them from the work of the grade next ahead.
11. As it is easier to promote than to demote, pupils coming in from rural or outside schools may at first be placed on trial a trifle lower than may seem their due, but proper allowance should be made for differences in type of preparation, and such pupils should be advanced to a grade of work which they are best fitted to do, regardless of whether they may have missed some parts of the course of study.
12. Occasionally a pupil ten to twelve years old will enter school for the first time. In such cases the first grade is not the place for him. It is better to place such pupils, if they are of normal intelligence, in the third or fourth grade, sending them to the first for reading, and to wait a half-year or so before definitely fixing their classification. Such pupils properly belong in an ungraded room, but where such is not provided the best possible makeshift must be substituted.

Special promotions. In a school lacking special teachers and rooms, or some form of parallel or differentiated class organization, the need for special promotions will be particularly marked, and to this phase of his supervisory problem the principal must give some study. His age-and-grade distribution sheets for the different rooms, his records as to the intelligence levels and school progress of the different pupils, and his study of the troublesome cases of the school will all serve to indicate the pupils who need his special attention. He will probably have to make, too, more special promotions than his teachers will approve. Especially are they likely to object to the promotion of those under age for the grade. Studies generally show that it is the bright child who is most held back by teachers and in consequence most retarded in our schools. The teachers may also be expected to object somewhat to the promotion of the slow and over-aged, as many grade teachers are firmly convinced that "skipping" means the loss of important work, and that the standard for passing to the grade next ahead should always be the passing on the work that lies behind. There are so many cases on record, though, that show the highly beneficial results to pupils of at times jumping whole grades or years of work that a principal, once he is convinced that such a jump would be to the best interests of the pupil, should not hesitate to stretch all the rules of the school in making a special promotion.

In handling the matter of special promotions, in the first type of school organization above described, the following principles should guide:

1. The initiative in the case of a special promotion may come from either the teacher or the principal, but before action is taken the principal should approve.
2. If the school can give a good physical examination before deciding, it will be a wise thing to do. If the results of such an examination are unfavorable, an extra promotion may well be a questionable proceeding.
3. In most cases it is best to consult with the parents before making the promotion. Especially is this desirable if the parents are intelligent people. Sometimes there are health reasons, unknown to the school, which might make a special promotion undesirable. Usually the parents approve, and are pleased at being consulted. In case of a demotion parental objections are likely to be encountered, and because this is so they should be consulted before such action is taken. Often they are able to do something to prevent the need for it.
4. Of the over-size and over-age pupils in a school, a few of fair intelligence can usually be singled out who will improve to a marked degree when placed in a grade ahead. A partial or trial promotion often spurs them to their best efforts.
5. When a bright pupil gives evidence of having too little to do

CLASSIFICATION AND PROMOTION

it is best to put him ahead where he will have to work harder. Trouble is often caused by lack of occupation. All troublesome cases should be looked up as to intelligence level and the character of their daily work.

6. A pupil of good physique, who has outside help that enables him to do more work, can often be spurred to larger effort by a promotion.

7. Partial promotions can often be made to an advanced section in the same room, the pupil sometimes reciting in both sections, in one or more subjects, until the transition can be made in full.

8. Special promotions ought in general to be made early in the term, to insure time for adjustment before the next promotion. A special promotion, also, ought ordinarily only be made when there is a strong probability that the pupil will be able to make the regular promotion also at the end of the term, as a hold over practically cancels the benefit of the special promotion.

9. In making special promotions *ad interim* it is best to make them as trial promotions. If good judgment is exercised in selecting the pupils nearly all will make good, but for the few who do not the dropping backward is made easier if the promotion is at first partial, or on trial. In one school system following such a plan, known to the writer, the special promotions during the past year equaled 9.7 per cent of the average daily attendance, while the failures to make good of those specially promoted was but 4.3 per cent, as against a failure rate of 11.7 per cent for the school system as a whole at the regular semiannual promotions.

10. Sometimes a whole grade or room will be ready for promotion before the end of the semiannual period, and in such cases it is a good thing to permit the group to proceed with the work ahead. Before approving such a procedure, the principal should take the class for half a day and convince himself, and the pupils, that the group is ready for promotion. This can best be done by means of an oral quiz, and offers the principal an excellent opportunity for group supervision. So valuable is this supervisory opportunity that some superintendents reserve such approval to themselves, in order that they may thus test the work of the teachers.

11. In the case of special promotions, good conduct, good school citizenship, punctuality, and good attention to duty may

very properly be insisted upon in addition to good scholarship.
12. To stimulate ambition, some prominence may be given, if done tactfully, to the special promotions which are made.
13. To prevent too rapid advancement, a good rule is that no child shall have more than one special promotion in any year, nor more than two in three years, unless shown by the Binet tests to be distinctly superior in intelligence, and of a mental age at least as high as that proper for the grade to which he is to go.

Securing results by individual study. However desirable and effective some of the special promotional schemes and differentiated courses may be in caring for irregular pupils and stimulating acceleration in a school, much that needs to be done can be done without their aid, in schools not themselves abnormal in type, by either more attention to individual cases or by a rather liberal use of the special promotion.

In Detroit, for example, the rate of non-promotion, for the entire school system, was cut down, in one year, from 14.7 per cent to 8.4 per cent, without lowering standards in any way as proved by the use of the standards tests, by means of a systematic city-wide attention to pupil cases, along the following lines:

1. Attention was centered upon the needs and difficulties of each individual pupil.
2. The principal or teacher interviewed each pupil privately, and the situation was frankly discussed in an effort to arrive at the cause and find a remedy.
3. Parents were visited, called into consultation, or otherwise informed of the impending failure, and their coöperation was requested.
4. Pupils were permitted to devote more time to the subjects in which they were weak.
5. Special help was given by the ungraded-room teacher, or by brighter pupils, during or after school.
6. Weak pupils were required to make special reports to the

principal, at stated intervals, daily or weekly, upon their scholastic progress.
7. Outside help and study for such pupils were encouraged.

The procedure was carefully worked out, tests were used to see that standards were not lowered, and the attention of principals and teachers was concentrated on the "flunkage" problem.

Value of, in school administration. The importance of such careful studies of promotions, and the use of special promotions where needed, cannot be questioned. There is little use for longer continuing a "lock-step" system of promotions in our schools. The special promotion also has a good effect on the teachers. Once they catch a vision of the possibilities of pupils, and come to regard the course of study as a means and not an end, it develops open-mindedness and leads them to make a new kind of study of both their children and the subject-matter. With the pupils, it does much to stimulate ambition and bring out leadership. They learn to look ahead, to plan, and to try to make good in a larger way. As one principal states it, it puts "pep" into a school. Pupils see their classmates advancing, and begin to inquire what they may do to advance also. The discipline of a school is frequently improved in a noticeable manner. Bright boys who have been troublesome because they found the work too easy develop into leaders for the school, once their best efforts are challenged. By holding to good conduct in class and good citizenship in the school as a necessity for special promotion, many troublesome cases can be transformed through the power of work and the stimulus of rivalry.

The usual experience of a pupil given a special promotion is that at first he falls below his former high standing, and is compelled to work harder than before to hold his place. Gradually, though, if the promotion was a proper one, the bright pupil pulls up and becomes at least a good average member of the new working group. It is good for pupils to have to make such a pull, and to succeed at it. To master the work of the new grade, day by day, is of much more importance than the work missed by skipping. Subject-matter is not so closely articulated or so intimately related that it must all be done. In arithmetic, spelling, reading, writing, composition, and language study there is constant review, and the bright pupil can soon master the particular points of the grade work passed over. Even in geography and history, where the clearest omissions will occur, there is usually a double cycle of study, and if not the loss is usually less important than the gain.

The use of the special promotion then, together with some shifting of pupils between stronger and weaker teachers in schools large enough to have duplicate grades, tends to keep more homogeneous working groups and in consequence to make classroom instruction both easier and more effective.

The whole plan, however, it must be freely admitted, has its limitations, and in schools having many pupils of low intelligence and poor home conditions it does not give the needed relief. The pupils are passed along when what they need is special help, they get beyond their depth, become discouraged, and tend to truancy and to dropping early from school. Such pupils need the help and classification that only special teachers and rooms can give.

The special, or ungraded room. Where a principal has in his building one or more teachers whose function is that of supplementing the work of the regular teachers by providing some form of help or coaching service, still more can be done to provide homogeneous working groups in the regular classrooms. Two main types of such special teachers are found. These are: (1) the special, or ungraded, or auxiliary, or a typical-class, or opportunity-room teacher; and (2) the disciplinary-class teacher. The first type has been provided for helpful educational service to particular children; the second is disciplinary, the room representing an intermediate stage between the regular classroom and the parental school.

To the disciplinary room, where such is provided, are sent, for indefinite periods, those who find themselves unable to conform to the established ways of organized society as found in the school. The better the adjustment of the promotional machinery to the pupils, and the more pupils are classified according to mental rather than chronological age and given work suited to their capacities and needs, the more the necessity for the disciplinary class will disappear. Nearly all disciplinary cases can be analyzed and reduced to some particular cause, other than mere perversity, though this does sometimes constitute the actuating motive. The special disciplinary class has its place and use, but its place and use are smaller the more intelligently the classification of pupils is attended to.

To the other type of special room are sent those pupils who need special instruction, either to enable them to keep up with their class or to move ahead to the next class. The ungraded or special room is thus a real Opportunity Room, and is often known as such, because it offers an opportunity to those who have fallen behind to catch up, and to those who find the work of the grade too easy to make up deficiencies and move ahead.

Still another plan would be to have at least two special or auxiliary teachers to deal with the retarded, to keep the slow-moving up to grade, and to forward capable pupils. The slow and retarded are relieved of some of the work of the course of study. The normal pupils who, for any cause, have fallen behind are helped up, being for a time relieved of some of the special work. Such rooms are sometimes designated as restoration rooms. For those who are to go ahead, instead of making a special promotion without preparation, the pupils are sent to this special room.

The special teacher in such a room can handle two working groups, of about ten to twelve pupils each, and she can handle about four such double groups a year. This will give about nine weeks to coach up each double group and get it advanced enough, in all the essential work of the grade, to fit it into the grade ahead. By so dividing the work of the teacher, and so selecting the pupils and timing their extra progress, eight working groups of accelerates can be handled each year, and from 80 to 95 pupils can be thus coached to gain a half-year in their school progress. A working group of capables from each class from 3B to 6A could thus be given nine weeks of coaching each year with a view to their acceleration.

Best use of such a room. In using such a room for aiding retarded pupils, two policies may be followed. The first and the more common one, is to send to this teacher all pupils who are retarded more than a fixed amount, or all who are falling behind in their classwork, and then expect the special-room teacher to bring them up to grade. This is often expecting the impossible, as some have not the mental ability to enable them to reach or to hold their age-grade level. A second and a wiser policy is to apply mental tests to all pupils before sending them to this room, and to try to do only what is possible and best. The mental subnormals can thus be located, and a type of work prescribed for them in which they may hope to succeed. If the school system makes such provision it is best to group the subnormals separately, but in many smaller school systems this is not possible. In this case the subnormals and the normal but retarded pupils will be in the same room, and the teacher will be called upon to adjust her teaching so as to meet the needs of both groups.

The best use of the ungraded room is that of helping pupils to keep up or to get ahead. It then becomes an opportunity, or an adjustment room. These, too, are better names for the room than ungraded or special. They give the room and service better standing in the eyes of all the pupils, and tend to prevent the room becoming known as the "dummy room" or the "bonehead room." Sending bright pupils to the room for special coaching, to enable them to move ahead by special promotion, does much to ward off such pupil terminology.

In many cases the special teacher will be able to coach pupils so that they may hold their grades. Pupils who have been absent or ill, or who have entered late, may be sent to this room to be helped back to grade. Some may need to be in the room all day, for a time; others will go to the room only for part-time work. Pupils who are fairly intelligent but who need help in the use of English may also be sent to this room. Pupils coming from rural schools and giving evidence of uneven preparation, or pupils retarded by much moving about, may also need the services of the special teacher. Timid pupils, those who are discouraged, those lacking in ambition, and those who have not found school attractive sometimes do well when sent to the special teacher.

Use of as a clearing house. The special, or ungraded, or adjustment, or auxiliary, or opportunity room can thus be made of large usefulness in any school in enabling the principal to keep more homogeneous working groups in the regular classrooms. Such rooms become, as it were, clearing houses, designed to handle all irregular cases, and thus keep the classroom groups more homogeneous. A large school could use two to three such rooms, specializing them somewhat as to grade and type of service. If there is but one such teacher to a building, she can be most useful by working largely with the pupils of grades three, four, five, and six, as there is more need for help in these grades than in others. From about twelve to twenty pupils, varying somewhat with conditions and needs and the character of the special teacher, is about what may be expected. If the teacher has too many pupils the individuality of the instruction and the effectiveness of the service rendered are alike interfered with.

In a few schools the ungraded room is organized on an eight-hour, two-section plan, with about fifteen to eighteen pupils each for the morning and the afternoon sections. The room may have even more pupils attending the class before school opens in the morning, or after it closes in the afternoon. The enrollment, too, will vary from week to week as the pupils come and go, and may vary with the different hours of the day, depending upon what use is made of the room.

Unless the room has been especially organized as a school for retarded or low-mentality pupils, those sent to it should be coached up and sent back as rapidly as can be done. The room should not be conducted as an asylum. To this end the teacher should have a good working program, with a proper time allotment for those fundamental subjects which the room is to teach. Special subjects, such as music, drawing, and gymnastics, have little place in the ungraded room.

The best use of such a room or rooms, too, calls for specially trained teachers who possess energy, enthusiasm, and personality; the use of educational and intelligence tests for diagnosis; special methods, such as a decrease in drill and explanation and discipline, and an emphasis on initiative and application and underlying principles; some special equipment; and an absence of school-grade rigidity. Such rooms, intelligently used, improve classroom work and school morale, strengthen weak spots, reduce retardation, help discouraged pupils to get a grip on themselves, and hold pupils better and longer in school. The extra cost for such work is more than compensated for by the advantages accruing to the classes from which the ill-adjusted children have been removed.

Acceleration and retardation in a parallel-course school.
When we pass from the common course of study to the parallel course of study, such as is illustrated in Figure 23, page 359, we find the adjustment of instruction to pupil easier to make. A glance at Figure 23, which may be taken as a type, will show the five natural transfer points for the two courses. The bright pupil can here find plenty of opportunities for acceleration, and pupils can be tried out in either course and easily shifted from one to the other. The special promotion now becomes of much less importance, and the ungraded room, while still of use in helping pupils to move forward, now finds its chief usefulness with the slow and the mentally subnormal. The apportionment of each year's work into three divisions instead of two helps to make a non-promotion less serious than under a semiannual promotional plan.

That the advantages of such a parallel course plan may be reaped in schools not definitely organized in this manner, by the formation of special working groups, the following quotation from a report made by the Superintendent of Schools of Montclair, New Jersey, will show:

In September, 1912, a group of fourth-grade children of fairly uniform and superior ability were put in charge of a strong teacher, who was instructed to allow the class to advance as rapidly as it desired. No pressure was ever brought to bear upon the pupils, but dawdling was discouraged. The class remained with the same teacher for two years, and in this time did three years of work. Four months after the special group entered the seventh grade, careful tests were made to determine to what extent the experiment had been a success or a failure. A comparison of the record of the special seventh-grade pupils with those of the entire seventh grade with which they had been merged, and with two other seventh grades of a similar type, showed a very gratifying situation. Tests in spelling, arithmetic, and English were given by the principal and a standard test in composition by the superintendent, while the penmanship was rated by the writing supervisor.

The following facts show the results of these tests:

School	Fractions	Fundamental Operations	English	Spelling	Writing	Composition
Special group (7B)	87	83	83	97	11.1	45.8
Watchung 7A	83.6	78	81	98	11.6	42.2
Watchung 7B	86.9	80	80	98	11.2	45.4
Grove 7A	77	69	71	97	11.4	45.4

The promotional problem in the differentiated-course school. When we pass still further to the differentiated course of study type of school, such as is shown in Figure 24, page 361, we find the promotional problem still easier to handle. Such a course of study, however, does not work out well in a small school, as it almost requires that a building have two rooms to a grade to carry it along to the best advantage. For example, supposing two fourth-grade rooms containing 72 pupils, we might expect to find that they would be classified by tests into approximately:

15 to 20 slow moving pupils, or 4C,
35 to 40 average pupils, or 4B, and
15 to 20 fast moving pupils, or 4A.

The pupils of this fourth grade could then be assigned to the two teachers and rooms, as follows:

Either (1) { 4C and 4A / 4B }   or   (2) { 4C and 4B (less able half) / 4B (more able half) and 4A. }

The second grouping is the better, as it makes transfers from group to group a little easier.

The champions of this type of grading and promotion plan claim that it is far superior to progress by special promotions. Pupils, they properly contend, should be doing

CLASSIFICATION AND PROMOTION

work that is adapted to their ability and their rate of speed, and the basis for classification should be the individual differences which tests and performance reveal. Instead of skipping a grade by an extra promotion, which leaves gaps in performance, the pupils are divided into three groups on the basis of mental and pedagogical tests, teachers' markings, health and strength, and actual schoolroom performance. The teachers will know the A group as the accelerated or superior group; the B group as the normal or average group; and the C group as the slow-moving group. To the pupils they will be known only as A, B, and C.

The course of study and the schoolroom procedure will then be adapted to the needs of each group, there virtually being three parallel courses. Group A will be able to take more abstract work, to cover a wider field, and to bring in much outside and supplementary material. Group B will not only cover average class work in the subjects of study, but will have the work more adapted to their interests and abilities. Group C will be given work at a rate best adapted to their needs, and a course with more emphasis on concrete work and practical everyday needs. Instead of imposing a uniform program on all, pupils will work and progress at rates of speed which are normal and natural for them. The pupil, rather than the course of study, becomes the measure for school work.

Special promotions and progress under this plan. From the diagram, Figure 24, it would be inferred that all children, during the first six years in school, would under this plan move forward at a uniform rate, that is a year to a school grade, the difference being in the amount of work done in each grade. Ordinarily this would be the case, the special promotions being of C pupils to a B division, and B pupils to an A division. Most principals, though, will find a few A pupils who, by reason of very superior ability, ought to go ahead faster. If an ungraded teacher is available the problem is relatively easy, but under the differentiated-course plan of grading and promotion the ungraded teacher is largely dispensed with. In case no such service is at hand the principal must then depend on home coaching, home study, and reciting in two grades at school, or else plain skipping to enable him to advance his A pupil to at least a B division of the grade ahead. The fact that the school, unless quite large, has year grades instead of half-year grades makes such a transfer more difficult. It can, however, be done.

A good example of the special progress of a superior group recently came to the writer's notice. A principal found six 5B and twelve 5A pupils of very superior ability in his school. By two intelligence tests all ranked as superior or gifted children. He organized them into a group by themselves and called them his "Special Fives." The group, working together, covered a year's work in four months, and even then the work had to be enriched for them beyond that ordinarily given. Checking the results of their progress by standard educational tests revealed a class median better than the standard medians for the tests, or of equivalent classes in the school. His conclusions were that gifted children work better when working with pupils of their own type; that they work with greater profit when moving more rapidly than normal children; that they demand a richer course of study; and that they are better students and happier when segregated into a group where all are subjected to competition of their own kind.

The two great advantages of the differentiated course of study plan lie in the provision of more homogeneous working groups, and in the adjustment of the effort demanded to the capacity of the pupils. The C course of study represents the minimum for the slow moving pupils; the A course the maximum load for the most capable children. By this type of segregation all three groups are benefited. The pupils make better progress when working with others of their own capacity, and they enjoy their school work more. The slow and timid are encouraged because they can now do the work and are not continually dwarfed by the competition of those whom they can never equal, while the capable pupils are worked up to capacity and in consequence largely prevented from developing into lazy and troublesome members of the school because they never have enough to do. To these specially capable pupils the school is under a special obligation, and for them working to capacity in a special group is better than extra promotions to get them ahead where the work will be more difficult. The writer is convinced that many a bright boy who later becomes a lazy loafer and never achieves any large success in life, does so because his teachers never taught him the joy of working to capacity. He loafed through school and he loafs through life.

Combination promotional plans. The different plans so far described have been set forth as though they were separate and distinct plans, and as though a principal using one plan would not make use of another. Such, though, is not the case. Instead, it is possible to combine them somewhat. To illustrate such combination we will take the school shown in Figure 6, page 96, and describe a possible combined grading and promotional plan for it. This school has a kindergarten, an ungraded room and teacher, nine grades, and a carrying load of 840 pupils. Grades one to six are organized on the grade plan, and grades seven to nine as a junior high school and on a departmental plan.

Let us now assume that grades one to six follow a common average-type course of study, with semiannual promotions, and that in the junior high school promotion is by subjects. Let us also suppose that the principal has power to make minor changes in the course of study for different classes, to make special promotions as may seem wise, and to organize special retarded or accelerated groups if the best interests of the pupils seem to indicate this procedure as desirable. We may also assume that in each of the first two grades the principal may now organize three working groups, C, B, and A, while in grades three to six two groups would probably suffice. The great bulk of the pupils will make normal progress, and the semiannual promotions, the ungraded teacher and room, and the special promotions will provide for their needs. There will be a certain number, however, at both ends of the scale who will need some special attention. The number of each kind will vary materially with the character of the neighborhood and the character of the parents who send pupils to the school. To care for these children some adaptation of the ungraded or the auxiliary room or of the differentiated-course plan may be introduced.

Adaptations for the slow and the capable. As this school is large, 840 pupils, there will probably be enough over-age and over-size and retarded pupils, by the time the sixth grade is reached, to organize them into special classes by themselves, one for boys and one for girls, putting them in charge of special teachers — a man, if the right type can be had, for the boys, and a woman for the girls. A few extra-large and over-age fifth-grade pupils may also be included. Because of their size and age these groups may be classified as specials, or as opportunity-room pupils, and may be placed with the junior high school part of the school organization. The room teacher for each of these groups will give most of the academic work they will need, but they should be allowed to elect such studies as manual training, cooking, sewing, millinery, hygiene, printing, typewriting, and agriculture, if they are interested in them and can do the work.

CLASSIFICATION AND PROMOTION

For the special subjects — music, drawing, writing, and science — they may recite with any class in the building with which they best fit. A pupil in one of these special rooms may then be doing 5A geography, 5B arithmetic, 4A language, 6B writing, 5B science, be excused from drawing except as he gets it in manual training, and be learning printing. Into these classes — special, adjustment, or opportunity rooms — are fitted as many of the slow-moving, over-age pupils as can profit more from work in them than in the regular grade rooms, and for them the course of study may be widely differentiated and no more attempted than can be done to advantage. Nearly all such pupils will leave school as soon as the compulsory years are over, and the purpose of the school should be to do the most possible for them before they go out into life.

There will also be a number of superior pupils in such a school who can do more than the regular work and who ought to be given the opportunity, but who probably ought not to be promoted too rapidly. By the time the fifth grade is reached these children may begin to do extra work, and after the seventh grade is reached, and promotion by subjects becomes the rule, these pupils can be cared for easily. In a few school systems the very superior pupils are segregated, after the sixth grade, with the consent of the parents, and sent to central schools where an enriched course of study is offered and an opportunity given them to do four years of work (seventh, eighth, ninth, and tenth grades) in three years. Without such central schools much the same results may be obtained in a school organized as is the school under consideration. Such a school should offer an opportunity for the superior children to study a modern language, do special work in music or drawing, more extensive work in some subject of study, or carry extra work in some of the manual or domestic arts.

To a casual visitor the upper grades of a school organized as just described may appear somewhat confused. It naturally lacks the military regularity of the old-type, lockstep, graded school. The pupils, in passing, seem to be going everywhere and to be all out of line. Each pupil, though, has a definite program, knows where he is going and what he is after, and is learning to assume responsibility. The capable and ambitious pupil has a chance to cut off a year in his school progress. The slow and backward pupil associates with those of his own age, and recites with those of his stage of advancement. By taking the over-age boys and girls out of the fifth and sixth grades the problem of discipline there is simplified, and by giving them a course of instruction suited to their capacities they are better prepared for life. By such flexible grading and promotional adjustments boys and girls make better school progress, are happier in their work, and stay in school longer. The problem for every school principal then is to so handle the classification and promotion of pupils as to introduce as much flexibility as is of advantage, and to keep the needs of the pupil rather than the course of study in mind in doing his work.

QUESTIONS AND PROBLEMS

1. Take the school shown in Figure 7, page 98, and the age-and-grade distribution of which is shown in Table VIII, page 341, and arrange a grade and room distribution of the classes in such a manner that the first two grades will be divided into three divisions or working groups — C, B, and A — and the remaining grades into two working groups — B and A.
2. What would you try to do with such a grade as is shown in Figure 19, page 346?
3. Suppose your lower grades showed some such mental-age distribution as is shown in Figure 22, page 353. Would an opportunity or development room be a useful adjunct to your school? If so, how would you use it?
4. Would you make any additional rules of promotion to the two lists given in the text, and if so what ones? Would you eliminate any of those given? If so, on what grounds?

CLASSIFICATION AND PROMOTION

5. Suppose, in the school shown in Figure 8, page 99, the retardation was found to be rather heavy, as shown in your age-grade distribution sheet, asked for in Question 12 of the preceding chapter, and on a showing of the facts the superintendent should give you two extra ungraded-room-type teachers, and two portables for your yard, with complete freedom to use them as you see fit. How would you use these teachers?
6. Could you use a companion-class organization, as described in Chapter VIII, pages 148–50, for the school shown in Figure 5 to help you with your promotional problems? If so, how?
7. How would the platoon-type of educational organization, as described in Chapter VIII for the schools shown in Figures 7 and 10, modify or help in solving promotional problems?
8. Work out a schedule for School 7 of Table VIII, showing how you would use a special coaching teacher to forward eight groups of accelerates each year, as described on page 374.
9. Show how a bright pupil might do four years' work in three in the junior high organization, as described on page 383 of this chapter.

SELECTED REFERENCES

Arthur, Grace. "Eliminating First Grade Failures through the Control of Intellectual, Physical, and Emotional Factors"; in *School and Society*, vol. 15, pp. 474–84. (April 29, 1922.)
   An interesting description of actual work, with results.

Ayres, L. P. *Laggards in the School.* 236 pp., New York, 1909.
   An old but valuable study of retardation and elimination of pupils.

Buckingham, B. R. "Promotion Rates of Pupils"; in *Journal of Educational Research*, vol. 4, pp. 308–11. (November, 1921.)
   A good editorial on how this may be determined.

Buckner, C. A. *Educational Diagnosis of Individual Pupils.* Teachers College Contributions to Education, No. 98. New York, 1919.

Callihan, T. W. "An Experiment in the Use of Intelligence Tests as a Basis for Proper Grouping and Promotions in the 8th Grade"; in *Elementary School Journal*, vol. 21, pp. 465–69. (February, 1921.)
   Descriptive of work in educational diagnosis by means of intelligence tests.

Cleveland, Elizabeth. "Detroit's Experiment with Gifted Children"; in *School and Society*, vol. 12, pp. 179–83. (September 11, 1920.)

Coxe, W. W. "School Variation in General Intelligence"; *Journal of Educational Research*, vol. 4, 187–94. (October, 1921.)
   Gives variations in twenty-four elementary schools in Cincinnati, and distribution of intelligence in each. Shows wide variations, and great need of reorganization of the course of study and other adjustments.

Elson, W. H. "Waste and Efficiency in School Studies"; in *Proceedings of National Education Association*, 1912, pp. 335–43.
   A good article on retardation, promotion, and the elimination of waste, with particular reference to the Cleveland schools.

Frasier, C. R. "At what should the ungraded school aim, and for what class of pupils should it provide?" in *Proceedings of National Education Association*, 1907, pp. 316–21.

> One of a number of articles, with discussions (pp. 310–27) on the topic "The Need for Special Classes." Old, but still good.

Freeman, Frank N. "Provision in the Elementary Schools for Superior Children"; in *Elementary School Journal*, vol. 21, pp. 117–31. (October, 1920.)

> Discusses the problems of classification, and results. What is being done, where, and how.

Hartwell, C. H. "Grading and Promotion of Pupils"; in *Educational Review*, vol. 40, pp. 375–86. (November, 1910.) Also in *Proceedings of National Education Association*, 1910, pp. 294–300; discussion, pp. 300–306.

> A very good discussion of the whole subject. Gives a digest of the New York City Teachers' Association's investigation of plans in use.

Henry, T. S. *Classroom Problems in the Education of Gifted Children. Nineteenth Yearbook, National Society for the Study of Education.* 125 pp. Good bibliography.

> A very important study of the problem, describing special room and experiments, school progress, the results of tests, methods of instruction, and a summary and conclusions.

Holmes, W. H. *School Organization and the Individual Child.* 197 + 211 pp. The Davis Press, Worcester, 1912.

> Part I describes plans for handling normal children, and Part II, subnormal children. An important volume.

Holmes, H. W. "The General Philosophy of Grading and Promotion in Relation to Intelligence Testing"; in *School and Society*, vol. 15, pp. 457–61. (April 29, 1922.)

> States the fundamental principles involved, and shows it to be an administrative problem. Favors differentiated courses rather than rapid promotion.

Kennedy, John, *The Batavia System of Individual Instruction.* 299 pp., Syracuse, 1914.

Phillips, D. E. "The Child *vs.* Promotion Machinery"; in *Proceedings of National Education Association*, 1912, pp. 349–55.

> An argument on the child side of the question.

Pintner, R., and Noble, H. "The Classification of School Children According to Mental Age"; in *Journal of Educational Research*, vol. 2, pp. 713–28. (November, 1920.)

> Good charts showing conditions before and after.

Saam, Theodore. "Intelligence Testing as an Aid to Supervision"; in *Elementary School Journal*, vol. 20, pp. 26–32. (September, 1919.)

> Work at Council Bluffs, Iowa. Facts and Figures.

Salt Lake City, Utah. *Report of the Survey of the School System.* 324 pp. Yonkers, 1915.

> Chapter IX, on the progress of children through the schools, deals with both retardation and the means employed to reduce the same.

CLASSIFICATION AND PROMOTION

Spaulding, F. E. "The Unassigned Teacher in the Schools"; in *School Review*, vol. 15, pp. 201–16. (March, 1907.)
   Describes the work of such a teacher in the schools of Newton, Mass.

Starch, D. "Standard Tests as Aids in the Classification and Promotion of Pupils"; in *Journal of Educational Psychology*, vol. 6, pp. 1–24. (January, 1915.)

Stockton, J. LeRoy; Davis, C.; and Cronin, A. "Criteria for Regrading Schools"; in *Elementary School Journal*, vol. 22, pp. 55–66. (September, 1921.)
   Use of mental tests in classifying and reclassifying children.

Strayer, G. D., and Englehardt, N. L. *Record Book for Elementary School Principals*. C. F. Williams and Son, Albany, 1918.
   A useful loose-leaf book of record forms.

Strayer, G. D., and Englehardt, N. L. *The Classroom Teacher*. New York, 1920.
   Chapter VIII, pp. 124–64, contains many illustrative tables and much good material on the classification and promotion of pupils.

Terman, L. M. *The Intelligence of School Children*. 362 pp., Boston, 1916.
   Contains interesting chapters upon how children differ in ability, the use of intelligence tests in sorting them, and the proper education of superior children.

Terman, L. M., and others. *Intelligence Tests and School Reorganization*. 111 pp., Yonkers, 1922.
   Chapter I of this volume, by Terman, is a resumé of our progress in the use of intelligence tests, and Chapter V, by Tupper, shows how they may be used in a small city in the work of pupil classification.

Washburne, C. W. "The Individual System in Winnetka"; in *Elementary School Journal*, vol. 21, pp. 52–68. (September, 1920.)
   Describes use of individual promotion plan, and results under it.

Zirkle, H. W. "Character and Results of Special Rooms as conducted in the Whittier School"; in *Elementary School Journal*, vol. 21, pp. 189–97. (November, 1920.)
   Types of work done and results in the Whittier School, Denver.

Zirkle, H. W. "Result of a Year and a Half with Special Half Period"; in *School Review*, vol. 24, pp. 219–21. (March, 1916.)
   Shows rather remarkable results in cutting down retardation, skipping grades, and preventing pupils from dropping by the use of a special help period for pupils from 3B upward.

First Yearbook of the Department of Elementary School Principals, National Education Association, 1922.

The following papers in this *Yearbook* form good reading in connection with the subject-matter of this chapter:

1. Campbell, Cora. The Intelligence Quotient as a Means of Classification in the Lower Grades, pp. 45–49.
2. Greenberg, B. B. Intelligence Tests as a Basis for Reclassification, pp. 55–58.
3. Krauskopf, Chas. C. The Individual Case; An Administrative Problem, pp. 59–65.
4. Marshall, J. Using the Results of Testing, pp. 49–55.
5. Merrill, John. Reducing the Percentage of Failures in the Detroit Elementary Schools without lowering Standards, pp. 126–28.
6. Smith, M. H. Finding the Individual, pp. 65–70.

CHAPTER XX

OBTAINING RESULTS FROM THE COURSES OF STUDY

Types of courses of study. Practically everywhere a principal may begin work he will find a course of study outlined for the guidance of himself and his teachers. Sometimes this course of study will have been laid down by the State, occasionally by the county, but most commonly by the educational authorities of the city in which he is to work. Occasionally it will have been formulated by committees of the teachers themselves, but more commonly it will trace its origin to the superintendent's office.

In character the course of study will vary much in different places. In certain places there will be a very rigid course of study, with what is to be done carefully laid down and uniformly required of all. Sometimes this will be in terms of fixed assignments in fixed textbooks, and sometimes in fixed directions as to what is to be done. Examinations for promotions may even be based on such assignments, and be uniform for the city. On the contrary, in places where the educational authorities have been blessed with a more intelligent conception of the educational process, the course of study may be a very flexible one, with optional work and optional textbooks. In some places it may be a minimum course, with authority left to principal and teachers to supplement it as they deem wise; in still other places two or even three parallel courses may be outlined for pupil groups of different working capacities.

Using the course of study as a stimulus to thinking. Even in school systems where the course of study is rigidly outlined, and even based on definite page assignments in definite textbooks, the principal will still find it possible to suggest some points for omission or emphasis, and to help teachers, especially new ones, to plan out the term's work for their classes. The problem then is not only to try to modify, where possible, with a view to providing as intelligent instruction for the pupils as can be done, but also to inject as much stimulus to thinking as is possible for the teachers, despite the rigidity of the instruction. There is always the greatest danger, under such a system, of the teachers becoming mechanical workers and the covering of the course of study becoming the end and aim of the work.

In school systems where a more modern type of course of study is in force, and where options are allowed to both schools and teachers, the principal will find it an important part of his work to help his teachers plan out their instruction and decide what and how much it is best to do. Since different groups will be traveling at different rates, and covering different amounts as they travel, the adjustment of the course of study to group needs will be one of the major problems of supervision in such a school. The principal now has an opportunity to use organization and adaptation of the course of study to group needs as one means of keeping his teachers thinking and growing, and he will in general do this best by giving them much liberty in making decisions rather than by taking it all upon himself.

Mapping out the instruction. In every school grade, and with every properly organized working group of pupils, there will be certain minimal work to be done, certain work that may be gone over very rapidly, and certain major points to be emphasized. There are also certain things that should be stressed for capable groups, and which may be minimized or omitted for other groups. The work of the grade or term, too, will have certain large objectives which should be reached. All of this should be set forth in relief to the teachers, that they may see their work as a whole and in its relationships, and in consequence be better able to organize their work for the grade or term into its parts or details. In many smaller city school systems this is done by the superintendent of schools, through his grade meetings, and if well done this is the most effective means. The larger objectives which each grade is to attempt may also well be set forth by the superintendent to the principals, at his principals' conference. If the superintendent assumes this function and gives his suggestions in a liberal spirit, it is of the greatest help to the principal in what he should later do. If the superintendent does not do this, then the principal should assume the work and incorporate it as a phase of his classroom supervision and service. In any case, he should reinforce and supplement whatever the superintendent may do, as it relates to his particular school, so that the minimal work and the larger objectives for the different grades may be clearly in mind. He probably will want to set up additional objectives for his own particular school.

Once these larger objectives for a term's work of a grade are in mind, the next thing for principal and teachers will be to lay out roughly into parts the work to be done, and then so to plan and space these requirements that the work may proceed rather evenly from week to week and from month to month. The older and more skillful teachers will need little help, and, if the principal finds them efficient, they may safely be entrusted with the organization of their own work. The younger and inexperienced teachers, though, should receive whatever help they may seem to need. With beginners, assistance in planning from week to week, with suggestions even from day to day, may at first be needed, until they grasp the idea of planning and attain some skill at it. Good organization of work and specific planning of what is to be done, and when, make for definite progress, eliminate waste, and promote thoroughness on the part of the pupils, but all this requires thinking the work through on the part of the teacher.

Distinctions as to major and minor aims should be clear, and as much liberty in the selection of materials and methods as can be used should be left to the teachers themselves. Where not prohibited from above, variations between classes and in different terms should be encouraged, and the major aim may be shifted from year to year or from time to time within the year. While carrying out the main thought of the course of study, it is well to allow variations and contributions from both teachers and pupils. The principal, too, should make his contribution. Both pupils and teachers are helped if they can exercise some choice in what they do.

Use and abuse of lesson plans. In mapping out the work to be done, some form of outline or lesson plan often is required, though lesson plans are not used to-day as much as they were twenty years ago. The idea has certain good uses, but some principals and superintendents carry it so far that it becomes a handicap rather than a help, and tends to develop and perpetuate mechanical work instead of serving the larger purpose of improving the instruction of the teacher. Some principals proceed on the theory that teachers generally do not know what they are trying to do, and to correct this require lesson plans for each week, and sometimes for each day, to be handed in at the office in advance. To such lesson planning serious objections are advanced, which may be summarized about as follows:

Seldom, it is argued, are such plans examined, and the time put on their preparation would better be put on other types of work. The principal or superintendent does not need them to tell what is being done when they visit the school, or to check up what is done when they do not. Public school teachers are seldom in the practice-teacher stage, and should seldom be required to follow practice-teacher methods and plans. The time spent in preparing detailed plans for the principal's desk would usually be better spent in reading, working with pupils, getting acquainted with parents and children, resting, playing, or sleeping. If a teacher possesses so little interest and enthusiasm in her work that a submitted lesson plan is the only assurance a principal can have that any thought has been given to the work of the day, then the sooner such teacher is eliminated from the school the better it will be.

On the other hand, some supervisors contend that the lesson plan has its use, but a use chiefly to the teacher who makes it. It represents, its advocates contend, evidence of some thinking as to what is to be done, some picking out of important points for emphasis, and some unit-planning of work to be accomplished. It aids the teacher in seeing her task for a week or a day as a whole, tends to secure better correlations, eliminates overlapping, usually insures a better organization of the instruction, aids in assigning new work, and is very useful to a substitute teacher if the regular teacher is forced to be absent. Used in this manner, a brief outline of the main points to be attempted for each week becomes a means to an end, viz., good instruction, and not an end in itself, viz., the plan.

How far such planning should go, and to what detail, will ordinarily vary much with the training and experience and skill of the individual teachers. Some teachers scarcely need to make any plan on paper for their own use, others only a brief page outline, while still others may need, for a time, to make rather full plans for what they are to do. So greatly do needs vary that lesson-planning is a poor subject for a principal to manage by uniform rules unless he knows

DAILY OUTLINE OF WORK

Teacher.....Della Denison....................Date....Nov. 2, 1922

Grade......4 A......Section or group....C......Room....15......

I plan to teach this day what is indicated after the following-named subjects:

Reading: Drill on enunciation and syllabification, based on Lesson 42, State Reader.

Language: Drill on use of capitals, and pronoun I. Written work from dictation. Exchange papers and correct and discuss.

Spelling: Speller, p. 39. Words of 3 syllables. Similarity of endings. Study for syllabification and accent, and then write from dictation.

Arithmetic: Mental drill. Four fundamental operations, whole numbers and simple fractions.

Geography: Study of State cont'd. Climate, rainfall, drainage.

History: Supplemental reading, "Story of Columbus," p. 23.

Nature Study: } Hygiene day: Keeping body warm and dry.
Physiology: } Oral work — clothing, food, shoes.

Writing: Copy Book, III, p. 6. Drill.

Music: Rote singing. "Suwannee River."

Drawing: Copying of colored design, cont'd.

Physical Training:

Manual Arts:

Domestic Arts:

FORM 3. A CARD LESSON-PLAN FORM, FILLED OUT

clearly what he is about, and wants to use the plans in his visitation and supervision.

Used for this purpose the lesson plan can be made of distinct use to the school principal, especially in a large school. In one, of the writer's acquaintance, where the principal spends a large percentage of his time in classroom supervision and plans this supervision carefully, the teachers are required to send to his office each evening or early each morning a penciled-in card-form plan-of-work for the day. Printed cards are supplied, of which the form given on page 393 is an example. Such a form is simple and easily prepared, leads to definiteness in planning the instruction, and is of use to the principal in arranging any visitation or special inspection he may desire to make.

Assistance to teachers. It is wise for a new principal, until his classroom supervision confirms the contrary, to take certain things for granted. He may with safety assume that his more experienced teachers have a good general grasp of the subject-matter to be taught, and will fill in the details from day to day as they are needed. He may also assume that they do some planning of their work, have fairly good methods which will bring fair results with the children, and have in mind certain definite aims toward which they work and which are in harmony with the proper progress of instruction and the larger objectives of the course of study and the school. Survey may show him that these assumptions are not valid, but they are good safe first assumptions. If some form of lesson planning seems necessary, it can be introduced later on.

This does not mean, though, that the young, the inexperienced, the weak, or even the strong and capable teachers need make no preparation for their work from day to day. The beginners, and some of the younger or weaker teachers, may need help almost on the practice-teacher level. Instead of making a uniform rule for all the principal should give such teachers individual help, having them plan out parts of their work for his approval. He should find their weak points and seek to strengthen them. He should discuss their plans with them, and in the room supervision show them how to develop better working plans. He must point out to them that they must know and evaluate the subject-matter they are trying to teach; that they must organize their day's work around the problems they want the children to solve; that they must think out a half-dozen pivotal questions to enable them to start the recitation well, and hold the discussion to the main issue; that they must make provision for summaries as they proceed; that they must have their future assignments clearly in mind, and make them very definite; and that they must use enough but not too much supplemental and illustrative material to keep the recitation going well. He must teach them to analyze and check up their work from day to day, in order to evaluate the strong and the weak points in what they do. Occasionally, instead of the principal taking the whole burden on himself, he can do a double service by asking some older, "know-it-all," and not-particularly-successful type of teacher to help in doing this service for some younger one — "out of the fullness of her experience" — and then sit back and watch them both.

Plans a means to an end. Teachers, new and inexperienced, or those who have never become accustomed to such planning of their work, can be materially helped in their profession by some training along this line. Effective and economical teaching demands just such preparatory thinking, whether or not it be reduced to writing. Written plans are most useful to new and inexperienced teachers, as well as to old teachers beginning to be seriously afflicted with "pedagogical cramp." It is necessary for them to think out their work more clearly, and to keep a better sense of proportion in what they do. Requiring written lesson plans from good and able teachers, on the contrary, is a waste of time and energy that ought to go to the children. Still more, an insistence on their preparation diverts the teacher's attention from the work to the plan, tends to set up the false standard of satisfying the supervisor, develops unnecessary routine work, and ultimately tends to produce lifeless teaching and teachers. The best lesson plans for able teachers are mental ones, because they involve the least expenditure of time and energy.

It is the principal's duty to so shape his supervision of instruction that every teacher will, of necessity, have to think out her work and organize some form of mental or written plan for it. How frequently he will discuss these plans with any teacher will be determined largely by the need for help of the teacher concerned. It is also the duty of the principal to so shape his interpretation of the course of study and the instructional work of the school that only the best lesson plans will be possible, and that only sound pedagogical principles will be employed in formulating these plans and in conducting the lessons themselves. If, in addition, the principal himself personifies the qualities which good lesson plans are supposed to cultivate, if he has good working habits and works to a purpose, if he can do constructive thinking, and if he studies the teaching problems of his teachers as well as he expects them to study them, it will go a long way in securing the qualities he desires his teachers to exhibit in their classroom work.

The course of study not an end in itself. In all discussion of instruction, lesson plans, and of work to be covered, both the principal and the teachers should keep clearly before them the important idea that any course of study is after all only a means to an end, and not an end in itself.

The purpose of all school instruction is the best possible development of the pupil taught, rather than the acquisition of subject-matter. After all, there is nothing especially sacred about the subject-matter of a course of study. If pupils are trained to think and work for themselves, and to stand on their own feet, the prime purpose of all instruction will have been accomplished.

No course of study, no matter how scientifically it has been worked out and mapped out, can accomplish its purpose in the education of youth without constant adaptations to the needs of the children taught. All our study of working groups has shown this clearly. New teachers need much help here in order to catch the vision of what modern education should attempt to do for young people. Because it is so much easier to have pupils memorize and recite from fixed material than it is to train them to think and work independently, new teachers require special attention and supervision to start them right. A principal who shapes the administration of the course of study in his school to this end, and who makes of it an important part of his school supervision, will find it one of the most helpful means at hand for developing and keeping a proper professional attitude on the part of his teachers.

Getting results by drives. While the great purpose of education is to train pupils to work independently and to think for themselves, there are still certain abilities and certain fact materials that must be mastered. Many studies along these lines have revealed the importance of concentrated study and work, for short periods, in such mastery. To this end the school grades will need, from time to time, to set up certain major objectives for short-period "drives," with the idea of concentrating attention on the rapid mastery of some skill or some set body of facts. Sometimes a selected group may make a drive to do a piece of work well in a brief period, as, for example, a term's work in arithmetic or language in half the regular time. The same principle will apply to review work, to which many courses of study seem to devote an unjustifiable amount of scattered time. Intensive one-week term reviews may be used to replace the term examination, the emphasis in the review work being placed on rapid, intensive work, with enough competitive work within the class to keep interest keen.

These "drives" will, for a time, become the major objectives of the group. Sometimes a term or even a year may be devoted to such objectives as improvement in English usage, better writing and spelling, new science work, or studies in civics. On the other hand, much valuable work can be accomplished by short, intensive efforts to fix some particular thing.

Types of such short-period drives would be:

1. For the school as a whole.
    a. Bringing up the health score.
    b. Best attendance for the month.
    c. Cleaner yard and building.
2. Special grade drives.
    a. Improving arithmetic scores.
    b. Improving writing scores.
    c. Elimination of composition errors.
    d. Elimination of common spelling errors.

Teachers should be encouraged to organize such campaigns from time to time, but the principal should give careful oversight to what is attempted. Most of the minor and short-period classroom drives can be left to the discretion of the teacher concerned; the major school drives should be decided upon by the teachers as a group. When once inaugurated, every such drive should be made to seem of much importance; the purpose of it should be clearly set forth; intensive work should be done; the results of the drive should be measured and graphically shown to both pupils and teachers; and the principal should show himself deeply interested in what is to be done and in the results obtained. Much of the value of any such drive lies in the enthusiasm it awakens and the pride of accomplishment that comes from success. All this tends to develop a school spirit that is worth much in many ways.

The question of home study by pupils. One of the important questions every principal will have to face, in the administration of the course of study in his school, will be what attitude the school will take toward the question of home study by the pupils. This is sometimes a burning question in a school, or even in a city. If an unreasonable amount of home work has been assigned by teachers it sometimes leads to a reaction that goes to the extreme of forbidding all home assignments. Just what position a school may assume will depend a little on circumstances, though there is a moderate and a median position that the school should take if it can.

A question that may be asked of a new principal, at his first meeting with his teachers, is, "Are you, or are you not, going to require home study?" As this is a very important question the new principal may very well reply that since it is so important, and since the right answer depends so much on conditions and attitudes, he would like to think the problem over before answering definitely. He may, on the other hand, inquire what has been the practice of the school in the past, and, if there seems to be no serious objection, the school may continue as before until there seems to be need for change. The subject, though, is one of much importance and should receive the most careful attention. Pupil progress in school, good teaching, and satisfactory relations with the home all in large part depend upon how the question of home study by pupils is handled by the principal and his teachers.

The home and home study. While a few of the better

middle-class homes like to have the pupils have some home assignments, the great majority of homes object to it. In many schools the most serious cause of friction between parents and school, and the basis of most of the criticism of the school, is this matter of home study by the children. In most homes there is no quiet place where the children may prepare their lessons; the children often do not know how to work alone, and bother their parents to help them; and to get the children to bed in time the parents often do their sums or write their sentences for them. The children in consequence develop poor habits of work, and are marked low by the teachers if they fail to get all that is assigned them. The tendency, too, of the poor teacher is to increase the home assignments if recitations are unsatisfactory. This only increases the dislike of the pupils for school and augments the friction between the parents and the teacher.

In schools where teachers assign tasks, hear recitations, mark grades, and send the children home at night with book assignments for the morrow, there is not likely to be any large number of satisfied children or parents. Such work denotes both poor teaching and poor school supervision, and a defense of such instruction is the refuge of poor teachers and poor principals everywhere. In ignorant families with bad home conditions little is accomplished; in better homes the parents turn teacher, do much of the work, and get the child off to bed. The general result is to make the children nervous and anxious, destroy their sense of honor, fill them with undigested information, prevent the development of their thinking power and good working habits, make them superficial, and arouse a sense of injustice in both parents and children. The parents rightly feel that the teacher should teach, rather than hear the recitations the home prepares.

What is good teaching? This attitude on the part of intelligent parents raises a fundamental question as to what, after all, is the purpose of the school. If the course of study is a fixed thing, if certain facts have to be learned and certain pages of textbooks covered, if term examinations are made out at the central office and are uniform for all, and if principals and teachers have little or no option to vary the instruction, then such antagonism between home and school as has just been described may be expected, and little that the school can do will diminish it because the emphasis in education is put at the wrong place.

The real purpose in education, aside from the learning of a few facts and the mastery of certain abilities that are found to be of use in later life, is to train young people how to analyze a problem and find out things for themselves; to form in them good working habits; to show them how to concentrate attention and to study effectively and independently; to teach them how to gather facts and marshal them to form a conclusion; and to awaken in them motives for work beyond what the school requires. That many teachers and schools fail to grasp such a conception of their work, and that many pupils get a wrong idea of what "to study" means, is common knowledge. Yet probably the most important element in good teaching is the development of good habits of study and the ability to do independent thinking. The beginnings of the formation of such study habits go down as low as the third grade.

It is in these important respects that home study for younger pupils fails most completely. Even under the most favorable conditions there is loss of time and working effectiveness, while in the poorer homes the neglect of preparation and the bad working habits developed are a distinct loss to the children concerned. Home study, as usually carried on, is destructive of the good habits of work the modern school should be laboring to establish, and tends to train young people to dilly-dally, waste time and energy, and in the end to dishonesty by their getting some one else to do their work for them.

New work for the school principal. It is the growing realization on the part of the school of these defects that has caused many schools to abandon all home-study assignments for pupils below the fifth grade, and often below the seventh, and to turn instead to teaching pupils to do effective studying in the school. This almost at once demands new attention to the teaching process, because the key to good teaching is found in the training given pupils as to how to study. Conversely, improper study habits on the part of pupils is an evidence of poor teaching and of poor study assignments on the part of the teacher. This in turn calls for new attention to the supervision of instruction on the part of the principal, for he will often find it necessary to show his teachers how to train their pupils to do effective studying. To this end he must himself be fairly well informed on the psychology of the learning process, as it relates to the different ages and the different subjects of study. He must also be able, in his classroom visitation, quickly to evaluate the instruction given by his teachers in its relation to pupil study. He must be able to explain in simple terms the principles underlying good study, and teaching pupils how to study, as these bear on programs, recitation work, and course of study assignments, and be capable of demonstrating what he means by at times taking the class from the teacher and showing her how.

He will naturally need to give more help and encouragement to some teachers than to others. To some it will mean a complete change of point of view. Those who talk too much will need to be shown how to question instead; those who waste time will need to learn how to work more economically; those weak in assignment will need to be shown how to organize their work better; those who make the recitation chiefly an exercise of memory will need to have revealed to them better aims and ends; those who use the textbook as a source of knowledge and an end in itself will need to be shown how to use books as tools. He may need to explain to his teachers the ways children can and do study, and to emphasize the importance of planning work and assignments so as to motivate what is to be done. A good insight into the problem to be dealt with, the ability to give helpful suggestions and encouragement, and above all the capability of actually demonstrating what he wants done by doing it with a class, will carry a principal along far in the training of his teachers to develop effective habits of study on the part of their pupils.

Organizing a school for directed study. Scarcely anywhere will a new principal find it to have been the practice to give home work to children below the fourth grade, though in a few places third-grade assignments may obtain. After the fourth grade home assignments usually increase gradually up to the high school age.

Let us suppose that a principal, after taking charge of a school, considers the matter with his teachers and that they decide to change to a school-study plan, with little or no home study before the seventh grade. There will, of course, have to be certain exceptions. Children may with advantage take home books for reading. A pupil interested in a problem may take it home for further inquiry or study. A perfectly well child who is slow and plodding, needing a little extra work to fix some point, may be given some definite home assignment. A well child, who is trying to gain promotion, may systematically take home assignments of extra work, as may a well child who is getting behind. Parental help in such cases may be enlisted, and be quite beneficial.

The first difficulty in inaugurating the new plan will be encountered in the school program, as the ordinary grade program, with two grades to a room, is adjusted to reciting rather than to studying. With but one class or section or grade to a room the matter is easy, but this is seldom the case. One plan, commonly followed, is that of rearranging the program of all grades from 3B upward, so that approximately forty minutes will be allowed for each directed-study subject. In the junior high school grades the time may be extended to forty-five or fifty minutes. Approximately one half the time is then given to recitation work, and the other half, directly following, to directed study, the teacher helping the pupils to make the transition and get to work.

With two sections or grades in a room there will, under such a plan, be but little time during which the teacher can give the pupils actual help in learning how to study. In such a case, and this is very common, it will be necessary to try one or more of a number of expedients. One is to reduce the time of the recitation somewhat and use the time thus saved for directions as to what is to be done for the morrow, and how to do it. This shifts the emphasis from reciting to working, and the teacher will often need training in how to handle coöperative group activity, where finding out something instead of telling is the purpose. Sometimes a whole recitation period may be given over to directed study. Problems in arithmetic, campaigns in history, map study in geography, and language study are types of work in which purposeful directed study may well replace reciting.

Another plan is to concentrate the saved time and use it for a directed-study period in the morning and another in the afternoon. Another is to organize an optional after-school period for helping those most in need of special service. Another is the adoption of some form of the Batavia plan, under which two teachers work in a room, one doing the drill and recitation work and the other the pupil-study direction. This plan, though, is not possible in the school of ordinary size, except as some special or ungraded teacher may give assistance. Under the platoon type of school organization directed study is easier to arrange for than under the grade-system plan. The best plan, but the one least possible of realization in most places at present, would be to lengthen the school day, have the studying all done in school, and compensate for it by freeing the pupils from all home work. If a six-hour school day could be provided, all needed study below the seventh or eighth grade, aside from reading assignments, could be done in school, under close supervision and with a maximum of effectiveness. This is one of the strong features of the Gary plan. A study of the school programs given in Chapter IX will show how little time can be saved by any of these expedients under the five-hour school day.

Redirecting the instruction. In making the transition from a home-study type of organization to a school-study plan it will be found that most of the pupils do not know how to study to advantage a lesson assigned. The same wasteful, wandering, dilly-dallying methods developed in the home work show in the school, and if the home work is cut off the pupils fail to get the assignments and the whole grade at first falls behind. Probably not over ten per cent of our teachers, on the average, have ever taken any special time or pains to show young people how to study, unless required to do so. Our teachers have not been trained to such service, and they think that the simple direction to "study" a certain assignment is all that is necessary to bring about intelligent and efficient work on the part of the pupils. If the pupils waste time and do not get their lessons in school, they have to get them in some way at home, or fail of promotion; the business of the teacher has been to see that they get them, not to help them get them.

The work of the principal now will be to try to focus the interest of his teachers in this new direction, and to build them up in the art of assigning work and showing pupils how to study. This will be much easier of accomplishment if the teachers themselves can be brought to see the need of such improvement, rather than having it forced on them by the principal. If some book that contains helpful material, such as McMurry, or Wilson, or some good magazine article on the subject, such as the ones by Hall-Quest, Merriam, or Holzinger, could be studied before the plan is tried it would be a decided advantage. Directed school study, too, would best be introduced gradually, that teachers may master its technique. Sometimes it is better to introduce the technique without saying much about the subject or plan itself, and gradually accustom the teachers to it and to a reduction and redirection of home assignments before any serious consideration of the plan in its entirety is undertaken.

The teacher's part in the work. The teachers must, in one way or another, be led to see that if the children are to prepare their lessons well they must be made to seem of importance to them, and that, to this end, the teacher must organize her own work effectively and make her assignments clear-cut and definite. She must have command of the needed facts, see what type of treatment the lesson calls for, see whether the problem is apparent or not and whether or not it calls for supplementary material, think out how best to attack the work and the steps in its solution, and then show the pupils just how to work, what to look for, and what to do. As in all good recitation work, there must be a specific purpose to the work assigned. Pupils, too, need training in how to use an index, a dictionary, a map, an encyclopædia, and a text, and how to judge values and form conclusions. The importance of directness, concentration, speed, and accuracy need to be brought before the pupils. Occasional talks on how to analyze a topic, get the thought of a lesson, run down a problem, or study a lesson in reading or geography or history or spelling may well be given the classes by principal or teacher. There is much representing the accumulated experience of adults that can be set before children to enable them to work more intelligently and effectively. Often the ideas and plans of the pupils, after they come to know how to work, can be used, and it is well to encourage them to help and suggest.

The teacher, too, must learn how to work intelligently at training pupils to study. She must direct and show the way, but not do too much herself. She should strive to give them the technique of proper studying, remove misunderstandings, and stimulate coöperative effort, but not do their work for them except when she wants to show them *how* to do some particular type of work. The study period must not be transformed into another recitation period, nor should the teacher use it as a time to do work herself while the pupils work. At times she will need to work with or show the whole working group or grade what and how to do, actually using texts, references, and going through the working processes with them; at times she will deal with smaller sub-groups; at still other times she will pass rapidly from individual to individual, overseeing what is being done.

Where directed study is needed. The elementary school studies in which special attention as to how to study them should be given are arithmetic, geography, history, language work, reading, and spelling. The drill subjects — drawing, music, penmanship, and physical training — and the work in science and the domestic and manual arts will not, on the other hand, call for such training. The study of those subjects which involve the formation of specific habits should be handled in school, while home assignments should be supplemental, review in type, or interesting and easily done. Spelling, for example, involves the formation of certain important habits, such as looking carefully at the word, seeing its parts, selecting out the special part for attention, visualizing it, pronouncing its syllables, noting similarities and contrasts with other words, etc. This is important habit formation, and the classroom is its place and the teacher its director. Review work in spelling is different, and may be done at home. Similarly, reading drill is school work; reading for pleasure or information is quite different. Language work and sums in arithmetic should be done in school and not at home, except in such cases as were previously noted.

Where home work, on the contrary, means reading a story or a geographical reader for pleasure, the following out from vital interest of some problem in science or history or geography or industry that has arisen in the school, or some experiment carried home, quite a different situation exists. Then home work is indicative of instruction that has challenged the pupils and awakened their interest, instead of being the refuge of a weak teacher who is either not skillful enough or too lazy to do effective teaching during school hours, and tries to conceal her inefficiency by home assignments and parent assistance to bring the pupils along.

In the junior high school grades it is well that the pupils should begin to learn how to do some effective home study. The work here is a little more difficult, and additional subjects come in which necessitate longer time for preparation than the school hours can provide. It is now that the value of the earlier training in how to study reveals itself, and now that supplemental instruction as to how to work alone is needed. The conditions for study — quiet, good light, a table where books and papers may be placed and kept, and a definite time for concentrated effort — need to be explained, that the pupils may begin early to develop the ways and habits of students. If the homes of the neighborhood do not provide such facilities, as many naturally do not, then a talk on the duty of providing them might be a good subject for a Parent-Teacher meeting.

What directed study may add. Directed school study, like the motivation of school work, project work, or special drives, is only a means to an end, and is not a panacea for all the difficulties a school encounters in its efforts to train young people to do what the race, after all, has done for but a very short period of its history. It is only one of many means that may be used to make easier what is no easy task, but it is one of the best of supplemental means because it heads the educational process in the right direction, tends to decrease the criticism of the school by the home, and is a simple but effective method of improving the teaching process. For that reason it has been selected for rather detailed explanation here.

Directed school study, too, offers both teachers and principal a reliable means for measuring the efficiency of the instruction after, of course, first evaluating the character of the working group the teacher has to deal with. The effectiveness of the teacher's analysis of difficulties and assignment of study-problems will appear in the recitations, and in the relative degree of progress which the class makes without home help. That teacher who finds her pupils growing in ability to do independent study, and their need for special help decreasing constantly, is well on the way toward becoming a successful teacher. The training of pupils in proper life habits, and the developing in them of independent power for effective work, is perhaps the highest evidence of teaching skill and probably the best thing a teacher ever does for boys and girls.

In the development of this type of instruction the principal plays an important part. It is one of his greatest opportunities for constructive work with his teachers. Whether or not his school takes up directed school study as a major idea, he should try, in his classroom supervision, to give to his teachers the best of its technique, in so far as it relates to assignment of work and training pupils for intelligent and independent study.

QUESTIONS AND PROBLEMS

1. Suppose, in taking charge of a new school, you find a Minimum-Essentials course of study, with options to schools to supplement this for working groups as may seem best. What part would you have (a) the principal, and (b) the classroom teachers, take in the selection of the supplemental work? Why?
2. Suppose, on the contrary, you find a fixed course of study, fixed textbooks and page assignments, promotional examinations based on uniform questions for the city, and central supervision that is essentially inspection. What could or would you do, assuming that you remain in the system as a principal?
3. Suppose the rules and regulations of the school board require that "all teachers in teaching history, geography, and science must prepare an outline for each day's instruction, and do their teaching from the outline and not from the textbook." What good uses could you make of such a rule, and how would you mitigate its severity?
4. Assume that a new principal takes it for granted that his experienced teachers have good teaching technique and properly plan their work, and that his classroom supervision shows him the contrary to be the case with a few of the older teachers. How should he proceed to improve conditions?
5. Assume that, instead of a simple grade school, the principal is the supervising principal of a group of schools, such as is shown in Figure 3, page 12. Show how he could plan for grade meetings of the teachers of the different schools so as to provide small working groups for discussion of the course-of-study aims and objectives.
6. What is your judgment as to lesson-planning, after reading the arguments pro and con?
7. Make a topical outline for a talk to a Parent-Teacher meeting on the home work and home study surroundings of children, to show what points you would emphasize.
8. Would it be safe to say that the amount and nature of the home study assignments of a school would form a rough measure of the efficiency of the instruction and supervision of it?

9. Suppose, in adopting a school-study plan of work, it was found necessary to organize a special help hour for a time, after school, for those most needing assistance in learning how to do their work. How would you plan it (a) supposing all teachers were willing to remain a short time, and (b) supposing one or more ungraded teachers were paid to remain?
10. Dr. T. D. Wood, in his *Health in Education*, in the *Ninth Yearbook of the National Society for the Study of Education*, Part I, gives the following table (page 54) as to the sleep of school children:

Age	Hours of Sleep Needed	Time in Bed	Hours of Schoolroom and other Mental Work
5 to 6	13	6.00 P.M. to 7.00 A.M.	3
6 " 8	12	7.00 " " " " "	3½
8 " 10	11½	7.30 " " " " "	4
10 " 12	11	8.00 " " " " "	4½
12 " 14	10½	8.30 " " " " "	5 to 5½
14 " 16	10	9.00 " " " " "	6
16 " 18	9½	9.30 " " " " "	7
18 " 20	9	10.00 " " " " "	8

What does this table indicate as to home study time, by grades? Terman and Hocking, in their study of the sleep of school children, found that children sleep less than the above amounts. Compare their studies, reported in Terman's *Hygiene of the School Child*, chap. xx.

11. Some schools find, after directed school study has been put into operation, that the children have more free time than they can well use. Some schools keep the playground open until six o'clock, with a teacher in charge. Others have made a schedule of home work, after the plan outlined in Alderman, and have required one school credit in home-work activities each term. Outline such a plan for home-credit activities, and state how you would administer it. What do you think of the value of such work?

SELECTED REFERENCES

Alderman, L. R. *School Credit for Home Work.* 181 pp., Boston, 1914.
Describes home-credit work, and various successful plans for carrying it out.

Bobbitt, Franklin. *The Curriculum.* 295 pp., Boston, 1918.
One of the best and most readable books on the subject.

Dewey, John. *How We Think.* 224 pp., Boston, 1910.
A good scientific presentation of the problem of thought training as it relates to the work of the school.

Earhart, Lida B. *Types of Teaching.* 277 pp., Boston, 1914.
Teaching types, training pupils to study, and making lesson plans.

Hall-Quest, Alfred L. "Training Pupils in the Effective Use of the Text Book"; in *Elementary School Journal*, vol. 20, pp. 57-64.
A good article on assignments, training to study, and habit formation.

Hall-Quest, A. L. "Supervised Study as a Preparation for Citizenship"; in *Journal of Education*. (January 1, 1920.)

Holzinger, Karl. "Periodical Literature on Supervised Study during the Last Five Years"; in *Elementary School Journal*, vol. 20, pp. 146-54. (October, 1919.)
A very helpful reference, with a good bibliography of articles on supervised study as found in periodical literature.

Hunter, Fred M. "The Superintendent as a Leader in interpretating the Curriculum"; in *Administration and Supervision*, vol. 4, pp. 271-80. (May, 1918.)
Good article. Clear definition of a modern curriculum.

Merriam, E. D. "Technique of Supervised Study"; in *School Review*, vol. 26, pp. 35-39. (January, 1918.)
A good topical outline of suggestions and plans for work.

McMurry, Frank. *How to Study, and Teaching How to Study.* 324 pp., Boston, 1909.
A very good simple presentation of the problem.

Richardson, J. W. "Campaign Method in Elementary Education"; in *Journal of Educational Research*, vol. 2, pp. 481-92. (June, 1920.)
Value of the method stated. Describes class that did a year of work in arithmetic in six weeks.

Starch, Daniel. *Educational Psychology.* 473 pp., New York, 1919.
Contains two excellent chapters, pp. 191-255, which summarize the important evidence on transfer of school training in mental functions and school subjects. Excellent for the principal to read on this controversial subject.

Stitt, Edw. W. "Home Work for Elementary Pupils"; in *Educational Review*, vol. 51, pp. 360-86. (April, 1916.)
A valuable study based on an investigation in New York City. Contains much information of importance to principals.

Strayer, G. D. *A Brief Course in the Teaching Process.* 315 pp., New York, 1911.
A very readable and useful book. Very good chapters on lesson plans, and the teacher in relation to the children of the school.

Strayer, G. D., and Englehardt, N. L. *The Classroom Teacher.* 400 pp., New York, 1920.
Chapter VII gives a good simple statement of the need for teachers teaching pupils how to study.

Terman, L. M. "The Sleep of School Children," in his *Hygiene of the School Child*, chapter xx.
A study of the amount of sleep needed, obtained, and the relation of sleep to intelligence and school success.

Terman, L. M., and others. *Intelligence Tests and School Reorganization.* 111 pp., Yonkers, 1922.
> This volume contains the following chapters on courses of study and school classification:
> II. Dickson, V. E. Describes the Oakland Three-Track Plan for handling Different Classes of Children.
> III. Southerland, A. H. Adjustment Rooms and Curriculum Materials.

Whipple, G. M. *How to Study Effectively.* Bloomington, 1918.
> A good small volume on the psychology of effective studying.

Wilson, H. B. *Training Pupils to Study.* 70 pp., Baltimore, 1917.
> Reprint of a monograph issued to teachers at Topeka, Kansas. Gives factors in such work.

Wilson, H. B., and G. M. *Motivation of School Work.* 265 pp., Boston, 1916.
> Designed to furnish concrete help in solving the daily problems of a teacher in an elementary school.

CHAPTER XXI

THE SPECIAL TEACHERS AND THEIR WORK

Types of special teachers. A phase of the work of the principal in the supervision of instruction which may possibly cause him much trouble relates to the work of the special supervisors and teachers who come to his building, either as specialists to oversee and direct the work of his own teachers, or to do special work themselves.

Different cities will provide different plans for such special supervision and instruction. In one city the principal may find a visiting primary supervisor, who will oversee the work in the first three grades, or possibly the first four; a grammar-grades' supervisor, who will cover the second four; and sometimes an intermediate-grades' supervisor for grades four to six, with the primary and grammar-grades' supervision then restricted to the three grades below and above respectively.

In other cities these supervisors may be lacking, and in their place will be a number of special traveling supervisors, distributed by subjects, as music, drawing, penmanship, science, domestic arts, manual arts, physical education, or foreign languages. The traveling school nurse, dentist, and medical inspector in part come in under this classification. Sometimes two or more of these will be combined with the primary and grammar-grade supervisors mentioned above.

There will also be teachers of special subjects who belong to the building, or who divide their time between one or two adjacent buildings, such as the ungraded-room teacher, special coaching teachers, playground teachers, the visiting nurse or visiting teacher, and teachers of cooking, sewing, or manual training. These latter have special rooms in which to work, do special work at stated program periods, and are more directly under the principal while at the school than are the so-called special supervisors.

The primary- or grammar-grades' supervisor. This type of special supervisor is usually a very helpful person. Interested in the development and progress of the pupils in all their subjects, and provided primarily to promote the welfare of the parts of the school system they oversee by giving to the school work a close and professional type of supervision which principals seldom find time to give, and frequently are not capable of giving, the visits of this type of supervisor can usually be looked forward to as days of professional help for both teachers and principal. Even should these supervisors not be persons of large knowledge nor possess distinct qualities of leadership, the principal, by dealing with them much as he must the more special supervisors, may secure considerable help from them despite any personal limitations that may be in evidence.

This type of special supervisor comes with something of the authority of the superintendent of schools himself, in that he or she usually represents and speaks for the superintendent in the interpretation of the purpose and intent of the course of study as it is carried into effect in the schools. They represent a form of specialized assistant to the superintendent, doing little except the supervision of classroom instruction in certain grades of the school system. Usually persons of good training and personality and experience, and visiting different schools from day to day, they are in better position than the principal to compare and evaluate the work being done in his building.

By helpful suggestions, outlines for supplementary work, organization of new teaching material, and personal conferences with the teachers, this type of special supervisor is one who may be of much assistance to the principal in solving his peculiar instructional problems, and from whom he may learn much of value. Able to take classroom work as they find it, calling for no special program or rearrangement of work when they visit, and possessed of a better understanding of the meaning of administrative organization and relationships than the usual supervisor of the so-called special subjects, this type of supervisor is a real help when visiting a school. Instead of leaving to them the work of the grades, as some principals do, he should follow them about and discuss the work done with them, that he may become as skillful at classroom supervision as they may be. If he can exceed them in supervisory skill, as he might well do, knowing his teachers and pupils better, so much to the good

The following outline for work, by a primary supervisor in a city of 45,000 people, will illustrate the nature of the work done by this type of special supervisor:

1. Visits each teacher in grades I–IV, once in four weeks.
2. Gives model work on visits.
3. Helps teachers to do work in better ways.
4. Holds a grade meeting with teachers of each grade, once a month.
5. Prepares bulletins to aid teachers in work.
6. Gives demonstration work at city institute.
7. Keeps accurate notes on all visits.
8. Gives criticisms directly to teachers.
9. Keeps principals informed as to work and progress of all teachers.
10. Does some testing of work done.

The problem of the special supervisor. It is the traveling supervisors of special subjects who are likely to cause the most trouble for the principal, and at times they, instead of the principal, run the school and direct the work when they are in the building. Coming as they also do with something of the standing and authority of an assistant superintendent, not infrequently they tend to regard the principal as a subordinate and to assume that the direction of their special work is something of which he knows little and over which he has no control. Much will depend on the traditions as to such service which have grown up within the city, and the place given to the principal in the educational organization by the superintendent of schools and the rules and regulations of the board of education. In some cities the superintendent will have established the conception that the principal is the head of the school, and that all directions for its control must be approved by him; in other cities this will not be the case, the special supervisors will largely ignore him in directions to the teachers, and when in his building will do about as they see fit. At times the first knowledge a principal may have that a special supervisor is in his building will be when he finds his programs disarranged and the regular work of the school upset to suit the requirements of some supervisor. As these special supervisors frequently have no regular schedule of visitation, the work of a school for a day may be completely upset by the unannounced arrival of two or three of them.

In addition to their actual classroom visitations the special supervisors frequently call the teachers together, by grades or by subjects, and give them instruction as to the work they are to do. Sometimes these are merely a restatement of a printed outline, and are onerous in character. Sometimes the work outlined is so excessive that it tends to destroy the needed balance in the work of the classes. The principals are not invited to these meetings, they are not met as a body by the special supervisors, and they must inquire of their teachers to learn what type of directions have been issued. Not only are the teachers not advised to talk over the work to be done with their principals, but at times they are advised to the contrary. Sometimes, in arranging the school programs, the special supervisors are very insistent that the arrangement be made with their work primarily in mind. Where but one or two supervisors are concerned this might be possible, but with three or four it is not. In the making up of school programs in the Autumn, delay is sometimes occasioned because the supervisors whose work calls for regular visitations have not made up their schedules. Some of the special supervisors, too, are possessed of the so-called "artistic temperament," and are not easy to get along with even under the best of circumstances. In consequence, many principals wash their hands of the whole business and do not attempt to direct in any way the work of the special subjects so supervised.

The principal and the special supervisor. Such conditions are bad for a school, and are fundamentally wrong attitudes for special supervisors or teachers to be allowed to take. They indicate a lack of proper organization of the work of school supervision, against which the principals of the school system ought politely but very firmly to protest. They represent a false perspective and a misconception as to the proper place and function of the principal of a school. That many of the school principals know little about the special work and would only interfere with the special supervisors if given control over them is not only a poor defense of a fundamentally wrong system, but one that tends to produce the wrong type of principal as well.

As was stated in Chapter II, school administration should tend to magnify the office of the school principal, and this office should be one of fixed responsibility and authority. All that relates to the work of the teachers or children in his building is his province, and in the organization and administration of his building he should be regarded as the head. Even the superintendent of schools for the city ought to consult with him before giving orders for changes in the organization or work of his building. Of course this does not mean that the superintendent could not advise a teacher as to better plans for instruction, or the school janitor for better heating or cleaning. Such directions will tend to strengthen and not to weaken the principal's authority, but even in simple directions the superintendent may wisely work through the principal instead of directly. In the case of special supervisors and teachers, even though they do come with the authority of assistant superintendents, they should be made to feel that they must respect the position and authority of the principal in his building, and where possible consult with and work through him. They should also be expected to meet approximately the same standards, in their supervision of the instruction, that the principal sets for himself in such work.

Types of difficulties encountered. The more school organization passes from the grade type toward the departmental and platoon type, the more the special traveling supervisors can be dispensed with. Under the platoon type of organization the teachers are employed and placed as special teachers, and the supervision of special subjects is then reduced to that of keeping up the tone and holding up the standards of the system, rather than of teaching teachers how to teach. The grade-type of organization calls for the largest number of special supervisors and the most classroom visitation by them, and consequently presents the possibility of the largest number of difficulties for the principal of the school.

Some special supervisors bring the name special into disrepute with the teachers by their exactions and their inspectorial and critical manner. Some so over-emphasize their work that they encroach seriously on the pupils' time. Some hold long teachers' meetings to explain "outlines," with a waste of the teachers' time and strength and with little pedagogical return. Some know their subject fairly well but do not know children, and keep the teacher busy with discipline while they are present and for an hour after they are gone. Some fuss at what is being done, and feel that their work is being slighted because it is not made to count or to count more in the promotions. Some demand so many changes in programs and classes that regular work is seriously disrupted. Some seem to have no conception as to a general school policy and administrative purposes, are left to do about as they please by the superintendent, and are much in need of expert supervision and advice themselves. Some, if not most, insist on rather uniform requirements, seemingly unaware of the great differences in the capacities and needs of different pupils and classes.

Many special supervisors, to be sure, are persons of good sense and good judgment, are businesslike in the matter of their hours and work, are careful as to their relationships, have a proper appreciation of the place of their work in the school program, and not only give no trouble to the principal but aid materially in giving tone and spirit to the school. Still more, as a consequence of such qualities and consideration, they secure an emphasis of their work by the teachers which leaves little to be desired and nothing to complain of. Still, it must be admitted that this desirable type of supervisor is not the most common type, and that one of the troublesome problems every superintendent faces is that of how to handle the work of his special supervisors.

On the other hand, the regular teachers of the building may have formed the habit of looking on the special supervisors as outsiders, their work as not entitled to the same consideration as the "regular subjects," and as a sort of necessary evil imposed on the school by the superintendent. There may, too, be a disposition on the part of a number of the teachers to feel little responsibility for the work supervised by the special teachers, and to leave it to them to do as completely as may be possible. If the special supervisors take charge of the class and do the teaching when they visit, instead of training the teachers to do it, this tendency on the part of the teachers will naturally become more and more marked.

The place of the principal in special instruction. If the school principal, in such situations as have just been described, possesses no definite powers of control and is not considered responsible for the special work, and in turn disclaims any duties connected with the special-instruction problem, the effect on the work of the school will be most unsatisfactory and may be positively demoralizing. If the instruction in the special subjects of study is to proceed properly, and if the teachers are to grow in ability to do their work, the principal must be in ultimate control and must keep and be kept in touch with what is being done. The principals of the city and the special supervisors, too, should work somewhat closely together, and the methods of the latter should be open to criticism by the principals individually or as a body. This much, at least, the principals of a city may properly ask.

If the following rather fundamental administrative principles are accepted as a basis for relationships, many of the difficulties so frequently experienced will disappear.

1. In the organization and administration of a school building the principal is in control, and changes in organization should not be made by special supervisors without his consent, and would best be made by his specific orders.
2. When the special teacher or supervisor enters his building to work, he or she comes under the professional supervision of the principal, and the relationship now established lies somewhere between that of a teacher in the school and that of a visiting superintendent.
3. The prime purpose of the special supervisor is to train the regular teachers, where this is possible, to do the special work, and to this end the special supervisor stands in much the

position of an assistant principal whose function is that of improving instruction within the school.
4. The principal, conversely, should keep closely enough in touch with the plans and work of the special supervisors to enable him to promote efficiency in the work, and to help his teachers in planning their teaching of the special subjects.
5. Special teachers who enter the building to do special teaching service, while in the building must be regarded as teachers in the school, and as subject to the same regulations and supervision as are other teachers.
6. The supervisor should usually reach the building before the opening of school, should inform the principal of his presence, should see that any changes in program desired meet with his approval, and in most cases should have a conference with the principal before leaving. If a teacher needs help, the supervisor should confer with her also.

Coöperation with the supervisors. The above principles are quite fundamental, though not generally understood. While the principal may well expect that this much authority and responsibility should be placed with him, he will do better to keep his ultimate authority in the background and proceed by trying to find out how he may be of assistance, both to the teacher and to the supervisor, and what is to be or is being done. By helping the special supervisors to arrange a good working program for their visits, by discussing briefly with them the aims and purposes and methods of their work, by dropping into the classrooms and observing them at work, by knowing what his teachers do when the supervisor is not present, by showing approval or appreciation of any particularly good work by either supervisor or teacher, by helping the supervisors to locate and handle any special difficulties experienced by the teachers of the building, and by frequently turning what they do or using their special knowledge for something of special value to the building, a good basis for coöperation between teachers, supervisors, and the principal himself will be laid. All such service tends to make teachers and pupils alike feel the importance of the work, and will greatly lessen the friction so common between the school and the special supervisors. It also enables a principal to diagnose the difficulties of a specialist who is not yet a teacher, and to hold somewhat in check the over-enthusiastic specialist who would distort the purpose of the school.

The principal, by interested coöperation with the special supervisor, can usually secure desired modifications of the work to fit the needs of his special school. Schools in different types of communities in a city have different needs as to work in some of the special subjects — notably cooking, sewing, music, and drawing. The principal and teachers, who know the home needs and know the children, are in a position to suggest many desirable changes in a uniform outline that will make the work more worth while to their pupils. If the grade teacher and the supervisor work together, and the grade teacher is given some liberty in modifying outlines, much more of value can be accomplished. Teachers often have ideas of value, and these too frequently are not sought for or utilized by supervisors. If the supervisors feel that the principal is anxious to help them make their work a success, they will be more willing to do their part in adjusting their work as he desires.

Best use of the supervisor's time. Whether the special supervisors visit on a regular schedule or come unannounced will depend somewhat on the purposes of the visitation and the requirements of the school system. In any case an even distribution of time and a similar type of work in each classroom is not the best use of the supervisor's time. The supervisor should always keep in mind that the real purpose of the work is to train the teachers to do without his help. Different teachers and schools naturally then call for different types and amounts of the helpful service the supervisor is supposed to be able to give.

There are three main types of teachers which a special supervisor may find in any building:

The first is the thoroughly capable teacher of the subject, who does the work well and who puts life into it. Such teachers need no visitation for inspectional purposes, and the chief service a special supervisor can render here will be by a word of encouragement, by giving them some new idea, or by using them for demonstration purposes while training others to teach.

Another type is that of the teacher who has sufficient knowledge of the subject-matter, and who proceeds with the work by methods which are pedagogically sound, but whose work is deadening on the pupils and tends to destroy their interest in the subject. It will be the chief work of the special supervisor here to develop — if this is possible — an interest in and an enthusiasm for the subject.

The third type, mostly the newer and younger teachers, are those who lack a real grasp of the subject-matter and whose methods are weak. While possessing less skill, this group will in general show more enthusiasm for the work and profit more from the instruction. They will need special attention and help to enable them to develop skill and a correct method of work, and likewise to increase their grasp of the subject itself. Often the principal can be of real assistance with this class of teachers, and if so it will be wise for him to help the special teacher.

The special supervisor in the classrooms. The bulk of the actual teaching of the subject should be done by the regular classroom teachers, and not by the special supervisor. The latter will probably desire to give occasional model lessons, and should do so, but this will still leave most of the teaching to the regular teacher, if she can do it. The same principles apply here as would apply to a lesson in geography or arithmetic. If the regular teacher can do the work reasonably well she should do it, the special supervisor taking the class at times to illustrate a point or a principle, and surrendering it again to the classroom teacher. New teachers will need extra help, as do new teachers in any kind of classroom work. The supervisor should be careful, however, not to let it appear to the pupils that the teacher is being taught how to teach.

In working in the classrooms certain principles ought to apply in the relations that are established between the special supervisor and the classroom teacher. These may be summarized as follows:

1. The regular classroom time should be carefully adhered to. The special teacher should not attempt work of a kind that cannot be done in the time allotted to the special subject.
2. Demonstration lessons by the special supervisor should be of the same general character as the classroom teacher is expected to give, and should be open to the same questioning as to purpose and plan and results, by teacher or principal, as would be a lesson by the teacher.
3. It is usually bad policy to interrupt a recitation by questions or remarks, although the teacher or supervisor may approve or request such. Breaking in by the supervisor tends to cheapen what the teacher does in the eyes of the pupils, and consequently weakens her authority with the children.
4. A supervisor should observe the same proprieties as a principal in not criticizing the work of a teacher before the pupils, or challenging a point of view in their presence.
5. A demonstration lesson by a supervisor should have a definite purpose, and this should be made clear to the teacher in advance.

If the regular teacher should be unable to learn to teach the special subject, as might happen in music or drawing, the principal should arrange some exchange of work between teachers in the building that will care for the subject, and not expect the special supervisor either to do the impossible or to instruct the class. The prime purpose of the special supervisor, it should always be remembered, is to train the teachers to do work for which they are not as yet fully prepared. Every visit of the special supervisor should contribute something toward making the teacher more able to do without the supervisor entirely, and the special supervisors will have achieved their largest influence when they shall have made themselves no longer necessary.

Departmental-type organization. Some of the difficulties so far stated disappear for the upper grades when we pass from the grade-school type of organization to the departmental type of school. The departmental plan, however, is not generally employed lower than the sixth grade, but in the grades from the sixth up it provides a form of specialization that makes it easier to secure good instruction in the special subjects without the necessity of so much oversight by the special supervisors. Teachers can now be placed, and new ones employed, with some reference to their competency to teach the special subjects. Still more, all the instruction in any one special subject may now be given in one room, which may itself be somewhat specialized in equipment and "atmosphere." The pupils move to this room, instead of the teacher moving, which is also an advantage.

A glance at Table IV, page 173, giving the daily program for grades six, seven, and eight of a departmental-type school, will show the degree of specialization of instruction that may be attained for the upper grades under such a plan of organization. Four teachers, it will be seen, are used to teach these grades, and they are specialized by subjects as follows:

A — Reading and Literature ($\frac{1}{2}$), History, Penmanship.
B — Mathematics, Drawing, Science.
C — Reading and Literature ($\frac{1}{2}$), Music, Hygiene, and Civics.
D — Composition and Language, Spelling, and Word Study.

Teacher D is also relieved for one sixty-minute period a

week, by special teachers who take the boys for work in manual training and the girls for work in sewing and cooking. The difficulties encountered in teaching the special subjects in these upper grades, either with or without special supervision, are in consequence greatly decreased. For these grades at least — and in these grades the most difficult special work is to be done — the teacher is specialized and the best talent the school affords may be selected for the work.

Platoon-type organization. The platoon type of school organization provides for a still greater degree of specialization, in that two types of teachers — classroom, and special teachers — are now employed for all the work above the first, or at most, the second grade. An inspection of Table V, page 176, will show the distribution of teachers in the school shown in Figure 9, page 101, when organized as a platoon-type school. Table VI, page 178, shows the weekly program for this same school, and reveals still more clearly the specialization of the instruction now provided throughout the school. Eight classroom teachers teach the drill subjects, while eight other special teachers handle the special subjects, the distribution now being:

8 Class teachers teach:
Phonics
Spelling and word drill
Reading
Language
Composition
Penmanship
Arithmetic
History

8 Special teachers teach:
Music
Drawing
Science and Geography
Manual Training
Domestic Arts
Gymnastics and Play
Auditorium
Literature

How much more effective instruction can be made, and how much simpler the supervision of the instruction will be for the principal, a glance at these tables will reveal. If the special teachers selected for this work are well prepared they will need but little assistance in their work from the special supervisors. In small cities, given good principals, or an assistant to the superintendent interested in the special work, this special supervision might almost be dispensed with; in large cities the special supervisors' staff can be materially reduced in size and used for a different kind of supervisory service.

The supervisory work of the principal. Under either the departmental or the platoon type of organization the supervisory work of the principal will now be changed somewhat in direction and purpose. Instead of having to keep in touch with what the special supervisors desire and do, and performing balance-wheel and corrective work, it will now be the duty of the principal to supervise the special work on approximately the same basis as the so-called regular subjects. All subjects now become regular subjects, and all now come definitely within the scope of his work as the supervisor of the instruction within his school. It will now be his duty to see that the teachers of the special subjects keep a proper balance in what they do, and that they do not let their enthusiasm for their special subjects run away with them. He will need to keep even more closely in touch with what is attempted and done, with the nature of the work-assignments, and with the standards set up for accomplishment than was expected under the grade-school form of educational organization.

The principal's work with all the so-called special teachers under a platoon type of organization, as was said above, will not be essentially different from what is called for in looking after the special teachers who are in or who come to a grade-type building. These may include ungraded-room teachers, coach teachers, teachers for classes of defectives of various types, disciplinary-class teachers, teachers of classes for the oral instruction of the deaf, playground teachers, and teachers of manual training, cooking, sewing, and printing. All such special teachers, when in his building at work, are regular teachers in the building, and his supervisory oversight and control over their work does not differ essentially from that over the regular classroom teachers. Neither is his responsibility for helping them in their teaching problems any less. He may not presume to know their special work, but the fundamental principles of the art of teaching, the teaching technique they employ, and in particular the results of their work with the children, are matters upon which he may properly offer suggestions and, in case of need, exercise certain control.

QUESTIONS AND PROBLEMS

1. Does a principal need to arrange any special program for a visiting primary supervisor? Why?
2. Assume that a special drawing supervisor arrives unexpectedly some morning at the building, has only the morning to spend, and wants to see the work in the third, fourth, fifth, and sixth grades. The time allotment for drawing is twenty-five minutes, and there are six teachers in these grades (two thirds, and two fourths) in the building. Leaving the fifth-grade program (Table III, page 171) as it is, arrange a schedule for the supervisor that will give him a chance to see regular work in all rooms, and a short conference with the principal as to the work before he leaves the building at noon.
3. Suppose, at the recess time of some grade, you find a room late in coming out, and on investigation you find a special supervisor has arrived, rearranged the programs, and held the class. What would you do?
4. Show that the demand for full school control by the principal does not arise from any desire to exercise authority or to show his importance, but represents sound administrative conceptions as to the office he holds.
5. Formulate the arguments for and against a regular schedule of visitation by the supervisors of special subjects.
6. In some cities special supervisors try to demand that principals arrange classroom programs so that the work in a special subject may come in sequence in the grades, in order to facilitate visitation and work. Show, by programs, that this may be possible for a few special teacher subjects (manual training, domestic arts, music), but would be quite difficult for many subjects. Is it necessary for subjects supervised, but not taught?

might be made of Teacher D (page 426) the sixty-minute
a week she is relieved of her class while the boys go to manual
...ning and the girls to cooking or sewing?

Does the companion-class form of school organization (Chapter VIII, Figure 14) decrease the need for special subject supervisors?

SELECTED REFERENCES

Bobbitt, Fr. "Supervisory Leadership on the Part of the High School Principal"; in *School Review*, vol. 27, pp. 733–47. (December, 1919.)
   The same principles laid down as applying to the supervision of high school departments would apply, in the elementary school, to the supervision of the work of the special teachers and supervisors.

Building Principal and Special Supervisors; How related at Atchison, Kansas. See *Elementary School Journal*, vol. 21, pp. 82–84. (October, 1920.)
   Gives rules of Board relating to. Gives principal but little authority.

Gilbert, C. B. *The School and its Life*. 259 pp., Boston, 1906.
   Chapter XX good on the special supervisor.

Greene, L. S. *Supervision of the Special Subjects*. 162 pp., Milwaukee, 1922.
   The powers and duties of, with special emphasis on the duties of a supervisor in the organization and supervision of instruction.

Harris, Ada V. S. "Influence of the Supervisor"; in *Proceedings of National Education Association*, 1906, pp. 117–21.
   A very sensible article on the work of the supervisor, the art of being helpful, and on teachers' meetings.

Hill, Sallie. "Defects of Supervision and Constructive Suggestions Thereon"; in *Proceedings of National Education Association*, 1919, pp. 506–09.
   On the supervisor of the special subjects.

Hunter, Fr. "How can Supervisors and Assistant Superintendents render the Most Efficient Service in their Relations to Principals and Teachers"; in *Proceedings of National Education Association*, 1913, pp. 300–03.
   Very good on the place of the superintendent in such service.

Kendall, C. N. "The Management of Special Departments"; in *Proceedings National Education Association*, 1904, pp. 271–76.
   A good article on special supervisors and their place in supervisory work.

CHAPTER XXII

PLANNING THE SUPERVISION

Supervision a supreme duty. In Chapter III the importance of the supervisory function was pointed out, and it was stated there that, of all the different aspects of a principal's work, this is the most essential and the one which he must in some way find time to do. This idea is not likely, under present conditions in the principalship in our American cities, to be emphasized too strongly. All else that the principal may do, important as this all else may be, is after all but getting ready for the most important service of all. All the work in the organization and the administration of a school is but the shaping of conditions so that teachers and pupils may meet together under the best possible conditions for instruction — the prime purpose of the school. To continually guide and improve this instruction, so that the children in the school may develop best and most rapidly under it, should be the deepest interest of the principal. If the responsibility for instructional progress is not placed definitely on him by the superintendent of schools or the rules of the school board, he should assume it any way, and should insist that he be given time to devote to this most important of functions.

One who has read even a few of the many school surveys published within recent years cannot but be impressed with the emphasis placed by the surveyors on this function of the school principal, and also how frequently they find that the function is either not assumed or is abused. The more recent scientific studies of grade progress, made by standardized educational tests, have all tended to fix the responsibility for the success of the school work still more definitely with the principal of the school. One of the most striking proofs of the principal's responsibility for results through supervision is found in the large differences revealed, by many of the surveys, in the achievements of the pupils in the different schools of the same city. These differences occur even when no marked differences are to be found in the course of study, textbooks, teachers, or pupils, and, in some cases where pupil — and population — differences are marked in various parts of the city, some of the better schools are found where they might least be expected. Dr. J. M. Rice, in his pioneer investigation of school results, discovered that "the striking differences are found not so much between individual classrooms as between buildings," and the more scientific school surveyors since his day have often confirmed his statement.

The supervision of instruction, then, must be regarded as the one supreme duty of a school principal, the one for which he must find time by minimizing other duties, and the one for which he must hold himself responsible whether the superintendent of schools or the board of education does or does not. That a great number of elementary-school principals throughout the country to-day are exerting little or no influence on the instruction carried on in their schools, and are contributing little or nothing toward the primary purpose for which their schools are maintained, cannot be accepted as excusing such neglect. The prime test of the competency of an elementary-school principal is his ability to improve the instruction in his school by helpful and constructive service to his teachers in their work of instructing children; the measure of his interest in such service is the means he employs to find time to do such work.

Supervisory mistakes. Some principals do not seem to know what to do; others have the idea that they are to act as detectives. The result is much misdirected effort and many mistakes. A common defect in the work of many principals who attempt to give some supervision is that they seem unable to offer constructive service to teachers after their visits. Some only criticize; many only observe and go away, leaving their teachers entirely in doubt as to what they may have thought of the work they saw. The principal forms his opinion of the teacher and keeps it to himself; the teacher in turn does the same of him. In consequence it not infrequently happens, in our cities, that a teacher is recommended for dismissal by a principal who has never made any definite attempt to help her, and who perhaps has never given her to understand that her work was other than satisfactory. Many a teacher's professional career would be quite different if she were taken in hand from the start by a strong principal, and helped to a firm foundation based on sound pedagogical procedure.

The supervisory function is sometimes abused, in that it is exercised in a harsh, severe, and dictatorial manner. "You do it this way"; "You should have done it this way"; "Don't do it that way"; "You don't do it right"; "You fail to get results," are types of supervisory criticisms not infrequently given. Notes are sometimes left on teachers' desks, in criticism of lessons observed, which lead to weeping on the part of the teachers. Some principals seem to visit only at times when conditions are unusual, as though their aim was to detect the poorest work done. Principals have been reported as having entered classrooms with a stenographer, taken down the words of teacher and pupils, left the room without comment, and never to have mentioned the work seen to the teacher afterward. Principals have also been reported as seldom visiting a classroom exercise except toward spring, about the time they would be called upon by the board of education to recommend teachers for dismissal. At that time they visit certain teachers for a whole day at a time, take notes, and offer no comments or suggestions.

All such types of so-called supervision are fundamentally wrong. They do not help teachers to instruct children better, they destroy the fine feeling that ought to exist, they make coöperation largely impossible, and they tend to drive teachers into labor unions and to agitation for life-tenure laws. Under such conditions it is the principal who ought to be changed, instead of the teachers. If the superintendent of schools were to deal with him by these same methods, he might appreciate better how the teachers feel who have to take this bitter medicine.

As a partial corrective of such errors, one superintendent recently issued the following cautions, in printed form, to the principals of his city:

MAY I REMIND YOU:
1. That the teachers are the real operators of the school plant.
2. That your chief function is to clear the way for them.
3. That their comfort, their self-respect, their potentiality, are to be safeguarded at every turn. The wise principal not only guards but nourishes these three.

LET ME COUNSEL YOU:
1. To show respect unfailingly for the judgment and abilities of the teachers.
2. To judge them not too soon nor too late.
3. To hear their side through patiently.
4. To use the question five times to the declaration once.
5. To encourage every one in your corps to find her way of doing her job better.
6. To seek out unfulfilled capacity in both your teachers and yourself.

Beginning supervision in a new school. Assuming a new principal taking charge of a school, one who is interested and competent, and who is skillful in arranging his time schedule so as to find the needed time for classroom visitation and the supervision of instruction, one important measure of his tact and skill will now be how he will begin, what he will do, and how intelligently he will plan what he does. Just how he will begin and what he will do at first should be determined much by what he finds needs to be done.

The most favorable situation will be where the new principal inherits a school in which a strong and masterful principal has been in control, and where the teaching body is alert, capable, and progressive. In such a case he may almost from the first plan a progressive and advanced type of school supervision, and may proceed along lines that we will indicate a little further on. It is more likely that the new principal will not inherit such good conditions, and will need to lead up to such a type of school supervision, for a time, at least, rather feeling his way. The most unfavorable situation will perhaps be where a principal succeeds to a school over which a well-meaning and very kindly administrative type of principal has presided for a quarter-century or more, and in which the teaching force has remained rather stationary and has come to accept his office-type of administration, and the freedom from supervision that it entailed, as the proper type of work for the principal of the school. Such a school may be quite well managed and orderly, and the teachers probably will be earnest, well-disposed, and well-satisfied with what they are doing, but inclined to resent at once any change in the *status quo*. Many of the teachers may have taught the same grade in the same room for so long that they have come to feel an ownership in both. The best advice to give a principal under such conditions is to "Go Slowly."

Good introductory plans. A good plan would be first to get the school going, study the organization, plan your work to have needed time for supervision, and then start in to visit and see and learn. Begin in the first grade and work upward, keep your opinions to yourself, say that you want to see the school and its work, note conditions, and try to find things to commend as you go along. Such general commendations as "a well-behaved class," "a well-kept room," "a bright-looking lot of pupils," "you questioned the class well," and "that was good drill work," are types of remarks that may be made when deserved. After two rounds of the school, conditions will become clearer and needs more evident, and then you can plan what to do and how to start. A magazine club may be suggested and started, some teacher may be asked to present an idea to a teachers' meeting that can be thrown open for discussion, or some teacher whom you have seen present a lesson with energy and some skill may be commended and asked to teach some new but similar lesson before all or part of the teachers, following with a discussion of it. This gives an opportunity for skillful questioning on the conduct of the lesson and the art of teaching, for which the principal should be prepared. "Did the lesson show motive?" "Was it well organized?" "Was it well based on the needs and knowledge of the children?" "Did it challenge their interest?" "Were they self-reliant?" "Were the questions thought-provoking?" "Did the lesson move?" "Was the teaching technique good?" "Are the educational principles (which have been brought out) applicable to instruction in other subjects, or other grades?" Such a discussion, if shaped to challenge thinking, will do so, and will probably show results in the classroom instruction.

Another introductory plan is to select problems applicable to three or four grades or teachers, propose that they and you stay some afternoon after school for a little while to consider them, prepare yourself so as to be able both to give help that will be recognized as such and will challenge the teachers and make them think too, and then to do follow-up work on the problems in the classrooms. Difficulties common to the school may be brought up at the general meetings. The work of the principal will be not so much to offer his ideas or to criticize as to challenge thinking, by continually asking questions and searching for pedagogical reasons for procedure. His larger knowledge and grasp of educational principles will be of much use to him in such a situation. After some such careful beginning, the next step would best be to ask permission to take a class and teach it before the teacher, doing good demonstration work and letting the teacher question his technique.

Accompany this procedure by loyal support of the teachers' authority in discipline, protect the teachers from petty annoyances, give the impression by actions rather than by words that you want to work with them rather than over them, and say words of encouragement whenever you can. Always give credit for any good work to the teacher rather than taking it for your school, be considerate, appreciate fully their difficulties, be just and impartial in dealing with all school problems, and in time a new principal will be received even into the worst of situations, and he may then proceed to assume control and begin active supervision of the instruction of his school.

Planning what is to be done. After a principal feels that he is able to proceed with the important work of helping his teachers to become better teachers, and of improving the instruction his children receive, it is essential that he lay out some plan or plans for what he proposes to do. Just as a principal's working schedule needs to be well organized, to enable him to find time for supervision, so his classroom visitation needs to be carefully planned if he expects it to be most fruitful in results for his teachers and in giving him firm control of his school. He must now lay out in his own mind what it is he wants to see and do, know why he wants to see it and what he will do with the results, and then plan his visitation carefully with his teachers' programs before him. The more definitely he plans what he is after the more certain will he be to get results that are valuable, the surer he will be to become interested in the work of supervision, and the easier he will find it to minimize the time given to routine work and to visitors and to find the needed time for systematic and helpful classroom service.

The poorest and most unprofitable type of classroom supervision he can give is the random visitation of classrooms, where he "just drops in, to see what is going on," and stays for from ten minutes to an hour, according to whether or not he finds the work interesting. While such supervision is of course better than none at all, it is far less effective, and does both teacher and principal far less good, than would carefully planned visitation. Some such brief and random visitation a principal will always want to do, especially at the beginning of a new school year, or where a substitute or a new and inexperienced teacher is at work, but it should not represent his regular procedure. During the first week of school it may be the best kind of visitation, as the principal can thus quickly get a line on the school and the work of its teachers and children. There will also be other times, throughout the year, when the principal will want to drop into the classrooms, for a few minutes at a time, to see how things are going and to get a measure of the health and sanitary conditions, the atmosphere of work, and similar items. A few minutes, though, usually will be sufficient for such inspectional visits, and not many of them will be needed after a school is once well under way. School inspection would be a much better term to apply to such work than school supervision, for it is not school supervision in any real or helpful sense of the term.

Types of supervisory plans. A principal who desires to make his classroom supervision effective and helpful will

PLANNING THE SUPERVISION

need to formulate some more definite plan for his work than mere random visitation.

One type of planning, sometimes followed, is the day-to-day planning, based on an inspection of such lesson plans as the one given on page 393. The principal can then plan to go at definite times to see definite things done, has an opportunity to evaluate the lesson from the points of view of aim, method, and results, and then may afterward offer the teacher suggestions as to more effective procedure or an improvement in teaching technique. With new teachers who are in need of special help, such visitation may be very useful, though a more detailed lesson plan for some of the subjects than the one shown on page 393 should then be expected. The day-by-day selective planning may also be useful as an alternate on days that are badly broken up, when careful systematic visitation is out of the question. Such a day-to-day planning of visitation is superior to the random classroom visitation so commonly followed, but it lacks good organization and continuity of effort, and still better plans are possible and in most cases ought to be used.

Good planning ought to be done for a longer period than a single day. Week-to-week planning is much better, and two or three or four weeks may profitably be laid out, though the type of work done may vary from week to week. Under such long-time planning the principal concentrates on one or possibly two subjects of instruction, and the accompanying teaching technique, and then follows the subject or subjects day by day through the grades; or he may study one or two grades as a whole; or he may take different types of working groups, as a C or an A group, and inspect the work in some one grade or in a succession of grades. Still again, attention may be centered for a week at a time on some general teaching problem, such as the motivation of the work, training the pupils to study, socializing the recitation, or effective questioning. Whatever the particular plan or aim it should not be random or indefinite, no one subject or type of work should be pursued long enough or often enough to become a fetich, and in the carrying out of any type of planned work the principal should systematically concentrate upon the most definite objectives he is able to select.

Definite long-time supervisory planning. If the aim of the principal is helpful supervision, and not inspection and detection, there can be no objection to his informing his teachers of the aims he has formulated for his supervisory visitation for a week or more in advance. This might be done at his regular teachers' meetings, or, better, a schedule might be posted on the principal's bulletin board for the inspection of the teachers. Still better would be a mimeographed outline, a copy to be placed on each teacher's desk. It is as fair for the principal to be expected to plan his work before the teachers in advance of visitation as it is for the teachers to be expected to plan their work and to reduce their plans to writing for his inspection. It is also a good thing for the principal to do, for its influence on the school. The more the teachers are taken into the confidence of the principal in his supervisory work, the more teaching is made to partake of the nature of coöperative work between teachers and principal for the good of the pupils, and the less it seems to be inspection and checking up, the more will teachers be encouraged to do their best and the better will be the spirit prevailing throughout the schools. The principal who can make his visits welcome, who encounters good will as he goes from room to room, and who because of this sees the best his teachers can do and draws from them their best work and ideas, has an asset of great value that he ought to strive to keep.

As an example of such long-period planning the Supervision Outline given on the opposite page is submitted. Such

PLANNING THE SUPERVISION

OCTOBER CLASSROOM SUPERVISION PROGRAM

Week of Oct. 2–6	**Supervisory purpose:** To ascertain the effectiveness and the extent of the correlation of the Language Work instruction, grade by grade, from 1st to 8th, A and B sections, oral work. **Main objectives:** Is growth regular and constant? Are there lapses? If so, where and why? Where most difficulties? Of what nature? Are we trying to do the best things, and in the best way? Special difficulties of our school? **Supplemental objectives:** Art of questioning. Thought-provoking instruction. Lesson assignments.
9–13	**Supervisory purpose:** Same as preceding week, but concentrated on the written work. Some written test work. **Main objectives:** Same as preceding week. **Supplemental objectives:** Character of the written work, with reference to suitableness, thought-provoking quality, and correlations. **Note:** Supervisory results of this and preceding week to form basis for discussion at building teachers' meeting of October 17th.
16–20	**Supervisory purpose:** Instruction in oral reading and phonics, grades 1–3, all sections, and transfer-value of instruction to silent-reading work of grades 3 and 4. **Main objectives:** Pupil growth in mastery of word forms? Growth in power to pronounce quickly and read accurately? Value or otherwise when transfer comes to silent thought-getting reading? Is the transfer easy and natural, or is there a loss that may be prevented? **Supplemental objectives:** Do we use a means to an end, as measured by subsequent power and growth, or do we overemphasize (or underemphasize) the means? Where is the desirable balance? Do we make the transition easily from the word and short sentence to the paragraph as a thought unit?
23–27	**Supervisory purpose:** Pronunciation, spelling, and word-analysis power of pupils grade by grade. Some written and oral tests. **Main objectives:** Is there a steady gain in power? Do the upper grades continue to increase power? Overemphasis? Lapses? Improvements? Time allowance and effectiveness? **Supplemental objectives:** Teaching technique. Pronunciation drills. Lesson assignments on words. Training in dictionary use. **Note:** Supervisory results of this and preceding week to form basis for discussion at building teachers' meeting of October 31st.

Interesting Readings: (Books in Principal's Office; Magazines on table.)
Freeman: *How Children Learn*, chapters IV (reading) and VI (spelling).
Jenkins: *Reading in the Primary Grades*.
Kendall and Mirick: *How to teach the Fundamental Subjects*, chapter II.
Strayer: *Brief Course in Teaching Process*, chapter XI.
Suzzallo: *Teaching of Spelling*.
Salt Lake City School Survey, chapter VIII.
State Series Readers, *Teachers' Manual*, Introduction.
Good recent magazine articles: — *Elem. Sch. Jr.*, May, p. 341; *Primary Educ.*, September, p. 61; *State School Jr.*, February, p. 241; March, p. 312.

FORM 4. A CLASSROOM SUPERVISION OUTLINE

an outline of proposed work, mimeographed and placed on each teacher's desk at the beginning of the month, would tend toward definiteness of work, economy of time, and effective supervision, because perfectly definite objective aims have been set up. Rightly used, such carefully planned supervision will lead to more invitations from teachers to inspect work and to visit classrooms than a principal can attend to.

Even such a well-formulated working plan as that given ought to be capable of some adjustment, and teachers ought to feel free to make requests of the principal to that effect. Some teacher may feel that her pupils would show their progress better to-day than two days from now; another might prefer a visit to-morrow instead of to-day; another may frankly say that what she is doing is not working out well, and ask the principal not to judge her work by the progress of a particular working group. Small happenings, too, disturb classes as well as teachers, and ought to be taken into consideration. Teachers, like other human beings, usually develop faith in themselves in about the same degree that the principal shows faith in them.

Professional leadership. Some pertinent reading has been suggested at the bottom of the outline, which teachers may or may not do, but with which the principal should be thoroughly familiar. It is perhaps best that any reading by the teachers should be voluntary, coming from a feeling of need for it. It will also be noted that each two weeks of work has here been made the basis for a teachers' meeting, in which the principal will present the results as he saw them and bring out discussion. Used in this way such a discussion is likely to be lively, and the principal will need to be well informed. Clearly beyond all but the most superior of his teachers the principal should know the best thought on the work he is attempting to supervise. He must lead in his school, as he expects his teachers to lead in their classrooms.

The planned outline gives him many advantages in this. Concentrated as it is on one subject for a week or more at a time, he can study up both the course of study material and the wisest thought on what should be the aims in the work. Teaching technique, in its different types, he will also need to know, but this is general rather than particular, and much the same principles apply to all instruction. With such a visitation outline he can also prepare himself much more easily to take a class and demonstrate his ideas, as he can now prepare on certain limited topics or lessons, and then demonstrate only with these. By making thoughtful preparation in advance his "impromptu" demonstrations will be much more effective.

A young principal would, for a few years, find that such work calls for a large amount of thinking and reading and preparation. This, however, will be good for him, and is just what he ought to be doing. Few investments he can make are likely to yield such large dividends in the future. He should keep notes on his reading, preserve his outlines, build up a working library, and mark his books. In time the work will become easier as he accumulates knowledge and experience, and the results will well repay the effort made. He may put it down as an axiom that it is only on a basis of some such broad and substantial knowledge of the teaching process, and of the aims and means and ends in education, that a principal may hope firmly to establish his professional leadership in a school. In organization and administration he may impose his leadership, and if things go reasonably well it will be accepted; in educational matters he must establish his leadership on the basis of understanding, consideration, human feelings, and in particular on broader knowledge and an ability to point the way to larger things, or his leadership will not be accepted by the teachers. There may be a form of lip service, but it will never be genuine and real.

Paving the way for helpfulness. The formulation of a good working plan for supervisory visitation, however, represents but the beginning. Even adequate professional knowledge in addition may not suffice to establish good relations and secure the best results. Nowhere in all the principal's work does his personality and method of attack play so important a part as in the work of classroom visitation and supervision. The principal is here dealing with the human factor at close range, and it is important that he establish the proper relationships before he goes very far, for he cannot help a teacher who does not repose confidence in him. He must, therefore, be careful to start right. He must remember that women are far more easily offended by even the most helpful of criticism than are men, and that a few women are especially resentful of any criticism from a man. Patience, kindliness, consideration, and helpfulness are necessary to win the confidence of teachers, and unless teachers come to feel that the principal is a friend working with them, and interested in their success, rather than a critical representative of the central office or the board of education, helpful relations are not likely to be established between them.

The principal's prime purpose in visitation is not to discover for himself or for any one else if he has weak teachers; in all probability he has, and it is one of his important functions to try to improve them. His purpose is rather to find where and how he can be of service. Helpful leadership, rather than inspection or dictation or criticism, is what the teachers need. Mere criticism, except as a basis for constructive suggestions, is deadening, while criticism based on sound pedagogical principles is a direct challenge to the teacher's knowledge and thinking. Encouragement, suggestion, practical demonstrations, drawing out the teacher's best, and with criticism only as a basis for constructive help, should represent the principal's chief line of approach. It is a good plan to make teachers feel that you believe them in earnest, that you consider what they are doing as of large importance, that you expect them to go ahead and keep busy, and that, as principal, you are there largely to be of assistance to them. Principals who inspire confidence will find that teachers will often come to them and tell them of their mistakes and ask for suggestions, instead of trying to conceal such for fear of making a bad impression. Such an attitude of frankness is very desirable, and the principal ought to encourage such confidence by confidence and helpfulness in return.

The technique of visitation. If the principal is visiting casually and without following a systematic plan, such as is given in the Classroom Visitation Program on page 441, and as he may frequently desire to do at times even though an outline is in use for the more thorough supervision of the instruction, the following suggestions as to procedure should ordinarily be observed:

1. Enter the classroom quietly, and disturb what is in progress as little as is possible.
2. Do not rush across the room, shake hands with the teacher, and make a general commotion. A quietly nodded "Good morning" is less disturbing and just as useful.
3. Preferably sit in the back of the room, or at one side, rather than on a chair in front. You want to be a quiet and largely an unnoticed observer, and not the center of what is going on. Sit at the teacher's desk or in front only if you expect to take charge of the class and conduct the lesson.
4. Make your presence in the room as little noticed as possible, and gradually train both teachers and pupils to go on with their work and pay little attention to your presence.
5. Appear to be an interested observer or listener, entering into

the spirit of the class work. Do not sit with "a mask on" — bored, expressionless, sour — or leave the room with an evident expression of disapproval.

6. After the novelty of your presence wears off, give attention to the teaching process. Try to analyze it.
7. Do not make notes on the lesson in a notebook or on a card while in the room, but do this outside after leaving.
8. If the teacher seems to be in difficulty and needs help, quietly move forward and suggest, in an undertone, the right procedure. Sometimes a question or two which changes the character and direction of the lesson may be all that is needed. If the teacher does not bring the lesson around right, it may be a good time for you to take the class and yourself demonstrate a better procedure.
9. Always ask the teacher's permission to break into a recitation, even with a question, or, if you desire to take the class, always let the pupils feel that you have full confidence in the teacher, and that you continually defer to her as in control.
10. After a teaching demonstration for a new teacher it is usually best to leave the room, to avoid any embarrassment to her in resuming charge of the class.

Whether visiting casually or by plan, it is best to try to see lessons as a whole. In doing so, the following additional suggestions will be found useful:

11. Examine the teacher's plan card or book, if you require or expect such, to see just what she is about to do. If no plan card is required, expect her to tell you, in a sentence or two, just what she plans to accomplish to-day.
12. Stay throughout the entire lesson, and note the beginning, the steps in the instruction as it proceeds, the assignment of new work, and how the teacher sets the pupils to work and starts the next class.
13. Give careful attention to the teacher's procedure, analyze it for good and bad technique, but as above make no notes while in the room.
14. Immediately after leaving the room make either a brief analytical summary, from which more detailed notes may be made later, or hastily fill out the desired record at once.

PLANNING THE SUPERVISION

Visitation records. It has just been stated, as a principle of supervisory technique, that the principal should not take other than mental notes while observing a lesson, but should give his undivided attention to the work of the teacher and pupils, making his notes after leaving the classroom. Some supervisory authorities, mostly those who have worked in teacher-training practice schools, would disagree here, and would contend that the principal should make full and exact notes on each recitation-whole he visits for supervision, embodying faulty questions and procedure, wrong aims, poor technique, etc. Some would even use a rather elaborate blank form for checking, with a carbon copy for the teacher. It is claimed that the teacher will soon become used to this procedure and not mind it. Perhaps the best answer to this point of view is that a supervisor should attempt to correct but a few things at a time; that an evident critical attitude always is disconcerting; that elaborate checking devices distract attention from the few large and central ideas; that a competent principal, after observing carefully a lesson-whole, ought to be able to analyze it sufficiently to make a brief card record; and that a collection of such records will be sufficient for all practical purposes.

Some principals keep rather full notes in a personal notebook; a few return to their office at once and dictate a record, with a copy for the teacher; some principals check their observations on a printed form, with a carbon duplicate for the teacher; and others use a card form of record as being easier to make, sort, find, and file, and which the teachers may see. A sample of a simple form of such a record is given on page 448.

While an elaborate form of record keeping is more likely to be time-consuming than useful, some brief record on each supervisory visit it is desirable to make and to keep. Such a record form may also well be filed for the work of the

[116—12-21—3M.]

SUPERVISORY VISITATION RECORD

Teacher.... Mary Craighead ..... **Date**.... 2/6/22.. **Tr. Card No. 16**..
Instruction seen....Reading....**Grade** 4A....**Gen'l Est. of**....D....

[Estimate Rating Scale:— A = Excellent; B = Good; C = Fair; D = Poor; F = Failure.]

Type of Lesson: Simple reading drill, from Supplemental Reader.
New reading; not review work.
Procedure: Called on pupils to rise and read, a paragraph at a time.
No discussion of material read.
No introduction to lesson; pupils told to open Reader to page 64, and reading began.
Good Points: Did not call on pupils in order.
Some selection of good and poor readers.
Teacher interested.
Weak Points: No audience situation created; all pupils had and looked on books; pupils inattentive.
Little attention to enunciation.
No questioning to determine thought-getting or to bring out meaning.
Supplemental Notes: Room too hot and somewhat close; pupils dull in consequence.
Discipline O.K. Posture of pupils poor.

Conference held with teacher: Yes; brief, in hallway, at recess following.
Suggestions made: Create audience situation by using one or two books.
Introduce lesson by a word as to what about. Have pupil called to read step to front and face class. Let pupils stop him if not heard or understood. Keep attention by questions as to meaning.
This card shown to teacher: No, but substance stated in conversation.

FORM 5. A CLASSROOM SUPERVISORY-VISIT RECORD

special teachers and supervisors observed by the principal. The invariable making of a record leads to system, careful observation, definiteness in analysis and thinking, is useful in discussing the recitation later on with the teacher, contains good material from which to compile supervisory notes for teachers' conferences, and is a useful record to file away. A series of such cards, numbered in order, will give an objective record of the defects and rate of progress and successes of any teacher. If it is thought desirable to have a conference with a teacher about the lesson observed, the date and general results of the conference should be recorded on the card.

Offering constructive criticisms. Different principals have different methods of offering their criticisms to their teachers. Some reserve their criticisms and suggestions for the general teachers' meeting, and then offer them as general suggestions. This plan is quite likely to prove ineffective. Criticisms and suggestions to be helpful need to be personal and given at the time when of most use, while general criticisms given to a group, later on, are likely to be accepted as fault-finding and forgotten, or be taken to heart by those least in need of them. The most helpful suggestions will always be those given before the first flush of success or failure has departed. Sometimes, with most teachers always, a word of suggestion at the close of a teaching exercise will be all that is necessary. Often the suggestions will be of such a nature that it will be perfectly proper to give them at that time, if it can be done quietly and so as not to attract the unfavorable attention of the pupils or embarrass the teacher in their presence. Sometimes the class may well hear that the principal thinks the teacher's work good, and why he thinks it good. Such comment, properly given, tends to strengthen the hold of the teacher on her class.

Should the suggestions the principal desires to give be of such a nature as to require privacy or more time, there is nothing so effective as a personal conference with the teacher before she leaves the building for the day. A verbal conference always gives an opportunity for questions and answers and for a tactful, sympathetic putting of criticisms and suggestions that no letter to a teacher can ever afford. Words, tactfully spoken, usually do not stir up the resentment that comes from reading cold type. If such personal conferences are held quite often, and the spirit of them is kept right by the principal, they ought not to cause apprehension on the part of the teachers. The work, the child, the good of the school are the elements to be kept in the foreground. Be impersonal, fair, just, and try to get the teacher's point of view. Remember that sound criticism seeks rather to discover and appreciate merits than to note faults, and to be helpful rather than destructive. Where such conferences are the rule, and the principal is helpful, the teachers come to expect them and the help they give and they are taken as a matter of routine.

Many a misunderstanding and many a failure in school work could be prevented by frank, constructive criticism given at the right time and in the right way. The unpleasant duty is likely to be put off until too late. Teachers are permitted to continue in wrong practices, even when they mean ultimate failure, because the principal dislikes the duty of changing their methods by constructive advice. This is not fair to the teacher or to the children under her, and is a clear evasion of duty by the principal. If the principal knows his ground pedagogically, if his criticisms and suggestions are constructive and not merely captious and fault-finding in nature, and if he has from the start established the right type of relationships between his teachers and himself, he ought not to find such conferences the disagreeable duty so many principals seem to find them. Should a conference prove to be disagreeable, though, through no fault of the principal, the best plan is to go through with it — as tactfully as possible, to be sure — and start right with such a teacher, for if he does not do so he can count with surety on more disagreeable encounters later on. Keep a sense of humor during it all. Sometimes a story or a laugh will relieve the situation and restore balance and good feeling.

Keeping the conference informal. The principal will do well to make such personal conferences as informal as possible. Ordinarily it is best to drop into the teacher's room later in the day, at recess or noon or after school, and begin the conference in a somewhat casual way by asking questions as to the teacher's procedure or purpose, and then gradually lead up to the suggestions intended to be given. "I was much interested, Miss Jones, in your recitation this morning, but I kept wondering through it all why you did so and so," or "just what it was you were trying to do," is not a bad way of beginning. It shows interest, commits the principal to nothing, puts the questionable procedure at once to the front, and gives the teacher a chance to explain. She will do this better in her own classroom and on her own ground and if taken unexpectedly, than if formally summoned to the principal's office, at a fixed hour, to receive what she will probably interpret to be a criticism of her work.

Where the case is one of long standing and serious, or where the teacher has habitually shown a rebellious attitude, and where the purpose is more the assertion of authority or the imparting of some straight advice or admonition, the principal may desire to call the teacher to his office and have the conference on his own ground. There is a certain psychological advantage in being in one's own room and on home ground that ordinarily the principal should allow to his teachers, but which in certain cases he may be allowed to capitalize for himself.

Keeping the criticism constructive. The most effective method to use in conferences with teachers will vary with the conditions, the purpose, and the matter under discussion, but the principal should not deviate from a constructive and friendly attitude, and a polite but frank consideration of the problem. No phase of the principal's work calls for such professional grasp as do these conferences with his teachers. He must be sure of himself and of the reasons — founded on sound educational theory and practice — for his point of view. A principal who does not know as much about teaching as his teachers cannot be very helpful in suggestions to them, nor is he likely to find himself on safe ground in attempting to improve their instruction. He must not only know that a particular recitation or piece of work was good or bad, but also why it was good or bad, and he must be able to defend his point of view and to offer concrete suggestions or materials for improving it when not satisfactory. It will always be the force of sound educational reasons, rather than personal authority, that will make criticisms or suggestions helpful and effective with teachers.

Even favorable comment on a teaching exercise should be sufficiently discriminating to enable the teacher to recognize the particular factors that made it a good exercise, and thus capitalize them in future work of a similar nature. For example, instead of merely telling a teacher that a particular class exercise was good, it will be much more helpful to tell her also that the particular things that made it good were the skillful questioning that brought out clearly the central thought of the lesson, and the alert attitude of the class. It will be still more helpful to tell her that the skillful questioning and the alert attitude of the pupils were the results of her own good preparation for the lesson, which enabled her to do the skillful questioning and to lead up to the central thought of the lesson in the very definite and logical and clear-cut way in which she did. A suggestion as to how to apply the idea to some phase of her work not so successful may also possibly be in place and be appreciated.

Conversely, merely to tell a teacher that a lesson in arithmetic, for example, was not successful or satisfactory, with no analysis of its defects and no constructive suggestions for making it better, is likely to still further weaken the teacher by robbing her of the little self-confidence she had. She doubtless has done the best she knew how to do, and if she is to do better work she needs to have shown to her — in all kindliness of manner — a better way. This, out of his larger experience and broader reading, it is the business of the principal to give. To tell her, on the other hand, that the reason the lesson was not successful was because she did not make her explanations clear, that this in turn was because she taught by a method too mature for the group, and that the remedy lies in simpler procedure and more concrete application, such as (illustrating), is to make her feel that the criticism was just and to look ahead with confidence to an improvement of her classroom methods. To say that, if she would like to have you do so, you will come in again tomorrow and teach the class for her, to illustrate what you mean, thus throwing yourself open to her criticism in turn, will inspire still more confidence.

Under such discriminating and constructive criticism teachers tend constantly to increase their ability in self-criticism, and to become more independent in correcting the mistakes in their own teaching procedure. This is not only a fundamental requisite for personal growth in teaching power, but it is also one of the best evidences of the presence of helpful and constructive supervision.

Supervision should liberate the teacher. An important purpose of classroom supervision, in addition to improving the teacher's technique, should be to liberate her and gradually free her from set procedure and definite prescriptions. Lesson planning, conferences on teaching procedure, demonstration lessons, teachers' meetings — all should tend toward freeing the teacher from the necessity of any close conformity to set plans and ways of doing things. In a few matters there will naturally still need to be definite prescription, but this is only in so far as may be necessary to secure a proper correlation and continuity of the work of the school. Otherwise the intent should be to extend liberty of action so far as liberty can be shown to be used intelligently, to place a premium on sensible originality and initiative, and to infuse the teaching force with such large conceptions of their work and of the aims and purposes of education as will illuminate procedure and stimulate the development of self-reliance and intelligent individuality. Nothing is more deadening to the growth of such initiative among teachers, nor more likely to result in arrested development, than a rigid, restrictive, and mandatory type of supervision.

On the other hand, this does not mean that teachers are to be freed from supervision because they have developed into good teachers, nor that the principal can now evade responsibility for making his school still better on the pretext of allowing wide initiative and large freedom to his teachers. No one who has caught the true significance of the modern liberalizing and democratic movement in education can believe that it places any lessened duty on the principal of a school in the matter of leadership. Instead, it will call for larger leadership and more real ability than did the older type of school administration. Under the older type the

PLANNING THE SUPERVISION

principal dominated the school and its instruction through mandatory requirements and the force of his position in the administrative organization of the city; under the new he must win and hold his place by virtue of his larger insight and knowledge and his qualities of leadership. He must still be the controlling factor in his school, but in the matter of the supervision of the instruction he must change from an inspector to an educational leader. No teacher really respects a principal who is an educational fossil, even though he makes life easy for her, as well as for himself.

QUESTIONS AND PROBLEMS

1. Explain why the different School Surveys so commonly report the elementary principalship as a seriously weak point in the school organization.
2. Assuming a day of selected visitation, based on teacher lesson-plan cards (Form 3 type) handed in, and a classroom supervision time schedule as given on page 47, make up a day's visiting program for work with grades 5 and 6 from the Platoon-type Class Program given in Table VI, pages 178–79.
3. Fill out Supervisory Visitation Records (Form 5) for two lesson-wholes seen during the day, planned as in Question 2.
4. Make out a Classroom Supervision Program (Form 4) for some other month and purposes.
5. This week you are going over the work in geography. You have a new teacher in 5B who seems to have little ability in geography teaching, though fairly promising otherwise. Yesterday she tried to teach drainage of the watersheds of the United States, but her work was over the heads of the children, and her questioning poor. She talked too much herself. You indicated her difficulties to her yesterday, at recess, and to-day you plan to go back, ask to take the class, start a review, and then turn the lesson into a skillful map-exercise to bring out the ideas of water-flow, watersheds, drainage basins, slope in relation to flow and uses of the river, why swamp lands, city and harbor locations and why, and similar information, to be thought out largely by the class under quick-fire questioning. Map out a card lesson plan outline that you will hand to the teacher as you take the class, that she may see what you want her to see and learn.
6. Suppose you have an older teacher who is hardly average, but who considers herself perfect, resents criticism, and will not let you be of help to her. You prefer not to use your authority, but rather to respect her position and rights and bring to bear a slowly cumulative

pressure that will in time produce either a change in her or a clear-cut issue with her. What will you do, and how will you do it?

7. Suppose, in visiting an arithmetic lesson, in the addition of fractions, the teacher first reads off a problem which each pupil copies and then proceeds to solve. After a proper time the teacher asks those who are through to hold up their hands, some one pupil to read his answer, and the class agree that this is right or wrong. The teacher then repeats the process, to the end of the period. Some hands are never up, and a few do most of the answering.

Write out a Supervisory Visit Record (Form 5) for this visit, and state what you would do afterward, and how you would do it.

8. Draw up a year's Supervisory Program for classroom and subject-matter supervision (main outlines only), by months, October to May inclusive, but with this main idea in mind: — Your teachers are weak in teaching technique, and you would like to have them read some of Strayer's *Brief Course in the Teaching Process*. If you asked them to do this as reading circle work for discussion in building teachers' meetings they would object, and do it only perfunctorily. Instead, you plan out a year's supervision of subject-matter instruction so that, week by week, you state, as a Supplemental Objective, one or more of the important phases of teaching technique as outlined in this book. Always cite the book and chapter under the "Interesting Readings," and always bring in the ideas of the chapter in the following teachers' meeting.

SELECTED REFERENCES

Allen, J. G. "The Supervisory Work of Principals"; in *School Review*, vol. 1, pp. 291–96. (May, 1893.)
   An old but very good article on the work of the principal in the supervision of instruction.

Bird, Grace E. "Teachers' Estimates of Supervisors"; in *School and Society*, vol. 5, pp. 717–20. (June 16, 1917.)
   Tabulation of results of an inquiry on the helpfulness and defects of supervisors.

Bobbitt, Fr. "Mistakes often made by Principals"; in *Elementary School Journal*, vol. 20, pp. 337–46, 419–34. (January and February, 1920.)
   Lists fifty mistakes, part of which relate to the supervisory function.

Burton, Wm. H. *Supervision and the Improvement of Teaching*. 450 pp., New York, 1922.
   Outlines the problems, aims, and procedure of supervision.

Coffman, L. D. "Control of Educational Progress through Supervision"; in *Proceedings of the National Education Association*, 1917, pp. 187–94.
   One of the best brief presentations as to the need for scientific supervision.

Gilbert, C. B. *The School and its Life*. Boston, 1906.
   Chapters XIII to XV good on visitation, conference, and judging teaching.

Gist, A. S., and King, Wm. A. "The Efficiency of the Principalship from the Standpoint of the Teacher"; in *Elementary School Journal*, vol. 23, pp. 120–26. (October, 1922.)
Results of an inquiry made by two Seattle principals.

Gray, Wm. S. "Work of the Elementary School Principal"; in *Elementary School Journal*, vol. 19, pp. 24–35. (September, 1918.)
An excellent statement of the principal's problem of supervision.

Gray, Wm. S. "Methods of Improving the Technique of Teaching"; in *Elementary School Journal*, vol. 20, pp. 263–75. (December, 1919.)
Very good on the supervision of instruction.

Greenwood, J. M. "How to Judge a School"; in *Educational Review*, vol. 17, pp. 324–45. (April, 1899.)
A helpful article on the work of a principal or superintendent in classroom visitation and supervision.

Hosic, J. F. "The Democratization of Supervision"; in *School and Society*, vol. 11, pp. 331–36. (March 20, 1920.)
On the work of a principal in supervisory instruction.

Kennedy, J. "The Function of Supervision"; in *Educational Review*, vol. 1, pp. 465–69. (May, 1891.)
A very good article on the characteristics of good school supervision.

Maxwell, C. R. *The Observation of Teaching.* 115 pp., Boston, 1917.
Nature of the problem; purposes; technique.

Maxwell, C. R. "Effective Supervision"; in *School and Society*, vol. 11, pp. 214–16. (February 21, 1920.)
A good short statement on supervisory visitation.

Morrison, J. C. "Methods of Improving Classroom Instruction used by Helping-Teachers and Supervisory Principals of New Jersey"; in *Elementary School Journal*, vol. 20, pp. 208–16. (November, 1919.)
The results of a questionnaire, tabulated. Contains good material.

Nutt, H. B. *The Supervision of Instruction.* 275 pp., Boston, 1920.
The job; devices; technique. Section C good supplemental reading for this chapter.

Palmer, J. T. "The Importance of the Teacher in the School Organization"; in *Elementary School Journal*, vol. 19, pp. 541–44. (April, 1919.)
The necessity of coöperation before supervision can be effective.

Power, L. "A Plan for the Supervision of Instruction by a Principal of an Elementary School"; in *Elementary School Journal*, vol. 19, pp. 408–18. (February, 1919.)
A very concrete and helpful article, with good details as to procedure.

Power, L. "How to make Visits profitable to Teachers"; in *First Yearbook of the Department Elementary School Principals, National Education Association*, 1922, pp. 11–19.
On the technique of visiting, lesson types, and conferences.

Rice, J. M. *Scientific Management in Education.* New York, 1905.
A book on scientific school supervision by a pioneer in the work.

Rugg, George. "Visitation as a Means of Diagnosis"; in *First Yearbook of*

the Department Elementary School Principals, National Education Association. 1922, pp. 7–11.
   On classroom visitation and results.

Stark, Wm. E. *Every Teacher's Problems.* New York, 1922.
   Chapters XI and XII contain a number of good problems relating to the work of the principal in supervision.

Strayer, G. D. *A Brief Course on the Teaching Process.* New York, 1911.
   Chapter XVII good on the teacher in relation to supervision.

Spencer, Roger A. "The Work of the School Principal in Supervision"; in *Elementary School Journal*, vol. 20, pp. 176–87. (November, 1919.)
   Coöperation; community study; plans; training teachers; improving instruction.

Taylor, Jos. S. "Some Desirable Traits of the Supervisor"; in *Educational Administration and Supervision*, vol. IX, pp. 1–9. (January, 1923.)
   A very good article for the principal to read.

Wagner, C. A. *Common Sense in School Supervision.* 201 pp., Milwaukee, 1922.
   Very good on the work of a principal, and how to make supervision profitable and enjoyable.

Wilde, A. H. "The Principal's Duty in Improving Instruction"; in *School Review*, vol. 24, pp. 617–25. (October, 1916.)
   A very sensible and readable article, containing much good material.

CHAPTER XXIII

HELPING THE TEACHER

Types of teachers. Any principal, on taking charge of a school, will find that the teaching force he inherits probably will represent a number of different types in training and experience and teaching power, and that several different kinds of human nature will also be in evidence. This he must expect, and he must learn to get along with the situation. Taking things as he finds them, it will be the problem of the principal to do the best possible for all his teachers, dealing with them as individuals rather than as a group, and remembering that in working to improve his teachers in instruction and management he is working primarily in the interests of the children in his school.

Except in cities where the best of standards for the selection of teachers have long prevailed, the principal will be fortunate if he finds a teaching force twenty-five per cent of which are really superior teachers — teachers who are well trained, ambitious and capable, who know what to do and why and how, and who will need but little help from a principal other than inspiration to do still better work. He will also be fortunate if not more than twenty-five per cent of his teachers are not either beginners who probably will need much help, or older teachers who have become set in partially wrong ways and are in consequence somewhat ineffective. Some of the older ones will be willing to do better work, if shown a better way; some, on the contrary, will be so set that they will be unwilling to change their ways or to make any effort at improvement. Something like fifty per cent of his force he may expect to belong to the fair-average type of teachers — teachers who do fairly satisfactory work, but who do not rise to any large conception of the possibilities of their work or attain to any high degree of teaching skill. Though standards as to training are constantly improving, the bulk of the teaching in our schools will still for some time probably have to be done by this fair-average type of teacher. Many of this type can be changed by helpful advice and education into better teachers; a few will not improve much even though they may seem to try.

It is with such types of teachers that a principal will have to work, and working through them do his work. He can do much to help them and make their work more attractive to them, though it will not be wholly by classroom supervision that he will accomplish the results he desires. The human factor will count for much. His interest in his problems, his energy and zeal for his work, his orderly habits, his businesslike attitude, his sense of humor, his appreciation of the human side of life, his understanding and sympathy, his kindliness and courtesy, his own desire for growth, his working philosophy of the educational process, his practical knowledge, and his ability to lead without driving — all will be important factors in moulding his teachers, in improving their methods, and in inspiring them with a larger vision of the importance of the work they do.

Types of service. The superior type of teacher the principal can both help and be helped by. The kind of help this type will need will be different from that needed by the other types. In handling children and in teaching technique they may be superior to the principal, and the lessons they teach probably will not need to be discussed at all. Many will be carried along by their own ideals of excellence, but all of them can be kept at maximum efficiency by evidence of appreciation of what they do, as well as by a form of professional helpfulness which consists largely of suggesting to them possibilities of further achievement of which they had not been aware. On the other hand, superior teachers strengthen the principal by showing him new standards for accomplishment, new technique that he can use, and by their stabilizing influence with the other teachers if they come to have confidence in the principal's leadership. Of all the teachers in a building, the aid and support of the most capable group is the backing most worth having. To win and hold this calls for a high degree of competence.

To the improvement in instruction and management of the other types of teachers the principal will need to give a varying amount of time and attention, and in doing so may need to employ a number of different supervisory devices. Of these devices some will be of more service in one school than in another.

The teachers most in need of help, and the ones who will profit most by the help given and usually be the most appreciative of it, are the beginning teachers. It is important that these be started right, and for these the principal should make his school a form of normal school. Each beginner, potentially, has the making of a superior teacher, but if neglected and allowed to struggle along may soon lose all professional enthusiasm and become confirmed in faulty procedure and teaching mistakes. It is easier and better to take these beginners and make good teachers of them, if this can be done, than it is to drop them and start over again.

The fair-average type of teacher also needs that constant stimulus to professional activity which a professionally alive and interested principal can give. The purpose is to change wrong ways of doing things, to eliminate mistakes in management and method that lead to a low grade of accomplishment and to discouragement, to awaken new professional interest, and to cause teachers of this type to catch a new vision of service and because of it to rise above mediocrity.

Often this type of teacher will do sufficiently well from year to year to warrant retention, yet without working or developing as she should.

It is these fair-average teachers who present a real problem to the principal. Yet so many cases are known in which a new principal, coming into a school, has taken a professionally dead teaching force and fired it with new life; we have so many instances of single schools, in cities that are professionally dead, being made centers of professional activity by a principal; and so great is the enthusiasm and optimism of women teachers when it comes to service for children that a principal possessed of the right type of personality and knowledge can be almost sure of success. A man or woman who knows what to do, and who has energy and imagination and fire can almost on a certainty count on succeeding if given a relatively free hand. The first meeting of such a principal and a body of teachers often gives the teachers a new sense of power, and they leave the room with a feeling of certainty that they will all be distinctly alive before he is through with them. Under the stimulus of leadership of this type a body of teachers responds and grows by leaps and bounds.

In helping teachers to improve a number of supervisory devices have been found useful, and these will be briefly mentioned here.

The beginning teacher. A principal often fails to appreciate the difficulties that a beginning teacher has to encounter. Often inadequately trained, timid, shrinking from assuming new responsibilities, unconscious of errors made, unable to diagnose a situation and apply a remedy when things go wrong — the beginning teacher is often in deep water before the principal realizes it. Even when a normal school graduate and possessed of a modern viewpoint, the beginner usually finds actual schoolroom conditions quite different from the small teaching groups and the close supervision of the training school. Both these types of beginners need oversight and attention. It is best that the principal should not assume the management of the room for her, except in extreme cases, for it is important that she learn quickly how to do for herself. To this end she should not at first be given much line or yard work or other types of duties that may lead to disciplinary difficulties, and for the first month or two she should be watched rather carefully and started right. To feel sure that there is a sympathetic principal who will respond with helpful suggestions during the learning period is a great help to such a teacher in establishing herself and learning to control the situation.

The young teacher usually runs into her first trouble with discipline. Not able as yet to teach effectively, her class gets away from her. The principal's work will be, not to do the disciplining for her unless things are serious, but to diagnose her difficulties, to tell her where and why the methods she uses fail, to point out what better methods she ought to employ, to keep her courage up by showing confidence in her ability to pull through ultimately, and by protecting her from all possible annoyances that may tend to impair her working efficiency. Many a beginning teacher fails here, is not given the help and support a principal should give her, loses self-confidence, becomes discouraged, goes from bad to worse, drags through the year, spoils a class, and is dropped by the school board at the end of the year.

The principal should keep every beginning teacher under observation, and be quick to detect and ward off trouble before it becomes serious. It is wise to have it definitely understood by every new teacher, at the beginning of her teaching in your school, that you expect to keep a close eye on her work and to help her all you can, and that you hope she will not become nervous under your observation nor object to any suggestions you may see fit to give her. At the first sign of trouble diagnose the situation, get at the causes and the probable remedies, and then give her the benefit of your larger experience and insight. Often the whole trouble will lie in that two or three boys can out-guess her, while things are new and little of the work has as yet become habitual. If she can get a grip on the situation well and good, but if she does not do so quickly, ask her to let you take her class and show her how you would handle it. To see how easily you squelch a disturbing youngster and to note your methods may be worth much more than any verbal instructions you could give her. Often a little reading on school management, a booklet on "does and don'ts," an article on how to handle an unruly room, or a book that will give her a better understanding of boys, may help her quickly.

Building up the beginner in teaching skill. As most disciplinary troubles have their origin in poor teaching, the best line of remedial treatment lies in building up the teacher in teaching power. Some simple book on teaching technique may be very helpful to her. Her trouble may lie in defective questioning, in talking too much and working the pupils too little, in giving her attention to but a few of the class, to an unfavorable voice and manner, in not being rapid and expeditious in her work, in poor assignments for work, or in other directions. Teachers who ultimately fail because of such faults may very properly ask of the principal, "Why did you not tell me?", and the superintendent of schools may properly ask the same question of the principal.

Here is the place for the principal to show his large skill in educational diagnosis and in suggestions for remedial procedure. He ought to correct mistakes from the first, and build up the teacher in teaching power as rapidly as possible. The first year a new teacher may require much help, but after a couple of years she ought to be able to care for herself in the main. While it usually takes five or six years to make a really good teacher out of a promising beginner, after the second year materially less guidance will be needed.

An important service by the principal during this early building-up process will be to keep the teacher from becoming discouraged. Most young teachers have been more or less impressed by stories of "born teachers," and technical skill seems so easy and natural to the expert and so hard for them to acquire, that many are depressed by their difficulties. A little wholesome encouragement along with advice as to better procedure, and some sound information as to how largely teaching must be learned, will often do much to keep up the spirits and courage of a beginning teacher.

Occasionally, on the other hand, the principal may draw a beginner who is very sure that she, or he, is right, and that the results obtained are much better than the principal thinks. This attitude is especially likely to be the case if the beginner is a man teacher in one of the upper grades, and still more likely if he is a normal school or college graduate. Such a case may call for some patience and much argument and education. Sometimes an arranged visit to another teacher may be helpful, sometimes reading can be suggested that will let in the light, sometimes a cock-sure individual learns best by permitting him, or her, to ride to a fall. If the principal bases his suggestions on sound educational principles he can usually afford to give these "heady" persons quite a large amount of rope, sure they will tangle themselves up in it in time. If the success of the school work is imperiled he may need to assert his authority, quietly but firmly, confident that he will be upheld in so doing if the teacher can be shown to be in the wrong and impervious to suggestions and advice.

The group conference. A principal can do much, for selected teachers in need of certain types of help, by organizing group conferences with those having the same type of difficulties or in need of the same kind of assistance. The groups may be quite flexible, and may change much in personnel and character. They are in effect short teachers' meetings, held with selected groups of teachers for some special purpose, and to consider matters that should not come before a general teachers' meeting of the school. Where the principal is a supervising principal, in charge of the supervision of a small group of schools, such group conferences can be arranged with greater advantage than where the principal has but one small group of teachers under him.

Such conferences probably will be most successful when they seem to have arisen somewhat spontaneously out of the needs of the teachers. Sometimes conditions can be so shaped that the teachers will be brought to ask for them; sometimes they can owe their origin to an offer by the principal to give some definite form of assistance. In these conferences real constructive help must be presented, and the principal must be sure to be ready to afford it. Fault-finding conferences will accomplish nothing. They must be constructive, must analyze conditions and difficulties for the teachers, ought to be based on needs that have been observed or felt, and should either point out better ways or lead to sound hard thinking about teaching procedure. Teachers ought to go away from them with a new feeling of mastery over their difficulties.

The following are suggested as types of possible special-group conferences for groups of new teachers, and possibly some of the older teachers who may be in need of similar help.

1. Special technique in the teaching of:
    a. Primary spelling.
    b. Upper-grade spelling.

HELPING THE TEACHER

     c. Primary number work.
     d. Mental arithmetic.
     e. Observational geography.
     f. Poetry in the upper grades.
2. The organization of lesson-wholes and plans.
3. Useful teaching devices.
4. The development type of lesson and its place.
5. The drill lesson and its use.
6. The review lesson and how to use it.
7. The appreciation lesson.
8. The assignment of new work.
9. Disciplinary difficulties.
10. Over-teaching by the teacher.

Analyzing one of the above, to show something of what the principal needs to have in hand for such a conference, we will take the first.

A. Primary spelling.
    1. Psychological processes involved in spelling.
       a. Perception.
       b. Image types (visual, auditory, motor).
       c. Habit formation.
    2. Application of these principles.
       a. Conditions of presentation, and errors in.
       b. Reproductory visual image desired
          (a) Written, not oral spelling.
       c. Habituation of the image.
    3. Method in teaching spelling.
       a. Writing and spelling at first coincident.
       b. Steps in teaching phonetic words.
       c. Steps in teaching non-phonetic words.
    4. Learning new words.
       a. Discover poor spellers early, and diagnose difficulty.
          (a) Correct work rather than speed.
          (b) Habituation to correct forms only remedy.
       b. Teach words in context.
       c. Teach limited number of fundamental words.
          (a) Use of Ayres' lists.
    5. Primary spelling don'ts.

In these conferences the principal will need to assume control and to lead, much as would a teacher with a class in a normal school. Some magazine articles or chapters in available books that may be read should be suggested, by way of follow-up work. Another form of follow-up work that is good is to enumerate various classroom applications that may be employed, and in the visitation watch to see if these are used. Occasionally some short and very pertinent book may be read by all, and later used as a basis for a further conference. Some suggestions along this line would be:

> Betts, G. H. *The Recitation.* 116 pp.
> Haliburton and Smith. *Teaching Poetry in the Grades.* 166 pp.
> Hartwell, E. C. *The Teaching of History.* 67 pp.
> Horne, H. H. *The Teacher as Artist.* 57 pp.
> Suzzallo, H. *The Teaching of Spelling.* 123 pp.
> Wilson, H. B. *Training Pupils to Study.* 70 pp.

Demonstration teaching. While the theoretical presentation of a problem and its solution has its place, the practical demonstration also has its function. It is surprising, after all, how much we learn by imitation. A demonstration lesson often teaches what it is desired should be taught better than any other plan could do. In taking charge of a class to do demonstration teaching the principal should be sure that he is prepared to do well what he attempts, so that it may be a real demonstration lesson, and he should explain the main points in his procedure in the light of sound educational theory. In taking charge of a class it is a good idea for the principal to work the class rather hard, that they may not think that the teacher asks too much of them. After the lesson, be glad if the teacher will question you about it, as this evidences a healthy interest. If she has criticism of your work, welcome that too. Show that you were right and why, or admit that you were not. If she is commendatory, explain to her, if she cannot herself, the educational principles that were applied and which made the lesson good.

Should the system employ a few so-called training-teachers — older and specially capable teachers, paid a little extra for the service, and charged with helping beginners and others to become efficient — they can be made particularly useful by a principal in helping his teachers to acquire needed skill. The primary supervisor is a form of such special service of help. The function of the training teacher is to visit, as needed, staying from a quarter to half a day with a teacher needing assistance, showing her how to handle her work, and then a few days later have this teacher, possibly in company with two or three others from other schools, visit the training teacher in her own room, for from half to a whole day, and see how she does the work with her own children. Such demonstration teaching is about the most valuable service that can be given new teachers. It has, too, the psychological advantage of coming from one of the teaching force, and not from a superior, and is in consequence more effective. The demonstration teaching by the primary supervisor, and visiting under her direction or with her, can be made very useful in the same way.

Every principal, in observing the instruction within his own school, or in his contact with visiting supervisors, will find opportunities for organizing an occasional demonstration lesson, to be put on before a part or possibly all of his teachers. It may be some particularly strong lesson work that he may like to have repeated before a selected conference group, or it may be a type of work representing common errors in aim or procedure which he finds occurring from grade to grade in his school. In the conference-group type it should be a real demonstration lesson, setting before the teachers who need it an example of excellent instruction which they may see, and upon which they may question as they wish. In the second case the lesson may also be of this same type, if that is what is desired, or it may be of the type mentioned above and the purpose of the principal will be to throw it open to questioning as to aim, content, and technique, with a view to tactfully bringing out in the discussion the errors he desires to bring to the attention of his teachers as a body. Needful criticism may thus be given without making it in any way personal, thus avoiding injured feelings.

The demonstration lesson has possibilities that as yet have been but little utilized. As one writer puts it, "some of the most expert teaching power of our best teachers is going to waste as far as imparting this power to others is concerned." After the lesson, the opportunity for analysis and constructive suggestion is very great. It would be well if all teachers could occasionally observe the work of a master craftsman, and be able to question as to the why and the how.

A visiting day. Many school systems allow teachers two or three "visiting days" a year, during which they are relieved of their room work and may visit other schools in the system or in adjacent cities. Teachers who are weak are often sent to visit some stronger teacher doing the same type of work. This device is useful now and then, if there is some specific purpose in view. Too much of the "visiting," though, is haphazard and not of any special value to the teacher or the school, being in effect a sort of a day off — a day when the teacher "dresses up and goes visiting." If training teachers are employed to help those needing it, as has just been described, there will be much less need for general visiting days.

On the other hand, the visiting day can be made useful and helpful if the visiting is done under direction, if it is arranged for with thought, and if some report on the visiting is expected. A superintendent of schools might with advantage provide that visiting be arranged for by conference, that certain definite objectives be kept in mind, and that, at least for teachers not as yet in the class of the strong and capable, a visiting outline be given the teacher by the principal, or by an assistant superintendent or special supervisor, indicating the main points she is to observe and be prepared to report upon on her return. For example, a teacher in need of help in teaching technique might be sent to visit one or two teachers who are noted for their skillful procedure, and might be given written directions as to what is to be looked for, of which the form on page 472 is supposed to be a copy. Such directions, of course, would not need to be filled out when superior teachers take their visiting day, only the permit part being used and the teacher left free to report on what she finds is worth while. Sometimes, especially when a superior teacher who is a good observer finds some particularly excellent work, it is a good plan to have a report on it made to a general meeting of all the teachers.

Another form of visiting that is occasionally useful is short room-to-room visiting in the same building. Sometimes, when a teacher is tired and nervous, the principal may take the class for a single lesson, often using the time to test the work of the class, and send the teacher to another room for a half-hour visit, to rest and to see some other teacher at work. To see how the teacher next below is preparing pupils to enter her grade, or how the teacher next above is using previous preparation may be helpful, as may also a short visit to some superior teacher doing an entirely different type of instructing.

Special teaching problems. All the suggestions as to devices so far given have been of the remedial or corrective type. The suggestion of special problems to teachers, on the contrary, represents a constructive type of device because the problem can be made to appeal to the teacher's interest and lead to study that is certain to improve in-

[129—2-20—½M.]

VISITING-DAY DIRECTIONS

Miss............Mary Carr,..................
...........McKinley..........School.

By permission of the Superintendent of Schools, you will be given leave of absence from your class work on Wednesday, October 23d, for all day, under the provisions of Sec. 79 of the Rules of the Board of Education providing for visiting days.

You are requested to visit the ......Lincoln......School on that day, and especially to see instruction by the following teachers:

    Geraldine Duffy, Grade 5B

    Margaret Marcus, Grade 6A

While observing their instruction, please note:

1. Dependence on or freedom from textbooks.
2. Organization of teaching procedure.
3. Character of questioning by teacher.
4. Attention and character of response by pupils.
5. Relative part taken by teacher and pupils.
6. Types of lessons seen.
7. How well the lesson was conducted, and brought to a proper conclusion.
8. Character of lesson assignment by teacher.
9. Strong points in teaching technique seen.

The principal of the school will be expecting you, as will the teachers named above. On your return to your school you will be expected to report to your principal on your observations. You are also requested not to comment on the work seen, other than favorably, to any one else than your principal.

                                                   William Jenkins

Date....Oct. 21,....1923.   Principal....McKinley....School.

FORM 6. A VISITING-DAY DIRECTION FORM

HELPING THE TEACHER

struction. An observing principal has constant opportunities for suggesting new ways of doing things that will challenge the attention of the teacher. By proposing some simple problem to her that will lead her to think more closely as to procedure, and to observe results more critically, he is quite likely to stimulate her to some activity. To suggest as many such teaching problems as teachers can use advantageously, and to be acquiring new problems, through reading, is one of the marks of a professionally alert principal. Similarly, to be able to use such suggestions is a mark of an alert teacher. In making his suggestions the principal should exercise care that the problems he proposes are very definite and concrete, are limited to a small segment of the subject, and are perfectly capable of solution by a teacher who will think. Large, vague, and general objectives will not give the desired results. If a teacher who is not strong and capable will not or cannot use the problem suggestions a principal gives her, it should be counted as one point against her when the principal comes to score her up for the information of the superintendent.

Any one of the possible teacher-conference subjects given on pages 466-67 might be subdivided into a number of simple problems which could be tested out in one or more rooms. Reading, geography, spelling, arithmetic, and English are fruitful of problems, and there is plenty of good literature on each. A principal, as he reads, ought to compile a card catalogue of simple teaching problems, with references to simple and easily obtained reading. A few such teaching problems, by way of illustration, may be mentioned here:

1. Locate any persistent errors made by pupils in different school subjects, and find out, if possible, why they make them.
2. Locate your bad spellers, diagnose their difficulties, and suggest remedial instruction for each pupil.
3. Locate the common errors made in composition, by type and by pupils, and plan a remedial procedure.

4. Organize your composition teaching to secure greater effectiveness and less after-school paper work.
5. What is the best use of illustrative material with intermediate geography work?
6. How best eradicate persistent errors in English?
7. Diagnose the difficulties of your poor readers, and see if the analysis of causes will not offer suggestions for improvement.
8. If intelligent thought-getting in reading requires careful attention to punctuation, how can we reverse the process and get proper punctuation in composition work by attention to expression of the meaning?

A teaching problem illustrated. To illustrate the type of solution that might be arrived at, let us take the first problem and cite an actual case reported to the writer by a principal. In a 3A class a little girl, apparently rather bright, could do little in arithmetic. Her reports were always poor. When asked about her, the teacher replied that "Marie just is n't able to learn arithmetic." The principal, in looking over her written work, discovered that her trouble was due to Marie making a constant error because of having learned a "carrying" direction wrong. She was very accurate, according to her conception of the multiplying process, but was constantly marked wrong by the teacher because she was wrong by the books. The following examples from her written work will illustrate:

(1)	(2)	(3)	(4)
463	567	323	4152
3	4	3	4
1589	3228	969	20208

The principal, seeing that problem (3) was right and the others wrong, soon diagnosed the difficulty. She had misunderstood carrying; instead of adding the number to be carried to the next product *after* the multiplication, she first added the number to be carried to the next number in the multiplicand, and then multiplied. By her understanding her sums were 100 per cent correct, instead of twenty-five per cent, and problem (3) would have shown the same error had the product at any time given a number to carry. To train teachers in such diagnostic methods leads rapidly to interest in teaching and to improved instruction. It also helps pupils to succeed and stimulates their interest and confidence. On the other hand, telling pupils that they will not pass if they do not improve, that they do not know anything, and that they do not work, only leads to discouragement and causes them to stop trying.

Course of study problems. Another type of special problem work, productive of much interest and personal growth, is that in which a principal is able to get teachers to work on phases of the course of study. This type of problem work, with the resulting discussion, is often one of the best means for bringing some older teacher to take a new interest in the professional side of her work, with a resulting improvement in the value of the instruction she gives the children. Where a principal is allowed something of a free hand as to modifications and minor changes and omissions, or in the determination as to what special groups may do, or where the daily contacts of teachers with children are capitalized in the formulation of course-of-study requirements and in making changes in established procedure, such course-of-study discussion by teachers can often be made useful.

This device for teacher stimulation should not be tried locally unless the principal is fairly well established in control of his school, and the teachers have come to have a fairly clear idea as to his aims and standards and are in sympathy with them. When this condition has been brought about the teachers may be started on the preparation of special syllabi, or a discussion of aims may be started. Often this will best grow out of the results of instruction measurement, described in the following chapter. A consideration of the work in spelling, of oral arithmetic, or the production of a syllabus for language instruction are types of simple work which do not involve any fundamental change in the city course of study, and which can be attempted almost anywhere. If the experiences and successes of other schools can be brought in, the interest is usually heightened.

At first the principal will need to keep control of the discussion and direct it; later on he may gradually withdraw and let committees of the teachers assume control. The results accomplished may not be of fundamental importance, but the exchange of experiences and ideas, the looking up and quoting of authorities, and the weighing of values in instruction are often very useful in awakening professional interest and in making teachers alive to the problems of their work and of the school. There is a training and an inspiration for work that comes from creative activity that the passive recipient of the work of others never knows. This is not a device that can be used generally and at any time, but when possible of use the principal should be alive to its value.

Professional reading. While a principal may expect to find a few teachers in any school who are not interested in improving the quality of their work, he will find that most teachers, on the contrary, are hungry for help. Perhaps one main reason why teachers do not progress professionally as much as they should, and why some experience an early professional death, is that the principals under whom they work so often devote almost no effort to keeping their teachers professionally alert. The details of administration absorb the thought and energy of the principal, and office work — always office work — in time produces that deadest of school men, the office principal. Such men, instead of being inspirers of others and instead of their school being a professional workshop, produce an institution which is lacking in spirit and which mechanically grinds out results. The teachers are faithful, diligent, punctual, morally upright, and interested in their children, but they lose enthusiasm and professional ambition.

To keep his teachers professionally alert and his school a sort of a continuation professional school ought to be one of the highest ambitions of a school principal. To be able to stimulate teachers to think, and from thinking to want to read, is the clear mark of a professional leader. The principal, though, should remember that teachers will get little from reading done from any other motive than a feeling of need for it. To create this need and then lead the way in satisfying it is the principal's work. When the principal finds a book that is helpful to him, and which he thinks will be helpful to some one of his teachers, he may properly bring it to her attention. If it proves to be of general interest he may pass it around. Particularly important magazine articles may also be brought to the general attention of teachers. The principal, however, must remember that teachers do not have the time or the energy to read much, and what is suggested should be short, pertinent, and attractively written. The principal himself must read and give his teachers the advantage of much professional literature that he cannot expect them to read. If he can get each teacher interested enough to read half a dozen magazine articles each year, a couple of good professional books, and two or three books giving an insight into child life or industry or world affairs, he may feel quite well satisfied.

To this end every principal ought to build up for himself a good working library of professional books upon which he can draw as needed. The school building ought also to have a small professional library of useful and pertinent volumes, and the ability further to draw on a central teachers' professional library for temporary loans. There should also be a few of the best magazines kept regularly at every school. As these are seldom furnished by the school department, a school ought to establish a magazine club and provide them itself. One way is for each teacher to give an equal amount; another is for each teacher to subscribe for some one professional or general magazine and deposit it at the building. It is best to let a committee of the teachers handle this, determine the magazines, and arrange the rules. The principal can well afford to put in two or three magazines himself.

Often some professional book that bears on classroom work can be adopted for reading and discussion. If this seems to be a desirable thing to do, it can be made very valuable. While the principal should prepare carefully on the work and be ready to keep the discussion alive and vital, it is best to appoint some one teacher to open the discussion each time. If chapters can be assigned so that teachers who are likely to be most helped by some particular chapter can be selected to lead, much good educational work can be accomplished without seeming intent.

Discovering special ability. Another type of device, sometimes used very effectively by principals, consists in studying teachers who are not doing their best work to see wherein they show signs of interest or ability, and then striving to develop that special interest or ability. A principal who is constantly finding his teachers able to do more than they had themselves thought possible, and who stimulates them by acknowledging their good work, is a type of leader most teachers will be willing to follow. Sometimes a fair-average or indifferent teacher, when thus encouraged and placed in a new type of situation, turns into an interested and good teacher. Often this is one of the best devices to use with older teachers who need, more than anything else, a change of work to wake them up.

Sometimes a grade teacher can be changed to a departmental type of work, or vice versa. Sometimes special ability in some one subject or type of work can be emphasized. Sometimes a teacher has been too long in one grade of work and would be improved by a change. Sometimes to allow a teacher to progress upward with her class, for a year or two, may develop new interest. Sometimes a change to another school may be a wise thing to suggest.

Training in working habits. Often teachers can be very much helped by a principal who gradually trains them in better working habits. To show a teacher how to do a thing more expeditiously is a service of value. The principal ought to have some of the characteristics of an efficiency engineer. If he has he can often show his teachers how to save time, how to get work done more effectively, how to concentrate on the essentials, how to organize and simplify the mechanics of their classroom procedure, how to mechanize their routine work, and how to cut down time spent on written work. Teach them that it is not necessary to correct and hand back all written work; that written work for the office does not need to be copied again for excessive neatness; that they must develop a time sense and a sense of proportion; and that it is important to save time for recreation and personal growth.

Conserve, also, the teachers' nervous energy as much as possible. Limit routine work, reports, statistical information, lesson plans, and records as much as the proper progress of the school will permit. Relieve them too, whenever possible, of the strain of adjusting difficulties with irate parents. One purpose of the presence of the school principal is to protect his teachers as much as can be done from everything that tends to interfere with their highest efficiency in instruction, and to promote everything that will tend to bring teachers and children together under conditions most likely to result in good instruction. Any device that improves the teacher results in an improvement of her school.

Rating the teachers. Many school systems now require principals to rate their teachers, once or twice a year, on individual score cards. The teachers are also rated, as is the principal, on similar cards by the superintendent, the assistant superintendents, and by special supervisors, and the ratings of all are frequently combined to form a composite score card. While these teacher rating cards may vary somewhat in form and items used, preparation, personality, professional attitude, teaching technique, and results attained are commonly included. The aim of all has been to provide a somewhat objective and practical method by means of which teachers may be rated and the efficiency of their work determined. One such rating card, on which three supervisory officers have rated the same teacher, is shown opposite. It will be seen from this that all unite in rating this teacher as a good to an excellent teacher. Some principals, after making up these cards, give or show copies of them to their teachers, as a supervisory device. Some principals ask each teacher to rate herself on one of these cards and turn it in to him, and some combine the teacher's rating of herself with their own by way of fairness to the teacher.

In making such ratings the principal will be aided in being objective himself if he has kept a series of numbered classroom supervisory-visit records for each teacher, after some such form as is shown in Form 5, page 448. When called upon to report on the efficiency of his teachers by the superintendent or the board of education he will then be able to base his report, or frame his rating card, from recorded data that will largely save him from being charged with personal bias and subjective opinion, in case he reports unfavorably

HELPING THE TEACHER

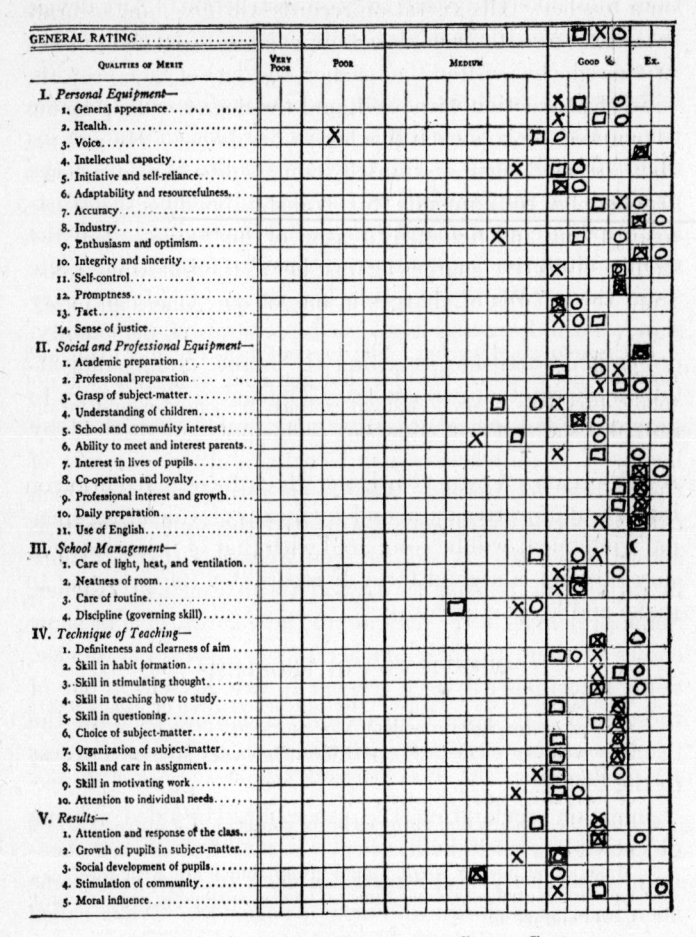

QUALITIES OF MERIT	VERY POOR	POOR	MEDIUM	GOOD	EX.
GENERAL RATING				□×○	
I. Personal Equipment—					
1. General appearance				×□ ○	
2. Health				× □○	
3. Voice		×		□○	⊠
4. Intellectual capacity					⊠
5. Initiative and self-reliance			×	□○	
6. Adaptability and resourcefulness				⊠○	
7. Accuracy				□ ×○	
8. Industry					⊠ ○
9. Enthusiasm and optimism			×	□ ○	
10. Integrity and sincerity					⊠ ○
11. Self-control			×	⊠	⊠
12. Promptness					⊠
13. Tact				⊠○	
14. Sense of justice				×○□	
II. Social and Professional Equipment—					⊠
1. Academic preparation				□ ○×	
2. Professional preparation				×□○	
3. Grasp of subject-matter			□ ○	×	
4. Understanding of children				⊠○	
5. School and community interest				○	
6. Ability to meet and interest parents			× □		
7. Interest in lives of pupils				× □	○
8. Co-operation and loyalty					⊠○
9. Professional interest and growth				□	⊠
10. Daily preparation					⊠○
11. Use of English				×	⊠
III. School Management—					⟨
1. Care of light, heat, and ventilation			□	○×	
2. Neatness of room				×□ ○	
3. Care of routine				×⊠	
4. Discipline (governing skill)		□	×○		
IV. Technique of Teaching—					△
1. Definiteness and clearness of aim				□○×	
2. Skill in habit formation				×□	○
3. Skill in stimulating thought				⊠	○
4. Skill in teaching how to study					
5. Skill in questioning				□ □⊠	
6. Choice of subject-matter				□ ⊠	
7. Organization of subject-matter				□ ⊠	
8. Skill and care in assignment				⊠	
9. Skill in motivating work			×□	□○	
10. Attention to individual needs			×	□○	
V. Results—					
1. Attention and response of the class			□	⊠	
2. Growth of pupils in subject-matter			×	⊠	○
3. Social development of pupils		⊠		○	
4. Stimulation of community				○ □	○
5. Moral influence				×	

FORM 7. A TEACHER-EFFICIENCY SCORE CARD

[Reprinted from J. B. Sears' Classroom Organization and Control, p. 254.]

Superintendent □; Principal ×; Supervisor ○.

This card shows the rating of a good teacher by three supervisory officers, and is in effect a consolidated score. Another plan of using the card would be for each to indicate rating by dots, and then to connect the dots by lines, using different colored ink for each rating.

on a teacher. His visitation records will give him accurate information as to each classroom exercise seen, the number of times he has visited the teacher, the date of each visit, the kind of instruction witnessed, and the degree of help he has attempted to give each teacher in his school. He will not then be in danger of himself being embarrassed, when a teacher he recommends for transfer or dismissal turns against him and fights, by reason of his having filed such highly subjective charges against her as the following, taken from the records of charges in one of our American cities.

She is not a good teacher. She does not do as I tell her to do, and does not get results. She does not get along well She will not follow directions. My judgment is that the school would be improved if she were sent elsewhere, or dropped.

A well-organized rating card, one which focuses attention on important objective data, and by means of which the principal's judgment will be compared with that of other supervisory officers, is a good form of record for the principal to make and keep.

QUESTIONS AND PROBLEMS

1. Compare the classification of types of teachers given on page 459 with that given by Superintendent Van Sickle (*Proceedings of National Education Association*, 1911, p. 437, or Cubberley's *Public School Administration*, p. 232). Does Van Sickle's classification set off the work of supervision more clearly?
2. State the fundamental purposes in the supervision of instruction by a principal.
3. Make an outline for conducting a group conference with three new teachers in grades two and three on mental arithmetic, or on the drill lesson and its use.
4. Plan a demonstration lesson outline either on some topic in observational geography (4th grade), or on the teaching of Longfellow's poem "The Day is Done" (5th grade).
5. Make out a Visiting-Day Directions (Form 6 type) for a fifth grade teacher of two or three years' experience, but who lacks good working habits and is weak in lesson assignment and discipline.
6. A good capable older teacher asks for a visiting day, to which she is en-

HELPING THE TEACHER

titled. What kind of a form would you fill out for her, if any? What type of report would you expect?
7. Propose three additional simple teaching problems, similar in type to those on page 473.
8. Can you suggest another illustration of the diagnosis of a pupil-difficulty?
9. What magazines would you suggest that a building group provide?
10. Suggest three books that would be good for general teacher reading and discussion, and state on what basis you selected each book.
11. On the Form 7 chart score up, by a series of dots connected by a pencil line, a "does-enough-to-get-by" type of teacher — one who does fair average work rather by reason of a strong executive personality and a pleasant manner than because of professional interest or preparation, and who is weak in teaching technique.
12. What changes or additions would you propose in the teacher rating card given?

SELECTED REFERENCES

Aitchison, Alison E. "Helping Teachers in Service"; in *Elementary School Journal*, vol. 20, pp. 65–67. (September, 1919.)
Descriptive of effort to improve geography work at Cedar Falls, Iowa.

Bagley, W. C. "The Test of Efficiency in Supervision"; in his *Craftsmanship in Teaching*, Chapter IV.
A description of work by a supervisor.

Boyce, A. C. *Methods for Measuring Teachers' Efficiency. Fourteenth Yearbook of the National Society for the Study of Education*, Part II. 83 pp. 1915.
A discussion of the problem, and rating forms.

Burton, Wm. H. *Supervision and the Improvement of Teaching.* 450 pp., New York, 1922.
On the problems and procedure of supervision, and its aims.

Carrigan, Rose A. "The Rating of Temporary Teachers after a Single Supervisory Visit"; in *First Yearbook of the Department of Elementary School Principals, National Education Association*, 1922, pp. 19–24.
The problem, and a score card.

Cranor, Cath. T. "A Self-scoring Card for Supervisors as an Aid to Efficiency in School Work"; in *Educational Administration and Supervision*, vol. 7, pp. 91–102. (February, 1921.)

Davis, S. E. *The Technique of Teaching.* 346 pp., New York, 1922.
On the teaching of the different common school subjects.

Gist, A. S., and King, Wm. A. "The Efficiency of the Principalship from the Standpoint of the Teacher"; in *Elementary School Journal*, vol. 23, pp. 120–26. (October, 1922.)
Results of an inquiry made by two Seattle principals.

484 THE PRINCIPAL AND HIS SCHOOL

Hall, J. W. "Supervision of Beginning Teachers in Cincinnati"; in *Twelfth Yearbook of the National Society for the Study of Education*, Part I.
> Set of notes, taken by supervisors during visits to teachers, given in full.

Hill, C. W. "The Efficiency Rating of Teachers"; in *Elementary School Journal*, vol. 21, pp. 438–43. (February, 1921.)
> Review, correlation, results, good summary. Use tends to better evaluation of teachers, and decrease of teacher's distrust.

Johnston, Jos. H. "Scientific Supervision of Teaching"; in *School and Society*, vol. 5, pp. 181–89. (February 17, 1917.)
> A teacher-rating scale, and its use.

Jones, Olive M. "The Relation of the Principal to the Teacher, and Standards for Judging the Effectiveness of Teaching"; in *School and Society*, vol. 14, pp. 469–77. (November 26, 1921.)
> Describes the new New York teachers' handbook and rating plan.

McMurry, F. *Elementary School Standards.* 218 pp., Yonkers, 1913.
> On standards in instruction and in supervision, as determined by the New York City School Survey of 1911.

Nutt, H. W. *The Supervision of Instruction.* 275 pp., Boston, 1920.
> Section B deals with devices in supervision, and Section C with the technique of supervision.

Rugg, H. O. "Self-Improvement of Teachers through Self-Rating; A New Scale for Rating Teachers' Efficiency"; in *Elementary School Journal*, vol. 20, pp. 670–84. (May, 1920.)
> Very good; gives rating sheet.

Sears, J. B. "The Measurement of Teaching Efficiency"; in *Journal of Educational Research*, vol. 4, pp. 81–94. (September, 1921.)
> History of teacher-rating schemes; requirements of an effective teacher measurement; and bibliography of 55 titles.

Strayer, G. D., and Englehardt, N. L. *The Classroom Teacher.* New York, 1920.
> Chapter III a good brief statement of the teacher's work.

Terman, L. M., and others. *Intelligence Tests and School Reorganization.* 111 pp., Yonkers, 1922.
> Chapter VI, by Grace Fernald, is very good on the diagnosis of spelling difficulties.

Wagner, C. A. "Construction of a Teacher Rating Scale"; in *Elementary School Journal*, vol. 21, pp. 361–66. (January, 1921.)
> Criticizes Rugg's scale (*Ibid.*, May, 1920), and proposes an alternative and better scale.

Wagner, C. A. *Common Sense in School Supervision*, 201 pp., Milwaukee, 1922.
> A very helpful book on almost every phase of helping teachers through the supervision of instruction.

Wilson, G. M. "Locating the Language Errors of Children"; in *Elementary School Journal*, vol. 21, pp. 290–96. (December, 1920.)
> Tabulation of common mistakes as revealed by four recent school surveys. Good material for principals.

CHAPTER XXIV

MEASURING THE INSTRUCTION

New scientific tools. There is another type of objective data, more important than any we have so far considered, which will be of very positive help to a principal in determining the efficiency of the instruction in his school and of each teacher in it, and of which he should not fail to avail himself. This is the type of data given by the use of the recently evolved standard tests and measures for determining the efficiency of the instruction given. Up to the present time some three hundred of these tests have been evolved and more or less standardized, and more are in process of construction. Of this number at least twenty-five to thirty are of enough importance for the work of the elementary school that the principal should be thoroughly familiar with them, and know how to give them and score and interpret the results.

The use of these tests enables the principal to substitute measurable and standardized results for personal opinion, and provides him with a series of clear and incontestable records of the achievement of the pupils and teachers in his school. They give him a scientific and objective basis upon which to build his supervisory procedure and defend what he proposes to do. As an instrument of supervision they are indispensable. Of course, testing can never displace constructive, helpful criticism, but the results furnish a rational basis for such criticism without which the best of supervision is relatively ineffective. So important is this new method in education that a principal can no longer be considered prepared for his work unless he is familiar with the use of the standard tests and measures and with simple statistical procedure.

Uses of these new tools. From an examination of the statistical array or the charted results of such measurements, a principal can tell, almost at a glance, whether pupils or rooms are making proper progress; when any working-group has made all desirable progress and should advance; how well a working-group is suited to continue working together; whether instruction is being directed to what are the weak points; where teachers who are carrying a heavy load or need help are located, as well as in what particulars they need help; in what rooms the load and the teacher are not properly adjusted; and whether the teacher is getting out of the pupils as much as they are capable of doing.

In diagnosing pupil and teacher difficulties, in planning remedial procedure, in the classification and promotion of pupils, and in evaluating the efficiency of the instruction, the standard tests and measures are of large value to the principal in the supervision of the instruction in his school. No single tool developed within the past quarter-century has meant so much for the scientific organization and progress of school work as has the introduction of intelligence and educational measurements. Still more, no addition to our procedure has done so much to change the emphasis, in the work of the school principal, from the duties of organization and administration to those relating to the supervision of instruction. The coming of standardized tests has changed the character of the service principals must render, and the character of the preparation they need for the work they are to do. Their use has now become a matter of routine supervisory procedure in determining and evaluating the results of instruction in a school.

The so-called informal tests. The old type of subject examination has long been used to test the efficiency of the instruction in school systems. Often uniform questions, based on the subject-matter of the course of study, have been formulated at the superintendent's office and given, at stated times, to the school system as a whole, the papers being graded and the results tabulated at the central office. The purpose has been to determine the efficiency of the instruction in the different schools, though we now know that this method was crude and that the results were unreliable. Such testing on subject-matter still has its place, where the aim is to test the mastery of definite subject-matter content, but such tests are now clearly subordinate to a more scientific examining procedure.

The so-called informal school tests, many of which have been evolved and published, and which can be worked out rather easily by principals and teachers, represent a first step away from the old type of examination and in the direction of a more scientific procedure. They have been called "scientific tests in the making," though but few of them will ever be perfected and standardized. Such is not the intention in constructing them. They are, however, patterned after the standardized tests, and are so constructed that the method of giving and scoring them is approximately the same as for the standard tests. The object in preparing them is to secure an accurate objective measure of the achievement of the pupils in a particular room or grade in some one subject or part of a subject. They are constructed so that they may be scored objectively, and thus avoid the wide divergence in marking of results so common on the old type of examination paper. Their diagnostic value is somewhat similar to the so-called standard tests.

A few selected samples, taken from tests described by McCall, will illustrate the nature of three types of these tests.

Type I — The True-False test. (Selected samples.)
GEOGRAPHY. (Underscore the correct answer.)
1. In general the mountains run east and west .... True False
2. Most of the rivers flow north .... "   "
6. The Cascade Mountains are nearer the Pacific Ocean than the Rocky Mountains .... "   "
13. The Mississippi River flows into the Great Lakes.... "   "
20. The central portion of the United States is more level than the eastern or western part.................... "   "

Type II — The Comprehension test.
ARITHMETIC. (Read the problem, and then write answers to the questions. Re-read the problem, if necessary, but *do not work it.*)
(The problem stated here.)
1. Whose names are to be used in making out the bill?..............
2. How many items are to be included in the bill?..................
3. Between what hours was the plumber away from the shop?........
4. How much per hour was the plumber to receive?................
5. What does the problem ask you to do?.......................

Type III — The Knowledge test. (Selected samples.)
CIVICS. (Write in the answer-column (3) the number of the civic term (1) which corresponds to the descriptive term (2).)

(1) Civic term	(2) Descriptive term	(3) Answer
1. Direct primary	The movement of foreigners to America	No...
2. Initiative	Method of removing public officers by vote	No...
3. Tariff	Power given voters to get new laws	No...
6. Recall	Power given voters to remove officials	Yes..
10. Spoils system	Wise use of natural resources	No...

Such tests are based on the instruction outlined in the course of study or given from the textbooks used; they are an attempt to measure objectively the desirable outcomes of teaching; they are useful in the diagnosis of errors and in revealing points that need further emphasis; they can be used to direct and motivate the instruction; when prepared by the teachers the work is of value to them; they are useful in checking up that mastery of facts or ability to think closely which the school is trying to emphasize; and they may be used to supplement or prepare for the use of the standard tests. The ability to score accurately such tests constitutes one of their main advantages over the older type of examination.

Use of the standardized tests. The use of the informal tests, as has been stated, forms a good preparation for both pupils and teachers for the use of the standardized tests. These tests have the advantage of much more careful preparation, and they have been used long enough and in a large enough number of places to have become standardized as to results. For all the older and better tests in the fundamental subjects of the elementary school — arithmetic, reading, spelling, handwriting, and language — well-established scores or norms have been built up, so that the accomplishment of any grade in any school can be objectively measured and compared with the norm for such grade and work done in schools generally. Fairly satisfactory tests also are available for history and geography. The usefulness of the standardized tests in improving the effectiveness of instruction has been so frequently demonstrated that progressive teachers and principals to-day use them continually to check up and standardize the ordinary schoolroom procedure. The norms provide schools everywhere with standards of attainment, based on the performance of tens of thousands of children in schools all over the land.

The course of study for a school system can at best give but general directions as to what teachers are to do, and the directions are usually stated in terms of textbooks, subject-matter acquirements, or of types of training to be given. Certain definite information is to be imparted — to read, write, spell, cipher, think, compose, learn geographical and historical facts; certain types of instruction are indicated to be used — drill work, reasoning exercises, directed-study work, lessons in appreciation; and certain aims are set forth as important — civic training, moral education, and health habits. These, however, at best are quite general specifications, and the same work naturally is indicated to be done with and for all pupils. Even when a differentiated-type course of study is provided, the same work is indicated for each of the groups. Such general aims in the more formal drill subjects are insufficient, in that they are not specific enough to lead to the type of results desired. The use of the standard tests and an interpretation of the scores obtained call the attention of the teachers to other aspects of the work of instruction — the results secured rather than the subject-matter covered; the needs of the pupils rather than the contents of the textbooks; the needs of individual pupils as well as the needs of the class as a whole; and to specific items and skills in teaching rather than vague general aims.

Diagnostic value of the tests illustrated by handwriting. One of the chief outcomes from the use of the standard accomplishment tests is the ability, from an examination of the scores obtained, to diagnose difficulties and to prescribe remedial procedure. For example, the results of a hand-

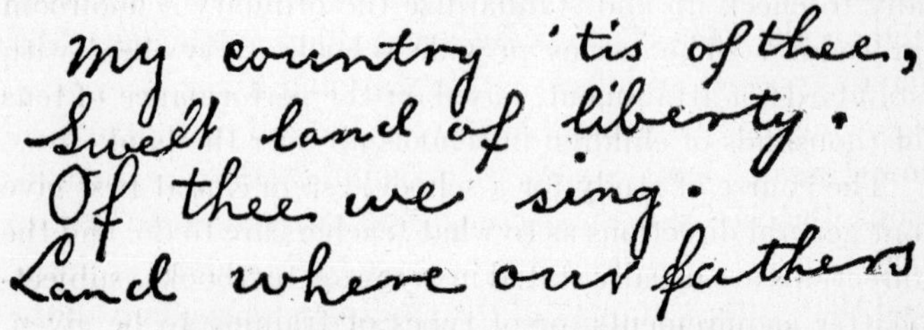

My country 'tis of thee,
Sweet land of liberty.
Of thee we sing.
Land where our fathers

FIGURE 25. A HANDWRITING SPECIMEN ANALYZED

The general quality of this 6B specimen is about average for the grade, but when analyzed into its elements the lines for future instruction are revealed. In size the letters are a little small; the letter formation is fair to good, but needs attention; the spacing throughout is good; the alignment of letters is fair, and of lines poor; the slant is variable and only fair; and the quality of the line is poor.

writing test may reveal undue perfection with too little speed, or too much speed coupled with low legibility. In either case the specimens can be analyzed as to size, letter form, spacing of letters and words and lines, alignment, slant, and quality of line, and individual remedial treatment can be indicated. This is well illustrated in the specimen of 6B handwriting reproduced in Figure 25 opposite, with the needed type of future instruction indicated beneath. Such intelligent diagnosis leads to handwriting instruction that is far superior to "just writing."

Diagnostic value illustrated by spelling. In somewhat the same way a spelling test, using standardized lists of

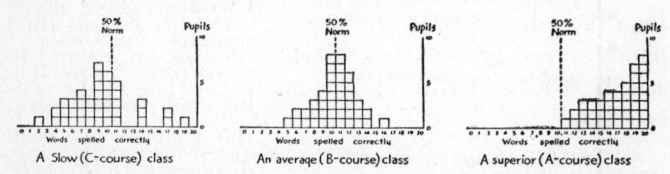

FIGURE 26. RESULTS OF A SPELLING TEST WITH THREE FIFTH-GRADE CLASSES

Based on words from the fifty per cent column of the Ashbaugh Iowa Spelling Scale. Three entirely different spelling situations are here shown.

words, may indicate much as to ability and needs of classes and pupils. The class averages may differ much, due to different types of situations. We may find a low class average, caused by a general low average of all or by the very low score of a few. Again, we may find good average conditions, the class as a whole doing good average work. Or we may find a class average much above the standard or norm, and that quite a number of the pupils (those spelling all the words of the test) were not tested at all. Figure 26, given above, reveals three such conditions in three fifth-grade classes, composed of different types of working groups.

Taking one of the three type situations there shown and analyzing it by individuals gives us Figure 27. This at once locates the poor and the good spellers of this group, as shown by the test. The next step is to diagnose the types of errors made by the individual pupils, and then to prescribe remedial procedure for the ones most in need of help. (See Form 8, page 493.) A fourth of this class, at least, probably needs spelling instruction by primary methods, while six of the pupils belong in quite another type of work. Still further, Figure 26 would indicate the need of somewhat different types of spelling instruction for the three classes. The C-course class needs primary methods — visualizing, pronouncing, and written work; the A-course class can dispense with this type of instruction entirely, shorten the spelling time, and do oral work. The B-course class may do best with a combination of both types of work.

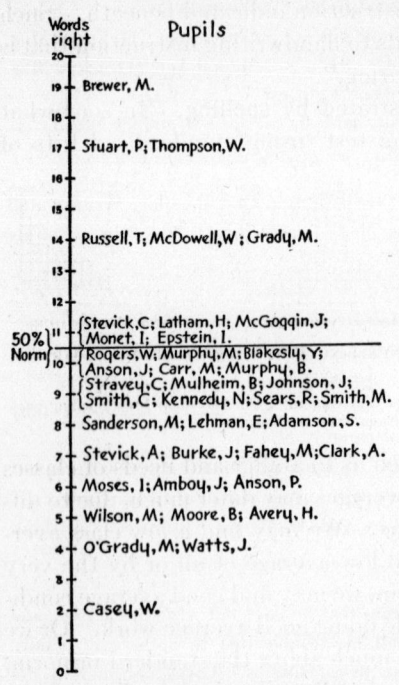

```
Words
right    Pupils
 20
 19  Brewer, M.
 18
 17  Stuart, P; Thompson, W.
 16
 15
 14  Russell, T; McDowell, W; Grady, M.
 13
 12
     {Stevick, C; Latham, H; McGoqqin, J;
50% 11  Monet, I; Epstein, I.
Norm    {Rogers, W; Murphy, M; Blakesly, Y;
     10  Anson, J; Carr, M; Murphy, B.
        {Stravey, C; Mulheim, B; Johnson, J;
      9  Smith, C; Kennedy, N; Sears, R; Smith, M.
      8  Sanderson, M; Lehman, E; Adamson, S.
      7  Stevick, A; Burke, J; Fahey, M; Clark, A.
      6  Moses, I; Amboy, J; Anson, P.
      5  Wilson, M; Moore, B; Avery, H.
      4  O'Grady, M; Watts, J.
      3
      2  Casey, W.
      1
      0
```

FIGURE 27. THE C-COURSE SPELLING CLASS ANALYZED

Each of the pupils listed as to words spelled correctly on the Fig. 26 Spelling Test.

Diagnostic value illustrated by reading. A reading test, similarly, may reveal varying conditions. A class may do very good oral reading, and yet be doing very little thought-getting. The pronunciation may be good, but the comprehension may be low. Again, both rate and comprehension in both oral and silent reading may be low or high. Still further there may be wide variations between different pupils in the same working group.

Figure 28 shows in table form the scores made by a sixth-grade class in silent reading, with the diagnosis. The score

MEASURING THE INSTRUCTION

[120—8-22—1M]
DIAGNOSTIC AND REMEDIAL PROCEDURE SHEET

To teacher of ..No. 2..Ungraded Room....Woodrow Wilson....School
Pupil...Max Eberhardt....Grade 6 B......Chron. Age..11 Yrs. 8 Mos.
Health ....Good ..........I.Q...94.......Mental Age..11 Yrs. 0 Mos.
Physical Defects.....Hearing poor, right ear........E.Q.....A.Q......
Type of Pupil.....Slow, serious, earnest...........Conduct..good....

Type of Special Help sent for: Drill work in Oral Reading, Writing, and Written Spelling. Needs coaching to enable him to keep abreast of his class.

Status of work:

Reading: Comprehension fair to good, rate good. Inaccurate in seeing and pronouncing words. Enunciation and attention to punctuation poor. A poor oral reader.

Writing: Irregular quality, alignment poor, letters often not fully formed, punctuation often omitted.

Spelling: Many inaccuracies. In some words omits whole syllable, but pronounces same as he spells. Poor visualization of words.

Other school work satisfactory; good in Mental Arithmetic; can think well.

Diagnosis:

Trouble thought to be largely that he does not visualize letters and words properly. Nearly all his trouble due to not seeing details. Sees in the mass and jumps to conclusions. Lacks accuracy in details.

Suggested Remedial Procedure:

Careful and accurate drill in pronunciation of words and syllables, and in expressive reading. Drill in letter formation, and accuracy in copying. Written spelling drills, from printed copy — not oral work.

Time sent for: Daily drill periods to be arranged; suggest two a day. Will recite with class otherwise.

Geraldine O'Grady....Teacher ....Kenneth Jackson...Principal.
Date..March 29/23 ......Room..15....Woodrow Wilson....School.

FORM 8. PUPIL DIAGNOSIS FOR TEACHER OF UNGRADED ROOM

indicates that the class is composed of careful readers, their comprehension score being but four points below the standard for the grade. Some emphasis in instruction should now be given to trying to improve the rate.

Use of tests to measure school progress. For arithmetic, language, geography, and history other scales have been constructed which indicate the progress of the instruction and the type of remedial procedure that may be called for.

Table 1 — Rate of Reading

SCORE IN WORDS PER MINUTE	NUMBER OF CHILDREN MAKING EACH SCORE
Over 400	
380	
360	
340	
320	1
300	
380	
360	
340	
320	
300	
280	
260	1
240	
220	1
200	4
180	7
160	4
140	3
120	6
100	
80	2
60	1
40	
20	
0	
Total	31
Median	176

Index of Comprehension

Diagnosis		Guesswork		Comprehension poor; additional training needed				Comprehension satisfactory	
Questions Answered	Total	Less than -5	-5 to +5	6-39	40-69	70-79	80-84	85-89	90-94	95-99	100
70											
65											
60											
55											
50											
45											
40	6							1		1	3	1
35	4						1				1	2
30	2						1	1				
25	4				1	1			1			1
20	11						2		4	1	3	1
15	4				1			1	2			
10											
5											
0											
Total	31				2	5	7	5		7	5

Median Number of Last Question Answered **25**   Median Index of Comprehension **91**

(Rate of work satisfactory / Diagnosis: Rate of Reading too slow. Additional training needed.)

FIGURE 28. SHOWING THE SCORES OF A SIXTH-GRADE CLASS ON THE COURTIS SILENT READING TEST, No. 2

This shows a fairly well-sorted class of thirty-one pupils whose comprehension is satisfactory, but whose rate of reading is too low. They are careful readers, but need attention to rate of work. (From Monroe's *Measuring the Results of Teaching*, p. 85.)

From the results obtained, which can be graphically and objectively set forth, principals and teachers are able to see conditions, diagnose difficulties, and prescribe types of pro-

MEASURING THE INSTRUCTION

cedure for a class as a whole or for individuals. Such work must inevitably lead to more effective instruction. As an example of the use that may be made of the results of the standard tests, we reproduced on the previous page a diagnosis and prescription for one pupil, sent to the teacher of an ungraded room for special help to enable

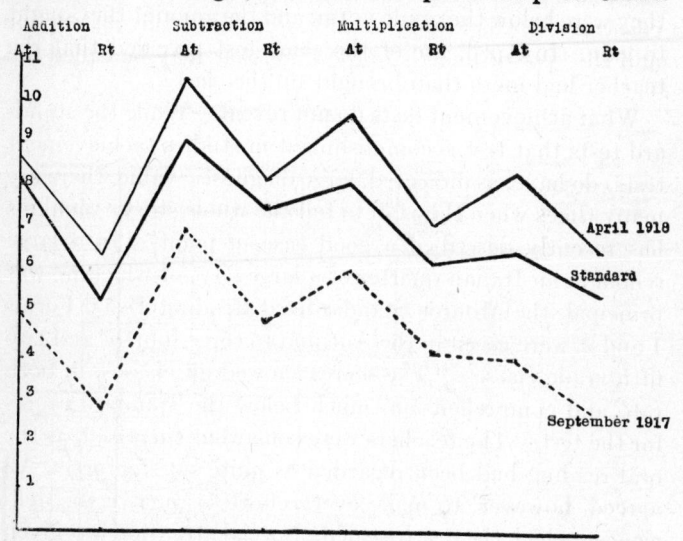

FIGURE 29. MEDIAN SCORES OF A SIXTH-GRADE CLASS IN SEPTEMBER, AND THE FOLLOWING APRIL, AS MEASURED BY THE COURTIS STANDARD RESEARCH TESTS IN ARITHMETIC, SERIES B.
(After Monroe.)

him to retain his place in his grade. Such information might be given orally to the special teacher, but is better written out on some such form as the one given.

The standard tests are also of use in revealing objectively to teachers and principals not only the status of an individual or a class at any particular time, but also the degree of progress made by a pupil or a class in any definite period of time. This use of the standard tests is well shown by Figure

29, which gives the status of a sixth-grade class in September, in the matter of both speed and accuracy in the four fundamental operations in arithmetic, and the results of seven months' work with this class by the teacher. By means of the tests the teacher knew definitely that the class entering her room in September was deficient, the amount they were below the grade norm, and the amount they ought to gain. In April, use of the same test revealed that the teacher had more than brought up the class.

What achievement tests do not reveal. While the standard tests that test accomplishment in studies (achievement tests) do have, as indicated, large diagnostic value, there are many times when they fail to tell the whole story. Jenkins has recently described a good case in point. In a large school in an Italian quarter of a large city, of which he was principal, the Monroe Standardized Reading Tests, Forms 1 and 2, were given in the Autumn to three fourth- and two fifth-grade classes. The scores showed all classes, in both rate and comprehension, much below the standard scores for the test. The teachers were somewhat surprised, as the oral reading had been regarded as quite satisfactory. All agreed, however, to make every effort to remove the deficiencies which the test revealed. Special attention was given to increasing both rate and comprehension. The work in silent reading was carefully motivated, daily drills for increasing rate were given, emphasis was placed on thought-getting, and the over-emphasis on oral reading was changed. A test later in the year showed that all grades had made good gains except one 5B class of forty-one pupils which still stood, despite all the teacher's labors, on about the same level as the 4B class in the same school. The teacher was a strong, energetic, and intelligent woman, interested in the problem, and capable of doing a high grade of work. After examining all the evidence, and the cumulative pupil-record cards, the conclusion was reached that this 5B class must be one of a lower mental level than the other classes. As Jenkins well says: "This, however, was only an opinion, and counted for but little in scientific education."

It is here that the intelligence test comes in to supplement the educational tests in determining the capacity of the pupils for learning. This test is an added scientific tool of the most fundamental importance in educational diagnosis. In view of the principal's estimate of the teacher, the above failure could hardly be attributed to poor instruction. From the results obtained from intelligence testing we now know that it is not safe to assume that poor teaching is the cause of the failure to make proper progress in their school work, either of pupils or of classes. Other factors enter into the problem which may be listed as follows:

1. *Success* may be due to:
    a. Superior intelligence, regardless of the teaching.
    b. Average intelligence and good teaching.
2. *Failure* may be due to:
    a. Average intelligence, and poor teaching.
    b. Low intelligence, regardless of the teaching.

It therefore follows that teachers can hardly be held accountable for the failure of pupils or classes to make normal progress until the intelligence level is known. Figure 26 illustrates well the differences in possibilities for instruction of three different classes of fifth-grade pupils, while Figure 22 shows still more clearly the impossibility of a teacher doing even average work with such a class. All our studies of pupil intelligence only emphasize the desirability of differentiating the instruction for different types of pupils, assigning different types of working groups to different teachers to handle, and then expecting quite different standards of accomplishment from the different groups.

On applying an intelligence test to the 5B class which

failed to make proper progress in the reading, it was found that the average mental age of the class was but eight years, eight months, or two years below normal, and that the average intelligence quotient (I.Q.) for the class was but 74. Grouping the pupils according to mental age the class was found to consist of:

Pupils		I.Q.
Feeble-minded	7	Below 60
Border-line cases	14	60–74
Dull and slow	10	75–84
Normal pupils	10	85–114.

A re-study of the achievements of the class, as shown by the reading tests, with their low mental age now taken into consideration, showed that the teacher had done excellent work rather than otherwise, the low mental age and the size of the class (41) considered. She had attempted the impossible, and had done as well as any teacher could have done.

Importance of the mental age (I.Q.). Such cases as the one just described bring forcibly to attention the desirability of finding some simple means of relating the two types of tests, and of being able to state the educational possibilities of a class or a pupil in some mathematical formula which will be readily intelligible. This we are now able to do.

In the beginning, both the accomplishment tests and the intelligence tests were developed separately, and for a time no attempt was made to establish any direct relationship between them. As the close relation of intelligence to school accomplishment was perceived, an effort was made to relate the two so as to be able to interpret achievement test scores in terms of mental rather than of chronological age. Stated another way, it was felt that the mental age, rather than the chronological age, should be taken as the basis of what a pupil should be able to do, whereas the school has in the past always based expectations on the chronological age. If the pupil's intelligence is 100, or approximately that, chronological age is a perfectly proper basis. If, however, the pupil has an intelligence quotient (I.Q.) of but 85 per cent of normal, or of 115 per cent of normal, the situation is quite different. A twelve-year-old pupil with an I.Q. of 85 would be, mentally, but ten years and two plus months old, and normally should be in 5B grade instead of finishing 6A. Similarly, a twelve-year-old pupil with an I.Q. of 115 would be, mentally, thirteen years and nine months old, and ought to be doing 8A work. The mental age of a pupil is thus seen to be a better basis for the grade classification of pupils than is the chronological age, and the giving of a mental test to all school pupils, as was pointed out in Chapter XIX, is seen to be a desirable routine procedure.

New achievement norms. Further study, however, revealed that even mental age was not wholly dependable as a basis for classification, as some children did better school work, as measured by the tests, than their mental age would indicate, and others did not do so well. This is readily understood if we remember that the test norms have been derived from results with tens of thousands of children, in many different cities and in different types of schools. Interest in the work, perseverance, seriousness of purpose, laziness, inattention, and good and poor instruction, have all come in as modifying factors. To express a pupil's accomplishment in terms of the standard scores for each of the tests, arranged as they have been on all kinds of numerical scales, would be unintelligible to any one but a professional. What was desired then was a simple decimal figure, analogous to the I.Q., by means of which both the actual educational accomplishments of a pupil and his possibilities of accomplishment could both be expressed by a figure that was based, as is the I.Q., on 100 as normal.

The first step was to develop age-score norms for the different test norms, so that any score made on a test could be at once translated, from prepared tables, from a test norm to an age norm, as, for example:

Test score	4.36 =	10 years,	0	months	age-score	
" "	4.74 =	10 "	6	"	" "	
" "	5.86 =	11 "	0	"	" "	
" "	6.13 =	11 "	6	"	" "	

The next step was to develop a "battery of tests," of both intelligence and accomplishment, which when combined would give a measure of the pupil's educational achievement. This has been done in "The Illinois Examination." Other somewhat similar combinations of tests have been formed for a similar purpose, and described, one of the latest being the new "Stanford Achievement Tests," devised by Kelley, Ruch, and Terman.

As a result of the studies which have been made we now have three indices of good reliability, by means of which we may now express the educational possibilities and determine the educational accomplishments of a pupil or a class, as well as the skill in instruction of the teacher teaching the class. The first of these is the Intelligence Quotient (I.Q.), by which we mean the percentage a pupil's mental age is of his chronological age. The second is the Educational Quotient (E.Q.), by which we mean the properly-weighted arithmetic mean of the age-scores made by the pupil on the different tests constituting the "battery" used. The third is the Achievement (or Accomplishment) Quotient (A.Q.), by which we mean what the child actually accomplishes, compared with what his mental age would indicate him as capable of accomplishing.

For example, suppose a boy in a 6A grade is 10 years, 10 months old, chronologically, but by an intelligence test he is found to be 13 years, 0 months old, mentally. His I.Q. then

$$\left(\frac{\text{Mental Age}}{\text{Chronological Age}} = \text{I.Q.}\right)$$

is

$$\frac{13-0}{10-10} = 120$$

and he presumably ought to be at least a year further along. On a properly weighted arithmetic mean of the different accomplishment tests used (battery), his work (age-score) is found to average up to that of a pupil 11 years, 4 months old. His E.Q. then

$$\left(\frac{\text{Mean Age Score}}{\text{Chronological Age}} = \text{E.Q.}\right)$$

is

$$\frac{11-4}{10-10} = 105+$$

His A.Q., then, which is the ratio of what he does to what his mental age would indicate him as able to do

$$\left(\frac{\text{Mean Age Score}}{\text{Mental Age}} = \text{A.Q.}\right)$$

is

$$\frac{11-4}{13-0} = 89+.$$

We now know his educational possibilities, and how hard he works. While his Intelligence Quotient (120) shows him to be able to do much better work than children of his age, and his Educational Quotient (105 +) shows that he does, his Achievement Quotient (89 +) shows that he is after all working to only

$$\frac{89+}{105+} = 84\tfrac{3}{4} \text{ per cent}$$

of his capacity to do. If this pupil is well and strong he ought to be put ahead in another grade, shifted to a maximum-work section, or given more work to do to bring his accomplishment nearer to his capacity. He is learning to loaf at his work in his present place. The A.Q. is the measure that tells the real story.

Importance of the Achievement Quotient. Suppose we now apply the above to a concrete case, by going back to the C-course fifth-grade class of Figure 26, page 491, whose work in spelling was analyzed by individuals in Figure 27, page 492, and take three cases from each end of the Figure 27 display and three from the middle, and list them in a table which may be assumed to represent the scores and the ability of each. We then get the following table:

TABLE X. SHOWING THE WORKING CAPACITY OF NINE 5TH GRADE PUPILS

Pupil	Chron. Age	Mental Age	Weighted Mean of 8 Tests, in Age-Scores	I.Q.	E.Q.	A.Q.
Brewer, Marion...	10– 8	10–0	10– 0	93	94	100
Stuart, Paul......	10– 6	10–0	10– 6	96	100	105
Thompson, Wm...	10– 5	10–1	10– 8	97	102	106
Monet, Irene.....	11– 6	10–2	10– 0	88	87	98
Epstein, Isadore..	11– 7	9–8	9– 4	84	80	97
Rogers, Walter...	10–10	9–0	9– 0	83	76	100
O'Grady, Michael	11– 6	9–3	9– 0	82	79	97
Watts, Jack......	11–10	9–4	8–10	78	75	94
Casey, Willie.....	13– 1	9–7	9– 2	73	70	96

The last column gives the important item, the A.Q. If the nine pupils selected are a fair sample of the whole class, it must at once be recognized that a very capable teacher is in charge of this C-course class, as she is getting capacity work from a class of very ordinary pupils.

It is evident that the Achievement Quotient is the only measure that fully takes into account the actual material with which the teacher works. For the teacher of a slow and backward class it is the only measure which fairly interprets her efforts and accomplishments. An inspection of the above table shows at once that the chronological age would be no measure, the range for fifth grade (see Table VIII, page 341) being 9–9 to 11–3 years. The I.Q.'s would be but little more reliable as an index, except that they would reveal the character of the group and that Casey, at least, ought to be removed to a border-line class. The mean age-scores would be better, but even these are not wholly indicative. The E.Q.'s reveal the possibilities for doing work, and the A.Q.'s tell what percentage of their possibilities for accomplishment the teacher is getting out of them. The low scores on the accomplishment test in spelling (Figure 26) now appear much better when compared with the capacity of the class. The same method applied to the A-course class shown in Figure 26, or to any class of bright pupils, might reveal that after all their rapid progress was no special credit to the teacher. The A.Q. of this 5A class might all be under 100, while the mean age-scores might show that the class ought to be doing sixth grade work instead of fifth.

The principal and educational measurement. In time our schools will come to have pupil records which will show, for each pupil, his standing and accomplishments at various dates, and battery tests will be used to determine periodically the progress of the pupils and the efficiency of the instruction in each class in the school. We may expect before long, too, that teachers will be supplied with such information regarding each pupil who comes to them to be taught, and that they will be expected by supervisory officers to get results according to the material they receive with which to work. A class of low intelligence capacity, or a class that has been poorly taught for a year or two before, will have such facts revealed on the records, while teachers who receive alert and well-taught classes will be expected to keep them up in accomplishment.

This new type of supervisory work will call for an entirely new type of preparation on the part of the principal, and somewhat on the part of the teachers. It will also call for the addition of an entirely new type of classroom supervision from that which principals have heretofore given. Just at present cities are trying to do this new work by creating "Efficiency Departments" and "Bureaus of Research," but the work is too large and too important to be handled long by such centralized methods, and soon we may expect that principals will be called upon to be familiar with educational and intelligence tests and statistical procedure, know how to give such tests and score the results, know how to interpret the scores and diagnose from them, and be able quickly, from prepared tables, to calculate I.Q.'s, E.Q.'s, and A.Q.'s. Teachers, too, may soon be expected to be somewhat more generally familiar with the nature of a few of the more important tests, and also sufficiently acquainted with the more important terms used to know their meaning when applied to their work. In tests and measures and scores and quotients and statistical procedure we have new tools of such large importance for education that the school will be forced to use them. To be able to evaluate the instruction by means of these will become one of the essential tests as to the competence of both principals and supervisors.

In time, too, new items will be added to the teacher rating sheets (Form 7, page 481) which principals will be asked to fill out relating to their teachers, and which will call for ratings based on the character of the class, and how much the teacher accomplishes considering the material given her. With such objective data a principal, against whose rating a teacher has appealed, will not feel as now that he has been placed on trial and lacks evidence for his defense.

All this new work is far larger and more important than the use of new symbols, the accumulation of tables, and the making of graphs. These are only the means to an end. This new work means the introduction of scientific management into the work of school supervision, and the direction of the activities of the school upon the basis of the best procedure known. It aims to measure as accurately as possible the actual results of teaching, as well as to pass on the methods used. Instead of debating whether or not a procedure is in accordance with a psychological principle, it goes directly at the results of the work with flesh and blood children. While there are, no doubt, intangible values in teaching, and especially in the personal influence of teachers on children which can be measured only in the lives of the pupils, inaccuracy in procedure because the school is not really aware of what needs doing cannot be excused on this ground. Most of the influence of a teacher is exerted through means which are perfectly tangible and which may be appraised in quantitative terms.

Teachers' marks and report cards. It may be expected that in time the influence of these important new tools may extend over to the marking of pupils and to the monthly and semi-monthly report card sent home to parents. An examination of many report cards in use shows that a report is usually made on each subject studied, the times tardy and the days absent are given, and then some kind of grade is commonly added on some one or more of such items as "interest," "effort," "attitude toward work," or "progress." The grading of the work in the school subjects is quite variable, and often without much of a standard. The personal opinion of the teacher or the results of an old-type examination form the usual basis for the marks, and not infrequently the basis for grading is wholly subjective. Teachers have been known to refuse to promote pupils because of poor deportment, or "because they do not deserve it" — that is because they had been disagreeable or offensive to the teacher or had not studied as hard as the teacher thought they should. Such considerations should have nothing to do with promotions, and leave the marks charged with subjective influences of which parents and pupils quite properly complain. It is a temperamental rating not supported by any objective evidence.

Even under ordinary grade-school conditions, with a uniform course of study, a principal can gradually introduce system and plan into the school marks by examining the pupil report cards, preferably at the teacher's desk in the rooms, before they are sent home to the parents. So meaningless are the reports at times that some principals would do away with them entirely, and send no reports home except when the pupil is falling behind. The pupil comparison, envy, excitement, charges of unfairness, discouragement, destruction of the reports, and forging of signatures represent the bad side of the monthly report card. Still, parents expect them and like to see them, and will blame the school when anything is unsatisfactory if they are not notified.

To use the standard test scores, or the translated age-scores would be meaningless, as would E.Q., A.Q., or any similar technical terms. It is possible, though, that a more standardized grading plan may in time be formulated that will take into account educational capacity and the ratio of actual accomplishment, rather than the comparison of a pupil's work with the teacher's idea of perfection. It will then be possible to develop a more scientific procedure in deciding upon the usual school marks to be sent home, and also in determining what kind of mark to give such desirable general terms as "effort," "progress," and "accomplishment." In formulating such new school grading and report-card standards and terms, the new scientific procedure in measuring instruction will of necessity play an important part.

Vocational guidance uses. There is another field in

which the new scientific measures as to intelligence and educational capacity are likely to become of increasing importance, even in the elementary school, and that is in advising young people as to possible life careers. The first main task of the elementary school in this direction is to make the school so attractive and so vital that pupils will remain in it until they have finished its work. There is no work worth while out in the world into which uneducated boys and girls can go. Only very limited "blind alley" work is open to them, and by twenty or soon after they see — then too late — the impossibility of getting ahead and amounting to much.

To hold pupils in school long enough to give them some educational equipment for life's work is a first essential. All the labors of a principal and his teachers in looking after the school attendance, making the school attractive, improving the physical welfare of the pupils, exercising good control, making the school work vital and strongly motivating it, and in building up a strong school spirit are steps in this direction. In the upper grammar grades or junior high school years much should be done to bring the pupils, through readings, discussions, vocational studies, and opportunities to try one's hand in vocational work, into some real contact with the industrial activity of the community about them. The manual and domestic instruction given, the visits to industries, the study of trade and transportation, and similar work offer good opportunities to set pupils to thinking along lines of their possible future life work.

While all this work of opening up vistas of opportunity is important and should not be neglected, nevertheless it must be recognized that the degree of intelligence a pupil possesses must after all limit his or her possibilities for usefulness in life. While a low I.Q. will not determine tastes and aptitudes or indicate the particular kind of life service in which a pupil can best succeed, it will, however, limit the level of the type of occupations in which that pupil can profitably engage. Conversely, the higher the I.Q. the more opportunities there will be open to a boy or girl, and the more they can be encouraged to stay in school and increase their preparation for life's work.

Intelligence requirements of the vocations. We are as yet in the mere beginnings of the study of vocational guidance by means of intelligence and aptitude tests, though the broad outlines of the field have been worked out. The preliminary studies by Terman and his students as to the I.Q.'s of certain groups of workers disclose an ascending level, by types of occupations, approximately as follows:

Groups	I.Q.'s
Professional classes	100–125 and up
College students	100–125 " "
Department store buyers	100–110 " "
Business men	95–110 " "
Railroad engineers	95–100 " "
Skilled labor	85–100 " "
Express Company employees	85– 95 " "
Motormen and conductors	80– 90 " "
Firemen and policemen	75– 90 " "
Barbers	75– 85 " "
Semi-skilled labor	75– 85 " "
Salesgirls	75– 85 " "
Unskilled labor	65– 75 " "

Other studies by other workers have confirmed the existence of such an ascending scale. Interpreting the figures, in terms of pupils, it would mean that many of those of the low I.Q.'s ought to be directed toward vocational courses and work, and that some differentiation in the school work ought to be provided in the junior high school years. Emphasis should be given in the case of the "finger-minded" pupils to their shop work, to nature study and agricultural instruction, and along the lines of the domestic arts. It is almost useless for a boy or girl with an I.Q. of 75 to try to go to the high school, or for a boy of 80 to 85 to expect to go to college. Certain occupations, too, do not call for large intelligence. An I.Q. of over 85 is probably wasted intelligence in a barber, street car conductor, or teamster, and 95 and over on a carpenter, plumber, or office clerk. On the other hand, studies of children's aspirations have shown the importance of directing many away from the learned professions and the white-collar employments. If all the children who in the elementary school think that they want to become lawyers and doctors and bank clerks were to do so, the present over-supply in these lines would be increased many times.

While the main place for vocational guidance studies will always be in the high school, and the elementary school must always largely concern itself with holding the pupils in school and teaching them the fundamental tools and the minimum essentials needed for life's work, the opportunities of the upper grammar grades for starting thinking and directing effort along vocational lines ought not to be neglected. As recent studies have shown, we are after all largely a nation of sixth-graders, and much of what the school can do along lines of vocational guidance must be done in the elementary school if it is to be done at all. In this work of guiding aptitudes and shaping ambitions and advising parents the results of the new intelligence and accomplishment tests are likely to play a rapidly increasing part.

QUESTIONS AND PROBLEMS

1. Construct an informal test of ten questions, of the Type III kind, for the geography of the United States.
2. Take any sample of handwriting available and diagnose its defects and indicate points to be looked after in future teaching.

3. Make up a diagnostic and remedial-procedure sheet for a good pupil needing special help to enable him to make a special promotion.
4. What new light do the studies of this chapter throw, for you; (a) On the problem of pupil progress — promotions, retardation, differentiated courses, and the proper basis for pupil advancement? (b) On the problem of teacher rating by supervisory authorities? (c) On the supervision of instruction by a principal?
5. Suppose you are superintendent of schools of a city and you find that your principals are unfamiliar with tests, scores, and testing procedure. Also that your board has no objection to the introduction of such work and will give you some money for it, but you can proceed only slowly. Outline a five-year program, showing what you would expect to do, and how you would proceed.
6. Suppose that you became principal of a school and found that pupil grades and report marks were based on highly subjective estimates, and that there was no scientific basis for the marks given or for their relative distribution. Suppose also that your teachers were willing to adopt a better plan, and that you submit the best plan that it is feasible to use in the school. What plan would you submit?
7. Point out the advantages of the platoon-type school in the matter of trying out pupil capacity and helping direct aptitudes for the vocational adjustments of life.

SELECTED REFERENCES

Brooks, S. S. *Improving Schools by Standardized Tests.* 278 pp. Boston, 1922.
   A very practical and concrete book on the use of tests in school supervision, with particular reference to town and rural schools.

Butler, W. F. "The Value of Informal Tests"; in *First Yearbook of the Department of Elementary School Principals, National Education Association,* 1922, pp. 94–119.
   Gives sample of informal tests that have been found helpful in diagnosis.

Courtis, S. A. "Educational Diagnosis"; in *Administration and Supervision,* vol. 1, pp. 89–116. (February, 1915.)
   Particularly good on advantage of definiteness.

Courtis, S. A. "Objective Standards as Means of Controlling Instruction and Economizing Time"; in *School and Society,* vol. 1, pp. 433–36. (March 27, 1915.)

Courtis, S. A. "Measuring the Efficiency of Supervision in Geography"; in *School and Society,* vol. 10, pp. 61–70. (July 19, 1919.)

Gray, W. S. "Use of Tests in Improving Instruction"; in *Elementary School Journal,* vol. 19, pp. 121–42. (October, 1918.)

Gray, W. S. "Value of Informal Tests of Reading Accomplishment"; in *Journal Educational Research,* vol. 1, pp. 103–11. (February, 1920.)
   Tells how to make such tests based on reading done.

Haggerty, M. E. "Measurement and Diagnosis as Aids to Supervision"; in *School and Society*, vol. 6, pp. 271–85. (September 8, 1917.)
: On language and composition. Illustrations and curves to show learning results.

Haggerty, M. E. "The Use of Educational Measurements"; in *School and Society*, vol. 4, pp. 761–72.
: An address to a body of school superintendents on use and value of objective tests. Good.

Hines, H. C. *A Guide to Educational Measurements.* Boston, 1923.
: A valuable guide to the best tests to use for each purpose, where to get them, how to use them, and their value.

Jenkins, A. U. "The Measurement of Teaching Efficiency by Means of Standardized Intelligence and Educational Tests"; in *First Yearbook of the Department of Elementary School Principals, National Education Association*, 1922, pp. 25–34.
: A very good article illustrating the use of combined tests to determine efficiency.

Judd, Chas. H. *Measuring the Work of the Public Schools.* 290 pp., Cleveland, 1915.
: One of the reports of the Cleveland Education Survey, made in 1916. Describes results found in the schools by the use of tests. An important volume, well illustrated, showing the use of standard tests in determining the efficiency of instruction in a school system.

Kelley, T. L., Ruch, G. M., and Terman, L. M. *The Stanford Achievement Tests.* Yonkers, 1923.
: A battery of primary tests in arithmetic, reading, and spelling, for grades 2 and 3, and advanced tests in arithmetic, reading, spelling, history, and literature for grades 4 to 8.

Leavitt, F. M., and Brown, E. *Pre-vocational Education in the Public Schools.* 245 pp., Boston, 1915.
: The education of children, and technical education.

McCall, W. A. "A New Kind of School Examination"; in *Journal of Educational Research*, vol. 1, pp. 33–46. (June, 1920.)
: Examination by informal tests. Gives many illustrations of.

McCall, W. A. *How to Measure in Education.* New York, 1922.
: The construction and standardization of tests; the technique of measurement procedure; and how to display results.

Monroe, W. S., DeVoss, J. C., and Kelly, F. J. *Educational Tests and Measurements.* 309 pp., Boston, 1917.
: An old standard text, now being revised, on the use of the standard tests for educational diagnosis. A valuable book for the principal.

Monroe, W. S. *Measuring the Results of Teaching.* 297 pp., Boston, 1918.
: Written more with the needs of the teacher in mind, but valuable for the principal as well.

Monroe, W. S. *Introduction to the Theory of Educational Measurements.* Boston, 1923.
: A very important volume on the construction and use of tests, their usefulness in school supervision, and the statistical interpretation of the results. A book the principal ought to master.

Monroe, W. S. *The Illinois Examination.* 70 pp. Bureau of Educational Research, Bulletin No. 6, University of Illinois, 1921.
> A description of this "battery of tests," with the results obtained from its use. A very important document.

Power, L. "The Principal, and Methods of Ranking Pupils"; in *Elementary School Journal*, vol. 20, pp. 285–91. (December, 1919.)
> Good statements on the dangers involved in the variability of grading standards on the report card.

Pressey, S. L., and L. C. *An Introduction to the Use of Standard Tests.* Yonkers, 1922.
> Types of tests, how to use them, and a testing program.

Saam, Theo. "Intelligence Testing as an Aid to Supervision"; in *Elementary School Journal*, vol. 20, pp. 26–32. (September, 1919.)
> Results of and conclusions from testing 2360 children in Council Bluffs.

School Surveys. In any of the recent School Surveys, such as the Salt Lake City, Grand Rapids, St. Louis, or the Boise Surveys, chapters will be found on the Measurement of the Instruction which will reveal the uses of the standard tests in evaluating the instruction. See also Judd's volume in the Cleveland Survey Reports.

Schultz, Fr. "Vocational Guidance in the Junior High School"; in *Educational Review*, vol. 63, pp. 238–46. (March, 1922.)
> Outline of a program by a junior high school principal at Erie, Pennsylvania.

Stebbins, Rona C. "The Accomplishment Quotient as a Means of Classification in the Lower Grades"; in *First Yearbook of the Department of Elementary School Principals, National Education Association*, 1922, pp. 34–44.
> A very good article on the usefulness of this measure in school supervision.

Terman, L. M. *The Intelligence of School Children.* 317 pp., Boston, 1919.
> Chapter 12 a good brief statement on the use of intelligence tests in vocational and educational guidance.

Terman, L. M., and others. *Intelligence Tests and School Reorganization.* 111 pp., Yonkers, 1922.
> Chapter 4, by R. H. Franzen, shows how to combine the results of mental and educational tests, especially as they relate to reading, language, and arithmetic.

Weeks, Ruth M. *The People's School.* 208 pp., Boston, 1912.
> Very good reading in connection with the vocational guidance of elementary-school pupils.

Woody, C. "Informal Tests as a Means for the Improvement of Instruction"; in *First Yearbook of the Department of Elementary School Principals, National Education Association*, 1922, pp. 87–94.
> Lists a series of informal tests.

Zirbes, Laura. "Diagnostic Measurement as a Basis for Procedure"; in *Elementary School Journal*, vol. 18, pp. 505–22. (March, 1918.)
> Description of an experiment in reading made by a second-grade teacher. An excellent illustration of use of objective tests in diagnosis with respect to pupil achievement.

CHAPTER XXV

MAKING TEACHERS' MEETINGS PROFITABLE

The teachers' view. In the estimation of the teachers concerned the after-school meetings held by principals vary all the way from a bore and a necessary evil to an invaluable privilege. With educational work changing and expanding as it is with us the teachers' meeting is a necessary feature in the administration of a school or a school system, yet in many schools the teachers' meetings are the most disliked of all school duties. The additional hour or more added to the working day, the lack of any vital import of what is frequently presented, and their usual unprofitable character are sufficient explanations for the very prevalent attitude. The principal who can get along with the fewest teachers' meetings, and who can make the ones he does hold short, usually is most approved of by the teachers. Yet the teachers' meeting, if properly handled, can be made a vital force in welding a group of teachers together, maintaining unity of purpose in a school, and building up professional ambition and spirit. It is too valuable an instrument to be neglected, and the quite common objection to giving time to it must rest on its improper handling by many principals.

Because of the objections so generally made many principals do not hold any teachers' meetings of a professional type, such meetings as are held being routine in character and of very brief duration. Others hold them as infrequently as the rules will permit. The writer has been acquainted with school systems where building teachers' meetings of a professional type were entirely unknown.

Reasons for this attitude. The reasons for this rather common attitude toward what conceivably could be made of large value to the teachers themselves lie in the character of the meetings commonly held.

Called at the fag end of the day, when tired nervous systems are demanding rest and relaxation, seldom beginning on time, lacking in plan or help or inspiration, unnecessarily protracted, the discussion often monopolized by a few, and usually getting nowhere, it is not surprising that teachers begrudge the time they take and look upon them as an unnecessary waste of energy.

Objectionable types of meetings. There are several types of teachers' meetings that will almost certainly produce this result, and it may be well to enumerate here a few of the more common of the objectionable types.

1. The bulletin-board type. This type is that in which the principal calls his teachers together in meetings to tell them what he ought to inform them of by means of a bulletin board, personal notices, or a daily or weekly bulletin placed on their desks. Often three fourths of the time of a meeting is taken up with reading notices, calling attention to reports that will be due, giving out statistical information, and explaining matters of a purely routine nature. If a teachers' meeting is to be made profitable, very little time should be taken up with such matters. It is not surprising that teachers object to staying to have read to them what they frequently already know, and if not should be informed of by some better method.

2. The grievance-day type. In these the time is taken up by the teachers in presenting their various grievances, and having them considered. The teachers keep a record of their troubles, trials, and tribulations, and unload them, often from recorded notes, at the teachers' meetings. Some teachers have few or none to unload; other teachers always have a plentiful supply. A half-dozen teachers consume the hour, the teachers leave the meeting dispirited and more fatigued than when they entered it, little or nothing of any consequence is decided upon, and the help teachers have a right to expect is not forthcoming. All such matters should be settled as they occur, and between the parties concerned. It is bad policy to start teachers to recording their grievances. Put the emphasis on the other side.

3. The grumbling type. In these the principal utilizes the meetings as an opportunity to find fault with what he has seen in the classrooms, on the grounds, and about the building. Some principals attempt to do their supervision of instruction in this manner, in an effort to avoid dealing directly and individually with teachers. Criticisms are made in general, to be applied by those whom they fit. Sometimes the occasion is used by the principal to "bawl out" some one without naming the person. It is a fundamental mistake to scold a body of teachers for the shortcomings of a few. Sometimes the teachers, trained by this kind of procedure, take the bit themselves and complain of existing conditions and requirements. This type of meeting soon promotes mutual dislike, distrust, and disloyalty to those in authority, and effectively destroys that *esprit de corps* and professional spirit which should animate a body of teachers.

4. The lecture-by-the-principal type. In this type the principal dominates the meeting and gives a professional lecture to the teachers. What he gives them may be good in itself without being useful. There will be times when a principal may properly take most of the time to present something that is vital to the work of the school, but after doing so he should leave some time for questions or discussion by the teachers. The principal who continually tries to "carry the ball" will find that the teachers soon lose interest in the game.

5. The routine-business type. Some principals devote their teachers' meetings entirely or almost entirely to pupil cases, formulating regulations, and other types of routine school business. This type of meeting is usually more acceptable than the other types mentioned because the teachers now have an opportunity to participate in the discussion and help in formulating the regulations for the school. Some principals find so many matters to bring before the routine type of meeting for discussion and decision that they excuse themselves from planning any more serious or more profitable work.

Certain routine business is likely to need attention by the teachers as a group, but to devote whole meetings, unless quite short ones, to routine matters is not profitable. If routine matters need consideration at a regular after-school teachers' meeting, bring them up first, handle them expeditiously, get at a decision quickly, and then proceed to more important business. Some principals hold two types of teachers' meetings — one a short one of ten to fifteen minutes, meeting at or just after the lunch hour and for routine matters only, and the other an after-school meeting for professional purposes.

It is not to be wondered that busy, hard-working, and sincere teachers look upon most of such meetings as an imposition and a waste of time. Thinking, well-educated teachers have a right to expect more from the leadership of a principal when he detains them for a teachers' meeting.

Responsibility of a principal. If a principal finds that a majority of his teachers have concluded that his teachers' meetings are uninteresting and unprofitable, he should seriously examine himself to see if he is not to blame. After all, a principal stands in much the same relation to his teachers that the teachers do to the children. When the work presented to the children fails to make an appeal the principal places the responsibility on the teacher or the course of study, rather than on the children. Do not the same principles apply to the teachers' meetings? That these meetings can be made a potent force in awakening and stimulating professional interest has been demonstrated too often to be gainsaid.

The principal should use his every endeavor to make his teachers' meetings live, interesting, and profitable. In a general way they should aim to develop and strengthen a spirit of unity, loyalty, and ambition among the teachers; they should contribute to the professional growth of the teachers, both in theory and in practice; and they should serve the principal as one of a number of means of effective supervision of his corps. Most teachers are, after all is said, anxious to grow, and it is the chief duty of the principal to stimulate them and help them to do so. The building teachers' meeting, rightly handled, is one means to this end.

There are few tests of the real qualities of professional leadership of a principal quite so exacting as the test of his ability to make his regular building teachers' meetings of interest and real professional value to his teachers. To do so calls for sound professional training and knowledge, some insight into human nature, genuine professional enthusiasm, and some administrative skill. If the principal can succeed in making his meetings of large professional value, and can stand out as the teacher and leader and master-mind of his group, he has an asset that will stand him in good stead and win for him the professional support of his teachers as almost nothing else will do. Far too many principals fail to realize the large possibilities they have for making good teachers into better ones, and that the greater part of the teacher's professional growth comes after she begins work as a teacher.

Types, time, frequency, and method. There are two types of teachers' meetings that a principal will probably want to hold — (1) short ones for matters of school business, and (2) longer ones for professional purposes. It is a good plan to keep the two types of meeting separate. The best time for the routine business meeting is at the noon hour, and the time limit for such meetings should be fifteen to twenty minutes. If the teachers lunch together, immediately after lunch is the time to hold such meetings, and they should be as informal and business should be expedited as rapidly as can be done. Such meetings might be held once a week, on a fixed day, or more often at times, if there seemed a necessity for so doing.

The other type of teachers' meeting, for professional purposes, should be longer, and is best held after school on a fixed afternoon. Some principals hold these professional meetings as frequently as once a week, others twice a month, some once a month, and some only occasionally on call. Unless there are rules to the contrary, the number held should be no more than can be made profitable and helpful. On the other hand they should be frequent enough to enable a principal to carry through a definite plan or campaign and accomplish something during the year. Remembering that teachers have other meetings to attend — grade meetings, special supervisors, superintendent's general, parent-teacher, and personal organizations — once in two weeks is perhaps the most desirable frequency.

As to time, hold the meetings early in the week, before the teachers get tired and "nerves" get on edge. The day and time might well be fixed, after consideration with the teachers at the beginning of the year, though Monday and Tuesday are perhaps the best days, and ten to fifteen minutes after school closes the best time. In some schools all pupils are dismissed a half hour early on teachers' meeting days, but it is doubtful if the cutting down of the school hours can be justified for a building teachers' meeting. As in the business world, teachers must be expected to take some little time to familiarize themselves with the best procedure in the business in which they are engaged, and to improve their qualifications as salesmen. Once the day is fixed it ought to be adhered to, so that teachers may know when to expect the meetings and may make their plans accordingly. As to place, hold it in the most comfortable room in the building. If the teachers can gather around a common table, it generally promotes discussion.

As the teachers are tired, it is not only restful but puts every one in a better humor if ten to fifteen minutes at the beginning are taken for social purposes, over a cup of tea with sandwiches or cakes. Such a "psychology tea" relaxes the strain of the day, promotes good feeling, and gives fresh vigor for thinking during the following hour. The principal could well afford to begin this at his own expense. Committees to handle the refreshments can easily be appointed, and the teachers will soon offer to share the cost.

The formal meeting can then begin by 3.20 to 3.25, and should close at the end of an hour. It is important that the meeting start promptly, know how and where it is going, and stop when it is finished. Conduct it as though it were a business proposition. You have a definite piece of work to do; do it and let your teachers go. Only when there is a general desire to continue longer should the meeting be allowed to run over the hour, and then not for more than five or ten minutes. The principal should then adjourn the meeting and let those who care to talk longer remain to do so. It is good psychology to stop before the group has talked the subject out. The principal will need to keep his program in mind, keep his eye on the clock, hold down irrelevant discussion, and proceed systematically to the desired end.

Have definite objectives. A principal should no more attempt to conduct a professional teachers' meeting without a clear outline of what he intends to do during a term, or year, and careful preparation for each fortnightly meeting, than should a professor in a university attempt to meet classes without knowing what he is going to do and how he is going to do it. The first thing a principal must decide upon is the general line of work he expects to carry out over a period of time at least as long as a half year. He should welcome suggestions from the teachers as to what they would like best to do, and if they seem profitable he may adopt some of them. Still he must be the master mind in the matter of the teachers' meetings if he hopes to be the professional leader in the school. His teachers' meetings, instead of being dry, routine affairs, should be sources of professional inspiration and new life, but if they are to be such it must come from his wider knowledge, more extensive reading, and larger professional insight and enthusiasm and skill. In the conduct of his teachers' meetings he stands somewhat in the position of an instructor in a normal school, and he must lead as he expects his teachers to lead in their classrooms. No work that a principal can do will do more to keep him alive and growing professionally than will the personal study and preparation necessary for good classroom supervision, and the conduct of vigorous and professionally helpful teachers' meetings.

The first thing then for him to do is to determine his objectives over a period of time, and then organize his meetings so as to cover some one part of his objective at each meeting. Just what kind of objectives he will decide upon will be determined somewhat by the needs of his staff, their general professional attitude, the special problems of his school, and the general policies which the superintendent is trying to put into effect for the school system as a whole. There are so many problems possible to a live and thinking principal that he might conduct normal school work with

MAKING TEACHERS' MEETINGS PROFITABLE

his teachers for a decade without duplicating what he has done before.

Types of objectives. Only a few types of objectives can be indicated here, but these may be taken as illustrative of what any live and intelligent principal may think out for himself.

I. A connected series of pupil problems. Many of these could be outlined. The following may be taken as illustrative:

1. Securing good attendance.
2. The drawing and holding power of our school.
3. Utilizing the play impulse.
4. Truancy; its causes and remedies.
5. Boys and their gangs.
6. Building up pupil coöperation.
7. Making special days useful.
8. Coöperation with the Parent-Teacher Association.
9. How make our school entertainments of value.
10. Building up the school spirit.

II. Practical classroom teaching problems. Dozens of these could be outlined. A few pertinent ones for which there is plenty of good reading are:

1. Types of teaching.
2. The drill lesson.
3. The inductive lesson.
4. The deductive lesson.
5. The lesson for appreciation.
6. The study lesson.
7. The review lesson.
8. The recitation lesson.
9. The art of questioning.
10. Artistic teaching.
11. Habit formation.
12. How and what to memorize.
13. Attention and interest.
14. Stimulating thinking.
15. Socializing the school work.

16. Repetition, wise and otherwise.
17. Awakening ideals.
18. Training for citizenship.
19. Economy in classroom management.
20. Variability of teachers' marks.

III. Pupil-differences problems. This is a very interesting field with plenty of live problems, and a year or two could be well spent on the general topic, with much profitable reading done by all. Terman's *The Intelligence of School Children* would be a good book for general reading, while centering the discussion of the meetings about some such list of practical schoolroom topics as the following:

1. Individual differences.
2. Promotions.
3. Best bases for promotion.
4. Use of the ungraded room.
5. Retardation and acceleration.
6. Differentiated courses of study.
7. Minimum essentials.
8. The average pupil.
9. The superior group.
10. Special opportunities for ability.

IV. Miscellaneous school problems. Often a principal will find it advisable to follow a number of lines during a year, taking up topics that seem of most usefulness without reference to any one objective. His objective now is a general-purpose objective. The following outline for a year's work will illustrate this type of planning:

1. Routine work on organization and administrative problems.
2. On what may we concentrate this year?
3. How are we using the educational resources of our community?
4. What do our boys and girls do outside of school hours?
5. Making our special school occasions profitable.
6. How may we build up our Parent-Teacher meetings?
7. Health factors which influence the progress of our children.

8. Devices for interesting careless and indifferent pupils.
9. Best methods for handling the written work of pupils.
10. Our school savings bank in relation to the corner grocery and drug store.
11. How preserve the teacher's health throughout the year?
12. Preparing our pupils for social usefulness.
13. Larger aspects of our civic work.
14. Forming ideals and ambitions.
15. School excursions and how to conduct them.
16. Mechanizing routine.
17. Reading for appreciation.
18. How to be happy as a teacher.
19. Why it pays to go to summer school.
20. Routine administrative work.

V. Objectives in the different subjects in the course of study. One or more meetings might be given to a consideration of what are the main objectives in teaching the different subjects in the course of study, and what the school should aim to accomplish in each. For example, three or four meetings might be devoted to the teaching of spelling or handwriting or reading, or the larger aims in teaching civics or science or play might be made profitable and helpful. With so many possibilities, the problem is rather the selection of that which is most needed and can be best presented.

Sometimes course-of-study work can be made into a coöperative study, with committees, to formulate new outlines or supplemental outlines for use along with the regular course of study. This often becomes quite prolonged, leads to much discussion, and can be made very fruitful in educating teachers in the aims and purposes and underlying theory of the work of the schools.

VI. Results of the classroom supervision. Form 4, page 441, gave a supervisory program of one principal for one month. Similar programs could be made out covering eight or nine of the months of a school year, and so organized in advance that the whole would represent a somewhat connected outline of work. The results of each two weeks' supervisory visitation would then be presented to the teachers at the fortnightly teachers' meetings. The results should be organized by the principal, some of the data charted, and the whole placed before the teachers with a series of questions which will lead to discussion and help to bring out the significance of the results obtained.

VII. Educational tests and measurements. A year's work in the use and interpretation of the results of the best of the educational tests, using as guides some such books as Hines' *Guide to Educational Measurements* and Monroe's *Measuring the Results of Teaching* in studying and giving the tests and interpreting the results. This is rather mature work, and might prove too ambitious a program. If so, it would be better to take up individual subjects, such as spelling, arithmetic, or handwriting, use the tests as supplemental aids, explain their use and how to give them, try them in the grades, and use the results at a later teachers' meeting.

VIII. Study of a book. Sometimes, when there is a general desire for a group study of some good professional book, such as one of the Reading Circle books, this can be made quite profitable, but too often this kind of work is rather dreary and without much value because it is poorly handled. A study of topics or problems is usually better. If a book is used the principal should not assign chapters and then conduct a quiz on the reading. This is deadening. Instead, organize the teachers into study or problem groups, have individual teachers take charge on different days, and keep plenty of time for discussion. If fifteen minutes were made a maximum for the presentation and criticism of the chapter by the leader, and the remainder of the time given to a group discussion of not only the chapter, but also of a dozen or so thought-provoking questions applying the chapter to schoolroom practice which the principal, or better still a group of teachers has prepared and given out, the work will be relieved of what most teachers find so deadening in the so-called Reading Circle discussion of a book. The principal can then keep largely in the background until the summing-up time comes.

IX. Capitalizing the successes of the teachers. Much of the fine work done by teachers goes to waste because it is not capitalized by principals and superintendents. At times some teacher may tell of some particular work she has made a success in developing, and stand a quiz on it. Occasionally some especially good work may be taught before the group, and the whole laid open to questioning as to purpose and plan and procedure. This has been mentioned before (Chapter XXII). The best place for this type of work, though, is at the grade teachers' meetings for a supervisory group or for the whole city, rather than at the single building teachers' meeting. A good principle to keep in mind is that what is presented at a building teachers' meeting should be of interest to all, and closely applied to the work the teachers are doing. If demonstration lessons are given before a building teachers' meeting the emphasis should be placed on method or procedure, rather than on subject-matter.

The principal as the professional leader of the group. The above types are illustrative of what might be done in the professional teachers' meetings. Sometimes, instead of following a single line, combinations of different types of work may be made. Occasionally, too, the principal should take full charge of the meeting, and tell the group what is going on in the educational world, suggest to them possibilities of accomplishment not thought of before, describe to them some significant educational experiment now being made, open up a new vision of usefulness in the profession, or digest for them the main contribution of some new and stimulating article or book. The principal should not be in the center of the stage all the time in a teachers' meeting any more than in a school assembly, but there are times in each when he should take charge and "put over" a talk that will not only be interesting and important, but also will do something to lift teachers out of the monotony of their daily work and give them a larger vision. He can usually base such a talk on some article or book he has read, or something that he has seen, and thus become an interpreter to them of the best educational thought of the day.

An important rule to follow in all he does is to keep what he attempts simple, concrete, and clearly applicable to the teachers' classroom problems. The principal must not expect his teachers to do any large amount of reading or work for these meetings; they have other things to do. Rather he must do the thinking and the preparing, and use the meetings to give them new inspiration for their work and to stimulate them to think. He must have read more and know more about every subject brought before the group than he can expect his teachers to do or know. He needs to be full of ideas and questions, and to know much more about the topic for the day than he will say or use. Still more, he must be enthusiastic about it, and be able to make his enthusiasm contagious. The better the principal is prepared the less he will need to say, and the more he will be able by skillful questioning to stimulate others to activity instead.

Rules and cautions. That a principal should make his teachers' meetings helpful and stimulating and vital has been said with sufficient emphasis not to need further mention. By way of summary a few rules and cautions may be given:

1. Avoid trying to do too much in any one meeting or series of meetings. Take time to follow up a good lead that teachers

MAKING TEACHERS' MEETINGS PROFITABLE

are interested in, even if the program you had formed for the term or year may not be covered. Much of what you planned to do may well go over to next year. Any one of the topics suggested above for a single meeting might prove so interesting that it might pay to devote two or three meetings to it.

2. Do not try to do all the work alone. Ask different teachers to take part. Organize working committees. Recognize that your interest in a subject has come largely from your study of it, and that the teachers are likely to become interested in proportion as you relate the topic to their daily work and get them to thinking and working on it.

3. Try to get all the teachers, as far as possible, into the discussion, by asking questions of them if they do not enter it voluntarily.

4. Keep the meeting as informal as conditions will permit, but be able to hold every one to the question so that the meeting will move along. A rapid fire of questions in which many take part is far better than longer talks by any one.

5. Keep the questioning and discussion constructive. Do not illustrate the point by mentioning some wrong practice you have seen in the rooms. On the contrary, frequently take occasion to illustrate with good things you have seen your teachers do.

6. If a professional book is used as a basis for the discussion, use teachers to present the work of the day, and small groups of teachers to plan the discussion. Keep somewhat in the background yourself, so as to keep alive the interest of the teachers in the book.

7. Do not hold the meetings too long. The teachers get tired, and they are not as interested in them as you ought to be. Keep the meeting moving, and leave the discussion at a point where the teachers are eager for more.

8. If a demonstration lesson is to be given, know in advance exactly what is to be taught and the outlines of the lesson plan, that you may be prepared to handle the discussion and keep it going well.

9. Permit interruptions by questions and illustrative contributions, as this is a good sign of teacher activity. Invite a challenge of every point involved.

10. While in general expecting all teachers to be present, do not wait for tardy ones, and be perfectly willing to excuse a teacher without requiring her to tell you why.

11. Keep the meeting balanced and well-timed. Do not use over fifteen or twenty minutes, ordinarily, for presentation of the topic of the day. Keep half an hour for general discussion, and be prepared with enough good questions and applications to make the discussion active and pertinent.
12. That the meeting may be brought to a proper conclusion, always save a few minutes to sum up the points, *pro* and *con*, that have been brought out, suggest a few applications and further questions, and summarize the discussion. This leaves the teachers with a consciousness that something has come out of the meeting, that it was worth while, and that the principal had a real purpose in holding it.
13. At the close of the meeting, announce the topic for the next meeting, and the leaders for the day. This is good psychology, as it awakens interest and stimulates thinking.
14. Keep the meetings largely for yourself and your teachers, and ordinarily do not bring in outside persons to talk to the teachers. Teachers hear far too many lectures, and think in groups far too little. If teachers from other schools want to come, that is a different matter.

Conducted somewhat as has been described, the building teachers' meetings can be made helpful and profitable. Adequate professional preparation on the part of the principal, and his willingness to organize efficiently the details of each meeting, are the prime requisites for success. They will require thinking and planning on the part of the principal, but it will be time and effort well spent. He will grow more under it than will his teachers. If he plans his meetings so as to present material for discussion having a close connection with their daily problems, if he keeps the meeting a discussion meeting, if he is a good presiding officer and knows how to keep the talk moving and to the point, if he prepares himself well so as to be able to inject ideas and questions and pertinent data, and if he can summarize well what has been done in the hour, it is safe to say that his teachers will soon come to feel that his teachers' meetings are not only profitable but an invaluable privilege as well.

MAKING TEACHERS' MEETINGS PROFITABLE

QUESTIONS AND PROBLEMS

1. Suppose a new and well-prepared principal, going to a school which has not had building teachers' meetings of a professional type for years. What type of professional meetings would you suggest that he begin with? Why?
2. Suppose you conduct two types of building teachers' meetings, as described in this chapter. List a dozen topics you would take up at the noon after-lunch meeting.
3. Take any topic given under Types of Objectives, I, II, or III, and prepare the kind of an outline you would make up on it for a building professional teachers' meeting. Add two or three good brief references, and half a dozen good questions that apply the topic to the school work.
4. Name some professional book you think would be good to use as a Reading Circle book with your teachers, state why you think it would be good, and indicate how you would plan to use it.
5. Suppose it is your day to take charge of the meeting and give your teachers a real message. What would you do?
6. It is often stated that the life of a school can be made to revolve about good teachers' meetings. Show how this might be true.

SELECTED REFERENCES

Gorton, Chas. E. "The Superintendent in Smaller Cities"; in *Proceedings of National Education Association*, 1900, pp. 222-29.
   Teachers; teachers' meetings; supervision of instruction.

Saul, E. L. "Professional Teachers' Meetings for the High School"; in *School Review*, vol. 30, pp. 371-77. (May, 1922.)
   Good article. Topics indicated for a year equally useful for the elementary school principal. One meeting outlined.

Stark, Wm. E. *Every Teacher's Problems.* New York, 1922.
   A good book for principals to know. Contains 241 assorted problems, with solutions for many of them worked out.

PART V
SCHOOL EXTENSION

CHAPTER XXVI

EXTRA SCHOOL ACTIVITIES

1. *Special school occasions*

Changed conception of the school. The progressive change shown in the character of the school buildings reproduced in Figures 5 to 10, pages 95 to 103, beginning with a simple, old-style school building of fourteen classrooms and an office and with almost no play space, as shown in Figure 5, and gradually progressing to the large, well-arranged, highly-differentiated community-center school building shown in Figure 10, with its regular classrooms, many special rooms, good play space, branch library, and assembly hall, is typical of the change in the conception as to the purpose of American education that has come in the past quarter-century. Once a somewhat isolated and purely academic institution and dealing only with children, the public schoolhouse is to-day in process of being transformed into a center for the community life.

With the coming of large numbers of foreign-born peoples, and the increased participation in the functions of government on the part of all the people, the demand has become stronger and stronger that the public school, as the one great, active, unifying, non-racial, non-political, non-sectarian force in our national life, should take upon itself a new service and make of itself a center for the formation and education of community sentiment. As the public school authorities have in turn been forced to ask the people for increased funds for the support of the many new policies and extensions the past quarter-century has brought, it has become increasingly necessary that each unit in the public school system do its part in the formation of that community sentiment, and in promoting understanding between the school and the parents who send their children to it.

In an increasing number of our cities definite community-center activities are being organized in connection with the schools by a special staff of workers, and the school building is being utilized extensively, outside the regular school hours, for many new types of educational and semi-educational work. Such work is quite generally under some form of special organization, and no attempt will be made to describe it here. Instead, only a few of the more simple things that a principal and his teachers may do, working without the aid of any community-center organization, will be indicated.

Building up school support. As was pointed out in Chapter III, in outlining the general nature of the principal's work, all these new social functions and relationships mean quite an extension of the older conception as to the work of an elementary-school principal. The progress of the school having outrun the thinking of the people, in a very real sense the principal must now act as an interpreter to the people of his community of the meaning and significance of what the school is trying to do for their children, and of the larger policies that the superintendent of schools and the board of education are trying to put in force for the city as a whole. It is one of his functions to help build up in his community a spirit of coöperation and willingness to back the schools in voicing their needs, and against hostile attacks. A school system that is moving forward cannot afford to have its public in ignorance of its aims and its achievements.

For the benefit of the school, then, as well as for the benefit of its public, each school ought to provide a number of opportunities during the school year when the parents may come and see to advantage the work of the school. These

EXTRA SCHOOL ACTIVITIES

special opportunities, or occasions, when the parents of the children are invited to come, are the school's chance to get in close touch with the parents. Well managed, they enlist solid support for the school; poorly managed, they generate opposition from those who ought to be the school's friends. They are opportunities for a form of educational propaganda, but unless the campaign is well thought out and the plan of action clear, with a quite definite purpose for each such undertaking, they may not contribute much to the promotion of better relations between the home and the school.

Just what it is best to do and just how to do it will depend much on the character of the people who send children to the school, upon the type of school, the neighborhood, the traditions of the city, and the degree of success or failure that has attended any past efforts in this direction. In general, three main types of special school occasions may be provided for by a principal and his teachers, viz., (1) special school visitation days, (2) special program days, and (3) annual exhibit days.

Special school visitation days. These are attempts to get the parents into close personal touch with the earnest and thoughtful service which progressive and capable teachers are rendering daily to their children. How to secure such visitation is sometimes a difficult problem, but the greatest appreciation usually results from it. One plan is to set aside three or four afternoons a year for this special purpose, have the pupils invite their parents, and have them visit the classrooms where their children are or see work in which they are interested. The program may be somewhat rearranged for the afternoon, though regular school work should proceed. It is often highly interesting and helpful for parents to hear and see how the old-line subjects are taught by modern methods, and it does much toward inspiring confidence in the work of the schools and the ability of the teacher. A few words of explanation given by the teacher before each exercise will serve to make clearer the work being done.

One principal of the writer's acquaintance, who has been particularly successful in building up school and home coöperation, holds one of these visitation-day afternoons once a month, on the afternoon that the Parent-Teacher Association meets at his school, and once a year he has a big evening meeting instead, intended to reach the fathers, and with all the instruction done by teachers and classes on the auditorium stage. For each such meeting his pupils write notes inviting their parents to be present, and copying from the blackboard the program that will be followed that afternoon. The following is a sample.

PROGRAM FOR MARCH 15
Room 9 — Grade 4A
Mary Brewer, Teacher

1.00 to 1.25	Music — Note drill — Rote singing.
1.25 to 1.50	Oral arithmetic drill.
1.50 to 2.05	Recess.
2.05 to 2.30	Blackboard drill work.
2.30 to 3.00	Home geography.

The parents are received and ushered to the rooms by eighth-grade pupils, and the teachers work in their classrooms until closing time. By keeping their programs wholly representative of the work of the school, both principals and teachers use these special days to build up home understanding and support and coöperation.

Special program days. Every school will have a number of special program days, when half an hour or more will be given to a special program celebrating some event or special day, and to which parents may or may not be invited to come. Such special days would be Columbus Day, Thanksgiving Wednesday, Lincoln's Birthday, Washington's Birthday, Longfellow's Birthday, Fire-Prevention Day, and Arbor Day. Every school bearing some person's name should have a special program on that person's birthday, that the pupils may become familiar with what he did and stood for and why the school came to be named for him. These, though, are school affairs rather than special school occasions.

In addition, a school may well afford to take time to organize one or two special programs, best carried out in the evenings, and which the parents are urged to attend. A good program illustrative of the school work should be prepared, the older pupils or the Scouts should do the ushering and manage the affair, and the principal should preside, welcome the parents, and introduce the numbers with a few words of explanation of each.

Another type of evening program occasionally used is that in which regular school work is carried on in the classrooms for an hour in the evening, the parents coming and being seated in the rooms. One principal who did this, in a school in a foreign community, found it so successful that the parents refused to send their children to a parochial school that was about to be opened in the neighborhood, and the attendance of parents at the public evening school greatly increased. Such occasions develop a community appreciation for the school and are helpful in many ways, provided they are not undertaken too frequently and do not involve too much special preparation.

It is usually rather easy to get out a good attendance for programs in the evening if held in a comfortable school auditorium equipped with good seats and a well-lighted stage. In such buildings as are shown in Figures 5, 6, 7, and 8 such a program would not be possible because of the lack of a school auditorium, but in the schools shown in Figures 9 and 10 much of importance could be provided. The preparation will of course require some extra work on the part of the principal and teachers, the crowd will get the building dirty, and there may be some disorder in the hallways, but these disadvantages are more than compensated for by the increase in home understanding and coöperation that come from a good program well presented.

Since the attendance frequently will be rather closely related to the number of different pupils participating, a principal is wise to see to it that in the choruses and exercises a large number of pupils have a part in the program. Single-pupil numbers should be avoided, and the work should be kept as truly representative of the regular school work as can be done. An orchestra number or two; some part singing by whole classes; a chorus; some physical exercise drills; some actual class exercises on the platform, such as rapid drill work and problem solving in mental arithmetic, a developmental lesson on some topic in American history, or a map-drill lesson in geography; with a closing song by the audience, led by the teacher of music; represent one type of program that might be profitable. Nothing should be continued for very long, the program itself should not be too extended, and what is done should be done promptly and rapidly.

Annual exhibit days. Many schools find it very profitable to hold, in the spring, an annual school exhibit of the work done throughout the year, to which parents are invited. Representative work is exhibited in the different classrooms and shops. The pupils not acting as ushers are dismissed for the afternoon. The teachers are present in their rooms to meet parents and explain the work, and some form of program is given in the evening. It is a sort of general reception and parents' day combined. A special effort is made to get the fathers out at the evening meeting. Since this exhibit is anticipated during the whole year, good work can be laid aside for it and the actual exhibit should not require much extra time for preparation and organization. What is exhibited, too, should be the regular work of the school, and not specially prepared work that is not only not representative of actual conditions but is wasteful of time and effort as well. If the principal is a good chart maker, and can have some good diagrams to hang up showing school results, it adds to the interest.

The purpose of all these special occasions is to bring the parents who send children to the school into closer contact with principal and teachers, and to build up understanding and support. A school system that is making progress needs to keep its parents in touch with what is being done. In so doing these special occasions are far more effective than articles in the newspapers, useful as these may be. All the special occasions so far described should be free of charge, that no family need be kept away by the necessity of paying an admission fee. This is an important feature.

2. *Entertainments to raise money*

The arguments against. In many schools, however, it is customary to have entertainments for the purpose of raising money for some school need. Whether or not this type of entertainment is desirable depends much on the type of parents and neighborhood sending children to the school. In some places they are quite successful and provoke little adverse comment, while in others they make trouble and cause much criticism of the school. In a few cities they have been forbidden by the general school regulations. Some principals believe in them heartily, while others regard them as a nuisance that should be suppressed. In school systems of moderate size or in small towns, where the school money is more limited and where the board of education has not as yet come to see that certain types of supplies and equipment should be provided at public expense, the entertainment to raise money usually works out better than in the larger cities. The admission-fee entertainment is often the device of the needy community, and the only means available by which the school can provide itself with needed play apparatus, musical equipment, or support some worthy school undertaking. Often, on the other hand, the community could well afford to provide the needed equipment, but has never been educated up to see that it ought to do so.

A very good case can be made out against entertainments to raise money for school needs. It can be argued that it is not the business of principal or teachers to raise money for school purposes, but that they should look to the school authorities to provide the necessary books, pictures, play apparatus, athletic equipment, musical instruments, and similar material. It can also be argued that any form of entertainment for school purposes in a public schoolhouse ought to be free to all, and that the school, being a state institution, should have its legitimate needs met by general taxation instead of trying to extract small sums of money from parents and children who often can hardly afford to pay, but who grudgingly contribute to keep up appearances. The preparation for these occasions, too, breaks into regular school work, takes the time of pupils and teachers that should be used for other things, imposes unnecessary extra burdens on principal and teachers and dissipates the energies of the school, while the net financial returns are not at all commensurate with the labor expended. Once begun, the board of education is likely to use their success as an excuse for not appropriating funds another year, and the abuse persists. The advocates of the above points of view would prohibit all entertainments in the school buildings or elsewhere for the purpose of raising money for the schools, and would permit only the free entertainment and school displays described in the preceding section.

The opposite point of view. While admitting the objections given above as important, there are other principals who believe that these objections can be obviated by proper handling, and that the advantages to be obtained from the pay type of entertainment outweigh their disadvantages. In the development of a strong school spirit, in training the pupils in group activity and friendly coöperation, and in interesting the parents in the school, it is held that one or possibly two pay entertainments a year are worth all they cost. Rarely, they contend, do the parents begrudge the dimes they pay, while both parents and pupils appreciate the school the more because by their efforts they helped to provide it with something it needed and which they can now enjoy.

The pupils, too, get valuable training and develop much fine school spirit from putting through some entertainment that to an adult might seem wasteful of effort and relatively unprofitable. It is what one gives to an institution rather than what one gets from it that counts, after all. The general result of a successful entertainment is a feeling of pride in the school, and an improved attitude toward it on the part of the pupils. The parents often give material help in preparing for these occasions, and this in turn frequently develops appreciation and support. Rightly handled they can be made to contribute to discipline and order by enlisting the activities of pupils who might otherwise be troublesome. The experience gained by the pupils, too, is of distinct value, and there is also an element of value in the business side of an undertaking carried through successfully.

Handling such an entertainment. Even admitting that the bad features probably outweigh the good, that the good features could be obtained for the school in some less wasteful manner, and that it would be desirable in most communities not to have pay entertainments at all, still the necessities of the school and the traditions of the community may be such that it will seem wise to hold an occasional entertainment for which an admission fee is charged. If so, then so far as possible the following principles ought to prevail in its organization and conduct.

1. See that the entertainment put on has some intrinsic educational value, and is worth while from an educational point of view as well as a money-raiser.
2. Do not have many pay entertainments in a year — one or two at most.
3. Keep the admission charge to the main entertainment moderate, but at the same time do not go to the trouble of arranging for it unless you expect to make some money by it. Some optional side-shows for which an extra fee is charged may help the fund.
4. The entertainment given should be worth the admission price.
5. As far as possible avoid individual-pupil exercises. Instead put on group activities, and in these give all pupils equal opportunities regardless of ability. Chorus singing, group calisthenic drills, pageants, dramatization, folk dancing groups, Boy Scout demonstrations, an inter-school debate, or a May Day entertainment are types of group activities that interest and do not awaken criticism as do such individual performances as where Rosie speaks a piece or Oscar plays the violin.

Minimizing the work of preparation. In one school which has handled the pay entertainment very satisfactorily, two such entertainments are given each year. One year the one in the late autumn is given by the first four grades, and the one in the spring by the four upper grades. The next year this order is reversed. The teachers of each group and the principal decide early on the date and general outline of the program, and divide up the work by assigning definite parts to each room. The exercises are planned, as far as possible, to take in whole classes, and are as representative of the school work as is the usual assembly program (Chapter XVII). This enables the teacher to train the pupils gradually, as part of their regular school work, to do some particular thing well. This avoids all after-school practicing and extra preparation, and in consequence removes most of the objectionable features. A week before the entertainment the practicing is transferred to the school auditorium stage by the teachers, separately, and one complete rehearsal is held the afternoon preceding the performance. This minimizes the labor of preparation and keeps the program representative of the school work about as much as is possible. The school fair or bazaar, often used to make money, represents the opposite. It is not typical of the school work, is burdensome on the teachers and principal and janitor, and does not give the parents any proper conception of the school as an educational institution.

As a means of awakening school spirit and loyalty on the part of the pupils the pay entertainment to raise money for some good school purpose doubtless exceeds in value the free exhibition of the school's work, because it develops team work and a group coöperation for success much better than does the free-exhibition type. It also probably awakens more interest in the school on the part of many parents. The clientele of a school, though, will determine to a marked degree the nature of the entertainment, free or paid, which can be undertaken with a good chance of success. In schools where the children come from the homes of the poor and the foreign-born, very simple and free affairs are best; with children coming from "the spoiled darling" type of homes such simple free affairs will not prove very satisfactory, and more elaborate entertainments will be necessary.

3. Inter-school contests

Value of if properly controlled. Competitive contests between different schools of the same school system, as between different groups in the same school, are almost certain to develop where playground sports are practiced.

Whether they are made useful as a teaching institution and influence properly the life of the schools, or otherwise, will depend much upon how they are organized and handled. If well managed they are productive of much good. They help to develop a strong school spirit that can be turned to account in getting other and less interesting things done. They can be made effective instruments in teaching self-control, in inculcating ideas of fair play and sportsmanlike conduct, and in training pupils to be good losers. For the boy and girl of mediocre intellectual ability they offer often the only chance to rise to any position of importance in the life of the school. On the other hand, when poorly managed they develop inter-school rivalry and jealousy that often leads to fighting, unsportsmanlike conduct in the games, and even to antagonisms between teachers in the different schools.

Whether or not there are to be inter-school contests is to be decided almost wholly on the ground of results they give. In American schools these contests do not have to be stimulated. They are the most highly motivated activities we have. What is needed is guidance and restraint, and the direction of the sport impulse into good channels. Like almost any other highly useful instrument for service, if not looked after carefully it gives very undesirable results. If the right kind of supervision and control is given to the inter-class and inter-school contests they form excellent tools for the development of fine manly qualities in the pupils. No people have secured better results with sports in this respect than have the English. Without the right type of supervision and control these contests are almost certain to bring harm to the pupils and to the school. Rightly handled they offer an excellent opportunity to work off surplus energy that otherwise would find an outlet in ways that might be injurious to the school.

While a help in developing school spirit, a good means of physical education, and a source of pleasure to many, all this should be held subordinate to the question of proper control with a view to character development. The contests should teach fair play, clean sport, an appreciation of good work, and develop self-control and an ability to lose without ugliness.

An opportunity to teach important lessons. The development of a sportsmanlike attitude on the part of both teachers and pupils is important, and no one can do more to further this than can the principal. By a talk in the school assembly on fairness and courtesy to the teams they are to meet, by stimulating others to talk on the conduct of a manly game, by cautioning the pupils to avoid "rough-housing" and "mud slinging," even if started by their opponents, and by setting clearly before the school the type of conduct that is expected of both the contestants and the bleachers, he can do much to build up a right attitude that will carry over into school work long after the contest has passed. To win a game fairly and manfully or else lose it ought to be the ideal of every school. Sometimes the teachers need as much cautioning as the pupils, since in their desire for victory for their school they sometimes exercise less judgment than do the pupils. Often the parents who attend are even worse partisans than the teachers.

Rules for handling inter-school contests. All inter-school contests need careful supervision. They are as much opportunities for teaching as are the classrooms, and a principal will save himself much trouble if he keeps a firm hand on the whole situation. The following regulations are usually desirable ones to enforce:

1. The contests should always be managed by representatives from the schools, and no games should be permitted to be matched without the presence of such representatives.

2. Unless there is a playground director who has charge of the sports, the principal or some teacher should have charge and go with the team when games are played.
3. The school, principal, and teachers, must let the pupils engaged win or lose the games, and must give to them as large a share as is possible in the direction and control of the games without leaving them unsupervised.
4. The principal must always reserve the right to choose or approve of the players, and to advise the captains as to their choice. Standards as to attendance and conduct and school work may properly be set up and enforced.
5. To reduce dissatisfaction to a minimum, care should be taken to secure responsible and competent officials for the contest.
6. The rules as to time limits should be enforced.
7. In traveling to and from the contest the contestants should go in a body, and under the supervision of the principal or some teacher.
8. The dressing rooms and showers used should be supervised.
9. It is not best to carry competition with any one school to the point where rivalry becomes intense; it is better to contest with a number of different schools instead.
10. Contests with schools outside the city should ordinarily not be permitted to elementary school pupils.

Handled in this way there is not much chance of things going wrong, provided the sports be kept clearly in the amateur class and free from the highly technical professional class that makes such an appeal to high school students. The sports are worth their cost in the chances they offer for improving conduct and building up sportsmanlike attitudes. They unify a school as few other things do, and they put forward the idea of selection on the basis of ability to do rather than on any other standard. The girls need more encouragement to play games than do the boys, and for both boys and girls as many different children as can play should be encouraged to compete. As the children come to school without the traditions of good sportsmanship, the school can render good service in training young people in the elements — manliness, courtesy, confidence, courage, fair play — that go to make up this important characteristic.

EXTRA SCHOOL ACTIVITIES

SELECTED REFERENCES

Alexander, Carter. "Public Opinion and the Schools"; in *School and Society*, vol. 4, pp. 913–18. (December 16, 1916.)
: An excellent article for principals and superintendent to read.

Averill, L. A. "Educational Possibilities of the Moving Picture"; in *Educational Review*, vol. 50, pp. 392–98. (November, 1915.)

Courtis, H. S. *The Practical Conduct of Play.* 330 pp., New York, 1915.
: A very good book for the principal to know. Good descriptions and sensible advice as to what to do.

DuBreuil, Alice J. "The Moving Picture and the School"; in *Educational Review*, vol. 49, pp. 204–12. (February, 1915.)
: Describes possibilities as an educational institution, and types of films.

Perry, C. A. *Wider Use of the School Plant.* 417 pp. Charities Publishing Company, New York, 1911.

Perry, C. A. *The Extension of Public Education.* 67 pp. Bulletin 28, 1915, United States Bureau of Education.
: A study in the wider use of school buildings.

Perry, C. A. *Community Center Activities.* 127 pp., New York, 1916.
: Description of recreation centers, with good bibliography.

Sechrist, Frank K. *Education and the General Welfare.* New York, 1920.
: School as part of the community life. Includes illiteracy, child labor, and non-attendance.

The City School as a Community Center; in *Tenth Yearbook of the National Society for the Study of Education.* 75 pp., 1911.
: Eight articles on the use of the school as a community center. Bibliography.

Williams, J. F. *The Organization and Administration of Physical Education.* New York, 1922.
: Chapter IX is good on the management of games, sports, and contests.

CHAPTER XXVII
THE PARENT-TEACHER ASSOCIATION

The new school-and-home organization movement. The school, the home, and the church stand as the three great constructive agencies of society for moulding the next generation along desired lines. The nature of our form of government makes any close coöperation between the public school and the church impossible, but between the school and the home there can and should be the closest coöperation and the most perfect understanding. This desirable condition can of course never be perfectly attained, and in different communities it will exist in all degrees from close and sympathetic understanding to almost no understanding at all. That sympathy and coöperation are desirable, from the point of view of both the school and the home, is generally recognized. How to get them while retaining to each its proper sphere of action is not always an easy question to answer.

With the increasing intelligence of the home, the coming of more leisure generally, and the extension of the suffrage to women, it has been but natural that the mothers of the children should direct new attention to the school with a view to a better understanding of its work and a greater coöperation with it in what it is attempting to do for their children. In consequence there has arisen in this country, within the past two or three decades, a number of organizations and movements which have for their purpose a closer affiliation of the home and the school. These have taken form under a variety of names — Home and School Leagues, School and Civic Leagues, Child Study Clubs, Special Committees of Women's Clubs, Patrons' Leagues,

Fathers' Clubs, Parent-Teacher Associations, and Mothers' Clubs — but their general purpose has been much the same. Next to the board of education these organizations stand closer to the school than any other official or non-official body, and they should form an intimate link connecting the home and the school. The organization which has attained the largest membership, and the only one to become national in scope, is the Parent-Teacher movement, sponsored by the National Congress of Mothers and Parent-Teacher Associations. This organization now has branches in nearly every state, over half a million members (1922), and is increasing in membership at a very rapid rate. It promises to become general within a short time, and is an organization of large possibilities for usefulness when its energies are directed into proper channels. With its purposes and possibilities and plans for work every school principal should be familiar.

Any such organization represents an interest in the school and an impulse toward constructive work. Just what it will succeed in doing will depend much on the intelligence with which it is directed, and the information and guidance given to it by those who know what is needed. Such associations in some form are almost certain to rise wherever there are schools. If largely ignored by teachers and school authorities and left to their own resources they will find their own work. Just what this will be will be determined largely by the energy and the character of the knowledge as to what ought to be attempted which the organization possesses. Like every other form of organization that is an expression of our democratic life, if rightly guided it can be made useful and helpful; if left to its own resources it can become a meddlesome nuisance to the school.

When to organize an Association. Whether a principal or a superintendent will want to try to organize a Parent-

Teacher Association will depend somewhat on conditions in the community. If the town or city is already over-organized with churches, lodges, and clubs, it probably will be better to try to do what is needed by working through committees of existing organizations. There are after all only about so many leaders in any community, and, if the energies of these are absorbed in existing organizations, an additional and less prominent organization may bring to the front only a group of poorly balanced but energetic souls who have failed to secure advancement in the older and more general community undertakings. Such a Parent-Teacher Association is likely to prove troublesome and hard to handle because of its lack of good leaders. In such a case it would be better to try to work through educational committees of the Women's Club, the Rotary Club, or the Chamber of Commerce, and to leave the educational direction of these club activities more to the central school authorities to handle.

As soon, though, as a school begins to interest its parents in the work its teachers are doing, and to have special school occasions which awaken interest, a demand for some form of a school organization analogous to a Parent-Teacher Association is sure to arise among the patrons of the school. When it does, the principal and teachers should coöperate fully with the movement, try to secure a good organization for it, strive to make its meetings profitable, and plan to keep it so busy on constructive undertakings that it will have little time or desire to engage in those of another type. All such organizations ought to come into being as the result of a need felt for association. When they arise they need real leadership, which the principal may for a time have to supply. Like the school assembly, the playground, inter-school contests, and pupil organizations to assist in management, the Parent-Teacher Associations can be made useful instruments for school ends if given attention, and if neglected can build up troubles for a principal and superintendent which will be both vexatious and time-consuming.

Troublesome organizations. The trouble with so many troublesome so-called Parent-Teacher Associations is that they are not parent-teacher associations at all, but merely parents' associations. Too often the parents desire to meet and coöperate, but the teachers, feeling that they have done their fair share of school work for the day, do not remain, and in consequence neglect their best opportunity to meet and know the parents of their children. They likewise neglect an important opportunity to help shape their thinking and their opinion of the school. While the avowed aim of such meetings is to bring the home and the school into closer relations, that greater things may be done for the children, the teachers, and sometimes the principal as well, leave the building and the meeting is forced to fall back on its own resources. Far too often a few over-zealous persons, lacking real knowledge, turn critic of the existing conditions and those responsible for them, and set up new goals for education that are both undesirable and unattainable.

If a principal can organize a Parent-Teacher Association from the start he can, if tactful, shape the organization and direct it at once into useful lines of service. It is not willfulness, but ignorance of what to do, that causes parents' organizations to give trouble. A principal coming to a building may inherit an association that has been neglected and gone wrong. In such a case the first thing for him and his teachers to do is to get into close touch with the organization and make of it a real Parent-Teacher Association, both in the social part and in the program part of the meeting. The leaders, especially, are to be gotten acquainted with, the program committee interested, and the work of the organization gradually diverted into new channels. It is redirection, not criticism, that is needed. It is much the same problem as that of helping a weak teacher, but with the difference that the principal should here attempt no exercise of authority. He is now only a member of a group, and he will be wise to remain somewhat in the background. As a properly organized Parent-Teacher Association always makes the principal a member of the managing committee, he has a good opportunity to help direct the organization without seeming to do so or being too prominent in the meetings. By attending the meetings along with his teachers, helping with the programs, taking part in the discussion, and accepting every challenge as an opportunity for enlightenment, much can be done by way of redirection that will be very valuable.

One principal known to the writer, inheriting such an association, accepted an invitation to address the first meeting. He outlined to them something of the great work of an American public school and the help that parents could give, said in closing that there were doubtless many questions they would like to ask which time did not then permit to be answered, and proposed a question-box for the future meetings. The proposal was adopted at once, and for the next three meetings there were more questions, mostly of a critical nature, than could be answered. The following are illustrative:

Why don't you teach reading by the alphabet method?
Why do you place so much emphasis on tardiness?
Why do you not have more book work in geography, and not so much of this home geography?
Why don't you teach arithmetic in the first grade?
Of what use is your so-called nature study?
Why does the school waste money on teaching cooking, and in furnishing baseballs and bats?
Why don't you stop fighting?
Why do we have part-time instruction in the first and second grades?

THE PARENT–TEACHER ASSOCIATION 553

Why don't the teachers teach the children in school instead of expecting the parents to do it at home?

Why do you punish one child for something and let another off free for the same offense?

These were all legitimate questions which represented interest and ignorance, and each gave an opportunity for enlightenment. The principal answered many of the questions, but asked some of the teachers to answer others. When the question "What are the policies of this school system anyway?" came, the principal proposed that the superintendent of schools be invited to come and talk to them in answer to that question. This was readily accepted, with excellent results. Before the year had gone by, the association was clearly in the process of transformation from a critical body of small usefulness into an organization helpful to the schools. What the organization was suffering from was neglect and ignorance, and the energy which led to its inception was being turned into destructive channels.

Need for a constructive program of work. Every such organization needs a worthy outlet for its activities, and the best way to reform a troublesome Parent-Teacher Association, as has been said before, is to set it to work on something useful. Many times such an organization will ask a principal what he wants done, or what it ought to do. This is his opportunity, and he ought to be ready to answer the question.

There are two main types of work which these associations may undertake with profit to the schools and to themselves. The first is in doing something needed by the school, and the second is in improving their own knowledge of school conditions and child needs by arranging meetings at which they will study or be told something of interest and value. The principal, when called on, should be able to advise as to a number of the most possible and helpful lines of effort, of both types, that a particular association may well undertake.

For the first type of work, there should always be something concrete for the organization to do — something to be provided which the school needs, or some new service for the children that calls for coöperative effort. To get the school a victrola, a picture machine, playground apparatus, instruments for the school orchestra, test blanks, shrubs and trees for Arbor Day, or anything that is difficult to obtain through the regular channels represents one type of constructive effort. Women have a peculiar genius for this kind of work and are happy in doing it. It does much to make them strong supporters of the school.

The organization of school lunches, the provision of shoes and clothing and food for needy children, the furnishing of dental service or a school nurse, or the backing of the requests of the school authorities for better provisions for the children represent a still better type of service, and one that is more useful than raising money for school needs that the public ought to supply. The same amount of energy, agitation, and persistent effort that money-raising for school needs requires, if directed toward the formation of a public sentiment in favor of higher taxes that the school may be provided with all needed equipment, will produce larger returns, leave the community in a better state of mind toward its schools, and free the energies of the Parent-Teacher Association for more useful service.

For the second type of activity there should be a group of topics of interest which can be taken up, and which will lead to better information as to what should be done both for the children and for the school.

Meetings, and types of work. The best results with these organizations have usually been obtained from meetings held once a month at the school building, the program

THE PARENT–TEACHER ASSOCIATION

usually beginning a very few minutes after the school dismissal. It is common to begin the meetings with a short program in which some school activity is shown, and which the teachers or the principal are called upon to provide. In all such work it is best to remember the cautions stated in the preceding chapter, use group or class activities rather than single-pupil activities, and keep what is presented as representative of school work as can be done. It is customary to adjourn the formal program at the end of an hour. After this a period of social intercourse should be provided. Frequently some light refreshments are served by the domestic science class or the eighth-grade girls, either just before or just after the formal program, though many successful association meetings are held without any such service.

As to the program, there are dozens of things that may be done, though just what would be best to do in one school might not be best in another. A few suggestions may be made to indicate possible lines of effort.

I. Things that may be done for the school. The following are possible and desirable things for most communities:

1. Furnish materials for the first-aid cabinets and sick room.
2. Supply money for purchasing food for undernourished children.
3. Establish and manage warm lunches in the schools.
4. Supply musical instruments for the school orchestra.
5. Equip the auditorium with a lantern, or a moving-picture machine.
6. Provide funds for renting slides or reels.
7. Make a home-conditions survey of the district.
8. Provide shoes and clothing for needy children.
9. Provide a school or a visiting nurse.
10. Provide for a dental clinic for the children.
11. Back the Junior Red Cross in its work.
12. Back the Boy Scouts and the Camp Fire Girls in their work.
13. Provide a good teachers' room in the building.

14. Purchase a few good pictures or busts for the school.
15. Conduct a campaign for better sanitary conditions in the buildings, and larger and better equipped playgrounds for the children.
16. Provide for a summer kindergarten and school playground.
17. Institute a strong home movement for simpler school dress, better social activities, and improved amusements for the children.
18. Establish a censorship of the "Movies," with a view to protecting the children from bad films.
19. Establish school savings banks, and teach children how to use money and leisure intelligently.
20. Study the needs and policies of the school system as a whole, and back legitimate demands for school bond issues and increased school taxes.

II. Talks that may be arranged. Every such organization needs to be told many things that will give them a better insight into the newer phases of education. The following are types of talks that may be made helpful:

1. The school nurse, on child feeding and care.
2. The domestic science teacher, on lunches and feeding.
3. The primary supervisor, on phases of primary work.
4. The principal, on problems of pupil administration.
5. A dentist, on care of the teeth.
6. A nose, throat, and ear specialist, on the hygiene of these organs.
7. A social worker, on community needs.
8. A mother, on bringing up children.
9. A play teacher, on the play needs of children.
10. The school nurse, on first-aid work and supplies.

One school of which the writer knows holds a useful but somewhat different type of parents' meeting at least once each year. Just after the reports go out, at the end of the first ten weeks, the teachers hold a parents' conference, in their individual classrooms, to which the parents of all the children are invited to come. By this time the school has become fairly well acquainted with its children, and the teachers now suggest ways in which the parents can be of assistance to the school in its work, such as seeing that the boys and girls are kept in school regularly, that their attendance at movies be restricted, that they have the proper amount of sleep, and that the parents give them a desirable kind of help and encouragement without doing their work for them. These meetings have proved helpful in promoting understanding, and have contributed toward keeping down retardation in this school.

The national Parent-Teacher Association organization has recently organized a division for the study of problems that relate to child welfare before the school age — baby clinics, child-welfare work, infant care and feeding, child discipline, and early education — that promises much of value for both home and school. It is known as The Pre-School-Age Mothers' Study Circle, and is intended to be a junior organization that will become a feeder of mothers into the Parent-Teacher Associations. This organization, too, considers the schoolhouse as a background and its proper meeting place, and the school kindergarten teachers and nurses and physicians as its supporters and instructors. This, too, a principal may be called upon to aid and encourage, and if so he should do it willingly. If he will carefully read Gesell's *The Pre-School Child* he will be better able to give intelligent aid.

Working through these organizations. Some form of parents' association is a natural development of the present-day interest of the American people in the education of their children. When they are started, principals and teachers should keep in close touch with them, that they may neither die early of inanition or become troublesome because their energies are misdirected. The policies of the school and the school system ought to be explained to them, that their support may be enlisted. In the last analysis it is public opinion that controls and limits school progress, and the Parent-

Teacher Associations are potent influences in the formation of public opinion.

A live principal, awake to his opportunities, will prefer to work in a school where there is a strong, active, and intelligent Parent-Teacher Association to working in one where the parents have not enough interest in the schools to form one, or keep it alive after it is formed. This organization offers opportunities for increasing the influence of the school and for building up school support that do not exist where these associations are lacking. The legitimate interest of the parent in the school is enlisted, recognized, and respected. Parents come to feel the sincerity of the teachers and their genuine interest in their children. Better results in instruction and discipline are obtained. Improved sanitary conditions almost invariably result. Play needs are recognized. Tardiness and absence decrease. There is a better understanding of school aims and school policies, because the people are kept closer to the schools. As an anchor to windward when trouble arises, or as a reliance for support in carrying through progressive school policies, there are few possible sources of backing superior to that of an intelligently directed and well-informed Parent-Teacher Association. As a phase of the constructive administrative policy of a board of education and a superintendent of schools it would be well to have such an association in connection with every school in the city. In carrying out such a school-and-home coöperative policy the superintendent must rely largely on the intelligent assistance of the principal and teachers of each school building.

SELECTED REFERENCES

Cabot, Ella L. *Volunteer Help to the Schools.* 130 pp., Boston, 1914.
    Demand for, types of, and guidance of the workers.

Cubberley, E. P. *Changing Conceptions of Education.* 70 pp., Boston, 1909.
    A simple statement as to the changes in the nature of our life and the consequent conception of the school, and present tendencies.

Denison, Elsa. *Helping School Children.* 338 pp., Illustrated, New York, 1914.
: An important book of suggestions for efficient coöperation with the public schools.

Gesell, Arnold. *The Pre-School Child.* 250 pp., Boston, 1923.
: A very important book on the needs and care and education of children from birth to the time of entering school. Of much importance for Pre-School-Age Mothers' Study Circles.

McAndrew, Wm. *The Public and Its School.* 76 pp., Yonkers, 1916.
: Contains many suggestions of value to a principal.

Mead, A. R. "Functions of Parent-Teacher Associations"; in *Educational Administration and Supervision*, vol. 8, pp. 503–06. (November, 1922.)
: The seven cardinal functions of, and the limits in each.

Patri, Angelo. *A Schoolmaster in a Great City.* 221 pp., New York, 1917.
: A New York principal's story of his lifework and efforts to help his children and parents.

Shuler, Marjorie. "The Parent-Teacher Movement"; in *The American Review of Reviews*, vol. 66, pp. 65–67. (July, 1922.)
: A good short article on the organization and its work.

Strayer, G. D., and Engelhardt, N. L. *The Classroom Teacher.* New York, 1920.
: Chapter XV is a good brief chapter on the teacher and the community.

United States Bureau of Education. *Health Bulletins.* The following numbers will be of value to Parent-Teacher Associations in their work:
: No. 2. *Diet for the School Child.* 14 pp.
No. 3. *Summer Health and Play School.* 12 pp.
No. 5. *Child Health Programs for Parent-Teacher Associations and Women's Clubs.* 16 pp.
No. 6. *Teaching Health.* 20 pp.
No. 7. *The Lunch Hour at School.* 62 pp.

Weeks, Mary H. "Purposes, Methods, and Results of the Parent-Teacher Coöperative Associations of the National Congress of Mothers"; in *Report of United States Commissioner of Education*, 1912, vol. 1, pp. 359–73.

Handbook of Information about Parent-Teacher Associations and Mothers' Circles. Free, from Secretary, 1201 Sixteenth Street, N.W., Washington, D.C.
: Contains good information as to organization and purposes.

CHAPTER XXVIII

THE PRINCIPAL AS A LEADER IN THE PROFESSION

His duty in leadership. In the two chapters which have preceded this final one the place and work of the principal in developing good community relationships and in helping carry out in his community the administrative policies of the school system have been indicated. However good the policy of the board of education or the superintendent of schools, it may largely be negatived in any school district within a city or a county-unit school system by the wrong action or lack of action of the principal and teachers of that particular school. "As is the principal so is the school" is as true here as elsewhere. The principal virtually decides the fate in his school of many constructive policies of the authorities above him.

Just as the school cannot to-day remain in isolation and apart from the people and life of the community which surrounds and supports it, but must assume its share of responsibility for the community attitudes toward it and for the educational progress of the school system as a whole, so the principal of a school cannot realize his largest efficiency if he is content to be merely the leader of his single school, however good a leader he may be. He owes a duty also to the educational profession, both within the community in which he works and to a certain extent in the state and nation as well. The same student-like qualities which have been emphasized throughout this volume as so important for the principal in his school should extend over into the principals' meetings which the superintendent holds, and into all local discussions of questions of general educational interest. Without being always on his feet or making himself too prominent, he should take his proper place and play his proper part in the principals' meetings and in the professional meetings of the teachers of his city or county. Outside he also owes a much more limited but no less certain duty as an upholder of professional standards, and as one deeply interested in the advancement of the work to which he is giving the best energies of his life.

The professional spirit. Perhaps the matter of first importance for the principal who would be a leader in his profession is that he become fully imbued with the professional spirit. He must see, more clearly than those around him, the great spiritual importance of the work in which he is engaged. Probably no service that one person renders to another compares in importance with the proper educational development of the boy and the girl. In a democratic nation such as ours, public education is the greatest of all our undertakings for the promotion of our national welfare, and the teacher in our schools renders an inconspicuous but highly important national service. In teaching the youth of our nation the principles which lie at the foundation of our democratic life; in awakening in them the conception of liberty guided by law, and the difference between freedom and license; in training them for self-control; in developing in them the power to shoulder responsibility; in giving them a sense of the greatness of that democratic nobility in which all may share; in instilling into them the importance of fidelity to duty, truth, honor, and virtue; in arousing in them a desire to be clean and strong, both in mind and body; and in unifying diverse elements and fusing them into the national mould, the teachers in our schools are rendering a service seldom appreciated and not likely to be overestimated.

The principal needs to grasp firmly these conceptions as to the great importance of the service in which he is engaged. His is not a small local but a great national service, yearly becoming more and more clearly recognized as public education comes to be understood by more and more of our people as the greatest constructive undertaking of the nation. Above all the petty trials of the day, the discouragements that are bound to come, and the short-sighted and often highly critical attitude of his teachers, he should see and feel clearly, and strive to keep alive in others, his fundamental faith in the vast importance of what they all are doing. If the parents of his children do not see that it is more important to "train the mind than to mind the train" he must do his part, by the life he leads, the service he renders, the stands he takes, and what he says when speech is the proper thing, to lead his people to see the importance of the work of the school and to respect the services and the devotion of those who give their lives to the training of the generation that is to follow. The mere fact that the mass of mankind does not fully appreciate the services of the teacher, and places higher values on less important community services, presents him his opportunity rather than being a cause for discouragement.

The professional spirit has its basis in knowledge. Such large conceptions as to the nature and importance of the work in which they are engaged come mostly to the men and women who are masters of their calling, and this results not so much from genius as from right attitudes, perseverance, concentration, and hard work. The man who decides where he wants to go and why he wants to go there, who embraces the opportunities that lead in that direction and rejects those that do not, will, given ordinary average ability, some day reach his goal. He will also be proud of the profession he is in.

Leadership in any field involves a broad fundamental knowledge of the work in which the man is engaged. Superficial information will not suffice. The principal who would become a leader in education must have built up by reading and study and observation and thinking a good clear philosophy of the educational process, and be deeply impressed with the conception of the improvability and advancement of the race by means of education. He must also be able to think through and beyond the current practices of his profession, and see the possibilities of doing things differently and in a larger and a better way.

To this end the principal ought to be a leader in professional improvement, not only as it relates to his own work in his own school, but also through his influence with those with whom he works. As was pointed out in Chapter II, the principalship is a student's opportunity, and one far too seldom realized, speaking generally, by the principals now in service in our schools. By personal reading and study, by attendance at the summer sessions of colleges and universities, by trying out new methods and procedures, by making numerous little studies, by being sure he has something to say and to give when he talks before parents and at institutes, and by the contribution of short articles from time to time to professional magazines and educational gatherings, a man or woman who works and thinks is almost certain to be looked up to as a leader and to become conscious of growth in knowledge and power to do. They come to think in terms of a personal philosophy for and definite knowledge as to the educational process, and learn to plan for and do things that to many would seem impossible.

Marks of the professional leader. A recent writer on educational leadership, writing in one of our professional magazines, characterized this ability to think through an idea, work it out clearly, and reduce it to such written form that it influences others and moulds procedure elsewhere as the first indication of developing professional leadership. Such a person is well on the way to becoming a leader in the profession. Without this ability to think things through in the light of sound knowledge, and to organize one's thinking in simple but concrete form, one is not likely to rise to eminence in the educational profession.

To impress one's ability for leadership on others, though, calls for certain other important characteristics. The writer referred to enumerated four others, the first of which was the ability to stand on one's feet and speak fairly well. A principal should embrace the many opportunities that come to him to express in simple form the concrete thinking which he does. Usually if he has ideas words will come; his work will then be to improve the manner of his presentation. Many schoolmen would be greatly benefited if they were to take a course in public speaking in some of the summer schools which they attend, and give some attention to practice which will improve their enunciation and platform presence and eliminate objectionable mannerisms.

For the three other marks of an educational leader, which the writer gave, we cannot do better than quote what he wrote:

There is a third attribute of leaders that is universal and not confined to the field of education. This is that all leaders are mentally active. They are always restlessly moving on to new thoughts, new acts, new methods of work. No one can exercise leadership through inertia.

Along with the mental activity of a leader goes intellectual courage. A leader is characteristically willing to take a chance. The man who always plays safe stays still, or follows. He does not lead.

Another characteristic, essential to educational leadership, and usually necessary in other sorts, is the ability to get along well with people. The Spaniards call this quality the *don de gentes*, or the gift of the people, and they recognize it as being as definitely a personal trait as eloquence, perseverance, or accuracy. This ability to get along well with other people is one which the educational leader must possess, and one he must not confuse with its counterfeit, which is being a professional mixer, or its imitation, which is being a glad hander.

The five attributes that have been described constitute, I believe, the fundamental essentials for educational leadership. Education for leadership largely means education for ability along these five lines, and, in the main, this means self-education.[1]

Maintenance of professional standards. The principal also owes a duty to his profession in the support of leadership in the organizations of the profession, and in the maintenance of professional standards. While individual progress may be made in isolation, it is in organization that professional progress is made. Man expresses himself best through the organized institutions of society. In education there are local, state, and national organizations that are important for him to be more or less connected with and to which he ought to give his support. In the teachers' institutes of his city or county he ought to be willing to put his shoulder to the wheel and do his full part. The state teachers' associations, despite their many defects, are on the whole rendering a valuable service in advancing professional interests and standards and promoting useful educational legislation. The hope for sound educational progress through legislation must lie almost wholly within the teaching profession, and it is important that those in a position to lead be well informed and actuated by sound professional motives.

In the matter of the ethics of his profession the principal also owes a duty analogous to that of a judge on the bench to the law, a leader in medical practice to medicine, or a minister to the ethics of a Christian life. In his relations with the school officers over him, with his colleagues in the work in which he is engaged, and with the teachers and pupils whose work he oversees and directs, he owes it to his profession to embody in his speech and actions the best ethics of the profession to which he is devoting his life.

[1] Leonard P. Ayres, in *The Phi Delta Kappan.*

SELECTED REFERENCES

Hyde, Wm. DeWitt. *The Teacher's Philosophy.* 88 pp., Boston, 1910.
An excellent little monograph, valuable for principals and teachers alike.

Mudge, E. L. "Professional Ethics for Teachers"; in *School and Society,* vol. 12, pp. 601–04. (December 18, 1920.)

Palmer, Geo. H. *The Ideal Teacher.* 32 pp., Boston, 1908.
A valuable little monograph on teaching as a profession.

Smith, W. R. "The Professional Status of Teaching"; in *Educational Review,* vol. 63, pp. 35–49. (January, 1922.)
On the growth of the professional spirit.

INDEX

Acceleration and retardation, 341-46.

Accident prevention teaching, 235-37; results of in Detroit, 236; use of Scouts in, 237.

Achievement tests, 496; norms for, 499.

Achievement Quotient (A.Q.), 500-03.

Administrative duties, 39, 42, 185.

Age-and-grade distribution sheet, 340-44.

Annual school exhibits, 538.

Apparatus, playground, 125, 126.

Assemblies, school, types of, 324; types of programs, 326; a month's program for, 329-32.

Assembly, the school, class responsibility for programs, 328; Gary-type programs, 330; importance of, 321, 332; period, use of, 320-33; on first day of school, 86, 90; use of in building up school spirit, 310.

Attendance of pupils, 247-63; compulsory methods, 262; devices for stimulating, 255-57; daily classroom check, 252; irregular attendance and causes, 247; monthly room record card, 253; principles to be followed in dealing with, 254.

Basement, the, 138.

Basements and toilets, supervision of, 132-37.

Binet tests, as aid in classification, 349-55; in first grade, 351.

Blank forms used, 201-05.

Boy Scouts, 237, 307.

Budget, small school, use of, 199-201.

Building and yard organization, 117.

Building inspection, the daily, 220.

Building, the crowded, anticipating conditions, 141; problem of, 140; solutions for, 142.

Building reconnaissance, 65, 79.

Building reorganization, 147.

Bully, the school, 272.

Business organization and administration, 185.

Callers, handling expeditiously, 49.

Camp Fire Girls, 237.

Census, school, and attendance, 339; checking of, 249.

Central office, relations with, 205-06.

Child hygiene, scope of, 224-26.

Children, play needs of, by ages, 122-23.

Chronological age, 346; and mental age compared, 353.

Class, increasing size of, 147; part time classes, 146.

Classification of pupils, 358; type plans, 358. *See also* Promotion of pupils.

Classification sheet, first day, 85.

Community, knowing, 338; relations with, 548.

Companion class plan, 148-50.

Conferences, group, with teachers, 465-68; types of work in, 466-67.

Control, self, building up of, 108.

Course of study problems, 475.

Courses of study, as a stimulus to thinking, 388; getting results by drives, 397-99; mapping out the instruction, 389; not an end in themselves, 397-99; obtaining results from, 388.

Crowded building problem, 140; anticipating, 141; solutions for, 142.

Demonstration teaching, 443, 468.

Departmental type of school organization, 169-72; and the special teachers, 426; programs for, 173.

Desk, organization of, 443, 468.

Diagnostic value of the standard

tests, in reading, 492; in spelling, 491; in writing, 490.
Directed pupil study, 403-10; what may add, 409; where needed, 407.
Discipline and control, 265-81; decreasing by prevention, 280; making productive, 279; minor disorders, 268.
Distinct lines, shifting the, 143.
Drives, for instructional results, 397-99; types of, 398.
Duties of the principal, range of, 37.

Educational Quotient (E.Q.), 500-03.
Entertainments, school, 536; to raise money, 539-43; arguments against, 539; arguments for, 540; handling of, 541; minimizing preparation for, 542.

Failures in school work, 341-48; by subjects, 349.
Feeding, school, 230.
Fighting among pupils, 269-74.
Fire drills, 109; captains for, 112; organization of, 110; rules as to, 110-11, 113-16; special points to be looked after, 113-16.
First aid case, 233-35; teaching, 235-36; work, 232-36.
First day of school, beginning work, 81; building in readiness, 79; call for executive ability, 78; forming the lines, 90; handling pupils, 82; planning for, 72; procedure that day, 73; pupil classification sheet, 85; starting the school, 84; starting with an assembly, 86.
Fresh-air rooms, 230.

Games of children, by ages, 122-23.
Gang fights, 272.
Girl Scouts, 237, 307.
Graphic methods, value of, 354.
Group conferences with teachers, 465-68.
Group, or supervising principal, 11.

Health department in a school, 238.
Health Leagues, 239.
Health record, a, 229.

Health service, a professional, 243-44.
Health supervision, 242.
Health teaching, 226-28; first-aid work in, 232-36.
Health work in a school, 223.
Home and school, 257-59, 548-59.
Home and home study, 400.
Home study by pupils, 399-403.
Homogeneous working groups, 363-65.
Hygiene, child, 224-26.
Hygiene, educational, five divisions of, 223.

Informal tests, 486-88.
Intelligence Quotient (I.Q.), use of, 499-509; in vocational guidance, 506-09.
Intelligence tests, use of in classification, 348-55; in first grade, 351.
Intermissions and lines, 93.
Interschool contests, 543-46; rules for handling, 545-46.
Instruction, redirecting the, 405.

Janitor, school, as a helper, 221; administrative principles in dealing with, 213-16; daily inspection of work of, 220; estimating work of, 219; placing responsibility on, 216; position and types of, 209; reasonable standards for work, 217-19; varied nature of work of, 210.
Junior Health Leagues, 239.
Junior High School type of organization, 9.
Junior Red Cross, 240, 309.

Knowing the school, 337-55.

Leagues, Health, 239.
Lesson plans, a card form for, 393; a means to an end, 395; use and abuse of, 391-96; value of to teachers, 394.
Lines and marching, arguments for, 100-06; arguments against, 106-08; minimizing marching procedure, 107; use in building up self-control, 108.
Lines, forming of first day, 90; or-

INDEX

ganization of, 102; rules as to handling, 104–05.
Lines, district, shifting of, 143.
Lunch hour, rules for, 131; teachers and, 132; supervision of, 130.
Lying and stealing, 274.

Major objectives for a school, 52.
Malnutrition, 230.
Marching and lines. *See* Lines.
Marks, teachers, 505.
Measuring the instruction, 485–509; achievement tests in, 496; achievement norms, 499; informal tests in, 486–88; standard tests in, 489; new scientific tools, 485; principal in this work, 503.
Meetings, teachers'. *See* Teachers' meetings.
Monitorial service, uses of, 306.

Objectives, major, types of, 52.
Obscenity and vulgarity, 276.
Office duties, 188–90; hours, 192.
Office work of a principal, 185; routine and system, 186; schemes for saving time, 190; with an office clerk, 191; without a clerk, 187.
Opening day, planning for, 72; procedure, 73.
Organization duties, 38.

Parent and teacher, improving relations between, 298; protecting the teacher, 295; supporting the teacher, 294.
Parent-Teacher Associations, 548–58; giving constructive work to, 553; handling when troublesome, 551; types of meetings of, 554–57; when to organize, 549; working through, 557.
Parents, classes of, 299; the complaining, 296; the irate, 296–98.
Personal equation, the, 26.
Personal relationships, 30.
Platoon plan, the, 150–59; applying in an old building, 151–53; applying in a modern building, 154–56; educational advantages of, 157–59; how program the school, 153, 174–81; special teachers and, 427.
Platoon-type assembly programs, 330.
Play, effects of good on youths, 130.
Play apparatus, apportioning the, 122.
Play needs of children, by ages, 122–23.
Play organization, advantages of good, 129.
Play space, apportioning grounds and apparatus, 122; per pupil needs, 93; dividing this off, 120.
Playground apparatus, 125–26; games, 307, 543–45; supplies, 126.
Portable buildings, 145.
Preliminary conferences and organization, 59.
Primary supervisor, 415.
Principal as a leader, 560–65; duty in leadership, 560; as a judge in disciplinary matters, 277; principles of action as to, 277–79.
Principal and special supervisors, 418; coöperation with, 422.
Principal and superintendent of schools, 19, 205.
Principal, creates school spirit, 304; in administrative organization, 20; place of in special instruction, 421, 428; range of duties of, 37.
Principalship, a student's opportunity, 33; important qualifications for, 23; importance of office, 27; personal qualities demanded, 22, 318; what it offers, 32.
Professional leader, marks of, 563–65.
Professional reading, 476–78.
Professional spirit, 561; based on knowledge, 562.
Professional standards, maintenance of, 565.
Program making, principles in, 163–65; standards, 166.
Programs, school, companion-class type, 148–50, 174; departmental type, 167, 170–73; platoon type, 150–56, 174–81; special supervisors, 165; time tables for, by grades, 168, 169, 171; types of programs, 162.

Promoted fights, 272.
Promotion of pupils, 358; by subjects, 174, 361.
Promotional-failure studies, 348; causes for, 349.
Promotional plans, combination plans, 381; differentiated-course plans, 361; parallel-course plans, 359; rules, 365–67; special plans, 361; type plans, 358.
Promotional procedure, 358.
Promotions, special, 367–74, 379; rules as to, 368–70.
Promotions in a differentiated-course school, 378; in a parallel-course school, 377; special promotions under either, 379.
Pupil-government idea in elementary school, 311–17; need for in modern society, 316.

Rating of teachers, 480–82; score card for, 481.
Recess periods, divided, 97; handling, 94.
Red Cross, Junior, 240, 309; first-aid work of, 333–36.
Report cards, 505.
Retardation and acceleration, 341–46; reduction of retardation in Detroit, 370; in differentiated-course schools, 378; in parallel-course schools, 377. *See also* Promotional plans.

Savings bank, the school, 311.
Saving time for work, 45.
School, changed conception as to, 533.
School and home movement, the new, 548.
School assembly, 310; captains, 314; congress, 315; councils, 313; contests, 543–46; entertainments, 310; feeding, 230; nurse, 242; support, 534; unruly, 266.
School spirit, and attendance, 260–62; building up, 302–18; how create, 305–11; principal makes, 304; school without, 302; what it is, 303; use in handling trouble in toilets, 137.

Scouts, use of, 237, 308.
Social duties of the principal, 44, 533, 548.
Special exhibit days, 538.
Special program days, 536.
Special school visitation days, 535.
Special rooms and teachers, 373–77.
Special supervisors. *See* Supervisors.
Special teachers and their work, 414.
Stealing and lying, 274.
Study, training pupils how to, 402–10.
Superintendent of Schools, visit to, 61; relations with office of, 205–06.
Supervising principal, the, 11.
Supervision, beginning in a new school, 434; effectiveness of, 15, 431; definite long-time planning, 440; good introductory plans, 435; leadership through, 442; offering constructive criticism, 449–52; planning what to do, 437; preparing way for, 337; purpose of, 444, 454; technique of visitation, 445; type plans for, 438.
Supervisors, administrative principles as to, 421; coöperation with, 422; principal and, 418; primary and grammar, 415; problems of, 416.
Supervisors, special, best use of time of, 424; principal in relation to, 428; relations with room teachers, 425; their work, 414.
Supervisory duties, 41, 42; function, importance of, 43, 431; mistakes, 432.
Supplies, and the store room, 193; giving out, 196; records and charging, 198; types of furnished, 194.

Teacher and government, 284; causes for poor control, 290–92; dependence on principal, 292; strengthening in control, 288–90; supporting, 293–95.
Teacher and lunch hour, 132.
Teachers, building up beginners, 462–65; discovery of special abilities in, 478; group conferences with, 465–68; marks, 505; neces-

INDEX

sary conditions for aiding, 286–88; protecting, 295; training in working habits, 479; types of, 285, 459; yard duty of, 118–21.

Teachers' meetings, definite objectives for, 519; end of first day of school meeting, 75, 76, 91; making the meetings profitable, 513–28; new teachers' conference meetings, 67, 71, 465–68; objectionable types of, 514–16; preliminary meetings in autumn, 66, 69, 76; responsibility of principal for, 516, 525; rules and cautions as to, 526–28; types and times of meetings, 517; types of objectives, 521–25.

Teaching, what is good, 400.

Teaching problems, special, 471–76; illustrated from arithmetic, 474; in course of study, 475.

Tests and measurements, diagnostic value of, illustrated by reading, 492; spelling, 491; writing, 490.

Tests, the informal type of, 486–88.

Tests, standardized, new tools, 485; pupil diagnosis with, 493; principal and, 503; use of, 486; use to measure school progress, 494; vocational guidance uses, 506.

Toilets, stopping trouble in the, 135.

Toilets and basements, inspection of, 134; shaping conditions in, 133; supervision of, 132; use of, 134.

Training pupils how to study, 403–06.

Type forms of school organization, 6.

Unruly school, transforming an, 266.

Visitation days for a school, 535.

Visitation, supervisory, records as to, 447–49; technique of, 445. *See also* Supervision.

Visiting day for teachers, 470; directions as to, 472.

Visiting teacher, the, 259.

Vocational guidance use of tests and measurements, 506.

Vocations, intelligence requirements of, 508.

Vulgarity and obscenity, 276.

Work, laying out of, 47.

Working schedule, 46, 47, 50; one for February, 51.

Yard duty of teachers, 118–20; an assignment sheet for, 121.

Yard organization, 117.

RIVERSIDE TEXTBOOKS IN EDUCATION

Edited by Ellwood P. Cubberley
Dean of the School of Education, Leland Stanford Junior University

History of Education

Cubberley: The History of Education
Cubberley: Readings in the History of Education
Cubberley: A Brief History of Education
Cubberley: Public Education in the United States

General Educational Theory

Almack and Lang: Problems of the Teaching Profession
Chapman and Counts: Principles of Education
Cubberley: An Introduction to the Study of Education
Cubberley: Rural Life and Education
Douglass: Secondary Education
Gesell: The Pre-School Child
Inglis: Principles of Secondary Education
McCracken and Lamb: Occupational Information in the Elementary School
Proctor: Educational and Vocational Guidance
Smith: An Introduction to Educational Sociology
Snedden: Problems of Secondary Education
Thomas: Principles and Technique of Teaching
Wallin: The Education of Handicapped Children

Methods

Almack: Education for Citizenship
Bolenius: Teaching Literature in the Grammar Grades and High School
Douglass: Modern Methods of High School Teaching
Freeland, Adams, Hall: Teaching in the Intermediate Grades
Kendall and Mirick: How to Teach the Fundamental Subjects
Kendall and Mirick: How to Teach the Special Subjects
Martz and Kinneman: Social Science for Teachers

HOUGHTON MIFFLIN COMPANY
BOSTON   NEW YORK   CHICAGO   DALLAS   SAN FRANCISCO

RIVERSIDE TEXTBOOKS IN EDUCATION

Edited by ELLWOOD P. CUBBERLEY
Dean of the School of Education, Leland Stanford Junior University

Methods

MINOR: Principles of Teaching Practically Applied
NEWCOMB: Modern Methods of Teaching Arithmetic
STONE: Silent and Oral Reading
STORMZAND: Progressive Methods of Teaching
THOMAS: The Teaching of English in the Secondary School
THOMAS: Training for Effective Study
TRAFTON: The Teaching of Science in the Elementary School
WOOFTER: Teaching in Rural Schools

Healthful Teaching and Healthful Schools

AVERILL: Educational Hygiene
AYRES, WILLIAMS, WOOD: Healthful Schools. How to Build, Equip, and Maintain Them
HOAG AND TERMAN: Health Work in the Schools
TERMAN: The Hygiene of the School Child

Administration and Supervision

ALMACK AND BURSCH: Administration of Consolidated and Village Schools
BRIGGS: The Junior High School
CUBBERLEY: The Principal and His School
CUBBERLEY: Public School Administration
CUBBERLEY: State School Administration
NUTT: The Supervision of Instruction
PERRY: Discipline as a School Problem
PITTENGER: An Introduction to Public School Finance
RUGG: Primer of Graphics and Statistics for Teachers
SEARS: Classroom Organization and Control
SEARS: The School Survey

HOUGHTON MIFFLIN COMPANY
BOSTON   NEW YORK   CHICAGO   DALLAS   SAN FRANCISCO

RIVERSIDE TEXTBOOKS IN EDUCATION

Edited by ELLWOOD P. CUBBERLEY
Dean of the School of Education, Leland Stanford Junior University

Administration and Supervision

SHOWALTER: A Handbook for Rural School Officers
WILLIAMS: Graphic Methods in Education

Psychology and Child Study

AVERILL: Elements of Educational Psychology
AVERILL: Psychology for Normal Schools
EDWARDS: Psychology of Elementary Education
FREEMAN: Experimental Education
FREEMAN: How Children Learn
FREEMAN: The Psychology of the Common Branches
PECHSTEIN AND MCGREGOR: Psychology of the Junior High School Pupil
PECHSTEIN AND JENKINS: Psychology of the Kindergarten-Primary Child
WADDLE: An Introduction to Child Psychology
WALLIN: Clinical and Abnormal Psychology

Educational Tests and Measurements

FREEMAN: Mental Tests
HINES: A Guide to Educational Measurements
MONROE: An Introduction to the Theory of Educational Measurements
MONROE: Measuring the Results of Teaching
MONROE, DE VOSS AND KELLY: Educational Tests and Measurements. Revised and Enlarged Edition.
RUGG: Statistical Methods Applied to Education
TERMAN: The Intelligence of School Children
TERMAN: The Measurement of Intelligence
   Test Material for use with The Measurement of Intelligence
   Record Booklets. Sold only in packages of 25
   Condensed Guide for the Binet-Simon Intelligence Tests
   Abbreviated Filing Record Cards. 25 in package

HOUGHTON MIFFLIN COMPANY
BOSTON   NEW YORK   CHICAGO   DALLAS   SAN FRANCISCO

240

Course of Study
Special Teachers
Planning Supervision